DATE DUE

			MAY 23 '63
GAYLORD			PRINTED IN U.S.A.

A HISTORY OF
LAY JUDGES

A HISTORY OF
LAY JUDGES

BY

John P. Dawson

HARVARD UNIVERSITY PRESS

Cambridge, Massachusetts

1960

ACKNOWLEDGMENTS

I acknowledge with thanks the permission granted by A. & C. Black, Ltd., London, and Van Nostrand, Princeton, to quote from J. E. A. Jolliffe, *Constitutional History of Medieval England;* by the Clarendon Press, Oxford, to quote from C. S. Orwin, *The Open Fields;* by George Allen & Unwin, Ltd., to quote from Sir Paul Vinogradoff, *The Growth of the Manor;* by the Harvard University Press, to quote from Volume II of James F. Willard and William A. Morris, *The English Government at Work, 1327–1336;* and by the Oxford University Tutorial Classes Committee, to quote from R. H. Tawney, *The Agrarian Problem in the Sixteenth Century.*

Distributed in Great Britain by Oxford University Press, London

Publication of this volume has been aided by a grant from the Ford Foundation.

Library of Congress Catalog Card Number: 61-5576

Printed in the United States of America

PREFACE

A HISTORICAL and comparative study of the jury was suggested to me in 1955 by colleagues at the University of Chicago Law School while I was serving as a visiting member of the Law School faculty. After a tentative start on such a study, I was induced by Dean Edward Levi to examine the muniments of the Bacon family, which are preserved in the Harper Library of the University of Chicago. The rolls of the Bacon manor courts opened new lines of inquiry into the effects of lay participation in the administration of justice in England. But it soon became clear that English experience, unique as it was, should not be viewed in isolation. To understand developments in England it seemed necessary to trace both the causes and the consequences of the displacement of lay judges in Roman, French, and German law.

In surveying the history of four legal systems over long stretches of time I have had to rely heavily on the work of others. Many authors have dealt with the topics that are discussed in this study. It has seemed useless to multiply citations on matters as to which there is little or no dispute. I have therefore referred to only a few of the secondary works consulted. My main object has been to provide perspective, by bringing together the results of much specialized work by numerous specialists.

I am much indebted to Mr. Robert Rosenthal of the Harper Library at the University of Chicago for facilities provided in reading the Bacon papers and for permission to quote from them. John Holt Wilson, Esq., the present lord of the manor of Redgrave, was extremely helpful during my visit to the manor in 1957. I am grateful to him for information supplied concerning the later history of the manor and for permission to examine its court rolls for the nineteenth and twentieth centuries. These rolls are in the possession of Thomas Wilson, Esq., solicitor in Bury St. Edmunds, who kindly consented to make them available to me. I have profited greatly from reading the unpublished study of S. F. C. Milsom, "The Origins and Early History of Judicial Review in

v

England," of which a copy is in the possession of Professor Samuel
E. Thorne of the Harvard Law School, who made it available to
me. I am grateful to him and also to Mr. Milsom for his permission
to refer to it as I have done in the appropriate places in Chapter
IV.

The text of this study has been examined and much improved
by several critics, to whom I am also much indebted. The most
helpful as well as the most critical has been my son, John Philip
Dawson, of the History Department of Harvard University. In
many conversations over several years I have drawn extensively
on the great store of learning possessed by Professor Samuel E.
Thorne of the Harvard Law School and to him I am most grateful for many suggestions and much helpful advice. Errors of fact,
of logic and of emphasis have been corrected by Professor Edgar
N. Durfee of the University of Michigan Law School, Professor
Roland Stanger of the Ohio State Law School, Professor Benja-
min Kaplan and Professor Mark De Wolfe Howe of the Harvard
Law School, Professor Franklin Ford of the Harvard History De-
partment, and Professor Samuel Shuman of the Wayne University
Law School. The remaining errors are of course my own.

J.P.D.

CONTENTS

Introduction   1

I. *GREECE AND ROME*   10
   1. GREECE   10
   2. ROME   14
      a. The Republican Period   15
      b. Principate and Empire   30

II. *POPULAR COURTS AND THEIR DISPLACE-*
   MENT IN FRANCE AND GERMANY   35
   1. MEDIEVAL FOLK-MOOTS   35
   2. FRANCE   39
      a. The Feudalization of French Courts   39
      b. Modes of Fact Determination   43
      c. Modes of Appellate Review   53
      d. The Disappearance of the Lay Element 60
      e. The Triumph of the Professionals (1500–1789) 69
      f. Political and Social Implications   83
   3. GERMANY   94
      a. The Survival of the Schöffen   94
      b. The Progress of Roman-Canonist Procedure 103
      c. The Surviving Mixture of Types   109
      d. Political and Social Implications   112

III. *THE ENGLISH ROYAL COURTS*   116
   1. THE SURVIVAL OF THE ANCIENT ASSEMBLY COURTS 116
   2. THE INTRODUCTION OF THE JURY   118
   3. THE ADVENT OF PROFESSIONALS IN COMMON LAW COURTS 129
   4. THE JUSTICES OF THE PEACE   136
   5. COURTS OF EQUITY   145
   6. OTHER ROYAL COURTS   172

IV. *THE ENGLISH LOCAL COURTS*   178

   1. THE COURTS OF COUNTY AND HUNDRED   178

   2. THE SEIGNORIAL COURTS   184

   3. THE ORIGINS OF THE COURT LEET   187

   4. THE ORIGINS OF THE MANOR COURTS   192

   5. SOME THIRTEENTH CENTURY MANOR COURTS   198

   6. A SUFFOLK MANOR IN THE SIXTEENTH AND EARLY
      SEVENTEENTH CENTURIES   208

      a. Court Baron and Court Leet   210

      b. The Redgrave Juries   215

      c. The Lord and His Steward   222

      d. Civil Litigation and the 40 Shilling Limit   228

      e. Copyhold Transactions   233

      f. Powers of Self-Government   244

      g. The Trial and Review of Presentments   255

   7. BOROUGH AND TOWN COURTS   264

   8. ATTITUDES OF THE CENTRAL GOVERNMENT   274

V. *SUMMARY AND CONCLUSIONS*   287

   Index   305

A HISTORY OF
LAY JUDGES

LIST OF ABBREVIATIONS

Brunner, *S.G.*	Heinrich Brunner, *Die Entstehung der Schwurgerichte* (Berlin, Weidmann, 1872).
Chénon, *HDF*	Émile Chénon, *Histoire Générale du Droit Français Public et Privé des Origines à 1815,* 2 vols. (Paris, Receuil Sirey, 1926 and 1929).
Esmein, *HDF*	Adhémar Esmein, *Cours Élémentaire d'Histoire du Droit Français* (Paris, Receuil Sirey, 2d ed, 1895).
Holdsworth, *HEL*	William S. Holdsworth, *History of English Law,* 13 vols. (London, Methuen & Co., 1922–1952).
Jolowicz, *RL*	Herbert F. Jolowicz, *Historical Introduction to the Study of Roman Law* (Cambridge, Eng., Cambridge University Press, 2d ed., 1952).
Kitchin, *Court Leet*	*Le Court leete et Court Baron collect per John Kitchin de Graies Inn* (London, Tottell, 1587).
Manorial Courts (S.S.)	*Select Pleas in Manorial and Other Seignorial Courts* (edited for the Selden Society by F. W. Maitland, 1889).
NRH	*Nouvelle Revue Historique de Droit Français et Étranger.*
Plucknett, *Concise Hist.*	Theodore F. T. Plucknett, *A Concise History of the Common Law* (London, Butterworth & Co., 5th ed., 1956).
Pollock and Maitland, *HEL*	Frederick Pollock and Frederick W. Maitland, *History of English Law Before the Time of Edward I* (Cambridge, Eng., Cambridge University Press, 2d ed., 1898).
Schroeder, *DRG*	Richard Schroeder and Eberhard von Künssberg, *Lehrbuch der deutschen Rechtsgeschichte* (Leipzig, Von Veit, 7th ed., 1932).
Tawney, *Agrarian Problem*	Richard H. Tawney, *The Agrarian Problem in the Sixteenth Century* (London, Longmans & Co., 1912).
Webb, *ELG*	Sidney and Beatrice Webb, *English Local Government from the Revolution to the Municipal Corporations Act* (London, Longmans & Co.): I (*The Parish and the County*), 1906. II (*The Manor and the Borough*), 1908. III (*The Manor and the Borough*), 1908.
ZSS (*röm.*)	*Zeitschrift der Savigny-Stiftung für Rechtsgeschichte, römische Abteilung.*
ZSS (*germ.*)	*Zeitschrift der Savigny-Stiftung für Rechtsgeschichte, germanistische Abteilung.*

INTRODUCTION

THE main theme of this study is the displacement of lay by professional judges in France, Germany, and England. Since French and German experience, and indeed also the English, include an important legacy from ancient civilization, the study also surveys briefly the use of lay judges in Greece and Rome.

For modern societies adjudication has become one of the primary means for achieving and maintaining social order. Its forms and procedures have become relatively stabilized. In reviewing the history of earlier societies, however, one soon discovers an astonishing variety of agencies and procedures employed in the settlement of disputes. In some primitive societies it has apparently been possible to achieve a high degree of social order without any specialized institutions for dispute-settlement and without designating any persons as specially qualified for the purpose. Then as procedures have been organized and responsibility more definitely assigned, the methods employed have depended at every stage on a variety of factors—the sources from which law itself has been derived, the types of sanctions available, and the alternative or competing means by which group decisions could be made. The manner in which the judicial function is organized at any particular time or place clearly must depend on underlying assumptions of the legal and political order at that time and place.

If courts are a product and a reflection of many forces in society at every stage in their growth, they also react on the societies that created them. This is especially evident in earlier times when courts had a central position as agencies for social control and group decision and usually combined other functions with that of adjudication. In these earlier times it was common to fuse with dispute-settlement some rule-making and executive functions. This fusion lasted late in many instances. Even where it did not, the prominent role of the courts meant that their formal structure, procedure and personnel had lasting effects on the societies in

1

which they were embedded, setting limits on growth and also opening new lines of growth. The survival of lay judges in many courts in England and the elimination of lay judges in France and Germany had far-reaching consequences in all three countries.

The approach will be mainly historical and will deal for the most part with events before 1800. As to France the year 1789 is taken as a terminus, since the French Revolution abruptly cut off many ancient institutions and started developments that in many respects were new. As to Germany some lines of survival will be traced into the nineteenth, and as to England, into the twentieth century. But in searching for causes of the great divergence that developed between these three countries, one must look far back of 1800. The influence of Roman law is a large factor, especially Roman law as it was transmitted through and remade in medieval Italy. In addition, the political and social environments in France, Germany, and England during the late Middle Ages brought major decisions which became irrevocable with the passage of time. The main directions were determined early, though they may not have been visible at the time.

I have approached these questions with all the biases of a twentieth-century American, trained in American case law. One of these biases certainly is that procedure is vital and, like court structure, provides both limitations on and impetus to change. It may be that this bias is reflected in a major thesis that will appear: that the adoption of canonist procedure in France and Germany was the primary cause of great changes in court structure which then had their own great and lasting effects on French and German society; whereas the procedural compromises of the English thirteenth-century common law fixed lines of growth in England for centuries.

I should confess also to another bias or strong inclination which developed as the study progressed, toward what might be called a political interpretation. The period mainly considered, prior to 1800, antedates the modern monopoly over adjudication that has been acquired by national states. As one moves back in time, one finds that there were strewn about many different kinds of courts. Some took shape in local communities, as the outward sign of their internal cohesion. Some were organized around the centers or transit-points of political power, like the courts of lords and vassals that linked into the lines of feudal relationship. Many were privately owned, though there were degrees of ownership. As one observes this abundant and varied growth and recalls the large role of courts in earlier societies, one cannot escape some concern with political implications. Courts were clearly an avenue to control and influence within the groups by which they were organized. Their decisions carried authority and could mobilize what we must call a public force, even though the force was only remotely or indirectly supplied by any central government. Contests over court-keeping rights were sometimes very bitterly fought and the outcome of these contests had major influence on political development. Since one of the crucial issues in the battle of courts was the choice of the personnel who would be empowered to render decision, the transition from lay to professional judges moves across the main battleground in greater political contests.

The terms "lay" and "professional," used over so wide a range in space and time, present some real difficulties that must be briefly mentioned. They seem to be the best shorthand expressions available to express the intended contrast. But the courts and judges encountered in this survey appear in a multitude of different types; as between some of the types the contrast becomes exceedingly blurred. I see no help for this. The words can actually be used to express a variety of meanings. As used in this connection, the term "professional" describes a person who applies a substantial part of his time and energy, with some degree of continuity, to the task at hand. In most instances this specialization is rewarded by paid income. For this reason, among others, I would hesitate to apply the term to the English justices of the peace, for example, or to the Roman classical jurists—the latter not being judges in any event except rarely and by accident. Specialization on judging also carries the implication that the office of judge has somehow been marked off and identified, even though other functions (rule-making or executive action) may still be attached to it. But identification of the office often came by slow degrees and in the minds of outsiders might be merely a byproduct, obscurely felt, of the specialized activity that they observed to be going on.

In much modern usage the term "professional" also carries some implication of specialized training and skill. In most instances this will be true here. But over the wide range of experience considered some exceptions are bound to appear. In the late Roman Empire and in prerevolutionary France the demand for trained persons far exceeded the supply and as a result men regularly assigned to judicial offices—perhaps owning the offices through purchase for cash—often had no training or skill and no incentive to acquire either. For such situations I have used the term "untrained professional". In most instances, however, regular attention to judicial duties in an office distinctly identified brought some extra measure of training and skill, even though training was on-the-job. Indeed at times the complexities that had come to surround the task created the feeling that trained persons were needed and became a strong force for specialization both of personnel and of function.

As used hereafter the term "lay" judge is simply negative—a judge who is not a "professional" in the sense that he is drawn from his community at random, is in no way distinguished from others by his tenure of an office, and works without continuity. The term "lay" judge is entirely neutral on such important issues as the judge's own place in society or the method by which he is chosen. The lay *iudex* of the Roman praetorian system was chosen from a panel of 900 or so eligible persons of high rank in Roman society. In other instances the judges were almost representatives of, and spokesmen for, some very simple folk. At the furthest extreme of democracy were the popular courts of Athenian Greece, a segment of the whole body of citizens. The method of choice is a crucial issue with large political implications, but in examining it I have tried to remember that direct translation into modern political ideology is very seldom possible. For purposes of this survey, then, a lay judge is simply a person who is empowered to share in some degree in rendering judicial decisions but who does so as a side-line, with unplanned irregularity. The question of skill or training enters only in the negative sense that skill or training in legal technique is no part of his qualifications for the judging work he does.

Even more difficult to define and more subtle in its gradations is the distinction between "public" and "private" courts. For per-

sons living in the twentieth century it might seem strange that
this should be so. For us adjudication that carries full authority
can be organized only by the state. Tribunals can of course be
created by consent of litigants but there are serious questions
still as to how far they can exclude or displace the judicial agencies
created by the state. In any event, the modern revival of arbitration as a method of dispute-settlement has not brought many
troublesome problems of classification of the kind that must now
be attempted. We think of arbitration as "private." Arbitration
tribunals may ultimately depend on state-created agencies to enforce their decisions and the decisions themselves when rendered
may have consequences that state officials must recognize, but
the consequences are attributed to private consent. The same is
true of discipline or grievance committees and other tribunals set
up by membership groups. Though the adjectives used may be
different, similar modes of analysis are used to explain courts or
commissions created for settlement of international disputes. In
this respect our thinking has been pervaded by a political theory
of the omnipresent state. Nowhere more than in adjudication does
the state's monopoly seem exclusive.

For much of the period that will be considered a monopoly in
the state did not exist. Both theory and means were lacking. In
early Greece and Rome as in other primitive societies there were
rules that we must call rules of "law," enforced at least by approved self-help, before means for full-scale adjudication had
been developed or power to apply force on the community's behalf had been permanently assigned to anyone. In Europe during
the early Middle Ages government was dismembered and widely
dispersed. The settlement of private disputes and the punishment
of wrongs were achieved through unregulated private adjustment
or later, increasingly, through assemblies of tribes or of neighbors.
These assemblies should be called "public," so long at least as
they could resist domination by powerful individuals, keep a diversified membership, and speak for the communities from which
they were drawn. "Public" courts at the national level, the an-
cestors of the courts of our modern states, grew out of the institution of kingship. But their growth was gradual, commensurate
with changes in the kingship itself. It was necessary for kings to
become something more than leaders among the chieftains or

mere symbols of national unity. Even after they had acquired wide powers to command, it was necessary for them to assume responsibility for ensuring justice to their subjects—a justice that transcended the immediate personal interests of the kings themselves. This complex transformation occurred at differing rates of speed in different countries. Even after it had gone quite far, the notion lingered that the courts of the king had a special duty to safeguard royal interests. They were "his" courts, long after it was felt and expected that they should be accessible to many and that the rules they applied should be rules of wide incidence within the king's realm.

The growth of feudalism throughout Europe brought other complications. It was characteristic of feudalism that courts of lords and vassals should be organized to deal with all matters affecting their interrelations. When confined to the terms of feudal tenure or to issues that might threaten the peace between their members, these feudal courts should clearly be labelled "private." Even when they acquired a broader jurisdiction over the general population, as occurred on a large scale in France and Germany, they will be described here as "private." Not only did the lords of such courts, as a rule, appropriate the revenue earned, but they acquired power to appoint the judges and other personnel and had some influence, therefore, on the course of decision.

The issue involved is much more complex, however, and relates to the central problems of this study. Even within a regime of private ownership, limits could be set to the court-keeper's power by a duty to follow rules of substantive law or procedure that derived from some external source. Still more effective limits could be set by a need to secure the concurrence of individuals over whom the court-keeper had no direct control. An example that will be considered at length is the English manor court. Here the revenues were normally paid to the lord. He appointed the presiding officer, the "steward." The court was held in the name of the lord and in one of its two phases at least—the "court baron" —it was held in theory on the lord's own authority. Yet in its other phase—the "court leet"—the English manor court was a royal franchise, exercising authority that in theory was delegated by the crown. More important, effective power of decision passed more and more from the lord and his steward to juries drawn from the neighborhoods, operating under a procedure that became well known and stereotyped, that was felt to be binding, and that left little room for intervention by either lord or steward.

In France and Germany it was otherwise. For different reasons and at different times, the nobility in these two countries acquired very extensive court-keeping rights. The laymen who originally rendered the judgments were excluded or became so disheartened that they generally ceased to attend; as a result the power of decision shifted to judges appointed by the court-keeping lords. The decisions of these seignorial judges are not reported, but one would suppose that they were not entirely free to invent the rules that they would apply. No doubt in theory they were bound like others by the applicable rules of local custom, by statute or perhaps by Roman law. Furthermore, the introduction of Roman-canonist procedure brought with it in both countries an elaborate system of appeals, so that the work of seignorial courts could be policed—by royal courts in France and by courts of feudal superiors in Germany. Partly as a result of this power of review and partly, perhaps, to promote its extension, royal lawyers developed a theory in France that powers of adjudication resided in the crown and were merely delegated to feudal lords; similar theories circulated in Germany in support of the claims of the rulers in the various principalities. If such theories were taken seriously, the courts of subordinate feudal lords would take on a "public" aspect, even though appellate review by the courts of crown or ruler was intermittent and ineffective. Despite all this, I shall persist in describing as "private" the seignorial courts of France and Germany. The adjective "private" is not meant to suggest that the judges who staffed them were free altogether from rule or review. Their wide powers were not due to their "privateness" but to changes in internal court structure and procedure, especially to the shedding of their lay membership.

The "public-private" distinction thus is a difficult distinction of degree and in itself is not the main theme. But it does provide a subordinate theme that will constantly recur. The location of court-keeping rights was a vital matter, even though less vital than the modes by which courts were organized and the procedure they employed. In England the courts of manors, though privately owned and essentially free from external controls, preserved the medieval fusion of powers, built their procedure around neighborhood juries and, as they enlarged their activities, became agencies of local self-government. In France and Germany the narrowing range of participation altered the whole balance of forces within French and German society and enhanced the power of their aristocracies. The continued survival and wide competence of seignorial courts in France and Germany lead, then, into a much larger issue—the fate of local self-government. Its decay in France and Germany was not caused by seignorial courts alone, but they played a part. As the decay progressed, large segments of authority were retained by seignorial courts, staffed by judges who were appointed by the court-keeping lords. The effects of this on social structure will be given some attention.

As between the various legal systems that will be considered, main emphasis will be placed on the English. This is partly because we have inherited so much from England, not merely the rules and institutions of the common law but more basic traditions and attitudes. There is also another reason. Despite the effort that has been devoted to the study of English history, certain aspects are not yet fully explored. Their interest and importance become much clearer when they are examined comparatively. For much of the English material, especially that concerning the common law courts, I have merely relied on standard authorities and assembled no new evidence. But I have tried to suggest a somewhat different view of the organization of the Chancery and its place among the institutions of the central government. The largest place is given to the study of English local courts. If the emphasis seems disproportionate, it is because the accounts so far given are inadequate and because for an American they have been an exciting discovery. They were microcosms of government, organized under judicial forms. The training they provided and the attitudes they shaped entered deeply into the experience that was transported to America and became part of our own inheritance.

The sharpest and most useful contrast with England is provided by France. The contrast is heightened by the numerous parallels between the institutions of the two countries in their earlier history. The ultimate divergence between them is all the more dramatic. Though the causes for this divergence have been searched for by many, the contribution of courts, especially courts at local levels, has been overlooked in the past and will be emphasized here.

Germany, on the other hand, will be briefly treated, although the diligence of German historians has produced a bulky literature. The developments in Germany came later, for somewhat different reasons and with different results. They are mentioned in the hope that they will add weight to the contrast with England.

The treatment of ancient Greece, with which the first chapter begins, will be briefest of all. For present purposes Greece merely provides a starting point and some interesting political theory. Rome will be considered somewhat more fully, both because Roman law had such lasting and pervasive influence and because the Roman development has some interest of its own.

CHAPTER I

GREECE AND ROME

1. GREECE

THE political theory that Greece contributes was stated best by Plato:

In the judgment of offenses against the state the people ought to participate, for when anyone wrongs the state they are all wronged and may reasonably complain if they are not allowed to share in the decision. . . . And in private suits too as far as possible, all should have a share, for he who has no share in the administration of justice is apt to imagine that he has no share in the state at all.[1]

But these opinions were not held by Plato alone. Aristotle too was quite explicit. His definition of a citizen was "a man who shares in the administration of justice and in the holding of office." [2] Among the essential elements of a constitution Aristotle included "the system of popular courts, composed of all citizens or of persons selected from all, and competent to decide all cases—or, at any rate, most of them, and those the greatest and most important." [3] In justifying the judicial functions of the popular assemblies Aristotle had this to say:

In the actual practice of our own day the people in their gatherings have both a deliberative and a judicial capacity, and in both capacities they make decisions which are all concerned with particular matters. Any individual member of these assemblies is probably inferior to the one best man. But the state is composed of many individuals; and just as a feast to which many contribute is better than one provided by a single person, so, and for the same reason, the masses can come to a better decision, in many matters, than one individual.[4]

---

[1] *Laws*, 767A–767B (transl. Jowett, Oxford, 1888). In his other writings Plato expressed misgivings as to the popular courts and proposed limitations on their powers, though he retained them as a primary element in his ideal political order. Glenn R. Morrow, "Plato and the Rule of Law," *Philosophical Review*, 50:105 (1941).

[2] *Politics*, 1275a (transl. Barker, New York, 1899).

[3] *Politics*, 1317b.

[4] *Politics*, 1286a.

Plato and Aristotle, writing in the fourth century B.C., were describing Athenian institutions that were already well established in the time of Pericles, a century before. It seems certain that these institutions were deliberately created, for they served so well the purposes of the democratic party. Their architects cannot now be precisely named but the purpose was clear—to promote direct participation by all Athenian citizens in the judicial function as in all other functions of the government. By the time of Pericles the design was complete. It was the product of minds that aimed, with clarity and firm purpose, to give the whole people command of the judging function as one of the most vital functions of government.

The institutions developed by the time of Pericles had grown by stages. The reforms of Solon somewhat more than a century earlier had given limited judicial powers to the general assembly of Athenian citizens—at least by way of appeal from magistrates' decisions.[5] The power to act as a trial court of first instance had been assumed by the assembly in the late sixth century, probably in cases of great political importance and public interest. The movement to broaden the assembly's judicial powers coincided with restrictions on the political power of the aristocracy and on the authority of magistrates. Dates are disputed, but it seems clear that by 450 B.C. the assembly had in principle acquired a universal competence in all civil and criminal cases. The resulting volume of judicial business was so great that the assembly was divided into sections or panels, probably about ten in number. The normal size of a panel (*dikasteria*) was probably 501, though they could be 201, 301, 401, 501, or more, and a court of 1500 sat in the attempted impeachment of Pericles. Every Athenian citizen of thirty years or more who was not indebted to the state and whose civil rights had not been forfeited, was eligible for election. Election was by lot, as for most other public offices. To ensure that all citizens could spare the time for judicial duties, Pericles introduced the system of regular pay for time spent in judicial services. This meant there was no lack of volunteers. Each day that the courts were open there might well be several hundred to more

[5] Robert J. Bonner and Gertrude Smith, *Administration of Justice from Homer to Aristotle* (Chicago, 1930), I, 153–166; Charles Hignett, *History of the Athenian Constitution* (Oxford, 1952), 97–98.

than a thousand citizens engaged in judicial duties. As a recent author has said:

As the control exercised by the people in the law courts extended to all departments of political life, the introduction of payment for the *dikasts* completed the revolution which the creation of the *dikasteria* had begun and crowned the transfer of power from the middle classes to the proletariat; the supremacy of the demos in the courts guaranteed its predominance in the state.[6]

These citizen courts should not be conceived as merely oversize juries giving verdicts on disputed issues of fact. They rendered judgment on the whole case presented, including both facts and law. Voting was by secret ballot, yes or no. From the vote of the assembly there was no appeal, nor were the individual voting members in any way accountable for the action taken. The magistrates who presided were merely chairmen with at most a duty to ensure that order was preserved and that the cases had been duly prepared in advance. In short, these popular courts had entire responsibility for decision. And this was because each court, though in fact a mere fraction of the whole Athenian citizenry, was a large and representative sample which in theory shared the sovereign power of the people as a whole.[7]

The political importance of this system lay first of all in the control it ensured over the actions and the policies of public officials. Beyond this was the whole matter of relations with subordinate cities in the Athenian Empire. Great numbers of cases, both civil and criminal, affecting them or their citizens were tried in Athens before the popular courts either by original suit or on appeal; such trials provided an important means of controlling these communities and of influencing the internal contests between democratic and oligarchic parties.[8] In Athens itself when the oligarchs recovered control of the state machinery temporarily in 411 and 404 B.C., the judicial powers of the assemblies were promptly

[6] Hignett, 221. The brief account given in the preceding paragraph is based on the admirable work of Bonner and Smith, I, 187–200. The differing views of Hignett (pp. 146–158) as to the dates and authors of the fifth-century innovations do not affect the issues that are of interest here.

[7] Bonner and Smith, I, 224–246.

[8] H. Grant Robertson, *Administration of Justice in the Athenian Empire* (Toronto, 1924), 72–87.

abolished. They were just as promptly restored by the democratic party when it returned to power.[9]

Yet this system of popular justice reflected something more than the political aims of the radical democrats. An inevitable result of such mass participation in judicial functions was a continuing legal education for all classes of Athenian citizens. This helped to prevent the growth of a class of legal specialists. The talents of ambitious men were guided toward acquiring skill in advocacy and declamation rather than toward study, analysis, and the accumulation of a legal tradition. In the modern sense of the term there were no lawyers in fifth and fourth-century Athens. Just as each citizen was prospectively a judge, so each citizen was a lawyer. The strong preference felt for the amateur was both a cause and a consequence of the judicial system of Athens. It is matched by the distrust of the specialist-expert that prevented the formation of a permanent class of officials or a professional clergy.[10] Faith in the judgment of average men brought resistance to monopolies, not only in deciding the main direction of public affairs but in all decisions, great and small.

It was at least consistent with these attitudes that arbitration by laymen was so much emphasized in Athenian practice. We can postpone for a moment the debated question whether state-sponsored courts developed in Greece out of a system of private arbitration, spontaneously organized. It seems highly probable in any event that arbitration persisted, parallel with court litigation, as an important and much favored means of settling disputes. In 403 B.C. a system of arbitration was formally organized. All litigation involving substantial values (above 10 drachmas) was submitted first to an arbitrator, chosen as a rule from citizens over sixty who had seen long service in the popular assemblies. If efforts at mediation failed, the single arbitrator proceeded to hear witnesses and try the case; his decision could be appealed to one of the popular courts, but on the appeal the record prepared by the ar-

[9] Bonner and Smith, I, 325–326.

[10] George M. Calhoun, *Introduction to Greek Legal Science* (Oxford, 1944), 47–48. J. Walter Jones, *Law and Legal Theory of the Greeks* (Oxford, 1956), 143–149, describes the work of the advocates before the popular assemblies and in chapter XVI (pp. 292–308) gives an interesting account of the effects on legal method generally of Athenian political (including judicial) institutions.

bitrator was the basis for decision and new evidence was not admitted. By this ingenious arrangement, the popular assemblies were relieved of much time-consuming litigation, without jeopardizing their ultimate supremacy or abandoning reliance on unspecialized amateurs.[11]

The clarity and logic of the Athenian solutions make them the center of interest, but we must recall that Attica was not the whole of Greece. Popular courts were not always used, as in Athens, to administer and to safeguard a system of radical democracy. In other parts of Greece, with quite different political systems, there were popular courts that ranged in size from 11 to 800 members.[12] Private citizens had participated in the administration of justice in earlier Greek communities under political institutions that were far from democratic.[13] A connection between lay adjudication and political democracy was therefore not inevitable. It was like so many other ideas that were first given shape in Athens during that time of inspiration, never to reappear in so pure or clear a form. Yet it was not lost or entirely forgotten, for the light of Greece was still to shine over the Roman world.

2. ROME

The Roman story is longer and much more complex. The whole record of Roman law extends over a thousand years. Yet one main point emerges at once: for the first and most crucial 500 years there was no such thing as a professional judge; all the judges were part-time amateurs. The difficulties begin when we distinguish, as we must, between criminal and civil proceedings and among various forms of civil proceeding. Altogether it seems best to bring together the developments of the first 500 years—the republican period—for all types of proceeding, and to start with the criminal cases. The second 500 years, down to the time of Justinian, will be discussed later.

[11] Bonner and Smith, I, 183–184, 346–351; II, 97–116; Calhoun, 37; Louis Gernet, *Droit et Société dans la Grèce Ancienne* (Paris, 1955), 103; Jones, 130–133.

[12] August Pauly and Georg Wissowa, *Realencyklopädie der classischen Alterthumswissenschaft in alphabetischer Ordnung* (Stuttgart, 1914–1950), V, 570.

[13] H. J. Wolff, "The Origin of Judicial Litigation Among the Greeks," *Traditio*, 4:31, at 62–63 (1946).

a. *The Republican Period*

The early Roman handling of criminal cases showed, externally at least, a striking resemblance to the Athenian, though there is no reason to suspect direct borrowing. A criminal proceeding against a Roman citizen was tried initially before a single Roman magistrate. But any citizen found guilty of major crime could suspend punishment by an appeal to the whole Roman people, meeting in a general assembly. This type of appeal, called *provocatio,* may have existed under the early Roman monarchy. It became a matter of right for every Roman citizen on the expulsion of the kings and the founding of the Republic. In voting whether to confirm or vacate the sentence of the magistrate, the citizen body of Rome under the Republic acted in its capacity as ultimate sovereign, free to choose indulgence or severity without limit from any rule.[14]

The privilege of *provocatio* was highly valued among the privileges of Roman citizenship, but it was available only where the sanction that could be employed against the accused was severe— the death penalty or a heavy money fine. Sentences of magistrates were not subject to review if they were enforceable merely by imprisonment or exile, moderate fines or seizure of goods. Furthermore, *provocatio* applied only to prosecutions commenced within the city of Rome; it lost much of its importance when Roman territory and the operating radius of Roman armies began to expand.

It is a matter of great theoretical interest that in the early centuries of the Republic no serious attempt was made to restrict the power or discretion of the magistrates by formulated rules, and that even the limited review of their actions by *provocatio* depended on the vote of a popular assembly functioning as a purely political body and equally free from restraint. There has been much romantic talk about adherence to order and the rule of law as representing the spirit of Roman society from earliest times. But it was only in private law and civil procedure that extreme rigidity and formalism prevailed. Over very wide areas of coercion

[14] Theodor Mommsen, *Römisches Staatsrecht* (Leipzig, 3d ed., 1887), III, 351, 358–359; James L. Strachan-Davidson, *Problems of the Roman Criminal Law* (Oxford, 1912), I, 136–138; Ernst Levy, "Statute and Judge in Roman Criminal Law," 13 *Wash. L. Rev.* 291, 295 (1938); P. F. Girard, *Histoire de l'Organisation Judiciaire des Romains* (Paris, 1901), 104–120.

and punishment individual magistrates, elected in annual elections, were left remarkably free from rules, of either substance or procedure. The same was true of the popular assemblies whose review could sometimes be invoked. The contradiction seems all the greater since it was through these avenues that public force could bear most heavily on the freedom and security of private individuals. Yet these great powers were left thus, at large, for the first four centuries of the Republic.[15]

It seems most likely that the setting of limits to the powers of magistrates was one of the principal motives for creating new criminal courts during the last century of the Republic. The origins of the new criminal courts must be found in a particular class of cases which were highly charged with politics—complaints of extortion by inhabitants of the provinces against their Roman governors. The first known case of this kind comes from 171 B.C. Here the Senate directed that a special commission of five senators, to be designated by the praetor, should sit as a court to try the charges.[16] Complaints of this kind lay in a borderland between civil and criminal law. They recurred so often that an assembly of the people in 149 B.C. passed a statute which set up a standing court of senators to hear and decide such cases. This statute expressed an important principle: appeal by *provocatio* to an assembly of the whole Roman people could be excluded through a delegation of the assembly's powers to a special tribunal. This was a useful and important idea, which was seized upon by that ardent but ill-fated reformer, Gaius Gracchus, in his contest with the senatorial party. Again the immediate issue was the politically explosive subject of extortion by Roman governors, who were almost always members of the senatorial class. In 122 B.C. Gracchus engineered the passage of a statute which

[15] The main theme of this paragraph is developed at length by Professor Levy in his admirable article in 13 *Wash. L. Rev.* 291, cited in the previous note. It is also discussed briefly by Girard, 125–126. Discussion of *provocatio* and its limitations will be found in Herbert F. Jolowicz, *Historical Introduction to the Study of Roman Law* (Cambridge, Eng., 1954), 322–327 (hereafter cited as *RL*); Strachan-Davidson, I, 96–110, 136–157, 170–173.

[16] Strachan-Davidson, I, 223–224 and II, 1–4. Authorization to existing *magistrates* to initiate criminal proceedings against particular individuals should be distinguished from appointment of a judging commission, which occurred in the case referred to in the text. Before 171 B.C. and at various times thereafter the Senate or assemblies of the people gave directives of this kind to magistrates. Strachan-Davidson, I, 225–227; Jolowicz, *RL*, 327.

transferred the judging function in such cases from senators to knights (*equites*). The knights were for the most part wealthy merchants, the upper upper middle class. The use of knights as judges in these *causes célèbres* was an important part of Gracchus' plan to divide the upper classes and stir antagonism between them.[17] The statute of 122 B.C. created a panel of 450 knights from which the judging commission was to be selected in each individual case; the commission so chosen was authorized to render final judgment in any case of alleged extortion by a provincial governor. This express authorization went far to ensure that no magistrate could prevent or obstruct a trial by exercise of a veto. Also, the inquisitorial powers of the magistrates were greatly restricted by using private complaint and private prosecution for the conduct of the trial and by giving control over proof to the private accuser.[18] The new procedure that was here taking shape was a radical innovation, like many of Gracchus' other schemes for reordering Roman society. The innovation was a double one—not only the exclusion of appeals to popular assemblies through *provocatio*, but subordination of the magistrates to rules that were laid down in advance. As this new procedure was gradually extended to other types of criminal conduct, it brought into the front line of political warfare the issue—who were to be judges?

It is common to speak of these new courts as "jury courts" and their membership as "jurors" (*jurés, Geschworene*). Their powers so sharply restricted the powers of the magistrates, which were in theory unlimited, that one author has tried to resolve the contradiction by describing these "jurors" as merely advisers to the magistrates.[19] They were much more than advisers. It is true that a magistrate presided at the trial in each case, but a majority vote of the whole membership was conclusive. Judgment was rendered on the whole case, including both facts and law. We do not know precisely how many persons were required to make a court in the earlier stages, but somewhat later, in Cicero's time, the range was between 51 and 75 members.[20] What is clear above all is that

[17] Theodor Mommsen, *History of Rome* (transl. William P. Dickson, New York, 1880), III, 113–117; Last, "Gaius Gracchus," in *Cambridge Ancient History* (Cambridge, Eng., 1932), IX, 45–93, esp. 69–78; Richard E. Smith, *The Failure of the Roman Republic* (Cambridge, Eng., 1955), 89–94.
[18] Jolowicz, *RL*, 329–331.
[19] Strachan-Davidson, II, 45–50.
[20] Strachan-Davidson, II, 97.

these large aggregations were courts in the fullest sense and that the presiding magistrates were at most their executive agents. In effect the sovereign assembly of the Roman people transferred the full power of decision in major criminal trials—not only its own, but the power of the Roman magistrates—to groups of lay persons chosen from a particular social class.

In the time of troubles that followed the murder of Gaius Gracchus, the membership of the criminal courts became one of the keys to control of the state. The knights, to whom Gracchus had entrusted the judging function, were wealthy capitalists who were heavily involved in tax collections, grain imports, and other large enterprises on both public and private account. To preserve their own investments and their influence in provincial affairs, the knights were just as ready as the senators had been to use violence and murder, as they did when their position was threatened for a time by a senatorial party of moderate reform.[21] Various attempts made to restrict or abolish the judging functions possessed by the knights came to no result until the counterrevolution of the conservative party, led by Sulla. In 81 B.C. Sulla transferred the monopoly of judging back to the senators as a part of his general program to restore the Senate's control of the machinery of government. Then in 70 B.C. an intermediate solution was adopted, by which the panel of eligible judges was composed equally of persons from three social classes—the senators, the knights, and the *tribuni aerarii,* a commercial class immediately below the knights. The total taken from each of the three classes was 300, for a total panel of 900. The panels were prepared each year by the urban praetor and were effective for one year. The selection of names from the panel was by a complex process of elimination, with proposals and counterproposals by private accuser and accused, and with a power to challenge on several grounds reserved to the accused.[22]

The functioning of these courts was not necessarily the same in all types of crimes. Separate statutes set up procedure for trial of each of the separate crimes, and in detail there were differences between them. However, through most of the first century B.C.

[21] Mommsen, *History of Rome,* III, 218–225.
[22] Joseph Lengle, "Die Auswahl der Richter im römischen Quästions-prozess," ZSS (*röm.*), 53:276, at 294–295; Strachan-Davidson, II, 97–111.

the major crimes—murder, treason, sacrilege, extortion, forgery —were regularly tried and decided by these lay tribunals, comprising usually somewhat more than fifty members. The statutes that provided for these forms of trial also defined the grounds of liability and the sanctions to be employed. The former discretionary powers of the magistrates and the general people's assembly were thus eliminated and the main body of Roman criminal law came to be quite precisely defined by statute.[23] The courts that applied these rules, however, were lay tribunals of considerable size, deciding by majority vote.

This general scheme survived, with minor variations, into the principate of Augustus. The main change of Augustus was to enlarge the lists of eligible persons to a total of 4000. Membership in the panels by then and thenceforward was sought only for honorific reasons. The contest over the power of judging in criminal cases, like other great issues that divided Roman society, was abated and submerged in the great Augustan compromise.

This system should not be confused with political democracy. It is true that Gracchus, at the time he used it for extortion cases in 122 B.C., was seeking to construct a kind of alliance between the commercial class and the city proletariat, and certainly at this time there were in circulation many radical democratic ideas imported from Greece. But Sulla, who confirmed and greatly extended the system in 81 B.C., aimed thereby to help restore the dominance of the senatorial aristocracy. Even later, when the membership in the panels was distributed somewhat more widely, the persons selected were all aristocrats of wealth if not of birth. In the accounts that have survived of criminal trials under the Republic, the judges and even the litigants belonged almost exclusively to a small ruling group.[24] Still less can one suspect that Augustus and his successors, in enlarging somewhat the list of eligibles, were inspired by Athenian conceptions of government by the crowd.

The development of the republican criminal courts has been described in such detail because it throws light on disputed matters in connection with civil proceedings. Before discussing the disputed matters in the trial of civil cases, I should like to mention

[23] Levy, 13 *Wash. L. Rev.* 291, 296–297.
[24] Strachan-Davidson, II, 119.

two promising types of civil tribunals, staffed by laymen, whose growth was stunted in adolescence.

The most interesting and mysterious was the court of the hundred men (*centumviri*). Its membership was chosen from the 35 Roman tribes, three men from each tribe, so that the membership of the court actually totalled 105. All proceedings before it were conducted by the archaic *actio sacramenti* with some ancient symbolism in addition that suggests antiquity for the court itself. But it is now generally believed that it was first created in the latter part of the second century B.C., about the same time as the criminal courts that have just been considered. The court of the hundred men dealt with civil cases. They were almost certainly not elected by the tribes on any principle of representation. They were probably chosen by the praetor or some other magistrate from the membership lists of the tribes. There is therefore no reason to suspect behind this new tribunal any radical plan for political reform. Yet it served at least to undermine the senatorial monopoly and provided a new source of eligible lay judges. It dealt only with cases between Roman citizens and apparently only with those of unusual interest or importance. It retained a high prestige and lasted well into the principate and empire, until the third century A.D. Yet it is neglected in the writings of the classical lawyers and even the scope of its jurisdiction is still under debate. At least in its later phases it probably sat in sections of thirty or forty members each. So it provides an example of a popular court created deliberately by state action in a time of crisis and political experiment. It had no known antecedents in earlier Roman institutions. It had no observable influence on later developments. It may well have been a deliberate imitation of Greek models and it is fascinating to speculate what its fate might have been if the class conflicts that destroyed the Republic had had a different outcome.[25]

Another type of lay tribunal, composed of the so-called *recuperatores*, can be traced back to the very early Republic. Such tribu-

---

[25] Pauly-Wissowa, *Realencyclopädie*, III, 1935 (*Centumviri*, by Wlassak); P. Koschaker, in ZSS (*röm.*), 50:679 (1930); Jolowicz, *RL*, 203–205; Olivier Martin, *Le Tribunal des Centumvirs* (Paris, 1904). The author last cited gives (p. 133) a somewhat different interpretation of origins.

The court of the *decemviri*, briefly discussed by Jolowicz in the passage cited, left so few traces that it seems not worth description here.

nals were created by early forms of interstate agreement and have an important place in the prehistory of international law. The need for such tribunals arose from the basic principles: (1) that the law to be applied to any individual was the law of the tribe or city-state of which he was a member and (2) that access to courts was likewise restricted to members of the court-keeping tribe or state. Thus the traditional Roman courts were competent only in cases between Roman citizens and a similar requirement of citizenship would normally exclude Roman citizens from foreign courts. In the centuries before a Roman peace was imposed upon them, some stable arrangements were needed between the city-states of the Mediterranean lands. The solution was to create by treaty special tribunals for cases of mixed citizenship. This became common practice among the Mediterranean city-states. As Rome absorbed or overpowered its neighbors, these treaty-courts survived; at first, perhaps, in cases between Roman citizens and foreigners in territories newly conquered and then between Roman citizens, even at Rome itself. Their chief advantage was their speed and informality. Cases were supposed to be decided within ten days from the start of suit. The members of the courts were always laymen, usually three in number but sometimes five. They were drawn from lists prepared in advance by a process of elimination, with proposal, challenge and counterchallenge between the parties themselves. They were something more than arbitrators, for they operated under known procedures and with a certain measure of state control. The courts of the *recuperatores* were small benches of lay judges that operated largely outside the ordinary law. They were widely used and might have played a larger part if other means had not been found for introducing flexibility within the formal structure of the civil law itself.[26]

The type of tribunal that triumphed over these competitors was the two-stage court of praetor and *iudex*. This was the arrangement described by the classical jurists, the central point in modern accounts of classical civil procedure, the final proof if proof were needed of the Romans' gift for innovation within a

---

[26] Pauly-Wissowa, *Realencyclopädie* (2d ser.), I, 406ff. (*reciperatio* by Wenger); Girard, *Histoire de l'Organisation Judiciaire des Romains*, 99–104; Strachan-Davidson, I, 211–224, the latter passage suggesting the important connection between the *recuperatores* and the early antecedents of the republican criminal courts developed by Gracchus and Sulla.

framework of order. It was in truth a most ingenious compromise. After a preliminary hearing of the whole case by the praetor, in the presence of the parties and perhaps of their counsel, a formula was prepared by the praetor. The formula appointed as *iudex* a single Roman citizen, defined the issues the *iudex* was to consider, and authorized him to render judgment according to his findings on these issues. The judgment, in all but very exceptional cases, was final and unappealable. The formula was thus both a directive and a grant of power by public authority. But it was more than this. The parties to the litigation must agree, not only on the choice of the individual judge but on the definition of the issues and on the powers conferred. The *litis contestatio* which concluded the stage before the praetor was thus in theory a contract between the parties. The praetor in the developed formulary system had means to compel assent, yet efforts were made to secure an assent that was more than nominal. The ultimate judgment rendered by the *iudex* was thus in theory and largely in fact "a state-reinforced arbitration award" with the double authority conferred by its mixed origin.[27]

The formulary system in its developed stage in the late Republic and early principate has been described in great detail by classical authors and modern scholars, with remarkable agreement on the main results. It is clear that the system provided great freedom for invention and flexibility in detail. By variations, large and small, in the formula the issues before the *iudex* in individual cases could be redefined and new doctrines or remedies thereby introduced. Experiments found useful or desirable could be incorporated as standard provisions in other formulas. When the doctrines thus worked out by experiment had found general acceptance, they could be incorporated by way of public notice in the edict issued by each praetor at the start of his year's term of office. Roman law and legal procedure were transformed by these means during the time when Roman power was expanding rapidly and the need of Roman society for internal readjustment was becoming irresistible. All these features and consequences of the developed formulary system are well known and not in dispute. The questions are—where did the formulary system come from, and when?

[27] The quoted phrase is that of Leopold Wenger, *Praetor und Formel* (1926), 30.

Modern opinions concerning the formulary system all stem from the work of Wlassak, who showed that consent to the formula by the litigants was a pervasive element of the system in its maturity. Wlassak also argued that the origins of the system must be found in private arbitration agreements entered into in earliest times quite independently of any state control.[28] Under this conception of origins, growth occurred through using the authority of public magistrates to reinforce the forms, procedures and results already developed by purely private agreement. In general support of this explanation, other authors have shown the great importance of arbitration in primitive societies—not only at Rome but in the Greek cities and Asia Minor. It is most difficult for us to project our minds so far back in human experience to a time when preservation of the peace stood so high on the scale of purposes for social action and when the means of social action were so feebly organized. There is much evidence to show that at such times friendly agreement, leading to peaceful settlement, was an objective consciously pursued and valued for itself.[29] The role of arbitration could then be very different from the role it has in our society, after internal peace has been made relatively secure, when courts can afford to wait for social disorders to be brought in for judicial treatment and the treatment itself is largely passive—the contest is worked out on the initiative of the parties through rulings by the court on matters submitted to its decision. For the stage of prehistory that we are trying to imagine, the explanation of Wlassak presupposes, in effect, that there was no legal order imposed and enforced by the group. It describes a condition in which the forces of society exhaust themselves when they have induced persons in strife to submit themselves to some trusted neutral outsider. It assumes that such submission would be mostly spontaneous, though indirect social

[28] This opinion is stated in many places, for example in Moriz Wlassak, *Gerichtsmagistrat im gesetzlichen Spruchverfahren* (Weimar, 1905–1907), 59.
[29] For Greece this is one of the main conclusions of Artur Steinwenter, *Die Streitbeendigung durch Urteil, Schiedsspruch und Vergleich nach griechischem Rechte* (Munich, 1924). Rudolf Düll, *Der Gütegedanke im römischen Zivilprozessrecht* (Munich, 1931), develops this general thesis also and aims to show that the notion of *iudex* as arbitrator had lasting effects on Roman substantive law and civil procedure by injecting needed elements of discretion. He also tried to show that public officials as part of their official duties undertook on a considerable scale to mediate affirmatively with litigants and promote the settlement of disputes.

pressure might sometimes be employed. From repetition would come rules which public agencies would then gradually adopt and invest with public sanctions.[30]

It is evident that the issues thus raised are of the most general nature and call loudly for help from students of primitive societies. It would be useless to attempt a review of all the opinions published about them. But some attention should be given to the strong dissent of Leopold Wenger, who was another great Roman proceduralist and in most matters a disciple of Wlassak. Developing hints that appeared in Cicero and other Roman authors, Wenger asserted first, that the absolute monarchy of the early Etruscan kings of Rome included a royal court with unlimited competence; second, that the unlimited judicial powers of the ancient monarchy were all transferred to the republican magistrates on the formation of the Republic; but third, that the introduction of a lay private citizen as judge, with a requirement of party consent to his appointment, was a "democratic" reform providing constitutional restraints on the inherited powers of magistrates. According to this view, the peculiar Roman split court of praetor and *iudex* was produced by action and reaction primarily at the political level and arbitration fades out as a causative factor. In arguing for his view Wenger urged the continuity of Roman political ideas: the theoretically unlimited *imperium* of the Etruscan-oriental monarchs was transferred to the republican magistrates and, despite the restraints introduced by "democratic" reforms under the Republic, it continued to brood over Roman institutions until Augustus and his successors appeared and resumed these ancient powers while the restraints gradually dropped away.[31]

For present purposes it should suffice to select only the most persuasive of the attacks made on Wenger's theories. First of all, it seems that he placed too early the conquest of extensive judicial powers by the Roman state. The evidence for an unlimited judicial competence in the kings is doubtful and late, a repetition

[30] It should be noted, in fairness, that Wlassak did not develop his thesis in the terms used in this paragraph or develop the comparison with modern procedure.

[31] The views of Wenger have been stated in various places in somewhat different ways. Summaries of his earlier views will be found in Leopold Wenger, *Institutionen des römischen Zivilprozessrechts* (Munich, 1925), sec. 3, and Paul Jors-Wolfgang Kunkel-Leopold Wenger, *Römisches Recht* (Berlin, 1935), 382. His later partial recantation is referred to below, note 37.

of ancient legends; it seems unlikely that at so early a time governmental powers could have been used to decide private controversies, full-scale and under an organized procedure.[32] Furthermore, the political theory developed by Wenger is based on very scattered evidence and seems to involve the reading back into early times of late Roman or even modern conceptions.[33] Comparison with Greek analogies reinforces the broad conclusion that the growth of state powers in adjudication was gradual and that it centered around the issue whether self-help measures were lawful or unlawful. This kind of administrative action by magistrates, chiefs or wise men—aiming either to inhibit or else to clear the path for private vengeance—could inject them some distance into contested issues and the examination of evidence, but full-scale adjudication would come very slowly and would expand only as controls succeeded gradually in limiting the use of private force.[34]

It now seems quite clear that the fateful decisions which determined the shape of Roman civil procedure were not made, as Wenger first contended, at the foundation of the Republic in the sixth century B.C. This much Wenger himself conceded shortly before his death. The use of the private citizen as arbitrator-judge, which appears in the legal sources of the very early Republic, would therefore seem to have had nothing to do with politics. Certainly if it had been conceived as a move toward popular control, it would have been resisted by the early patricians who acquired command of the state on the expulsion of the kings. Furthermore, as a device for limiting governmental power, trial before the citizen-judge could not have had much effect, for the rigidity and formalism of both substantive law and procedure would have left little scope for the judge's influence or discretion

[32] Max Kaser, "Zum Ursprung des geteilten römischen Zivilprozessverfahrens," in *Festschrift für Wenger* (Munich, 1944), I, 106, 109–110; E. Levy, book review in ZSS (*röm.*), 46:364, at 369–372.

[33] Alfred Heuss, "Zur Entwicklung des Imperiums der römischen Oberbeamten," ZSS (*röm.*), 64:57 (1944); Gerhard Wesenberg, "Zur Frage der Continuität zwischen königlicher Gewalt und Beamtengewalt in Rom," ZSS (*röm.*), 70:58 (1953).

[34] The conclusions stated in the text depend largely on the work of Professor Hans Julius Wolff, especially in his article "The Origin of Judicial Litigation Among the Greeks," *Traditio*, 4:31 (1946). Professor Wolff's conclusions in this article were forecast and the issues conveniently summarized in his book review in 5 *La. L. Rev.* 367, 369–371 (1943).

in the trial of civil cases. It could be that the early *iudex* was at times a referee appointed by one of the magistrates—that is, a specially qualified expert or reliable person authorized to find facts, not in order to restrict the powers of the magistrates, but to aid in their exercise.[35] And if this were true, it would not exclude the possibility that party-consent was secured in other cases, as a means of facilitating action and promoting acceptance of the ultimate judgment. In the 300 years from 500 to 200 B.C., it seems quite likely that different expedients were tried. We are therefore not required to choose between private arbitration or state authority as the exclusive source of an ultimately mixed procedure.

But no matter what view of origins is adopted, certain mysteries remain. When the formulary system emerges into the light of day in the first century B.C., it has main features that are directly contradictory. On the one hand, the praetor in preparing the formula in each case had an enormously wide discretion. On the other hand, his discretion was limited by the two requirements that the function of rendering judgment must be transferred to a private citizen-judge and that the litigants must consent to the choice of judge and to the powers conferred upon him. The surviving Roman sources attribute the praetor's discretion to a statute, the *lex Aebutia,* but do not give its date. Modern authors on the whole agree that it came somewhere between 150 and 120 B.C., though this does not dispose of the question whether some freedom of action had been acquired by the praetors before the statute and quite independently of it.[36] The power to manipulate the formula was the key to the later praetorian reforms. For present purposes the source of this power is not so interesting as the source of the limitations upon it. If one can conclude that the main elements of the formulary system were not established until the second century B.C., the whole problem takes on a new aspect. The compulsion to employ a private citizen as judge in a second, separate stage and the requirement of consent by the parties would then emerge at about the time when assembly-

---

[35] This suggestion by Kaser, "Zum Ursprung des geteilten römischen Zivilprozessverfahrens," *Festschrift für Wenger,* 106, 114–126, is developed by Wenger in *Studi in Onore di Siro Solazzi* (Naples, 1948), 47, at 54–57.

[36] Jolowicz, *RL,* 226–233, argues persuasively that such freedom probably existed before the *lex Aebutia.*

courts were being created for criminal trials; when new experiments in government were very actively discussed and Greek conceptions of total democracy were in general circulation. This suggests that the famous split in Roman civil procedure was probably part of a broader movement to limit the powers of magistrates in the second century B.C.[37]

The political results achieved, if any were intended, could not have been very large. Civil litigation was much less likely than criminal prosecution to raise highly charged political issues. The use of a single lay judge, instead of assemblies of 40, 50 or more, meant that there was no attempt to secure a cross section of opinion. The panel of eligible judges did not have the political importance in civil that it had in criminal cases, for the parties in civil cases could choose from outside the panel; any mature male Roman citizen who was not under physical or legal disability could be appointed as *iudex* provided the parties agreed. Therefore the citizen-judge, deriving his powers both from litigants' consent and praetor's appointment, was not a very effective instrument for introducing at Rome an Athenian style of direct democracy. If the measures adopted in the second century B.C. were "democratic" in motive, their chief political result was to limit the discretionary powers of the praetor in civil litigation, by subjecting the choice and the powers of the *iudex* to a requirement of litigants' consent. To the Roman citizen this amounted to a guarantee that in disputes with another Roman citizen he was entitled to a judge of his own choice. One can call this guarantee "democratic" as some have done.[38] It seems much better to omit

[37] This much seems to be agreed by various persons who reject or qualify in other ways the views first advanced by Wenger, such as Paul Koschaker in ZSS (*röm.*), 50:724; Kaser in *Festschrift für Wenger*, I, 106. Wenger himself before his death withdrew his contention that the split procedure originated at the beginning of the Republic and argued instead that it became compulsory in the period of the Gracchi—"a political phenomenon of a democratic nature." Wenger, "Vom zweigeteilten römischen Zivilprozesse," *Studi Solazzi* (1948), 47, at 61–63. But Jolowicz, who also joined the controversy, offered another solution which minimized the degree of real freedom possessed by the parties in agreeing to *iudex* and formula, and rejected all political motives, either in the sixth or in the second century B.C. "The Iudex and the Arbitral Principle," *Revue Internationale des Droits de l'Antiquité*, 2:477 (1949).

[38] Carl W. Westrup, *Introduction to Early Roman Law* (Oxford, 1934–1954), IV, 151–152, calling the bipartition of civil procedure "undoubtedly a republican-democratic reform"; Rudolf Düll, "Iudicet iudicarive iubeat," ZSS (*röm.*), 71:348 (1954), arguing strongly that "this basic democratic principle" was imported from

the word. A distance much wider than the Adriatic Sea separated the Roman *iudex* from the Athenian people's courts.

The principle of free choice of the *iudex* by the parties survived as long as the formulary system itself. In practice it seems that in the choice of judges the chief source of supply was the album of eligibles prepared for criminal prosecutions.[39] This may have been due to suggestion from the praetor in the hearing before him [40] or it may have been due to the assurance of competence and impartiality implied by membership on the list. For the album was revised annually by the praetor (at least after 70 B.C.); with the advent of the principate Augustus and his successors added the scrutiny of the lists to their other tasks and found here, no doubt, a useful and harmless form of political patronage. Those listed on the album were bound to serve unless they had a sufficient excuse, for judging was conceived as a public office.

The fact was that as time went on judging became a burden from which many citizens sought to escape. The power to vote in criminal trials was no longer an avenue to control of the state. In civil litigation the role of the judge was honorable but for the most part it represented merely civic duty. For prominent or ambitious men other things were more worth doing. And so the lists grew longer in the effort to secure an ample supply of judges. Augustus created a fourth class of judges, eligible only for civil suits involving "smaller sums," though even these fourth class citizens had to be worth in the census at least 200,000 sesterces. Caligula later added a fifth class, bringing the list to a total of 5000 persons.[41] Yet even with these extensions, the public office of judge was clearly reserved for lay persons of rank and high

---

Greece. Girard, *Histoire de l'Organisation Judiciaire des Romains*, 79–82, seems to adopt the same views, though more guardedly.

[39] Jean Mazeaud, *La Nomination du Iudex Unus sous la Procédure Formulaire à Rome* (Paris, 1933), 5–6; Wenger, book review in ZSS (*röm.*), 68:424 (1935). Both writers agree (Mazeaud at pp. 40–48) that the album was used in the republican period as a source for *iudices* in civil litigation, and not merely for criminal cases as some authors have contended.

[40] Mazeaud, 104–105, argued for an increasing influence of the praetor in the choice of the *iudex*, though conceding that in principle the consent of the parties was needed. Wenger (at pp. 440–442) was willing to concede only that the influence of the praetor could have been increased through the great lengthening of the lists of eligibles under the principate, which aggravated the problem of choice.

[41] Pauly-Wissowa, *Realencyclopädie*, VI, 289 (*Equites Romani*); IX, 2466 (*Iudex*).

social standing, from the beginning to the end of the praetorian system. In view of the general trends in Roman society, one would hardly expect that its willingness to entrust the judging function to laymen meant that every man could be a judge. Adjudication by laymen was clearly not a means of achieving political democracy.

Yet it is surely a remarkable thing that through all the great creative phase of Roman law for the first 500 years, there was no such thing as a professional judge for whom judging was in any sense a career. Down to the end of the Republic all decision-making in every form of state-sponsored court was by unspecialized laymen—in the assembly courts for criminal trials, in the court of the hundred men set up for civil cases, in the three- or five-man courts of the *recuperatores*, in the split two-man court of praetor and *iudex* in standard civil procedure. The setting up of some of these courts surely involved some major political contests. But the contests were not between laymen and professionals; in first instance at least they were contests over the powers of elected magistrates. And these magistrates themselves were no more professionals than the persons who bore the title of *iudex*. They were elected, normally for one year. They knew no more law, as a rule, than any other Roman needed to know to perform his civic duties.

It is not that the Romans lacked legal specialists. Unlike the fifth- and fourth-century Athenians, they had jurists who applied themselves most diligently to the study of law and achieved a very high standard of technical skill. It was the jurists who supplied to praetor, *iudex*, and other public officials the information and guidance they needed to perform their duties. The influence of the jurists was universal—in developing the main lines of the formulary system, in rendering opinions as to the proper solutions in individual cases, in advising both praetor and *iudex* on cases pending before them, and in many other ways. It was purely accident if one of them was elected praetor in any particular year or was chosen as *iudex* in a particular case. The function of the jurist was entirely different. Holding no public office, owing his influence only to his proved competence in the work, the jurist was custodian and transmitter of doctrine. He, not the judge, was the oracle of the law.

The influence of the praetorian system of procedure, with its

split court of praetor and *iudex*, lasted after the system itself had
been displaced in usage. The displacement was by the new system
of imperial courts which took shape as the principate was being
transformed into empire. In most of the provinces the praetorian
system was displaced quite early and in some (such as Egypt)
it was apparently never used at all. At Rome itself the last known
evidence of private citizens chosen as *iudices* from lists of eligibles
comes from the early third century A.D.[42] Yet the classical jurists,
centered in Rome, continued to discuss and describe the praetorian system as though it were regularly in use, and if they did
not discuss it they usually presupposed it. This survival in lawyers'
discourse of institutions almost obsolete is proof enough, if proof
were needed, of the traditionalism of the great Roman jurists and
the narrow range of their assumptions.[43] But it also means that
the Digest, the largest by far and the most admired part of surviving Roman law, was strongly focused on praetorian procedure
with its two laymen—praetor and *iudex*.

Here we approach a great paradox, the first of several that appear in the history of judges. The legacy of Roman law to the
later history of Europe included the conception of the judge as
a trained, specialized professional with complete command and
active duties at every stage of the proceeding. This conception
and the procedure built around it were to drive the laymen out
of the courts of continental Europe. Yet Roman law throughout its
creation and greatest flowering knew no such thing as a professional judge; when professional judges began to emerge in the
late classical period the great classical lawyers preferred not to
discuss them.

b. *The Principate and Empire*

A new system of judicial administration began to develop
quite early in the principate. Its central element was the authority of the *princeps*-emperor which soon began to pervade every
element of public administration. The process started gradually

[42] Moriz Wlassak, *Der Judikationsbefehl der römischen Prozess* (Wien, 1921),
77–78. The latest reference in an inscription to membership in the album of judges
is that of a man who served as consul in 261 A.D. and who had apparently been
listed on the album early in his career. Mazeaud, *La Nomination du Iudex Unus*,
38.

[43] General comments on this subject appear in Hans Julius Wolff, *Roman Law*
(Norman, Okla., 1951), 112.

but the rate acclerated. In the early principate the immense personal authority of Augustus and his immediate successors was carefully disguised under republican forms. The disguise soon wore thin. New institutions and new lines of authority developed, stemming from the general administrative powers of the emperor.[44] In court organization as in other phases of government, innovation came mainly from the provinces. But in Italy and even in Rome itself administrative officers, acting under the authority of the *princeps*, quite soon undertook specific lines of action that called for hearings, findings, and adjudication. These administrative proceedings, leading to the formation of administrative courts, were described as *extra ordinem*, outside the order of praetorian procedure. The power to judge in proceedings *extra ordinem* did not depend in any sense on the consent of the parties. The official concerned would conduct the hearing and render judgment under the emperor's authority.

The need for new machinery was probably greatest in criminal cases. The rules set up in the republican statutes had greatly limited the discretion of the assembly courts and of the magistrates who presided. Sanctions were strictly defined and trial procedure was formalized. But this system produced real difficulties where the conduct of the accused diverged somewhat from the conduct described in the statutes. Furthermore, prosecution depended on the initiative of private accusers and qualified judges were growing harder to find. The republican statutes did not in general apply in the provinces, or even in Italy to other than Roman citizens. So it is not at all surprising that imperial officials began to try, convict, and punish offenders in geographical areas and for types of misconduct to which the statutory schemes did not apply. Since their actions did not depend on statute but on imperial authority they were free to employ different sanctions or redefine standards of conduct, without effective limitation. The discretion soon acquired by imperial magistrates thus brought Roman criminal law full circle. The powers of the magistrates, originally very wide, had been limited by the strict rules of late republican legislation. Now these rules were supplanted by discretion in the magistrates, carried even further than in the early republican

[44] On the evolution of imperial powers and institutions the best short account in English is Jolowicz, *RL*, 336–355.

period. Reliance was placed increasingly, not on rules of law but on the personal integrity and judgment of officials who now clearly acted as full-scale judges under imperial authority.[45]

Similar developments occurred in civil procedure. The rate of change was different in the various parts of the empire. In Egypt, where the formulary system was apparently not introduced at all when Roman control was established, the pre-Roman public courts of Egypt, fully staffed with judicial officers, were simply carried over under Roman authority.[46] In other provinces that were administered directly by the emperor the formulary system probably disappeared quite early. Even in those whose governors were named by the Senate, the wide powers conferred on the governors probably gave great freedom in selecting and empowering judges in civil litigation. There were traces in some provinces of panels, composed of wealthy and prominent provincial citizens who were eligible to function as judges or referees.[47] Even later there survived in usage copies of the standard formulas of praetorian procedure. But these forms may have been nothing more than convenient descriptive forms or models, like some of our older pleading forms that are used long after their original functions have disappeared. The use of the praetorian formulas was not forbidden expressly until 342 A.D. Long before this the Roman system of judicial administration had become a hierarchy of public officials, surmounted by the emperor himself as highest appellate judge and deriving its powers by delegation from him.[48]

The transfer of the judicial function to permanent officials helped to produce a radical recasting of Roman procedure, whose total effect was to increase greatly the powers and the influence of the judge. The trial judge acquired continuous control over the proceedings before, during, and after the trial. He ruled on the sufficiency of pleadings and on exceptions or objections introduced at every stage; he directed service of papers and employed

[45] Levy, "Statute and Judge in Roman Criminal Law," 13 *Wash. L. Rev.* 291 (1938); Levy, "Gesetz und Richter im kaiserlichen Strafrecht," *Bull. dell'Ist. di Diritto Romano*, 45:57 (1938); Jolowicz, *RL*, 411–413.

[46] Moriz Wlassak, *Zum römischen Provinzialprozess* (Wien, 1919), 4–6.

[47] Wlassak, *Zum römischen Provinzialprozess*, 13–16.

[48] Wlassak, *Zum römischen Provinzialprozess*, 23–30; Wlassak, *Der Judikationsbefehl der römischen Prozess*, 77–78. In these passages Wlassak develops his suggestion that the forms and classifications of praetorian procedure could have continued in use for some time after the disappearance of the citizen-judge.

state authority to compel attendance of the parties and testimony by witnesses; he entered judgment and supervised execution. Though the proceeding before the judge remained at this stage an oral hearing, there was an increasing reliance on documents, both through written pleadings by the parties and in the written records that the judge himself prepared. Compulsory oaths by the parties, the prelude to an inquisitorial system, came into wider use. Trials ceased to be public. Appeals, which in the modern sense had been unknown in the praetorian system, were early introduced and became formally organized with two or more levels of appellate jurisdiction. Judging had in short become a steady if not a full-time job, captured and administered by the state as one of the essential functions of autocratic government.[49]

This did not mean at all that the judges appointed under the late empire were highly trained lawyers. Poverty and ignorance in this time of somber twilight meant that trained personnel were everywhere in short supply. Responsibility for judging was often mixed with other kinds of official duties or intentionally assigned to persons without formal education. To meet the needs of such persons, lawyers were appointed and paid by the state to act as legal advisers of the courts. These court assessors not only informed the official judges of the applicable rules of law but often drafted orders and advised on the conduct of trials and the disposition of cases. The available legal talent was thus mobilized for the service of a largely untrained imperial bureaucracy, on whom the new legal procedure placed greatly increased demands.[50]

It was of course through Justinian's Corpus Juris that knowledge of Roman law was transmitted to medieval Europe. In this huge miscellany the traces of the praetorian system with its citizen-judge were not by any means obliterated. The late imperial system was described as a kind of parallel with no real attempt to resolve the discord between them. There might have been some problems of choice for medieval lawyers if they had read the Corpus Juris with full comprehension of the historical changes that the compilers crudely telescoped. But the medieval lawyers

[49] The general account in this paragraph is based mainly on Jolowicz, *RL*, 459–467; Paul F. Girard, *Manuel Élémentaire du Droit Romain* (Paris, 8th ed., 1929), 1140–1146; and Wenger, *Institutionen des röm. Zivilprozessrechts*, sec. 29.
[50] Jolowicz, *RL*, 469.

lacked almost wholly the time-dimension. They also had faith in Justinian's claim for his text of a perfect internal harmony. With the assumptions they used they could hardly have failed to be impressed by the explicit account of imperial innovations. These innovations, and the theories of government they presupposed, happened also to meet the needs of the canon lawyers, who were to become in the Middle Ages the great proceduralists. For the canon lawyers the choice was easy. Seeking a system of courts and procedure that would promote the organization of a universal church under strong papal control, the canonists accepted the version that the late empire had constructed. The lead of the canonists was readily followed by secular jurists. Thus it was that canonists and civilians in a friendly alliance imposed on the continent of Europe a system derived from late Roman law and left to modern historians the reconstruction of the procedural system around which Roman law itself had been built.

This was not to mean a sudden shift to a program of judge-made law. On the contrary, medieval practice was to maintain the classical Roman division of responsibility, between the judge who merely decided cases and the legal expert, the custodian and transmitter of doctrine. So far as theory could do it, the judge was suppressed as a factor in legal development and cast in a wholly dependent role. But in the decision of particular cases, the canonist procedure based on late Roman law was to magnify the office of judge and enlarge its duties. This meant a constant pressure toward professionalizing the judicial function. Time was needed for the effects to be felt but the effects when felt were enormous.

CHAPTER II

POPULAR COURTS AND THEIR DISPLACEMENT IN FRANCE AND GERMANY

As Roman authority disintegrated there spread over the continent of Europe new institutions of government brought by the Germanic invaders and inspired by profoundly different conceptions of society. The inheritance from Rome was never wholly forgotten. These new institutions showed, in local adaptations, many differences of detail. But they rested on a common fund of ideas, derived from a common experience and producing similar modes of action, which were spread through the north and east of Europe and in the west to England, France and Italy. They must be briefly sketched, since later developments stem from them.

1. THE MEDIEVAL FOLK-MOOTS

In the earliest records of the Germanic tribes it appears that the central agency of government was the assembly of the people, which every free and law-worthy member of the group had a duty to attend. Membership depended on kinship through blood-ties, real or supposed. Meetings of the assemblies were held at regular intervals and usually in the open, perhaps in places rendered holy by religion or providing some other outward symbol of community. Any matter of interest to the group could be brought before the assembly. The settlement of disputes was part of its business but this part was distinguished in no formal way from other kinds of business. The rules applied came from no lawgiver or other external source. They were known to all law-worthy men, as an inseparable part of common group experience.

35

There has been a great temptation, which not everyone has resisted, to paint these assemblies of free, self-reliant blonds in exceedingly bright colors:

In free nature, in the woods or on a spacious hill, under old trees or
by salubrious springs the Germans found their law. Just as the law itself sprang from the free womb of the people, so law-finding was not
hemmed in by walls and tents.[1]

Modern political terms have been used to describe them, such as
"democratic peasant republics." [2] Such modern ideas may easily
mislead when applied to barbarian communities, yet they contain
a measure of truth. Jolliffe stated it well:

Since blood-relationship was accepted as the bond of society, the
folc was normally equalitarian in its public life, equal, that is to say,
within each of the birth-grades of which the folk was composed. This
found expression in the law, in the courts in which it was administered,
in their composition and procedure, in the rights and duties of individuals. . . . The right of all free individuals of the race, and—upon
the level of dearer birth—that of all nobles, was identical, a common
racial inheritance. . . . There is little scope for interpretation since
the law expresses the simple facts of life adequately and with the
sanctity of race heritage; equally little for authority since the state is
not a party to any cause. There are thus at first no royally made judges.
Our oldest law, like that of Germans and Celts, is one in which the
appropriate maxim is on every man's lips as soon as the facts of any
case have been determined. From this it follows that the court is a
meeting of common men, neighbors, a folk-moot. Freed from question-
ings about law, since it has the acknowledged rules of folkright to
apply, it expends its full force upon establishing the efficacy and integrity of its means of arriving at right judgment.[3]

From very early times, it seems, leadership in the folk communities was assumed by individuals who had some special claim
to pre-eminence, especially those priests who had channels for
communication with supernatural powers.[4] As secular law was
detached from religion, there emerged in many Germanic tribes

[1] Hans A. Fehr, *Deutsche Rechtsgeschichte* (Berlin, 5th ed., 1952), 9.
[2] Richard Schroeder and Eberhard von Künssberg, *Lehrbuch der deutschen
Rechtsgeschichte* (Leipzig, 7th ed., 1932), 132. This work will hereafter be cited
Schroeder, *DRG.*
[3] John E. A. Jolliffe, *Constitutional History of Medieval England* (London, 3d
ed., 1954), 7–8.
[4] Westrup, *Introduction to Early Roman Law,* III, 47–50.

the "law-speakers" who had no claim to priesthood but who were honored for their wisdom in legal matters. The function of the law-speakers was to propose a judgment, the assembly expressing its approval by cries, or clashing of weapons, or indeed at times by silence. This use of wise men as judgment-proposers was not exclusively Germanic, for similar phenomena appeared in early Greece and elsewhere.[5] Certainly it seems unlikely that even the German arrangements, widespread as they were, could have conformed to a single formula. In the choice of leaders there was every variation from popular vote to appointment or simple inheritance. The crowd of bystanders (the *Umstand*) must have shown every degree of participation from active discussion to sullen acquiescence. But the twin principles remained, very deeply built in, that the consent of the assembly was needed to render a valid judgment and that the members of the assembly were responsible for the judgment rendered, no matter how proposed.[6]

Among the many variations on the original theme, most interest attaches to developments in the Frankish kingdom, for in them lay the path to the future. The main impetus came from the Merovingian conquerors who re-established a central government in the seventh century. The Merovingian kings desired a judicial system under direct royal control but encountered a shortage of trained personnel and also the complications arising from the competing systems of Germanic, Roman, and king-made laws that survived in the ruins of the western Roman Empire. So the presidency of the local courts was transferred to royal officials. To inform and advise them law-finders were chosen—lay persons with special knowledge of law and prestige in their own communities. For some time the law-finders for each district continued to be elected. For some time also the consent of the community to the judgments proposed was probably required. Yet the emphasis on royal power must have reduced the influence of the bystanders. By the eighth century it became fairly clear that

[5] Westrup, III, 90–97; *Max Weber on Law in Economy and Society* (ed. Max Rheinstein, Cambridge, Mass., 1954), 87–89.

[6] Schroeder, *DRG*, sec. 8; R. Schroeder, "Gesetzsprecheramt und Priestertum bei den Germanen," ZSS (*germ.*), 4:215 (1883); Heinrich Brunner, *Deutsche Rechtsgeschichte* (Leipzig, 2d ed., 1906–1928), I, sec. 20.

judgments rendered in this type of court rested on the authority
of the royal presiding officer and the law-finders alone.[7]

This system was given lasting influence by the reforms of Charlemagne, effected perhaps two decades before 800 A.D. These reforms were in a sense a compromise, between the more ancient
institutions that survived in parts of his large domain and the
remodelled version created by the Frankish crown. One motive
expressed by Charlemagne was to relieve ordinary freemen of
the burdens of court attendance. Another was to ensure a higher
standard of decision-making and conformity to law.[8] His solution
was to provide in each district a permanent group of law-finders
(*scabini*) who were to be appointed by central authority with
a somewhat vague requirement of popular consent.[9] These law-
finders, normally seven in number, were to have as president and
executive officer the royal district governor—the count or *Graf*—
and were empowered to give judgment in less important matters
with the count's concurrence and without reference to any assembly. General meetings of the people were reserved for the full
courts held three times a year. At these general courts there was
the same traditional duty for all freemen to attend and it seems
likely that decisions still required some kind of assent from the
whole assembly.[10]

The system devised by Charlemagne spread widely through
and beyond his dominions. From the viewpoint of his officials it

[7] Wilhelm Sickel, "Die Entstehung der Schöffengerichte," ZSS (*germ.*), 6:1,
14–56; Schroeder, *DRG*, sec. 25.

[8] Capitulary of 802 A.D., expressing the desire *ut judices secundum legem juste
judicent, non secundum arbitrium:* quoted by Artur Engelmann-Robert W. Millar,
History of Continental Civil Procedure (Boston, 1927), 98.

[9] One capitulary of Charlemagne provides for appointment of *scabini* "*totius
populi consensu.*" Schroeder, *DRG*, 179.

[10] The power of the "by-standers" is, however, a much disputed subject. It is
discussed by Édouard Beaudouin, "La Participation des Hommes Libres au
Jugement dans le Droit Franc," *Nouvelle Revue Historique de Droit Français et
Étranger* (hereafter cited *NRH*), 1887, 450 and 557; Emile Chénon, *Histoire
Générale du Droit Français Public et Privé des Origines à 1815* (Paris, 1926),
I, 240–243. (Hereafter this work will be cited as Chénon, *HDF*.) The most
radical view is that of Ernst Hermann, *Die Entwicklung des altdeutschen
Schöffengerichts* (Breslau, 1881), who denied that from earliest times the people
had any effective part. Believing (pp. 149–150) that "all human development
starts from aristocracy," Hermann claimed that judgment-making was throughout
the whole post-Roman period a function of kings or royally appointed aristocracy.
An excellent general account of Charlemagne's reforms appears in Brunner,
Deutsche Rechtsgeschichte (2d ed.), vol. II, sec. 88. A useful summary appears
in Helen Cam, "Suitors and Scabini," *Speculum*, 10:189 (1935).

had the advantage of preserving central control over executive functions and large influence in the choice of local law-finders. The law-finders selected were usually great landowners but their standing and influence might well be enhanced by appointment to this imperial office. From the viewpoint of the communities concerned, the principle of collective action was preserved but made more workable through the use of smaller groups of persons in whom responsibility was concentrated. For important matters it was possible to secure the consent of augmented assemblies, and where this was felt to be desirable the consent might be something more than nominal. Altogether it was a skillful combination, acceptable at the time and adaptable in the future.

Then the Northmen descended. Central governments, weak and divided, lost their power to command. Out of the ruin of the ninth and tenth centuries a new order was painfully built in western Europe. Each part of Europe went its own way and the paths diverged.

2. FRANCE

a. *The Feudalization of French Courts*

In France the powers of government were widely dispersed by the year 1000 A.D. By royal grant or by usurpation great landowners acquired immunities from interference by crown officials, with corresponding freedom to govern their private domains. Of the functions of government that were thus distributed, court-keeping was perhaps the most vital. As Goebel has said:

In France and in Germany, the great abbeys, the bishops and the powerful landlords had possessed themselves duly and in good legal form of powers which deflected the administration of justice from a centralized royal supervision, and which gave them at once the profits and the determination of form and procedure. This was the culmination of something long under way. Certain powers of justiciation men with sufficient substance to maintain an establishment had had from the days of Roman rule. The acquisition of additional powers through the grant of a benefice or an immunity had been going on since Merovingian days. While centralization was proceeding, the means of its disintegration had been simultaneously contrived. It was the debacle of the late ninth century which completed the process.[11]

[11] Julius Goebel, *Felony and Misdemeanor* (New York, 1937), 124.

Through the confusion and terror of the ninth and tenth centuries it is impossible to trace any lines of continuity. There are only clues. In Flanders and northeastern France there were public courts with a general civil and criminal jurisdiction functioning in the eleventh and twelfth centuries and bearing every mark of descent from Carolingian models. In the towns the judicial powers of the *scabini* (now Gallicized to *échevins*) were enlarged into broad powers in general administration. As the towns were organized the *échevins* in some cases became the governing councils and officers.[12] This line of growth is most easily traced in northeastern France. In other parts of France the growth of the towns was based on other forms of community organization, some of them inherited and some recently created.[13] Outside the towns, adjudication by lay assemblies survived in French procedure through the thirteenth century at least, but mostly in courts that had been fully feudalized. The problem then is to explain how through most of France the public courts of Carolingian times were captured by private hands.

From the period of transition, the tenth and eleventh centuries, very little survives. Yet what there is shows a common pattern in widely scattered instances. The Carolingian *scabini* were from the outset recruited from the upper ranks of society and many of them must have become involved through land tenure in the bonds of feudal homage that were slowly being forged. Grants by the crown of fiscal and judicial immunities helped to concentrate power in the crown's grantees, just as it marked the weakening grasp of the crown itself. As new centers of power were organized in the great lordships and in local communities, the dominant personalities gathered courts around themselves and enforced attendance from their vassals as a condition of tenure. Law-finders (*scabini*) who were not vassals of the court-keeper continued to attend for a time, side by side with vassals. But

[12] François Louis Ganshof, *Recherches sur les Tribuneaux de Chatellenie en Flandre avant le Milieu du XIIIe Siecle* (Paris, 1932), 65–84; Yvonne Bongert, *Recherches sur les Cours Laïques du Xe au XIIIe Siecle* (Paris, 1948), 80–85.

[13] Chénon, *HDF*, I, 623–640; Adhémar Esmein, *Cours Élémentaire d'Histoire du Droit Français* (Paris, 1895), 334–335; Eleanor Lodge, "The Communal Movement, Especially in France," *Cambridge Medieval History* (Cambridge, Eng., 1926), I, 632–633.

regular attendance was a burden, to be escaped by those whose attendance the territorial lords had no power to compel. As the circles in attendance grew smaller, the burdens on those remaining grew heavier. The duty of attending court became more and more a form of feudal service. The functions of the law-finders, over most of the land, became fused with the functions of vassals in courts held by their lords.[14]

All this presupposes strong pressures to maintain older modes of adjudication under the newer forms imposed by feudalism. That such pressures must have existed is shown by the record of feudal societies throughout western Europe. It is true that the distinction between the presiding officer, in whom resided the executive power, and the assembly, which "found" the judgment, was ancient and familiar, long antedating feudalism. It is also true that frequent, mutual consultation was a natural incident to the feudal relation, which placed so high a premium on the loyalty and mutual trust that were symbolized in the ceremony of homage. We should not underestimate the force of the demand for justice and the "all-pervading respect for law" that governed the relations of lords and vassals and made it the lord's duty to see that justice was done among his men.[15] Beside these ideal factors, whose force was perhaps intermittent, one can place some very practical considerations. In times when there were few written records and few places of safe-keeping, the best informed witnesses on the terms of feudal grants would ordinarily be other vassals who had been present at ceremonies of investiture. Much more important was the dispersal and weakness of executive power. It was by no means always that a feudal lord, however great his estates, could be sure of his ability to put judgments in execution without help from his vassals. In rendering any judgment it was wise to engage with responsibility those persons, already bound by duties of service, who might be needed to enforce it. On the side of the vassals, there was some reassurance in having matters of vital concern decided by fellow vassals who

[14] The text depends heavily on F. L. Ganshof, "Contribution à l'Étude des Origines des Cours Féodales en France," *NRH*, 1928, 644.

[15] The phrase quoted is taken from Jolliffe, *Constitutional History of Medieval England* (3d ed.), 152–160. Similar comments appear in Frank Stenton, *The First Century of English Feudalism* (Oxford, 1932), 44.

were usually united by common interest under similar conditions of tenure.[16] It was for reasons such as these that the standard type of feudal court, not only in France but elsewhere, placed the power of rendering judgment in the assembled vassals and required at most the concurrence of the feudal lord who was the court's executive agent.

Yet it would have been possible for a vigorous and useful system of feudal courts to concern itself only with feudal business—disputes between lord and vassal over the terms of feudal tenure or the limits of feudal service, disputes between vassals that might threaten the peace between them. Both in Germany and in England, as we shall see, feudal courts restricted to feudal matters existed parallel to the older "public" courts. The outer lines of feudal jurisdiction might be somewhat indistinct, but there was a line that marked it off from the jurisdiction of the ordinary courts over the general population. When the French courts emerged, in the twelfth century, from the darkness that had surrounded them, they had already crossed this line. There were wide variations from place to place. Some feudal justice was "high" and some was "low," depending on the scope of civil and criminal jurisdiction. Within these two broad classes there were many variations.[17] Some lords had courts that concerned themselves only with feudal business. In Flanders and Normandy strong government maintained by territorial lords preserved judicial powers in ducal, if not in royal control.[18] But in most of France court-keeping functions had been distributed into innumerable private hands. Much of the evidence is negative or indirect, but we can judge by the result. When the French crown belatedly, in the thirteenth century, commenced to reconstruct a system of royal justice, it found at hand no analogue to the English county and hundred courts which the Norman kings in England had already proceeded to reinforce and make agents of royal will.

In medieval and early modern societies, including the French, it is clear that the administration of justice represented by all odds the most important function of government, especially since

[16] These suggestions are taken from Barnaby C. Keeney, *Judgment by Peers* (Cambridge, Mass., 1949), 5–6.

[17] Bongert, *Recherches sur les Cours Laïques du Xe au XIIIe Siecle*, 86–90, 119–124.

[18] Cam, "Suitors and Scabini," *Speculum*, 10:189, 192–195.

so much rule-making and general administration were carried on under judicial forms. In the absence of standing armies, poor relief or other welfare functions, there was no continuing service of government that loomed so large or reached so far through all levels of society. The capture of the courts by the feudal lords therefore had great consequences for the general population and interposed whole thickets of obstacles to the restoration of royal power. The rebuilding of a royal system of justice was both a primary object and a measure of success in the broader effort of crown agencies to recapture powers of government that had been fragmented and dispersed. The means by which this broader program was carried forward ranged all the way from political marriages and punitive raids to the invention of new institutions of government. Within the area of judicial administration there were two main problems that confronted the framers of royal policy and are important for present purposes—the modes of fact determination that would be used and the forms and scope of appellate review. The solutions adopted for these problems had effects that could hardly have been foreseen. Changes in procedure brought changes in court structure and personnel, for the procedure chosen was quite complex and called for expertise.

b. *Modes of Fact Determination*

The modes of proof employed in the early Germanic courts, both public and private, left little room for expert inquiries. Proof was chiefly by way of oath of the litigant (or accused), either taken alone or reinforced by the oaths of friendly supporters. But the oath of neither litigant nor oath-helper was testimony in the modern sense, for it merely affirmed the truth of the allegations made by the particular litigant; if the number and form of the oaths were sufficient they were decisive and further inquiry was foreclosed. Even less room for inquiry was left by appeals to the supernatural, such as the judicial duel or the various forms of ordeal. Proof by written documents filtered in gradually, but low standards of literacy and the resourcefulness of forgers preserved the ancient distrust of written evidence. Witness proof in the modern sense existed, but it was for long limited to attestation of documents and the testimony of specially credible persons of high standing. The whole court proceeding, conducted publicly and orally before lay assemblies, was framed so as to relieve these assemblies of serious burdens in settling issues of fact.[19]

In developing more rational modes of proof and investigation, the officers of the French crown had a major choice to make. There was on the one hand the group inquest, developed in the Frankish empire for fiscal and other matters of paramount interest for the crown. By it a selected group of local inhabitants was compelled to answer under oath the questions put before them by royal inquisitors. This device, inherited by the Norman dukes, had already been imported by them into England and was later to be transformed into the common law jury, but that is another story. In its origins the group inquest had been an exercise of high prerogative power by the crown.[20] Through the disasters of the ninth and tenth centuries the central authority had been too weak to employ it, but as the powers of the French kings expanded there were examples in the twelfth and early thirteenth centuries of a similar procedure, employed to ascertain and enforce crown rights. For a time there was indecision whether responses to questions should be made by the jurors individually or by the group collectively. Yet the procedure used in instances scattered through central France was in the main so similar to that employed in Normandy by the Norman dukes as to suggest a common origin and an equally promising future.[21]

The chief alternative to the Frankish crown's group inquest was the Roman-canonist system of proof by individual witnesses, whose evolution was still far from complete in the early thirteenth century. The church had borrowed the essential elements of its procedure from late Roman law, in which the state-appointed judge had already emerged as an active, indeed dominant figure. By the time of Justinian compulsion to respond under oath had been introduced, at least as to the litigants. In the development after Justinian of church court procedure the use of oaths had

[19] Engelmann-Millar, *History of Continental Civil Procedure*, sec. 58–60, gives an adequate summary of the matters here referred to.

[20] Heinrich Brunner, *Die Entstehung der Schwurgerichte* (Berlin, 1872), 87–106. This work will be cited hereafter as Brunner, S.G.

[21] Brunner, S.G., 223–233, 279–287; Hippolyte Pissard, *Essai sur la Connaissance et la Preuve des Coutumes dans l'Ancien Droit Français et dans le Système Romano-canonique* (Paris, 1910), 102–105; Bongert, *Recherches sur les Cours Laïques du X° au XIII° Siecle*, 263–264.

been expanded: first as a form of purgation for accused persons and then by way of interrogation under the judge's own authority, especially in cases of corruption or misdeeds of the clergy.[22] The revival of Roman law studies around the year 1100 produced very soon an extensive literature on procedural questions, inspired by the Corpus Juris though including some important medieval accretions and directed, like so much of the glossators' work, to immediate practical ends.[23] It was natural if not inevitable that the leadership in the reworking of these materials should have been assumed by the canon lawyers. The canonists were close students of the Corpus Juris themselves and had learned all that the secular lawyers could teach them on legal problems of church administration. The church courts were enlarging their activities greatly and were being rapidly marshalled under common standards and firm control by the advancing power of a universal church. The great compilation of Durandus, the *Speculum Judiciale,* was not written until the latter part of the thirteenth century.[24] Well before that time canon law procedure had become a largely written procedure, involving an exchange between the parties of written statements of claim and defense, written interrogatories prepared by the parties to be administered to the witnesses, and written records that the judge was required to keep of his rulings, findings, and judgment. For present purposes it is even more important that the basic mode of proof was the testimony of individual witnesses under oath, under interrogation by the judge who then proceeded to make his own findings of fact.

As compared with the hazards of litigation before secular tribunals with their archaic modes of proof, the procedure of the church courts offered immense advantages. Knowledge of the new methods was disseminated as part of the new learning that drifted northward from Italy. Clergy knew it best, for this was the law of holy church and the clergy represented a major fraction of those who knew how to read. Yet many lay persons who were engaged in controversies preferred this better way of ascertaining truth. And here we must pause to consider the interesting

[22] Adhemar Esmein, *Histoire de la Procédure Criminelle en France* (Paris, 1882), 66–78.

[23] Engelmann-Millar, *History of Continental Civil Procedure,* 432–444.

[24] Engelmann-Millar, 448–454.

suggestion that it was chiefly by means of private arbitration that canon law procedure became common coin in France. The argument rests on several points. The feudal courts were often lacking in executive power, their modes of proof made lawsuits a gamble, they were not subject to effective review by appeal. To end armed conflict and achieve internal peace was the declared object of kings and of most articulate leaders and above all of the church. If arbitration by trusted neutrals was agreed to, it would have been most natural to follow the procedure used in church administration, especially since it was strongly supported by common sense and had not yet been elaborated into bewildering complication. During the twelfth and thirteenth centuries, at any rate, there is much evidence of resort to arbitration, governed by canon law rules of procedure. Without direct aid from kings or counts or other court-keepers, private arbitration may well have prepared the way for a general reception of canonist procedure.[25]

In the early thirteenth century the choice between the group-inquest (jury) and the canonist modes of proof had not yet been decisively made. Proof by individual witnesses was becoming more common in ordinary litigation.[26] Examination of individual witnesses on the initiative and authority of the judge was permitted by local custom in some specific situations and the king's court ordered inquests of this type in some instances before 1250.[27] There was, however, a procedure in criminal cases—apparently derived from the Frankish group inquest—which permitted conviction on group verdict.[28] For proof of customary law another form of group inquest was organized in royal courts during the second half of the thirteenth century. It came to be known as the *enquête par turbe* and was required to give a collective answer through the spokesman chosen by the jurors. The *enquête par turbe* survived for centuries as the standard mode of proving custom in those regions of France that were governed by customary law. It seems strange indeed that the only de-

[25] Bongert, *Recherches sur les Cours Laïques du Xe au XIIIe Siecle*, 97–111, 159–182, 273–278.

[26] Bongert, 257–261.

[27] Brunner, S.G., 443–445, 448–449; Esmein, *Histoire de la Procédure Criminelle en France*, 82–84.

[28] Esmein, 78–81.

scendant of the Frankish group inquest that survived in France was a type devoted to proving, not facts, but local law.[29]

The decisive step in choosing between the two available modes of proof was taken by Louis IX in 1258 by his ordinance abolishing the judicial duel in royal courts. The problem confronting the framers of this ordinance was evident: if duels were to be abolished, something must take their place. The same problem had appeared in England some forty years before when the crown had deferred to the church's newly declared hostility to the duel and had abolished it, thereby giving a sudden impetus to the growth of the common law jury.[30] The abolition of the duel in France had still another implication, in that it removed the threat to witnesses that they might be required to defend themselves by battle against charges of perjury. In some parts of France this threat was so serious that witnesses were not compelled to testify unless they were exempt from the risk of challenge to a duel.[31] So it was that elimination of the duel in royal courts operated both directly and indirectly to promote the use of witness-proof, with which many Frenchmen were becoming familiar. Louis IX ordered that instead of the duel his judges should use secret examination of individual witnesses under oath, through questions administered by the judges themselves.[32]

Some of the reasons why this course was chosen are plain enough. France had lain for 150 years in the main paths of advance for Italianate ideas. Influential persons, both clerical and secular, had become steeped in these ideas. The king's government in France did not make its own choice as to modes of investigation until nearly 100 years after Henry II in England had introduced the group inquest—the jury—as a standard feature of the royal remedy for novel disseisin.[33] During this century of experience many people in France must have become persuaded that interrogation of individual witnesses under oath was a far

[29] Brunner, S.G., 385–393; Pissard, La Connaissance et la Preuve des Coutumes, 102–153.

[30] Frederick W. Maitland, Pleas of the Crown for the County of Gloucester, 1221 (London, 1884), xxxviii–xliii.

[31] Beaumanoir, Coutumes de Beauvaisis (ed. Salmon, Paris, 1899–1900), secs. 1762–1768.

[32] Brunner, S.G., 446–447.

[33] Frederick Pollock and Frederick W. Maitland, History of English Law Before the Time of Edward I (Cambridge, Eng., 1898), I, 146.

more rational mode of ascertaining truth. But there were other great differences between France and England, centering around the power and resources available for governmental action. Even in 1258 the French king's writ did not run through all the lands that owed him nominal allegiance. Even within his own domain it would have been no easy task to assemble groups of local inhabitants and compel them to give collective answers to questions from royal officers. Where the power existed, as it no doubt did in some parts of the royal domain, exercise of the power on any scale would have imposed an immense task of local administration. So far as theory was concerned, it might have seemed almost as high handed for royal judges to take individuals into secret places and ask them questions under oath as it was to extract group verdicts. But in civil litigation the individual witnesses would not normally be assembled by the crown or its agents: they would be brought forward by the parties themselves. Even in criminal cases, the procedure was still usually founded on private accusation with initiative in the accuser; criminal investigation by the judge ex officio, reinforced by torture, did not come into vogue until the fourteenth century.[34] When one considers the difficulties in drawing six or twelve or more trustworthy persons to some central place and extracting a verdict under oath, it must have seemed far easier, as well as far more rational, to address the questions to individuals who had been presented by the litigants or who were believed for some other reason to be especially well informed. So it might well be that in the choice of means the framers of royal policy were influenced not only by their familiarity with canon law procedure but even more by the weight of local inertia and resistance, which they had no means to overcome. If this is true, we encounter another paradox. The canonist methods of proof were soon to require a vast increase in the royal bureaucracy and the criminal inquisition came later to symbolize the overriding power of unlimited monarchy, but the initial choice of this procedure by the central government may well have been due much more to weakness than to strength.[35]

[34] Esmein, *Histoire de la Procédure Criminelle*, 89–108.
[35] This thought is also suggested by Bongert, *Recherches sur les Cours Laïques du X² au XIII² Siecle*, 269–270.

The royal ordinance of 1258 abolishing the judicial duel applied only in royal courts. Even seignorial courts within the royal domain were not directly affected. Actually the force of tradition was so strong that even in royal courts as a concession to the nobility, the privilege of using the duel was restored to them in some criminal cases in the early 1300's, and it survived on a limited basis into the 1400's.[36] At the same time, judicial examination of witnesses under oath was deemed enough of a usurpation so that the nobility succeeded in securing for itself a series of specific immunities from royal inquests.[37] The new inquest procedure in royal courts was therefore only a model and it had some trouble making its way. It had large influence nevertheless, for it threw a bright light on the utter irrationality of the older modes of proof. The main alternative to court-directed witness proof was the jury or group inquest, and this was surely too much for the lesser nobility to organize if the crown did not lead the way.

To mark the progress of the new procedure in criminal cases, it is worth taking a sample from some thirteenth-century private courts that were owned by various abbeys near Paris. These were not ecclesiastical courts, concerned with internal church discipline and administration. They were courts of general jurisdiction but completely feudalized. The abbots were feudal lords who administered justice not only for their own vassals but for all other residents of their territories. The records of these courts that have survived are almost entirely concerned with criminal prosecutions though they mention other matters—the deaths of foreigners or persons without heirs, whose assets were forfeited to the feudal lord; [38] wandering pigs that were apprehended and deposited with the abbot; [39] and similar sources of revenue that were mixed with the profits of justice. The monks were engaged

---

[36] Esmein, *HDF*, 468.

[37] Esmein, *Histoire de la Procédure Criminelle*, 85–89.

[38] Louis Tanon, *Histoire des Justices des Anciennes Églises et Communautés Monastiques de Paris* (Paris, 1883), 395: "In the year of grace 1272 or thereabouts there was a bastard at St. Germain who had the name Ermengon, daughter of Heloys the Drunkard, who died without heirs and whose property we took." Entries concerning forfeited estates are frequent in the registers.

[39] Tanon, 324: "In 1274 in St. Maur des Fossés *quidam porcus inventus fuit in foro Fossatense, extraneus. Ductus fuit ad granchiam abbatie.*" Similar entries relating to alien pigs appear on pp. 338 and 394.

in constant battles to maintain their court-keeping rights against
encroachment by royal officers, for it was often difficult to fix
the location of offenses and offenders within jurisdictional lines
that bisected the streets of a turbulent urban settlement. Many
of the entries seem to have no purpose except to provide to royal
officers some proof that the powers claimed by the abbeys had
in fact been exercised. The records are usually most laconic. A
few quotations will give the spirit:

In the year of our Lord 1277 on the day of Good Friday there was
captured in the house of the Count of Champagne, a thief who had
stolen the surcoat of a knight, and he was hanged the day after Easter
at Saint Germain. All the neighbors know this and all the town of
St. Germain.[40]

In the year of our Lord 1277 a certain man, Roger by name, was
seized in the town of St. Maur des Fossés while selling an iron chain
that had been stolen; who because of this and other acts was hanged
on Monday before the feast of the Apostles Philip and James.[41]

1273. Likewise in this year Emeline of Holland and other old pimps
were taken in our lands and burned in the street before the church of
St. Andrew.[42]

These entries provide types that were often repeated: the offender caught in flagrant delict and the offender (often a re-
peater) whose guilt was a matter of common knowledge and
required no specific testimony. Outside these categories difficulties arose. Judicial duels had lasted in the Paris abbey courts even
after the royal ordinance of 1258, though only for a few decades.[43] The abbey courts seemed to prefer above all a confession
by the accused. To extract confessions, it seems, abbey officials
used torture even before 1300.[44] After 1300 torture was certainly
used by them and by other courts, both feudal and royal, and in
later French procedure it became a standard method of criminal
investigation. An alternative to torture was for the accused person to "accept the inquest"—that is, to agree with the judge
that he would abide the result of an examination conducted by
the judge. This had the effect of enlarging the judge's power to
punish and of dispensing with strict rules of evidence; for the

[40] Tanon, 416.
[41] Tanon, 326.
[42] Tanon, 413
[43] Tanon, 16–27.
[44] Tanon, 58–64.

accused it had the advantage of excluding torture. This sort of procedural contract had come into use by 1300 in the Paris abbey courts [45] and was soon to become an important means for extending the use of inquisitional procedure in courts all over France.[46] But where the suspected person would neither "accept" an inquest nor confess his guilt there was for decades no clear course of action. The older modes of proof, by oath-helpers or ordeal, had apparently disappeared from the abbey courts altogether by the latter part of the thirteenth century. Apart from the unsatisfactory solution of releasing the prisoner for lack of proof [47] the most attractive possibility was for the judge to undertake an inquest on his own authority. The few scattered examples of such procedure suggest that it was well enough known but that difficulties were felt in establishing power to compel testimony under oath.[48] Certainly we cannot assign as cause any overdelicacy of feeling or excessive concern for the rights of suspected persons, who were promptly hanged or mutilated when summary inquiries seemed to establish guilt. It was a different matter where the court, in order to proceed, must assert for itself a generalized power to compel answers under oath. This meant an assumption of initiative by the court itself and an important addition to judicial powers as defined by ancient procedure.

In civil cases the new modes of proof did not require a similar assertion of judicial authority. Responsibility for selection of witnesses and for persuading them to testify was thrown on the interested parties. While the judge supervised the preparation of the questions and examined the witnesses himself or through his delegate, his role in civil cases was mainly to assemble and evaluate the evidence that the parties presented. The term *enquête*

[45] Tanon, 368.

[46] Adhémar Esmein, "L'Acceptation de l'Enquête dans la Procédure Criminelle au Moyen Age," *NRH*, 1888, 13 and 107.

[47] As in a case of 1281 before the abbey court of St. Germain des Prés (Tanon, 419).

[48] The court of the Abbey of Ste. Geneviève conducted inquests ex officio in 1290 and 1296 (Tanon, 349 and 408). The Abbey of St. Maur des Fossés used an inquest in a criminal case as early as 1278, though this may have been with the consent of the accused (Tanon, 333).

The term "inquest" was also used to describe inquiries made by royal officers to determine jurisdictional limits as between royal and abbey courts, but it would seem that this was quite a different matter. Many illustrations appear in the registers published by Tanon—e.g., pp. 336, 339, 353, 357, 374, 376, 385, 408.

was soon applied to this kind of investigation, but it was not an inquisition of the kind that the canonists were developing for criminal or disciplinary proceedings, conducted by the judge ex officio. The *enquête* in civil cases was a court-conducted examination of individual witnesses, made available to private litigants to settle disputed issues of fact.[49]

The older modes of proof persisted for some time, side by side with the new. Beaumanoir, writing about 1280, described the judicial duel as still used in the court of the Count of Clermont. He also described a system of interrogation of individual witnesses by court-appointed auditors, who were free to take an active role in questioning and to depart from the questions prepared in advance by the parties. The testimony was taken down in writing by the auditor and reported back by him under seal. Where interrogatories were used, Beaumanoir asserted that the court had power to compel attendance of witnesses before the auditor and to force replies to questions.[50]

It was not until the fourteenth century that these methods of fact determination were firmly established in northern France, though in the southern *pays de droit écrit* they had made headway sooner. By the period 1332–1357 the abbey court of St. Martin des Champs in Paris was run by a specialized (apparently full time) judge, employing a procedure that was highly developed along canonist lines.[51] A few decades later both abbey courts and lower royal courts of the Paris area seem to have accepted the whole apparatus of canonist methods of proof—written exceptions, repliques and draft interrogatories submitted by the parties, interrogation under oath by court-approved interrogatories, and a written report (*procès verbal*) of the examiners as the basis for fact-finding.[52] Surviving evidence suggests that

[49] Paul Guilhiermoz, *Enquêtes et Procès, Étude sur la Procédure et le Fonctionnement du Parlement de Paris au XIVe Siècle* (Paris, 1892), introduction, xxx.
[50] Beaumanoir, *Coutumes de Beauvaisis*, secs. 1225–1249.
[51] Tanon, 455–556, published the register of the abbey court.
[52] Louis Tanon, *L'Ordre du Procès Civil au XIVe Siècle au Chatelet de Paris* (Paris, 1886) including the Registre Civil of a local seignorial court for the years 1371–1373. As early as 1340 and 1341, the normal method of proof before the royal *bailli* of Senlis was the *enquête* by court-appointed commissioners, though in rare cases the court could receive oral testimony of witnesses before the court itself. E. de Rozière, "L'Assise du Bailliage de Senlis en 1340 et 1341," *NRH*, 1891, 714, at 727–729. A survey of criminal procedure in Auvergne has likewise indicated that the transition to inquest procedure occurred in the early decades

this procedure spread rapidly everywhere during the fourteenth century and at the end of the century had won the whole field, in civil and criminal actions of every type, in feudal as well as royal courts. Together with these methods of fact-determination —and an active agent in promoting their adoption—came a new type of appellate review.

c. *Modes of Appellate Review*

Under ancient Germanic procedure a judgment already rendered could be reversed only by a direct attack on the court that rendered it. To participate in a false judgment was deemed a dishonorable failure of duty. All those who had a share in it were subject to attack and were in principle required to defend themselves. If the judgment was proved to be false, the result was not correction of the judgment but punishment of the judges.[53]

These ancient ideas survived in France long after the collapse of the Carolingian system. In the thirteenth century Pierre de Fontaines explained that a false judgment proceeding should lead to penalties and damages assessed against the false judges but should not lead to a reversal, "since the party for whom the original judgment was rendered should not lose his claim through the fault of another." [54] Beaumanoir, writing about 1280, was explicit that a false judgment proceeding must ordinarily be settled by a duel between all the judges and the aggrieved party, though if the aggrieved party was unwilling to fight them all he could specially request the lord of the court to name a single adversary, who would then do battle on behalf of his colleagues in defense of their common decision.[55]

The type of appeal developed in Roman law under the late empire was of course well known to medieval students of Roman law. In the southern part of France, governed by vulgarized Roman law, there appeared in the twelfth and early thirteenth cen-

---

of the fourteenth century. R. Grand, "Justice Criminelle, Procédure et Peines dans les Villes aux XIII° et XIV° Siècles," *Bibliothèque de l'École des Chartes,* 102:51 (1941).

[53] Schroeder, *DRG,* secs. 37 and 63.

[54] *Conseil à un Ami* (ed. Marnier, Paris, 1846), XXII, 8, discussed by Chénon, *HDF,* I, 674–675.

[55] Beaumanoir, *Coutumes de Beauvaisis,* secs. 1752–1755. This method, which Beaumanoir described as a method of "appealing wisely," was not available to serfs except by special local privilege.

turies a type of appeal that was modeled on the Roman and that led to correction of error rather than punishment of the judges.[56] In the northern sections of France, governed by customary law, a similar form of appellate proceeding was sufficiently well known so that the king could authorize its use by special grant in individual cases. The first major step toward general adoption was again inspired by the efforts of Saint Louis to abolish judicial duels in royal courts. The same ordinance that forbade the use of duels provided that any complaint on the ground of false judgment should be heard and decided by the royal court to which the complaint was presented; this court was then to approve or reverse the judgment attacked. Power merely to modify, without complete reversal, was asserted successfully by royal courts thereafter, apparently without express legislation.[57] It is important, however, that these new powers were in a sense merely grafted on the old complaint of false judgment. In northern France (not in the southern *pays de droit écrit*) the new royal appeal required formal summons, not only to the opposite party but to the court appealed from and exposed the latter, in the event of reversal, to money fine or other penalty imposed by the higher court.[58]

One cannot consider the effects of the new appellate procedure without taking a glimpse at the subordinate royal officers, whose judicial activities came quite early under appellate review. The competence of these officers was rapidly expanding through the thirteenth century, for the re-establishment of Crown authority meant an increase in local administration and an expansion of the judicial powers of inferior royal officers. The central figure was the *bailli* or *sénéchal*, the territorial representative of the crown who, like the English sheriff, combined in his office financial, military, administrative, and judicial functions. To extend the judicial powers of the *baillis* and their subordinates, two main devices were used: (1) the theory of *cas royaux*, roughly comparable to the English crown pleas—cases like counterfeiting, *lèse-majesté*, or (later) some crimes of violence—in which crown officers alone were competent; and (2) direct competition with seignorial

---

[56] Marcel Fournier, *Essai sur l'Histoire du Droit d'Appel* (Versailles, 1881), 190–195.
[57] Fournier, 204–210; Chénon, *HDF*, I, 677.
[58] Chénon, *HDF*, I, 677–679.

courts by *prévention*, that is, by accepting cases in which the seignorial courts were fully competent and surrendering them only if the dispossessed lord protested and demanded their return. The group of *cas royaux* was extensible and over the centuries was slowly extended, though it never came near the enormous sweep of the English pleas of the crown. *Prévention* was a more effective means of extending royal judicial powers. The competition with seignorial courts, through the concurrent powers of the royal courts, had no limit except that defined by the vigilance and tenacity of private court-keepers in defending their positions against royal attacks from the rear.[59]

For the expansion of central authority it was necessary to establish controls not only over the local royal officers, with their widening powers, but also, gradually, over the various types of seignorial courts. In some parts of France the private court-keepers began quite early to tolerate appeals from their courts to the royal courts. The great seigneurs resisted longer. Yet by the middle of the fourteenth century the private jurisdictions almost everywhere had come under the wide umbrella of royal appellate review. The feudal hierarchies were left intact. Appeals had to proceed from vassal's court to lord's court along established lines of fealty. The feudal courts might lie three deep, and in some places deeper. Yet at some point in the series, perhaps from a high feudal court at the summit of a feudal pyramid, an appeal could be taken to a court of the king, the ultimate justiciar.[60]

[59] The *cas royaux* and *prévention* are discussed by Chénon, *HDF*, I, 685–688, and Esmein, *HDF*, 471–475. The study of Ernest Perrot, *Le Cas Royaux* (Paris, 1910), reveals how little progress had been made by the end of the fourteenth century in displacing seignorial justice through the theory of *cas royaux*.

The remedy of *prévention*, awarded to court-keepers for defense of their jurisdictions, is comparable to the writ *de non intromittendo* by which English feudal courts were permitted to reclaim cases brought by writs *praecipe* in English royal courts. Plucknett, *Concise Hist.*, 356.

[60] Chénon, *HDF*, 688–694; Esmein, *HDF*, 480–481. It is worth noting that the canonist form of appeal had been early adopted within their own domains by some of the great feudal lords, even before the subjection of their courts to appellate review by the Parlement had put pressure on them to do so. In contests with their own local nobility the canonist appeal evidently offered advantages to the great feudataries when administered by trained judges that they themselves had appointed. *Histoire des Institutions Françaises au Moyen Age* (eds. Ferdinand Lot et R. Fawtier, Paris, 1957), I, 97, 147–148, 222, 295, 304, 311, 331–332, 386–388, 413–415.

For the student of English history, the power of the Parlement of Paris to en-

There was thus distributed all over France an appellate procedure that was heavily influenced by the royal model. As appellate procedure developed at high and intermediate levels, it had in its turn a large influence on trial procedure. In fact the rapid increase in appellate business had already brought growth at the summit of royal justice. In the court that surrounded the kings of France there had been some specialization of function as early as the twelfth century, but the assignment to particular persons of purely judicial duties was not a regular feature until after the year 1250. Still more time was needed to shed the extraneous lay personnel—tenants in chief of the king, leading clergy, and administrative officers—and to organize a court of trained professionals. This occurred gradually during the late 1200's—not quite 100 years after the formation of the English Court of Common Pleas. The high court thus formed appropriated to itself the title of Parliamentum or Parlement, the great colloquy of the king's great men. Whether it acted as a court of first instance, as it sometimes did, or in its normal aspect as an appellate court, the Parlement employed a procedure that was modeled on the canonist system. What this required in personnel is suggested by the amazing growth in the size of the court, a forecast of things to come. In the year 1296 a royal ordinance fixed the membership of the Parlement at 51 judges. Twenty-three years later, in 1319, the official total was 67. By 1343 the total had risen to 180, but this total was reduced by drastic retrenchment and from 1345 for several decades the total was just over 80.[61]

The reasons for this aggrandizement must be found primarily in the court's procedure. There was no doubt much competition for jobs and some weakness in the appointing authority, but it

tertain appeals is important for its bearing on the protracted contest over the power of the French kings to control and supervise the administration of Gascony, held as a fief by the English crown. An appeal was entertained by the Parlement as early as 1271 and in later years it became a major objective of English officials to counter and to circumvent its harassing intervention. Staffs of jurists and clerks, occasionally supplemented by higher officials, had to remain on the watch in Paris to safeguard the interests of Edward I but in effect a power of appellate review by the Parlement was conceded by him as early as the 1290's. Powicke, *The Thirteenth Century, 1216–1307* (Oxford, 1953), 287–293, 296–298, 310–318.

[61] Félix Aubert, *Histoire du Parlement de Paris de l'Origine à François I* (Paris, 1894), I, 11–16, 21–27, 34–37. After the recapture of Paris from the English in the next century, an ordinance of 1454 fixed the total membership of the Parlement of Paris at 94, of which 42 were assigned to the *Chambre des Enquêtes*.

seems unlikely that so vast a court could have been maintained so long (and later much further enlarged) if there had not been real need for judicial personnel. A full picture of the Parlement's procedure does not emerge until the fourteenth century but all the evidence from the time of its first organization strongly suggests that the Parlement adopted a procedure which involved in most cases a full retrial of issues of fact through full-scale canonist inquest. A crude index is offered by the internal organization of the court. As early as 1296 it had been found necessary to divide the Parlement into three chambers or divisions, a *Grand' Chambre*, a *Chambre des Enquêtes*, and a *Chambre des Requêtes*. Thereafter the decision to order inquests was normally made by the *Grand' Chambre*, but the burden of conducting and reporting them was assigned to the *Chambre des Enquêtes*, which by 1319 comprised 40 judges out of the total of 67 and in later fluctuations of the Parlement's membership remained quite consistently about 50 per cent of the total.[62]

Within a century after its organization as a court, the procedure of the Parlement of Paris had reached a high stage of elaboration. Cases before it were always commenced by an oral statement of claim and defense, made in the *Grand' Chambre*.[63] But it was seldom that the merits could be decided without resolving disputed issues of fact and for this purpose an inquest would be ordered. In the fourteenth century the first step in preparing an inquest was a written statement drawn up by the parties, repeating the allegations and claims that each had presented in oral argument. This document, called the *intendit*, governed completely the content of the proof (by documents or by witnesses) that each party would be allowed to present; but in addition to the *intendit* each party was required to state in written "articles" a summary of the witnesses and documents that he would present and the questions that should be asked. After one or more members of the court had examined the *intendits* and

[62] Aubert, cited in the preceding note.

[63] The account of the Parlement's procedure that is given in the text is based on the article of Paul Guilhiermoz, "De la Persistance du Caractère Oral dans la Procédure Civile Française," *NRH*, 1889, 21, and on the same author's important work *Enquêtes et Procès, Étude sur la Procédure et le Fonctionnement du Parlement au XIV* Siècle* (Paris, 1892). An account based largely on fifteenth-century sources also appears in Aubert, *Histoire du Parlement de Paris de l'Origine à François I*, II, 81–113.

the articles, had checked them for internal consistency, and had considered and ruled upon objections by opposing counsel, commissioners were appointed to travel to the localities where the witnesses were to be found. These *commissaires-enquêteurs* would include at least one member of the court itself, often augmented by lawyers or prominent local laymen. After meeting in the locality to review the questions about to be asked, the witnesses were privately and separately examined and a written *procès-verbal* was prepared by a clerk of the examining commission. The whole written record of testimony, objections, rulings and other proceedings was then placed in a sack under the seal of the commissioners and carried back to the central court. Copies of the *procès-verbal* and of the documentary evidence presented were then supplied to the parties but none of the testimony presented by individual witnesses was disclosed to either party.[64] It should not be surprising that the court with which such reports were filed could handle the mass of material only by appointing one of its members—the *rapporteur* of classic French procedure—to read the whole record, to summarize issues, to mark the significant testimony, and to recommend both specific findings of fact and ultimate disposition. The procedure was not organized, like the English system of common law pleading, to sift out and simplify so that the case could be submitted to the collective verdict of a lay jury. The drift was strongly in the other direction. The litigants were entirely responsible for formulating their claims and presenting their witnesses for examination. Thereafter the preparation of cases for trial, the assembly and evaluation of evidence, and the drawing of conclusions on both facts and law were functions of the court. It is no wonder that so many judges were used or that the judges who administered the system were in need of specialized training.

It may well be that French courts generally would have developed the kind of procedure they did without any pressure from the Parlement. The Parlement itself required several decades to

---

[64] In standard canon law procedure the practice was, after completion of testimony, for the evidence presented by the witnesses to be "published," with copies of their depositions being supplied to the parties. This practice, adopted by Louis IX originally, was abolished by order of the Parlement of Paris in 1276, except for proprietary actions. Most lower courts, though not all, followed the example of the Parlement. Guilhiermoz, *Enquêtes et Procès*, 73–74.

perfect its own system, and even before it had been perfected, the lower courts had moved strongly toward the adoption of canonist procedure, especially its modes of proof. For all French courts, from the Parlement of Paris to the courts of the smallest lordships, the crucial decision had really been made in the thirteenth century when the group inquest had been allowed to disappear as a mode of establishing facts. By following the lead of the canonists in more refined methods of investigation, French courts committed themselves to a system that was likely to develop according to its own internal logic. When it was decided that witnesses were to be examined individually and in secret, a reliable examiner was needed and some record must be kept. If the examiner was to ask all the necessary questions, he would have to be prompted by a list of questions beforehand. In a case of any complexity it would be imperative that the questions be put into writing; it was natural to cast on the parties involved the burden of preparing the questions. To be sure that the draft interrogatories prepared by the parties were relevant and proper, it was convenient to have the initial statements of claim and defense put into writing.[65] When this stage of documentation was reached, objections of each party to the other's claims or proposals would often need to be put into writing and the prolongation of the proceedings would make it imperative that the judge keep a written record of his actions at each stage. There was heavy and continuous pressure, in short, to move toward a written procedure. Though French law maintained till the end a principle of orality, the effort to ensure that oral statements were precisely duplicated by a written record merely added more complication.[66] Complications had certainly been achieved as early as 1337, when two treatises written by a member of the Parlement showed the demands placed on its membership.[67] By then it

[65] The requirement of written statement, the *intendit*, appears in the procedure of the Parlement of Paris through an order of the court in 1291. Guilhiermoz, *NRH*, 1889, 21, at 26.

[66] This theme is developed at length by Guilhiermoz in the article cited in the preceding note.

[67] Published by Guilhiermoz in *Enquêtes et Procès*, 181–234. Written by a judge of the *Chambre des Enquêtes* who had had long experience, for the instruction of his junior colleagues, the two interconnected treatises no doubt set forth standards of care and thoroughness that were not always followed. They nevertheless give a vivid picture of the complicated paper work required of any man with an equally stern sense of duty.

was already essential that the judge have not only an ability to read—a skill that was rare enough in itself—but an ability to dissect and scrutinize the contents of several layers of manuscript. As specialized personnel were assigned to these tasks and the paper work grew more complex, there was increasing distrust of informal, oral procedures not evidenced by writing. Each element of the system reinforced the rest.

Yet one can doubt whether the triumph of Roman-canonist procedure would have been so early and so complete if the Parlement of Paris had not influenced lower courts both by example and by direct pressure. In the rapid development of the Parlement's procedure during the fourteenth century, lawyers' technique entered largely. Indeed only lawyers could have used logic so remorselessly or constructed so ponderous a procedural machine. Around the Parlement, in the capital city, there was gathered trained legal intelligence in high concentration. The system constructed by the Parlement's lawyers had the prestige not only of the high court itself but of the highly trained professionals who built it. In this sense it was a model for other courts to follow. Yet it was more than a model. By the fourteenth century, as we have already seen, the Parlement had acquired power to review the judgments not only of subordinate royal judges but of the seignorial courts. As will be seen, reversal meant money fines on the erring court, especially if it was a seignorial court. The pressure to conformity was intermittent but nation wide.[68] Forces already at work were given added momentum. Their effects were soon felt in other directions.

d. *The Disappearance of the Lay Element*

The feudalization of the French local courts did not necessarily mean exclusion of the laymen. On the contrary, as already suggested, organized feudalism served to maintain the practice of regular mutual consultation between the feudal lord and his vassals. It would be impossible to prove that this practice survived everywhere in France, in all territorial courts that had been feudalized. Direct evidence is scanty, for these aggregations of laymen could not have felt much pressure to record their proceed-

---

[68] The splitting off of the provincial Parlements does not require qualification of this comment, since the procedures and practices of the provincial Parlements so closely imitated those of the Parlement of Paris.

ings. Yet there is evidence as late as the thirteenth century that ancient forms of court organization had survived in a feudal context.

Beaumanoir, for example, writing around 1280 concerning his own experience as a judge in Clermont en Beauvaisis, spoke of "the districts where the *baillis* (lord's or king's stewards) make the judgments and those others where the vassals of the lord make them." He first explained that even in those districts where the steward made the judgment, the steward should assemble the "wisest" persons to advise him and should follow their advice, since he would then be excused from blame if the judgment was later found to be false. In those districts where "the men" made the judgment, the whole duty of the steward was to compel them to render judgment, using imprisonment or seizure of their lands as sanctions if needed. As for his own experience, Beaumanoir stated that nowhere in the domain of the Count of Clermont was there a district in which judgment was otherwise than by "the men." [69] That this was proving somewhat cumbersome is suggested by his qualification that in matters that were "clear and evident" under the applicable rules of customary law, the steward might render judgment unaided; only in those cases that were important or that raised some doubt was it necessary for "the men" to decide.[70] Yet on the main issue he was clear. Even if the action was brought by the lord himself, no objection could be raised that in the lord's court he was judge in his own cause; "the men," not the lord or his steward, were the judges and if they decided against the lord, his recourse was a complaint of false judgment against the men, a complaint that would be decided by battle.[71]

Elimination of the judicial duel and introduction of a new ap-

[69] Beaumanoir, *Coutumes de Beauvaisis* (ed. Salmon), secs. 23–24, 1853, and 1862.

[70] Beaumanoir, sec. 31: "Since it would often be long and burdensome for the men who make the judgments to be present in all the cases that come before the *bailli*, the *bailli* should take great pains to settle matters that have been pleaded before him when he knows what should be done in the case according to the custom and when he sees the matter is clear and evident. But whatever is in doubt and the great quarrels should be reserved for judgment."
In sec. 42 Beaumanoir says that since it would be a great burden to the litigants and to "the men" to have all the men present at all pleadings and arguments of every case, it will suffice if two or more—only "a part"—of the men are present, provided those present record what occurs and report it to the whole group when it assembles.

[71] Beaumanoir, sec. 36.

pellate procedure diminished notably the risks incurred by these lay judges. They were no longer bound to defend their collective decisions with their bodies and their personal liability was reduced to a mere money fine. According to a writer of the early fourteenth century, judgments were rendered by "the men" in seignorial courts "in many places" and when such judgments were appealed to the Parlement of Paris "the men" were required to appear personally before the Parlement itself. If they failed to appear but their judgment was affirmed, they could not collect the fine due them from the appellant for his false appeal. If their judgment was reversed, they were in any event liable to such money fine as the appellate court might assess.[72] As a measure of protection against this unlimited liability, a royal ordinance of 1358 or thereabouts fixed a limit of £60 as a group fine or £10 per man if the court under attack comprised fewer than six men.[73] For men of modest means such sums were large. Yet there is evidence from near the end of the fourteenth century that lay judges were still rendering judgments—even in some lower royal courts —and were still being subjected to fines for their mistakes.[74]

A compromise between the ancient collective courts and the single professional judge survived even longer. This was a system by which routine matters were entrusted to a single judge and important or doubtful matters were brought before an assembly for collective decision. This kind of distinction had formed an

[72] Guillaume Du Breuil, *Stilus Curie Parlementi* (ed. Aubert, Paris, 1909), 49–50, 159–160. Even if the appellee defaulted so that the appellant was entitled to a default judgment against him, Du Breuil pointed out that the case must proceed as an action between the appellant and the judges "for the fine due to the King and the said judges in the event it is found that the appellant falsely appealed."

[73] Du Breuil, 160. The text in which this ordinance is referred to is a later addition to Du Breuil's manuscript, which Du Breuil had probably written shortly before 1332. It may be that the scribe who made the addition confused the supposedly general ordinance of about 1358 with an edict of 1368 that contained similar provisions but applied only to the district of Vermandois. The text of the latter edict is quoted in full in the *Ordonnances des Rois de France* (Paris, 1723– 1849), V, 140.

[74] Du Breuil, 160. The addition made in the latter part of the fourteenth century, referred to in the preceding note, mentions a decree of the Parlement of Paris imposing a fine for a partially erroneous judgment rendered *"per homines judicantes in curia Belvacensi."* On pp. 159–160 both Du Breuil's original manuscript and the late fourteenth-century addition refer to "men of the king" who decided certain cases and who, unlike the king's judges, were liable to fine for their false judgments.

Jean Bouteiller, *Somme Rurale* (ed. Charondas, Paris, 1603) writing in the four-essential part of the Carolingian system, though there the routine matters were dealt with by a group of law-finders, meeting frequently, unlike the general assemblies which met only three times a year. Whether or not there was a direct line of descent, the general assembly of vassals was well known in medieval France and was usually described as an assize. In the abbey courts of Paris during the late thirteenth century, judgments in several important matters were recorded as made "by the assize." [75] But the line between full collective responsibility and mere rendering of advice was crossed fairly soon. In the Paris abbey courts, for example, it seems that the assizes held by the abbeys had become merely advisory by the middle fourteenth century.[76] For most of France the shift cannot be traced in detail. Assizes continued to be held in many places until 1789. In some they were attended by considerable crowds. Edicts were often published there, and announcements made, and even judicial business transacted. Yet by the sixteenth century the collective responsibility of the assembly, almost everywhere, had quietly

---

teenth century, emphasized the importance, in appeals, of summoning by individual notice "hommes de fief," "hommes censiers," or "hommes cottiers" who judge jointly with their lord or his steward, "because these judges so judging defend the judgment at their own expense and risk and their lord is not made liable thereby."

Jacques D'Ableiges, *Grand Coutumier de France* (eds. Laboulaye and Dareste, Paris, 1868), vol. III, chap. 19, p. 478: "Nota quod ubi judicatur per homines regis, si propter eorum malum judicium emenda committatur, homines solvere debent pro se, sicut debent habere pro se ab alio qui appellavit quando bene judicatum fuit per eos." (D'Ableiges died in 1391.)

The journal of the royal *bailliage* of Senlis for 1340 and 1341 shows that the function of rendering judgment had already shifted to the royal *bailli* who conducted the court, assisted by an advisory council in important cases. E. de Rozière, "L'Assise du Bailliage de Senlis en 1340 et 1341," *NRH*, 1891, 714, at 720. But in the *bailliage* of Vermandois fourteenth-century sources reveal judgments being rendered by "hommes du roi," who sometimes signed and sealed the record of the royal court themselves and who showed the human propensity to delay in rendering judgments because of the threat that they might be fined for false judgment. In a charter of 1368 "hommes du roi" were defined as "nos hommes de fiefs qui, en raison de leurs fiefs, sont tenu de rendre la justice au conjurement de notre bailli ou de notre prévôt." Henri Waquet, *Le Bailliage de Vermandois* (Paris, 1919), 56–63.

[75] Tanon, *Histoire des Justices des Anciennes Églises et Communautés Monastiques de Paris*, 80–84, 331, 336. This may also be the thought behind Beaumanoir's suggestion that important or doubtful matters should be reserved for decision by "the men" (above, note 70).

[76] Louis Tanon, *Registre Criminel de la Justice de Saint-Martin des Champs à Paris au XIVe Siècle* (Paris, 1877), lxv–lxix.

faded away. The judging function had been transferred to specialists.[77]

This great transformation occurred with almost no commotion. No district rose in revolt to preserve the share of its people in the judicial process. The infiltration of professionals was not listed among the grievances that the crown was asked to redress. There are no records so far published that describe any efforts by "the men" to force their way back into the judges' seats.[78] For attendance at courts was a burden. As the volume of cases increased, it was entirely out of the question for people otherwise occupied to attend regular court sessions twice or three times a week—the frequency with which sessions were held, for example,

[77] The institution of the assize is described in legal treatises, such as Pierre Jacques Brillon, *Dictionnaire des Arrests* (Paris, 1771), I, 170; Laurent Bouchel, *Bibliothéque ou Thrésor du Droit Français* (Paris, 1666), I, 273–278; Jean Baptiste Dénisart, *Collection des Décisions Nouvelles* (Paris, 1771), I, 177. Some customs published in the sixteenth century required the holding of assizes at regular intervals, such as 2 or 4 times a year (Angoumois, art. 7, Poitou, art. 19), or once a year (Clermont en Beauvaisis, art. 119). In La Rochelle the published custom contained the negative statement that assizes could not be held *more* often than four times a year. The most convenient collection of the published customs is that of Charles A. Bourdot de Richebourg, *Nouveau Coutumier Général ou Corps de Coutumes Générales et Particulières de France* (4 vols., Paris, 1724). The provisions of the customs referred to (Angoumois, Poitou, Clermont en Beauvaisis and La Rochelle) will be found in De Richbourg, IV, 780; IV, 840; II, 774; and IV, 853.

Charondas le Caron, in his 1603 edition of Bouteiller, *Somme Rurale* (vol. I, Tit. 83, p. 488), made this comment on Bouteiller's description of the liabilities of "the men" in group judging: "This the lords anciently caused to be well observed and with money penalties; but at present it is not so frequently used, except in assizes if the feudal lord has a right to hold assizes." For more general comment see Esmein, *HDF*, 467–469.

External evidence of the decreasing importance of assizes held by royal officers during the fourteenth and fifteenth centuries, and the corresponding promotion of judicial "functionaries" is assembled by Gustave Dupont-Ferrier, *Les Officiers Royaux des Bailliages et Sénéchaussées* (Paris, 1902), 319–336.

The fifteenth-century custumal prepared by private practitioners in Poitou in 1417 stated in Article 4 that "chascun seigneur chastellain est fondé d'avoir grande et petite assize," but that for the holding of such assizes "peut et doit avoir deux juges," one for the small assize and one for the great assizes. Article 7 added that the *sénéchal* or *bailli* holding the great assize could call up for his own hearing any case pending before the judge of the small assize. *Le Vieux Coustumier de Poitou,* published by Professor René Filhol (Bourges, 1956).

Survival of the practice of judging by "the men" in certain assizes is suggested, however, by the comment of the seventeenth-century lawyer Charondas le Caron, quoted below, note 86.

[78] I have found no evidence whatever to support the statement of Julius Goebel in his Introduction to Joseph H. Smith, *Appeals to the Privy Council from the American Plantations* (New York, 1950), xi, that in France there was a "popular reaction against the spread of professional judging at the expense of the ancient community exercise of this function."

by the court of a Paris abbey in the fourteenth century.[79] The problem was to compel attendance, by fines or other sanctions. When attendance was poor there was constant temptation for presiding officers to get on with the business, to dilute requirements of attendance or to decide the cases themselves.[80] But the sacrifice of time by "the men" was the least of it. For judging still involved risk of liability, collective and individual. Even after their own bodies had been withdrawn as the stakes in the contest, the lay judges could lose heavily if they were found to be wrong. One would not expect much discussion of a "right" to perform such a risky and burdensome duty.[81]

If the lay judges saw nothing worth fighting for, it could be otherwise with the litigants. A desire to be judged by one's own kind might provide powerful motivation. In medieval France, as in medieval England, this desire reached the level of conscious expression as the *right* to be judged by one's peers. Similar emotions might have been at work much earlier, in the Frankish or the still earlier Germanic assemblies. It has even been suggested that the right of Roman citizens to be judged by their fellow citizens was a principle of Roman law, expressed not only in the two-stage procedure of the praetorian system of remedies but in the immunity from review of judgments rendered by the Roman *iudex*.[82] In early Germanic assemblies it is at least conceivable that communal methods of adjudication might have been inspired and preserved not only by the community's broad interest in dispute-settlement, but by the specific interest of individual litigants in being judged by their fellows.[83] This is a most attractive idea, for it means that our own principal reason for venerating the jury would have its roots in very ancient times, among the blond barbarians who met under their old oaks or by their salubrious springs. The difficulty lies chiefly with the lack of evidence. If in these early times there were individuals who successfully

[79] St. Martin des Champs, whose register was published by Tanon and is referred to above, note 76.

[80] Beaumanoir, *Coutumes de Beauvaisis*, sec. 31.

[81] Compare the comment of Pollock and Maitland, *HEL*, I, 537, concerning the English county court: "And first we must notice that of any right of attending the county court we read no word. Of the duty of attending it we read much, and obviously this duty is irksome."

[82] Wenger, *Institutionen des römischen Zivilprozessrechts*, sec. 18, pp. 182–183.

[83] Chénon, *HDF*, I, 657–658, presses this idea quite strongly.

asserted the right to be judged by their peers, no record was kept. It was in the context of the feudal relationship that this idea was first articulated in records that have survived. It became a right of the individual vassal to be judged by his fellow vassals, especially in contests with his lord.[84] In the legal sources of thirteenth-century France it appeared as a special privilege of nobility—of counts and dukes and barons. Very clearly serfs could claim no such privilege and even free peasants were not treated in this matter "as though they were gentle folk." [85] By skillful work of royal lawyers and evasive action by the crown, this privilege of nobility was narrowed even further. It was confined to great lords only and became a right to be tried by the Parlement of Paris with other lay peers added, in cases involving life, limb, personal honor or the ownership of the estates that made them Peers of France. Whatever political or emotional content may have been left in the idea of trial by peers was drained away after 1300. The idea was left as an empty symbol of highest aristocracy.[86]

So there were no effective barriers to the retreat of the judging "men," who quietly deserted. For those who guided the growth of the new institutions it must have seemed good riddance. The attitude prevailing in canonist circles appears in a decretal of Gregory IX, written as early as 1199 and addressed to the Bishop of Poitiers. It dealt, it is true, with lay adjudication in matters of church administration, an excessively touchy subject, but its overtones are suggestive:

You should know that it has come to our attention that in your diocese there is observed, even in ecclesiastical matters, an unreason-

[84] Keeney, *Judgment by Peers*, 5–12.

[85] The quotation is from Beaumanoir, *Coutumes de Beauvaisis*, sec. 1507. Other references to the same effect are collected by Esmein, *HDF*, 296–298 and Chénon, *HDF*, I, 658–660. The idea was formulated somewhat more broadly in Norman sources, but it seems that the substance was much the same. Keeney, *Judgment by Peers*, 27.

[86] Keeney, *Judgment by Peers*, 12–31. Bouteiller, *Somme Rurale* (edited by Charondas le Caron, 1603, p. 653), describes a criminal case appealed to the Parlement of Paris in which the accused claimed that "he wished to be treated and judged by men" or else by special commission. The Parlement by decree in 1377 refused to set aside the judgment of the royal *bailli* in Vermandois, and according to Bouteiller the Parlement declared that the *bailli* was empowered to decide "par luy seul et par tel conseil que bon luy sembleroit." The marginal comment of le Caron says: "At present royal judges decide both civil and criminal cases without being obliged to call the men of the fief; except in the assizes in places where the judges hold assizes at certain times with the men of the fief."

able custom according to which, when any case is being dealt with there and after the allegations and claims of both parties have been heard, all persons present, whether literate or illiterate, wise or unwise, are asked what the judgment should be and whatever they or some of them say is taken to be the judgment.

The Bishop of Poitiers was of course directed that this "custom" should be no longer observed.[87]

Yet it took some time for the new procedure to drive out the laymen. It was perfectly possible for the written *procés verbal* of an inquest to be reported back to an assembly of "men" and this did occur.[88] The new appellate procedure could be superimposed on trial courts of laymen, who were restrained from irregularities by the money fines imposed on them personally when their judgments were reversed.[89] Wide variations in detail persisted in the procedures employed by various courts all over France. The shift from oral to written procedure and the pile-up of complications occurred in some courts more rapidly than in others. But as the successive steps in lawsuits were extended and the mounds of paper grew, lay judges—many of them surely unable to read—must have grown more and more bewildered. In their confusion and trouble they must have used often the escape route described by a writer of the early fourteenth century:

If the men who judge in any court say they are not sufficiently trained (*dicant se non peritos*) to decide a particular case, they are justified even after they have been sworn in remitting the case to their superior, who, with the men entirely excluded, will then have to decide; and the men will be required to pronounce the judgment in accordance with his decision.[90]

[87] The text is quoted in Paul M. Viollet, *Histoire des Institutions Politiques et Administratives de la France* (Paris, 1898), II, 455.

[88] Beaumanoir, *Coutumes de Beauvaisis,* sec. 1225. Though in a passage shortly thereafter (sec. 1254) Beaumanoir mentions the kind of mishap that could so readily occur. In a particular case the results of the examination were reported back under seal, the seal was broken, but after an interval the "men" took an adjournment without arranging to reseal the documents, which were thus rendered invalid.

[89] It is interesting to note that Du Breuil, a reliable witness, stated in the early fourteenth century that the fines for false judgment imposed on "the king's men," judging apparently in lower royal courts, were not imposed on "the king's judges" who made similar mistakes and were reversed on appeal. *Stilus Curie Parlamenti* (ed. Aubert), 159–160.

[90] Du Breuil, 79.

The writer went on to say that if "the men" were thereafter attacked for false judgment, they could call on their lord as guarantor. To most it must have seemed safer to stay away, as they surely did by thousands. Yet decisions had to be rendered and responsibility assumed. The silent retreat of the laymen made it absolutely essential that professionals be recruited and assigned to duty. The professionals in inferior royal courts were exempt from personal liability for simple error in their decisions.[91] While many of these, even in royal courts, must have been pitifully unprepared, there were enough good brains with legal training to add new refinements and roll up more complications.

The thesis I advance is that the active agent in driving out lay judges in France was the Roman-canonist system of procedure, especially its modes of investigation and proof. It was adopted, I have argued, not merely because of its superior accuracy and refinement but also because, at the crucial times, the French monarchy lacked the means to organize and adopt alternative forms of procedure. Once adopted, the canonist system was further refined and elaborated under the pressure of its own internal logic. As a result the whole function of adjudication was transferred from the ancient forms of community court, leaving the local assemblies with only scattered functions. Once the process was well begun, it is a question whether it could have been arrested. But the most significant fact is that no effort was made to arrest it. The French monarchy on its first rebuilding had started with the same materials as the Norman kings of England: the group inquest from which our own juries have descended and local courts composed of laymen and possessing a mixture of judicial with other functions. These institutions could have been maintained only through active intervention of government, of the kind that occurred in England. They needed to be organized and greatly strengthened, to have their purposes redefined. The effort to organize, strengthen, and redefine was not seriously attempted by the framers of crown policy in France. Even if they had the power to do so, they could not have thought the effort worth making, for it was difficult for men of the fourteenth century to foresee the immense but hidden pos-

[91] Above, note 89.

sibilities of these institutions as instruments of government. So political authority held its hand while these institutions were silently destroyed. So far as it could, by action and example, the Crown took the lead in destroying them.

e. *The Triumph of the Professionals* (1500–1789)

Through the last three centuries of the Old Regime the displacement of lay by professional judges was almost everywhere complete. In Alsace and Lorraine there survived till the seventeenth century some ghostly reminders of the ancient *scabini*— assembly courts with permanent members (usually fourteen) who were locally elected.[92] In two of the customs officially published in the sixteenth century, there was expressed an affirmative duty of vassals to participate in judgment-making at the assizes held by their lords.[93] A very diluted version of older conceptions appeared much more widely and lasted late—a requirement that judges, royal and seignorial, attach to themselves councils of local advisers. Whatever ties it may have had with the ancient tribunals, this practice soon brought lawyers, not laymen, to the judge's entourage, though he was left free to reject their advice. In the form it took after 1500 this was not a means to channel in lay opinion as an element in the judging process. It had precisely the opposite effect of confirming the dependence of judges on the organized legal profession.[94]

By the sixteenth century the canonist methods of investigation

[92] Albert Babeau, *Les Assemblées Générales des Communautés d'Habitants du XIIIe Siècle à la Révolution* (Paris, 1893), 75–77. In Normandy it may have been a similar echo from the past when the published text of the Normandy custom of 1583 required "all judges, both royal and subordinate," to judge "in accordance with the will of the assistance." Article 12 (De Richebourg, *Nouveau Coutumier Général*, IV, 60).

The comparable institutions of the Channel Islands—Jersey, Guernsey, Alderney, and Sark—bear every sign of inheritance from ancient times, though their revival and persistence into later centuries were due to the large measure of local self-government permitted by the English monarchy. Their tie with the ancient *scabini* is left in doubt after careful review of the evidence by J. H. Patourel, *The Medieval Administration of the Channel Islands* (London, 1937), 88–99.

[93] Amiens and Clermont en Beauvaisis (De Richebourg, *Nouveau Coutumier Général*, I, 185; II, 774).

[94] Chénon, *HDF*, I, 662. The reduction of the attending *conseil* to a purely advisory role had apparently occurred in the *bailliage* of Senlis as early as 1340–1341. At a hearing held Dec. 12, 1340, the *conseil* employed by the royal judge comprised 11 persons of whom one was a local noble and the rest were lawyers. Rozière, "L'Assise du Bailliage de Senlis en 1340 et 1341," *NRH*, 1891, 714, at 720.

and proof had been adopted everywhere, in trials as well as appeals.[95] Perhaps the most striking consequence of the new system was the incredible number of judges required to administer it. The Parlement of Paris, which had reached a total of 51 judges within the first half century of its organization,[96] was steadily increasing in size. A factor in this increase was the sale of judicial offices, not unknown before the sixteenth century but a regular means of enhancing royal revenues after the time of Francis I. By 1715 the Parlement of Paris was composed of 240 judges, not counting 21 royal law officers assigned to the court or the 40 on its clerical staff. This vast concourse of judges was divided into nine chambers or divisions. Of these the *Grand' Chambre* with 42 judges assumed the leading role and dealt with the more important matters. There were five separate *Chambres des Enquêtes*, each composed of 33 members—a total of 165.[97] This might be described as a massive growth, yet it is the least of the story. The volume of judicial business was so great that during the fifteenth century there appeared the series of provincial Parlements, all modeled on the Parlement of Paris and all possessing, within their own territories, the powers of a supreme appellate court. The Parlements of Toulouse in the south and Normandy in the north began the series, then Grenoble, Bordeaux, Dijon and so on to a total of twelve provincial Parlements when the Revolution came to submerge them all. Most of these had a membership in the neighborhood of 100.[98] In addition there were four courts of appeal without formal title as Parlements but with independence in fact. To these should be added hundreds of lower royal courts conducted by royal *baillis*, some of which had powers as intermediate appellate courts by appeal from the multitude of minor royal judges. That the minor royal judges did exist in a multitude is suggested by the medium-sized royal *bailliage* of Vermandois. There were 140 royal judges from whom appeals

[95] Jean Imbert, *Practique Judiciaire* (Paris, 1616), vol. I, chap. 43, pp. 283 ff., gives a full account. For the fifteenth and sixteenth centuries Dupont-Ferrier, *Les Officiers Royaux des Bailliages et Sénéchaussées*, 364—377, gives a more general statement. The private compilation made for Poitou by local practitioners in 1417 gives quite a full picture in articles 254–282 and 752–762. *Le Vieux Coustumier de Poictou* (pub. Filhol, 1956).

[96] Above, sec. 2c.

[97] Chénon *HDF*, II, 508–509.

[98] Chénon *HDF*, II, 506–509.

were taken to the royal *bailli* of Vermandois. In the sixteenth century there were in France as a whole about ninety such intermediate appellate courts.[99] If one leaves out entirely the judges of the seignorial courts, which will be considered in a moment, and concentrates exclusively on royal courts, the total number of judges in the supreme appellate courts (Parlements and the equivalent) was about 1200 during the early decades of the eighteenth century.[100] The total number of royal judges at this stage must certainly have exceeded 5,000.

These estimates for France should be compared with figures from England: from 1300 to 1800 the judges of the English central courts of common law and Chancery rarely exceeded fifteen. These fifteen judges, furthermore, conducted most of the trials and all the appellate review that English central courts undertook. This meant, as will be seen, that a great deal of the work that French royal judges did was assigned in England to other agencies, under very remote control by the central courts. There were in England also various specialized courts like the Admiralty and the ecclesiastical courts, so that the figure of fifteen is incomplete. One must also allow for population. Within the boundaries of France as defined in the fourteenth century there were probably four or five times as many people living as in England at the same time. The ratio remained about the same as French territory was enlarged in later centuries. Around 1700 there were probably about twenty million people in France and four or five million in England minus Wales.[101] Yet even after

[99] Amédée Combier, *Les Justices Seigneuriales du Bailliage de Vermandois sous l'Ancien Régime* (Paris, 1897), 3.

As to the number of *bailliages* and *sénéchaussées*, a list of 86 is supplied for the end of the fifteenth century by Dupont-Ferrier, *Les Officiers Royaux des Bailliages et Sénéchaussées*, app. I. The later practice of elevating lower courts (*prévotés*) to the rank of *bailliages* brought the total of *bailliages* close to 400 though this did not in itself mean a net increase in the number of judges.

[100] Franklin L. Ford, *Robe and Sword* (Cambridge, Mass., 1954), 53.

[101] Any estimates of population are subject to the hazards that inhere in medieval statistics. For both France and England the most reliable figures date from the fourteenth century.

For France modern estimates are mainly based on the census of households (*feux*) ordered by the crown in 1328 to determine local liability to taxation. The studies of Ferdinand Lot indicate that the census itself was made with care and was remarkably complete as to the royal domain, which in 1328 comprised about three fifths of the territory of modern France (after 1918). The problem comes with the multiplier, since there is no direct evidence of how many persons lived in each household. Levasseur in his earlier studies had taken four as the average

correctives have been made for differences in population, the contrast is striking. If French royal judges could have been deployed on European battlefields, they would have made a considerable army by the standards of those times.

The supply of trained personnel could not be expected to meet a demand on so vast a scale. So far as the Parlement of Paris itself was concerned, from as early as the fifteenth century its permanent membership had been quite uniformly composed of persons with formal training and degrees in Roman or canon law,[102] though there were some occasions on which the Parlement was augmented by the attendance of lay peers. How proficient these permanent judges were is another question, since policing of the requirement rested with the Parlement itself. There is plenty of evidence that after the sale of judicial offices had brought inheritability and free transferability, the examinations conducted by the Parlements were extremely perfunctory

membership of a household. Lot took five except for Paris, where he used 3.5 as the multiplier. This gave a total of 16.5 to 17 million for the kingdom as its boundaries existed in 1328. F. Lot, "L'État des Paroisses et des Feux de 1328," *Bibliothèque de l'École des Chartes* (1929), 90:51 and 256, esp. 293–301. It is generally agreed that the French population recovered slowly from the ravages of the Black Death and the Hundred Years' War and even by 1600 had probably not come to exceed the 1328 figures. Joseph J. Spengler, *France Faces Depopulation* (Durham, N.C., 1938), 16–17. The figure for 1700 is based on a royal census and seems to have been about 20 million for France as it then was with a rise to about 26 million by 1789. Emile Levasseur, *La Population Française* (Paris, 1889–1892), I, 201–217; Alfred Cobban, *History of Modern France* (London, 1957), I, 47.

For England the poll tax survey of 1377 came at a point when the English population was probably near its lowest level after the successive epidemics of plague. The most recent student estimates that the total population of England minus Wales was 2.23 million in 1377. Projecting this backward through estimates of loss from the plague, he reaches a figure of 3.76 million for 1348. When population growth was resumed after 1430 the rise was gradual, reaching 3.78 million by 1603 and about 4 million by 1690. Josiah C. Russell, *British Medieval Population* (Albuquerque, 1948), 119–146. It may be that Russell's figures are too low. It has been pointed out that estimates based on the 1377 poll tax run the risk of taxpayers' evasion and the omission of some classes of nontaxable persons. May McKisack, *The Fourteenth Century, 1307–1399* (Oxford, 1959), 312–313. As to later periods, the widely used estimate of King would indicate 5.5 million population for England and Wales in 1690. George N. Clark, *The Seventeenth Century* (Oxford, 2d ed., 1947), 5. If Russell's figure of 390,000 for Wales in 1690 is added to his 4,000,000 figure for England alone, his estimate is at least a million less than King's. As for the period 1720–1750, English population gained probably about a million, and between 1750 and 1820 it nearly doubled, rising from 6,400,-000 to 12 million. Mabel C. Buer, *Health, Wealth, and Population in the Early Days of the Industrial Revolution* (London, 1926), 22–23.

[102] Aubert, *Histoire du Parlement de Paris des Origines à François I*, 77–78.

for candidates whose family connections and social standing were acceptable.[103] For the intermediate levels of the royal judiciary, a royal ordinance of 1499 required a degree in Roman or canon law [104] but it seems unlikely that this requirement was enforced. For the lowest echelons of the royal system no similar requirement was even attempted until the edict of Louis XIV in 1679 which demanded two years of law study of candidates for royal judicial offices.[105]

It was the seignorial courts, however, that must have felt most acutely the shortage of trained personnel. If one were to look to the conventional sources of information on French law, one would hardly anticipate that the problem was serious. The picture drawn by the French law books is essentially that described by a modern writer—of nonroyal courts being in a state of "full-scale decadence" from about the fifteenth century.[106] The lawyers did not write about them. They contributed almost nothing to the continuity or growth of legal doctrines. But for people then living they loomed very large. Even the formal sources suggest this.

To the medieval categories of "high" and "low" seignorial justice there had been added, by the sixteenth century, an intermediate type described as "middle." No one of the three had exactly the same content in all parts of France. Yet generally "high" justice included both "medium" and "low," in the absence of a special grant to an inferior lord exempting his territories from the higher jurisdiction. In many of the districts of northern France whose customs were published in the sixteenth century, the official texts described in some detail the limits of each type of jurisdiction. "High" justice ordinarily gave power to punish all crimes except for those on the limited list of *cas royaux*, and it was often expressly stated that "high" justice gave power to administer the death penalty or bodily mutilation. In civil matters "high" justice usually had no limit of subject matter or value. As to "middle" justice there were somewhat wider varia-

---

[103] Ford, *Robe and Sword*, 112–118.

[104] Chénon, *HDF*, I, 847–848; II, 516–517.

[105] Isambert, Jourdan et Decrusy, *Receuil des Anciennes Lois Françaises* (Paris, 1823–1829), XIX, 195. This series will be cited hereafter as Isambert, *Anciennes Lois Françaises*.

[106] Chénon, *HDF*, I, 865.

tions from district to district; most commonly it included all types of civil action, without limit of subject matter or value and in criminal proceedings no sanction more severe than a fine of 60 sous could be imposed. "Low" justice represented a type of small claims court; for criminal sanctions the upper limit was often 6 sous or 7 sous 6 deniers, with a similar (perhaps somewhat higher) limit on the values in civil actions.[107]

The depreciation of the *livre tournois* meant that a jurisdictional limit of 6 or 7 sous, measured by that standard, was low. Though the sou corresponded nominally to the English shilling,

---

[107] The following references are to the texts of the published customs as they appear in De Richebourg, *Nouveau Coutumier Général:* Melun, arts. 1, 16, 20 (III, 434–436); Sens, arts. 1, 16, 18 (III, 505–507); Auxerre, arts. 1, 18 (III, 593–594); Grande Perche, arts. 1, 4, 9, 21, 24 (III, 647–648); Blois, arts. 14, 21, 23, 27, 28 (III, 1048–1049); Senlis, arts. 96, 98, 99, 108, 120 (II, 715–716); Valois, arts. 2, 4, 5 (II, 796); Nivernais, chap. I, arts. 13 and 15 (III, 1124); Bourbonnais, arts. 2, 4 (III, 1231–1232); Eu, arts. 1, 2 (IV, 177–178); Maine, arts. 4, 6, 12, 44, 45, 49 (IV, 465–470); Anjou, arts. 2, 3, 11, 39, 42 (IV, 530–533); Touraine, arts. 1, 39, 55 (IV, 643–648); Poitou, arts. 3, 4, 15, 16, 17, 68 (IV, 775–781); Amiens, arts. 223, 236 (I, 185). As to Paris, the most important of all, provisions on the subject were drafted by a group of practitioners in terms quite similar to those above referred to, but these clauses were never adopted by the assembly of the three estates for the Paris district, though it was generally agreed that they represented the usages of the district. The draft clauses appear in Jean Bacquet, *Traité des Droits de Justice* (*Oeuvres,* Paris, 1664), chap. II, and are discussed by Pierre Lemercier, *Les Justices Seigneuriales de la Région Parisienne de 1580 à 1789* (Paris, 1933), 40–48.

Among the deviations from standard usage were the provisions as to "middle justice" in Grande Perche (jurisdiction given as to all personal actions but none as to real actions) and Blois and Touraine (a limitation of 60 sous value in all civil actions).

As to "low justice" the customs of Sens and Bourbonnais gave the court-keepers jurisdiction of *all* civil actions without limit of value; the jurisdictional limit of value for civil actions was 60 sous in Auxerre, Valois, Nivernais, and in the draft articles never adopted for the custom of Paris. For "low justice" Sens and Bourbonnais provided no limit of value whatever for civil actions concerning movables and batteries without bloodshed.

A considerable number of published customs contained no provisions as to the competence of the seignorial courts. Perhaps it was in such districts that one might apply the "maxim" reported by one law reporter to have been approved by a decision of the Parlement of Paris on Aug. 23, 1605: that "the officers of a lord having middle or low justice . . . are competent to decide all civil and mixed actions without any limitation of value," as well as all criminal cases in which the fine cannot exceed 60 sous. Laurent Jovet, *Bibliothèque des Arrests* (Paris, 1669), 405. It is impossible to accept this "maxim" with the full sweep given it by Jovet. Nothing as broad as this appears in such standard accounts of high, middle and low justice as Daniel Jousse, *Traité de l'Administration de la Justice* (Paris, 1771), I, 188 ff.; René Choppin, *Commentary on the Custom of Anjou* (Paris, 2d ed., 1662), I, 68–72.

the purchasing power of the sou was perhaps an eighth as much in the sixteenth century and grew relatively less as time went on.[108] In the early part of the sixteenth century, for example, 7 sous could be two days' wages for an unskilled male farm worker.[109] The great upward surge of prices in the last two thirds of the sixteenth century, pushed by the tide of silver from the mines in the New World, brought in France roughly a tripling of prices.[110] This meant a corresponding contraction of seignorial justice whose jurisdictional limits were expressed in money terms. By the eighteenth century, for example, an unskilled farm worker might be found who would work for 7 sous a day or even somewhat less, but more probably he would be paid 16 or 20 sous for a single day's work. Seven sous would buy a chicken, a pound of pork, or somewhat more than a dozen eggs.[111] Jurisdictional limits expressed in figures like these would, where enforced, exclude all but the pettiest litigation. Thus international economic pressures, helped by kings who debased the coinage, undermined the outer barriers of a system that was too firmly fortified for direct attack. The effects of inflation must have been chiefly felt by "low" justice, owned by the smaller gentry. But not even "low" justice was everywhere subject to low money-value limitations; in many districts of France, furthermore, the ancient rules were not firmly fixed by custom or charter and could therefore be evaded. All one can say is that the main course of

[108] Georges d'Avenel, *Histoire Économique de la Propriété, des Salaires, des Denrées et de Tous les Prix en Général Depuis l'An 1200 jusqu'en l'An 1800* (Paris, 1894–1926), I, 38–39. There are obvious difficulties in stating these relationships with any exactness, not only because of the scattered and unclassified nature of the price data available but still more because of the large variety of coins that circulated in France, both of domestic and foreign mintage. As d'Avenel makes clear, the *livre tournois* was the most common standard but by 1200 it had become a money of account only, representing 98 grams of silver. Successive debasements by kings and other coiners, plus legislative attempts to alter the nominal value of coins already in circulation, led to frequent changes in public estimates of the value of this ideal entity, with a strong though fluctuating trend downward. D'Avenel, I, 35–75; also Georges d'Avenel, *Histoire de la Fortune Française* (Paris, 1927), 44–47

In administering the jurisdictional limits on seignorial courts there was the further difficulty that references were not always or necessarily to the *livre tournois,* especially in areas that were strongly addicted to coins of local manufacture.

[109] D'Avenel, *Histoire Économique,* III, 500–501.

[110] D'Avenel, *Histoire Économique,* I, 16–20.

[111] D'Avenel, *Histoire Économique,* IV, 272–275, 396, 175–177.

events was favorable to the "high" and squeezed many of the "low" justiciars. The question how many did survive will be considered shortly.

In seignorial as in royal courts, the judging function had passed by the sixteenth century into the hands of professionals appointed by the court-owning lords. This meant not only that the lay entourage had vanished but that the lords themselves had surrendered their claims to be judges. This latter result had some importance and it was by no means inevitable. For court-keeping was conceived as a subject of ownership like other lordship rights that gave revenue as well as control. In the texts of the codified customs that were published in the sixteenth century, rights of "justice" were all mixed up with rights to seize straying animals and treasure trove, to forfeit goods of convicted persons or foreigners, to appoint guardians and notaries, to have grain ground at the lord's mill or to give special grants of the lord's protection to individuals on his lands. If numerous feudal lords had made a strong demand to act as sole judges in their courts, it might have been difficult to frame a theory by which such a demand could be denied. It was practicality that prevailed, no doubt, rather than theory. The same procedural complications that drove out the "men" would produce boredom in the lords. If there was widespread contest, it has not been recorded. By the sixteenth century it was taken for granted that a seignorial court must have a judge, someone other than the lord himself. Some published customs stated this expressly.[112] Reliable authors of the *ancien régime* testify that this was the practice.[113] Modern studies in particular districts confirm the

[112] Poitou, art. 7 (De Richebourg, IV, 775); Grande Perche, art. 14 (De Richebourg, III, 648); Paris draft, arts. 2 and 13 (Bacquet, *Traité des Droits de Justice,* chap. II, in *Oeuvres,* 1664). In two customs it was stated that the lord could have a specified number of judges, the number being stated as a limitation (Angoumois, art. 4 and Blois, arts. 15 and 28; De Richebourg, IV, 840 and III, 1048–1049). The custom of Eu, art. 2 merely recited that the justice of the Count of Eu "a esté toujours exercée par son bailly" (De Richebourg, IV, 177).

It is interesting that in the *Vieux Coustumier de Poictou,* written by private practitioners in 1417 (published by Professor René Filhol, 1956), the requirement is stated explicitly: every *seigneur chatellain* "can and must" have two judges, one for his *petite assise* and one for his *grand assise.* Above, note 77.

[113] Guy Coquille, *Histoire de Nivernais* (*Oeuvres,* Paris, 1665), I, 395, refers to a case of 1329 in which a lord had exercised justice in person and then says:

conclusion that seignorial justice all over France was exercised by special judicial officers appointed by the lords.[114]

The central government attempted in 1560 to set minimum standards of qualification for the judges of the seignorial courts.[115] It did not attempt to impose any requirement of legal training, but merely set up a procedure for examination by local royal officers into the "life and morals" of persons appointed to such posts. All the sources agree that this provision was ignored in practice.[116] One reason for this disregard of the royal command was that reversal of a judgment rendered by a seignorial court meant a money fine payable by the lord of the court, not by the judge himself. In the case of a very "high" court—one from which appeals were taken directly to a Parlement—this fine was £ 60; in other cases it was 60 sous.[117] From this it was inferred that the court-keepers needed complete freedom in choosing their judicial officers—even, indeed, complete

"Mais depuis a esté ordonné et ainsi est observé, que les Seigneurs justiciers doivent establir des Juges sans eux-mesmes exercer: Imo leur est défendu d'assister à l'expédition des causes."

Charles Loyseau, *Traité des Seigneuries* (*Oeuvres*, Lyon, 1701), chap. X, nos. 69–71. In another of his works Loyseau, who was himself most critical of seignorial justice, argued that the court-keeping lord was incapable of participating even as a member of his own court and added that the Parlement of Paris had found such attendance of a lord in his own court to be "bad" (though not indicating how bad). Loyseau, *Traité des Offices* (*Oeuvres*, 1701, p. 281), C., chap. I, nos. 45 and 46.

[114] André Giffard, *Les Justices Seigneuriales en Bretagne aux XVIIe et XVIIIe Siècles* (Paris, 1903), 71–74; Amédée Combier, *Les Justices Seigneuriales du Bailliage de Vermandois sous l'Ancien Régime*, 10–12; Jacques Henri Bataillon, *Les Justices Seigneuriales du Bailliage de Pontoise à la Fin de l'Ancien Régime* (Paris, 1942), 44–45.

[115] Ordonnance d'Orléans, art. 55 (Isambert, *Anciennes Lois Françaises*, XIV, 79).

[116] Georges Louët, *Receuil de Plusieurs Arrests Notables du Parlement de Paris* (with notes of Julien Brodeau; Paris, 1712), O, no. 3, citing 5 decisions of the Parlement of Paris between 1595 and 1644 to this effect; Giffard, cited note 114, stating that the provisions of the ordinance were "absolutely disregarded" in Brittany; Lemercier, *Les Justices Seigneuriales de la Région Parisienne de 1580 à 1789*, 80–83.

[117] These fines for erroneous judgment by seignorial courts had of course existed earlier. D'Ableiges, *Grand Coutumier de France* (eds. Laboulaye and Dareste), vol. IV, chap. 10. They were confirmed by royal ordinance in 1563. Ord. d'Orléans, art. 27 (Isambert, *Anciennes Lois Françaises*, XIV, 166). Both Brodeau and Louët, however, testified that by the seventeenth century the £ 60 fines were seldom imposed by the Parlement in the absence of serious fault in the court appealed from. Brodeau sur Louët, *Arrests Notables*, O, no. 3.

freedom to dismiss them except where the judicial office in question had been sold to the incumbent.[118] Of course it did not necessarily follow that the judges chosen would be wholly untouched by legal training. By a royal edict of 1680 two years of legal studies, leading to a certificate, were required for appointment as judge in those very "high" seignorial courts from which appeals were taken directly to the Parlements.[119] Quite apart from this legislation, samples taken in particular districts show a fairly high standard of skill and training in the judges of the great lordships. It was quite a different story in the lower ranges of the seignorial jurisdictions.[120]

The question as to qualifications of seignorial judges is important, for it seems plain that conventional sources of French legal history give a most misleading picture of the role of seignorial courts. They were no mere decadent survivals. "High" justice in most districts was unlimited as to subject matter or sanctions in both civil or criminal cases, except for the small reserved area of *cas royaux*. "Middle" justice dealt only with less serious crimes, though in civil cases its jurisdiction was often unlimited. "High" justice could hang or mutilate. The owners of both "high" and "medium" justice had jails and these jails were certainly used, even though the prisoners were immortalized in nineteenth-century opera rather than in published law reports. It is true that the competition of royal courts cut in on seignorial justice, through the practice of royal judges in taking cases subject to remand if the lord protested. But there was quite a lot left. The only attempt at a tabulation relates to the province of Brittany, which was not fully representative since feudalism in Brittany was probably more highly developed than in any other province of France. An eighteenth-

---

[118] Bacquet, *Traité des Droits de Justice*, chap. XVII (*Oeuvres*, 1664).

[119] Isambert, *Anciennes Lois Françaises*, XIX, 228.

[120] Giffard, *Les Justices Seigneuriales en Bretagne*, 97–100; Combier, *Les Justices Seigneuriales du Bailliage de Vermandois*, 10; Loyseau, *Traité des Seigneuries* (*Oeuvres*, 1701), chap. X, nos. 69–71, p. 58. In the last cited passage Loyseau argued strongly that for "high" justice, which gave power to impose the death sentence, the judges "devroit en bonne Jurisprudence etre lettré et gradué." He conceded that for "medium" and "low" justice this was not necessary, provided that the judge hear no criminal cases, and no civil cases above £10 value, unless he had a graduate lawyer to advise him. In this proviso, as in his argument generally for having law-trained judges in "high" justice, it seems that Loyseau was not so much reporting as exhorting.

century estimate, approved by a careful modern historian, indicates that during most of the eighteenth century nine tenths of the judicial business of Brittany was handled by seignorial courts.[121]

A crude index of the volume of business is supplied by the number of judges employed in seignorial courts. In the *bailliage* of Vermandois, to the northeast of Paris, there were 210 seignorial courts, most of them administering "high" justice. Each court as a rule had two judges, as well as a clerk, two *procureurs*, a sergeant and a notary, so that for the 210 courts in question the court officials appointed by the court-owning lords would total nearly 1500.[122] Among the judicial districts of France—approximately 90 in number in the sixteenth century—Vermandois was a district of medium size. Brittany was much larger and the figures for Brittany cannot be projected over the whole of France since, as already suggested, the system of seignorial courts in Brittany was relatively overbuilt. But when every discount has been made, it is still remarkable that a census made in 1711 showed a total of 3700 seignorial courts operating in Brittany. At the time of the revolution in 1789 this total had been reduced to about 2500, an average of two seignorial courts in every parish. Some country parishes had 10 or 12 or even 30. The city of Rennes alone had 27 seignorial jurisdictions. Perhaps a third of the provincial total were "high" justice.[123] The number of judges that sat in these 2500 courts would be hard to guess. But one modern estimate for the period immediately before the revolution does not seem extreme—that all the full- and part-time judges in all the seignorial courts of France totalled 70,000 to 80,000.[124]

What this meant in confusion and conflict we can only dimly imagine. The lines of division between the seignorial jurisdictions had for long been territorial, but transfers and divisions and subinfeudations had produced many crazy quilts. The ownership

[121] Giffard, *Les Justices Seigneuriales en Bretagne*, 107–109.
[122] Combier, *Les Justices Seigneuriales du Bailliage de Vermandois*, 3–12.
[123] Giffard, 34–45.
[124] Introduction to Combier, ix. The qualification that many of the seignorial judges worked part-time needs to be emphasized. The studies of particular areas that are referred to below indicate that there was much duplication of functions, a judge of one court being *procureur* or process-server in another, etc.

of courts was rooted in ownership of land, at least in the sense
that transfers of court-keeping rights were no longer tolerated—
if they ever had been—apart from transfers of land ownership.[125]
Yet the deposits of centuries, modified by erosion through inertia
or disuse, left local patterns unclear. For example, at the start
of the seventeenth century there were in the City of Paris alone
25 private court-keepers, the most important being the Bishop of
Paris whose "high" justice covered one-third of the City. Some
of the smaller courts had jurisdictions limited to groups of
houses on different streets (three houses on the rue du Moulin,
twelve houses on the rue St. Martin, etc.). In the suburbs "high"
justice was exercised over tracts as small as two, three, or four
acres.[126] The fragmentation can be seen in extreme form in a case
in Brittany in 1769. One Guichaut had died and the contest of
jurisdictions was over power to administer his estate and the at-
tendant fees. The kitchen and dining room of his house were admitted to be subject to the seignorial court of Chairval, but the
bedroom in which he died was subject to the lord of Fougeray.
The officers of the court of Chairval claimed the right to make
an inventory and sell the assets because the domicile of the
deceased was "not in the room where he was only husband" but
in the kitchen and dining room "where he was both husband and
father." Despite this impressive argument, it was apparently
decided that he spent more time in the bedroom and that this
was his domicile.[127]

The truth seems to be that the seignorial courts had acquired
not so much a corps of judges as an army of predators. The king
by ordinance had exhorted the court-keeping lords to pay their
judges "honest wages," but like many other pious hopes this one

[125] There has of course been great controversy over the question whether feudal
rights of justiciation were dependent on land ownership (whether fief and justice
were "one and the same"). But the arguments were basically directed to a different issue—the issue whether land ownership without more gave rights to administer feudal justice. A convenient summary of the arguments appear in Chénon,
HDF, I, 650–656. When a transfer of high, medium or low justice was attempted
in the seventeenth century without transfer of the lands with which it was connected, the Parlement of Paris held the transfer to be wholly void despite royal
letters confirming it. Lucien Soefve, Nouveau Receuil de Plusieurs Questions Notables (Paris, 1682), II, 196.
[126] Lemercier, Les Justices Seigneuriales de la Région Parisienne, 2–31.
[127] Giffard, Les Justices Seigneuriales en Bretagne, 56–57.

was disappointed.[128] The judges, like the clerks, the process-servers and the other officials, lived off the fees and gifts of litigants. They had every possible incentive to engage in jurisdictional battles, to pile up unnecessary papers and prolong litigation, for fees and exactions provided their livelihood. It is quite amazing to read the sums that were paid by buyers of the higher judicial offices—in Brittany £23,200 were paid in 1717 for a hereditary seignorial judgeship and £2,500 in another case for a mere twelve-year appointment.[129] At the lower levels of the feudal hierarchy, to which most of the personnel were condemned, it is quite certain that income was smaller than these sale prices would suggest. Offices had to be doubled up—a judge for one lord was a process-server or part-time clerk in another lord's court. A critic of seignorial justice claimed that many judges became rent collectors or domestic servants for their lords and were thus for their employers a convenient pool of cheap labor. If the judge had not bought his office from the lord of the court, he could be dismissed "like the lord's valet." [130] With so vast a number of courts and officials to accommodate, quarters were insufficient and court sessions were held without regularity, in private homes, in taverns and under the trees. The judges were mostly ignorant and untrained, vested with great power but in reality dependent on the lords who appointed them. Exceptions of course existed. There were honest and competent judges even in "low" justice and many more in the upper scale. Yet the main design that emerges is one of organized rapacity. The judges and other judicial officers were professionals in the sense that they devoted themselves regularly to judicial duties and earned an intermittent income through fees and money fines and gifts extracted from litigants. They were parts of a massive system that undoubtedly helped to maintain order, eventually settled disputes, and provided a livelihood to a large and not especially deserving class. If this system had any other social function it

[128] Giffard, 86.

[129] Giffard, 86–88. Compare the judgeship in the court of the Abbey of St. Germain des Prés, which sold for £48,000 in 1654. Lemercier, Les Justices Seigneuriales de la Région Parisienne, 75–76.

[130] Loyseau, Discours sur l'Abus des Justices de Village (Oeuvres, 1701), 11. The Discours was first published in 1605.

was to maintain the status, prestige, and authority of the French nobility.[131]

It should be noted also that appeals from judgments of seignorial courts followed the lines of the feudal hierarchy before they reached royal courts. The point at which the lines of appellate review crossed over to the royal system depended on the "height" of the feudal justice concerned. In many cases feudal courts piled up three deep. In Brittany, where the feudal pyramid reached its most monumental proportions, appeals could rise through as many as five feudal jurisdictions, so that when the stages of royal justice were added there could be in a single case eight appeals before the Parlement of Brittany was reached.[132] Among all the oppressions of seignorial justice, it was the multiplication of appeals that contemporaries described as most burdensome and universal.[133]

Even before the revolution of 1789 there were some who considered that seignorial justice had outlived its usefulness. Shortly after Louis XIV re-established his authority after the Fronde, some quite respectable persons urged that the whole system be abolished. But this drastic action would have been a breach of the tacit alliance of Crown and nobility by which the new state was to be maintained. Instead Louis XIV contented himself with modest measures, such as buying out the abbey courts of Paris. More than a century earlier Francis I had tried to abolish the abbey courts which bisected the streets and alleys of that brawling city. He had met with such fierce resistance from the monks that the proposal was shelved. In 1674 the Sun King

[131] These conclusions are based on Giffard, *Les Justices Seigneuriales en Bretagne*, 100–106 and 235–253; and Combier, *Les Justices Seigneuriales du Bailliage de Vermandois*, 19–29. These two modern studies deal only with Brittany and Vermandois, but there appears no reason to consider that in these respects the two districts in question differed from the rest of France. A contemporary indictment, not restricted to any particular district, is that of Loyseau, *Discours sur l'Abus des Justices de Village*. One modern author has concluded that the indictment by Loyseau was exaggerated so far as the records of the district of Pontoise disclose. Bataillon, *Les Justices Seigneuriales du Baillaige de Pontoise à la Fin de l'Ancien Régime*, 142–161.

[132] Giffard, 58–62.

[133] Imbert, *Practique Judiciaire*, chap. 3; Loyseau, *Discours sur l'Abus des Justices de Village*; Esmein, *HDF*, 438–439. It is interesting that the multiplication of appeals was a major complaint in the system of seignorial courts that was transplanted to Canada in the seventeenth and eighteenth centuries. William B. Munro, *Documents Relating to the Seignorial Tenure in Canada* (Toronto, 1908), 78–81.

bought out the rights of the monks, paying them generous in-
demnities.[134] There the matter rested. The rest of the seignorial
courts were left unscathed until 1789, when they were swept
away with all that they symbolized.

f. Political and Social Implications

The full impact of this mixed system of public and private
justice will be more evident after English developments have
been described. The English story must be postponed for the
present, but some points of comparison can be anticipated now.

The French judicial system, taken as a whole, surely helped
to hold French society under the *ancien régime* in equilibrium,
an equilibrium that seemed so firm at the time but that was so
easily and suddenly destroyed. The Parlements, led by the Parlement of Paris, were vitally important in eighteenth-century
politics. Their role depended essentially on a right of public
remonstrance and a limited power to deny registration (and
thereby enforcement) to royal legislation. Resuming an active
political role in the eighteenth century, the Parlements provided
the main centers of resistance to authoritarian government. Indeed it was the refusal of the Parlement of Paris to register royal
edicts introducing urgent and needed fiscal reforms that drove
the king to convoking the Three Estates and thereby brought
on the ultimate disaster.[135] But the role of the Parlements included much more than these dramatic acts of political opposition. From medieval times they had inherited powers of legislation which they exercised over a wide range of public and private
matters. These majestic assemblies could thus inject themselves
into general administration and policy in many ways and at many
levels.

It was therefore of crucial importance that the sale of ju-

[134] Tanon, *Histoire des Justices des Anciennes Églises*, 120–122; Esmein, *HDF*,
483–484. The subject is fully discussed by Lemercier, *Les Justices Seigneuriales de
la Région Parisienne*, 229–276. He makes it clear that the project of 1674 did not
aim at a full-scale attack on seignorial jurisdictions generally but only at reducing
the conflict and confusion in the rapidly growing capital. Even so the crown re-
ceded from the terms of the edict of 1674 and restored an important part of the
private jurisdictions originally abolished.

[135] These well-known events have been often described, e.g., by François J. M.
Oliver Martin, *Histoire du Droit Français des Origines à la Révolution* (Paris,
1948), secs. 505–510.

dicial offices, in the Parlements as elsewhere, had made the
office holders irremovable except for gross misconduct. As judicial offices became ever more clearly subjects of private
ownership, they became inheritable and, within certain outside
limits, saleable. The transmission of offices within families that
were related by blood or marriage built a strong sense of corporate solidarity. Then as the status of the Parlements was
steadily raised and as judgeships in the Parlements came to
ennoble their owners automatically, there developed something
more than solidarity within and between the Parlements. The
nobility of the robe in the eighteenth century discovered a
community of interest with the nobility of the sword and the
ties grew closer between them. This meant that these judicial
assemblies, immune to royal pressure or control, became powerful
defenders of the nobility as a class. A recent study has shown
with great skill how this "regrouping" of the French aristocracy,
under the leadership of the Parlements, paralyzed efforts at
moderate reform and guaranteed that change when it came
would be catastrophic and complete.[136]

But private justice too had its part to play. The developing
alliance between the nobility of the robe in the royal courts and
the noble owners of seignorial courts meant, first of all, that no
sustained attack on seignorial courts would be made by the royal
judges. Many of the judges were court-keepers themselves on
their private estates and had interests of their own to preserve.[137]
When one seeks to analyze the nature of these interests, shared
by all court-keepers alike, it seems evident that their primary
stake was not in money income. It is true that private, like
royal, justice was expensive to the litigants, but the intake was
largely siphoned off by the swarms of officials who staffed and
surrounded the seignorial courts. In part the court-keepers'
interest was in symbols of status, for the holding of court in
the name of the lord was an accepted mark of rank. The contest for
honors was continuous among some 200,000 nobles who differed
widely in wealth and position.[138] Privileges that were empty of

[136] Ford, *Robe and Sword.*
[137] This point is made by Ford, *Robe and Sword*, 168–169, and Giffard, *Les
Justices Seigneuriales en Bretagne*, 230–231.
[138] Ford, *Robe and Sword*, 22–34, gives an excellent account. He accepts the
figure of 20,000,000 as an estimate of the total French population at the start of

content like the privilege of marching first in public processions or sitting in the front pew in church, could be defended as vigorously as those that gave real power.[139] But the judicial work of some seignorial courts certainly gave them power. "High" justice that could imprison, mutilate, or hang offenders gave something more than the honor of having a gallows erected on one's estate; even though their work in criminal law enforcement became more and more sporadic as time went on, there were occasional bodies that swung in the wind to provide a grim reminder.[140] In civil cases the jurisdiction of each seignorial court was in principle exclusive within its own district, subject to

the eighteenth century within the boundaries as they then existed, so that the ratio of nobility to the rest of the population would be about 1 to 100.

[139] The *droits honorifiques* of the nobility that the authors discussed were mostly concerned with the deference due in church ceremonials. These *droits* were conceived to be an incident to court-keeping rights, and the highest honors were of course attributed to the owners of "high" justice. They inspired much litigation, some of it between competing claimants of lordship rights but most of it in contests with clergy who resisted the pretensions of the lords. It was generally conceded that the owner of "high" justice was entitled to march in church processions immediately behind the priest, to have a pew in the front of the church or in the choir (on the right, as "more honorific" than the left), to receive incense and be sprinkled with holy water specially, to be named with his full name in requests to the congregation for prayers in his behalf, to have the church draped with black as mourning for his death, and so on. Pierre Jacquet, *Traité des Justices de Seigneur* (Lyon, 1764), vol. I, chap. 22; Edmé de la Poix de Fréminville, *Pratique Universelle Pour la Rénovation des Terriers et des Droits Seigneuriaux* (Paris, 2d ed., 1759), II, 41–99. The Parlement of Paris ordered in decrees of 1704 and 1716 that the lord and his lady must each have incense three times and each of his children once, but the Parlement of Dijon decreed that it was sufficient for him and his lady each to receive incense once and their children once as a group (Jacquet, I, 279–280). Holy water was the subject of even more vigorous contests. The Privy Council in 1646 decreed that the local lord must be separately sprinkled with holy water by the *curé* and this was confirmed by a general assembly of the clergy of France in 1656 and by a "solemn decree" of the Parlement of Paris in 1699. But local clergy sometimes resisted. In one case a lord secured a court decree against the local *curé* directing that the lord be given holy water separately, "with distinction and before the people" in the church. The *curé*, after this decree, waited until the lord appeared with a new wig and then manipulated the sprinkler so that it drenched the wig, producing a "lawsuit greater than the first." In another case the *curé* secured a sprinkler of enormous size and on a cold day drenched the lady justiciar so that she had to leave church and change her clothes (De Fréminville, II, 65–66). The abundant litigation on these and similar issues is summarized by Jacquet and de Fréminville in the passages cited above.

[140] In the late seventeenth century and throughout the eighteenth the inertia and inefficiency of the seignorial courts in criminal matters led throughout France to a reduction of their importance in cases of major crime and to increased initiative by royal officers. This abstention seems to have been motivated primarily by the high costs of maintaining an adequate staff of law enforcement officers. Giffard, 119–129; Lemercier, 145–153.

limitations of value or subject matter that were often wide; in "high" justice there were usually no such limits at all. The court-keeper's opportunities for influence and control through the work of his court would depend on the training and integrity of the judges he employed, but the assurances of impartiality were, to say the least, incomplete. It must have been true in many places beside Brittany that they

did not have the authority and independence of true magistrates. Without training, without morality, without private resources of their own, maintained solely by *chicane,* the officers of the lord, subject to his dismissal, were not merely fiscal agents and judges without independence; they were managers of their lord's affairs, his devoted agents, his humble and faithful servants. This is the way they appear in the correspondence they exchange with their lords; the lords speak to them as they speak to domestic servants and the judges reply as to their masters.[141]

In the relations between social classes the most important feature was that even the "lowest" justiciar was entitled to litigate in his court all disputes that arose in enforcing the lord's own rights. In such cases the value limits on seignorial jurisdiction would ordinarily not apply. The seignorial rights were numerous and harassing to the general population, though they varied widely from place to place—rents, dues and services (in kind or commuted), tolls and monopolies (over the grinding of grain or the pressing of grapes), exclusive rights to hunt and fish. Contests between lords and peasants over commons of pasture and other ancient rights of usage produced widespread bitterness and could bring some local communities very close to civil war.[142] In most places it was a further aggravation that absentee lords had delegated to estate agents the task of extracting income from their lands and this often meant that their rights were pressed to the limit. One does not need to emphasize individual examples of violence or arrogance shown by these servants of the nobility to build a picture of frustration and helplessness in those who felt oppressed. Though review by royal justice could be secured by way of successive appeals, the costs and delays and often the bias of royal judges made this remedy

[141] Giffard, 242.
[142] Henri Sée, *Les Classes Rurales en Bretagne* (Paris, 1906), 208–240.

an illusion. In the last decades before the Revolution there is much evidence that seignorial exploitation grew harsher.[143] Whether or not this can be proved for all of France, the judicial power possessed by the nobility in their own courts was the strong-point in the defense of their inherited privileges. In French society as a whole, it seems clear that the surviving wide scope of seignorial justice helped to build up pressure behind the dam and ensure that it would burst.

When one contrasts French developments with English, it seems that in France there was not only a general absence of representative institutions but a failure of local self-government. The reasons for the failure of local self-government lie far back of the eighteenth century, in the thirteenth century and before. As has already been suggested, the "public" courts of the Carolingian empire were absorbed in France by feudataries so that the late medieval monarchy did not have at hand a functioning system of local courts, like the county and hundred courts that survived the Conquest in England. This meant in the thirteenth century that royal justice must be rebuilt from new foundations. But a main thesis advanced in this whole argument has been that the choices made by the framers of French crown policy—chiefly the critical decision to adopt the canonist modes of investigation and proof—had lasting effects on the structure of the courts and their relations to political authority. The laymen who still composed most of the courts in the thirteenth century faded away in the fourteenth. The whole responsibility for conducting trials and rendering decisions was transferred to professional judges, however untrained they might be. Many of them later were wholly untrained, especially in seignorial courts. It might be said that lay participation was preserved by appointing to judicial positions vast numbers of ignorant men. But the men who took over the judging function were in no sense spokesmen for or responsible to the communities in which they lived. Their ap-

---

[143] Sée, 178–207. This account deals primarily with Brittany but attempts some generalizations. The classic account in Alexis de Tocqueville, *The Old Regime and the French Revolution,* part II, chap. 1, can still be read with profit. Lemercier in his study of seignorial justice in the Paris region (*Les Justices Seigneuriales de la Région Parisienne de 1580 à 1789,* 89–90) was unable to find any direct evidence of exploitation in enforcement of seignorial rights and was forced to leave the question unanswered.

pointment they owed to the court-keeper, whether he was the
king or a feudal lord; what security they had they paid for by
buying the office itself. For present purposes it is more important
that this transfer of the judging function to specialists meant
the loss by lay assemblies of the central core, the continuing element, around which other functions could be built.

It was difficult, especially in the beginning, to distinguish
between dispute-settlement, rule-making and general administration. In the surviving sources of medieval France there are not
many clear examples of this fusion of functions, because of the
poverty of the materials. But the Abbey Court of Sainte Geneviève in Paris did not hesitate to issue in 1291 a general order
to all tavern keepers in the enclave controlled by the Abbey,
forbidding them under penalty to give food or drink to "dis-
solute persons, male or female, or to those suspected of evil-
doing." [144] The manorial courts of Alsace that continued to meet
through the sixteenth century issued ordinances concerning the
use of common lands, the cutting of wood, the impounding of
pigs and other matters of local concern, and chose their own
officials to enforce their legislation.[145] In this they acted with the
same freedom as the English local courts of manor and town
that will be later described. There is no reason to think that
local assemblies in France would have failed to develop along
similar lines if their meetings had been regularized and organized with the support of central authority.

This is not the place to describe in detail the effects of royal
intervention in paralyzing French local government. But it seems
worth while to sketch very briefly the history of the chartered
towns, whose remarkable growth and vitality in the late Middle
Ages were an outward sign of general social revival. In France as
in the rest of Europe, common needs and interests and a deeper
sense of shared human values had preserved ancient forms of
social organization; but the growth of economic activity, centering in the towns, pushed them irresistibly toward new forms

---

[144] Tanon, *Histoire des Justices des Anciennes Églises et Communautés Monastiques de Paris*, 366.

[145] Auguste Hanauer, *Les Constitutions des Campagnes de l'Alsace au Moyen
Age* (Paris, 1864), 160–162, 211–217, 316–320.

of group action and decision. The forms employed differed widely. In each region the types of community organization that were known or remembered were adapted to newly felt needs— the Carolingian *scabini* in the north and east, Roman forms of municipal government in the south, the merchants' guilds, religious confraternities, or local organizations for military self-defense. The powers they acquired varied widely, as did the degrees of independence they could wrest from crown or feudal control. Through much of the thirteenth century the crown saw the larger communities as a counterpoise to the power of the nobility and gave them support through royal charters and otherwise. In the fourteenth century, however, internal dissensions within the towns and fiscal mismanagement gave the crown pretexts for revoking many charters and installing royal officers to administer town affairs; even where crown intervention was not so direct the central government began to develop forms of supervision, explained by the theory that the chartered towns were like minors who needed "administrative guardianship." Through the sixteenth century, nevertheless, much independence remained; many towns had relative freedom in electing their own officials, and their courts, police officers and administrative functions gave a large measure of local autonomy. But even in the sixteenth century crown officers and the Parlements interfered frequently in municipal elections and local administration. These interventions certainly did not arrest and on the whole promoted the trend toward concentration of power in local oligarchies. The drive toward centralization under Henry IV and Richelieu brought increased dictation by agents of the crown, especially the intendants, in the choice of municipal officers and the direction of municipal affairs. Then late in the reign of Louis XIV the crown attempted to suppress election altogether and, in order to meet its pressing financial needs, to sell municipal offices to buyers who would hold them perpetually. Extreme vacillation in carrying out this policy during the eighteenth century discouraged prospective buyers and dried up municipal offices as a major source of revenue. But the policy could be described as successful in the sense that it destroyed the last remnants of real independence and left town governments in disorder and confusion, protected from their own officials by the increasingly vigilant "guardianship" imposed by the central government.[146]

The same needs for cooperation and mutual aid that had inspired the growth of self-governing towns were felt in the countryside. From the thirteenth century onward inhabitants of rural communities met regularly in many different parts of France to discuss, decide and regulate matters of common interest. Their purpose often was merely negative, to present collective resistance to the exactions or oppression of some local lord or prelate. A constant need was to regulate the use of common assets, such as pasture or woods or waste land, or to ensure the maintenance of bridges or roads. They quite often elected their own local mayors, as well as wardens of pasture and woods, shepherds and guardians of beasts on the common fields. The meetings were held in the open air, on common lands or in the church square after mass. Since the powers they claimed were limited and the matters dealt with were of purely local interest, the crown for long was tolerant, especially because the assemblies began to be used to collect royal taxes and were encouraged to elect their own tax collectors to receive and pay over the sums collected. Judicial functions they very soon lost, if they ever had them at all; though we should note again that in Alsace, which remained part of the Hapsburg empire until 1681, the local assemblies still functioned as full-scale courts until shortly before that date.[147] If France had been able to maintain the national gathering of the Three Estates as a representative assembly the local assemblies would no doubt have acquired a political role, for in the sixteenth century many localities elected their representatives

[146] This sketch is based primarily on the account in Chénon, HDF, I, 623–648 and 698–701 (for the tenth through the thirteenth centuries), I, 855–858 (for the fourteenth and fifteenth centuries), and II, 472–488 (for the sixteenth through eighteenth centuries). For the sixteenth century there is a good short account in Gaston Zeller, Les Institutions de la France au XVI⁰ Siècle (Paris, 1948), 38–47. Franklin Ford, Strasbourg in Transition (Cambridge, Mass., 1958), chap. IV, gives a more detailed account of how similar processes of erosion wore down the powers of self-government that Strasbourg had retained until the union of Alsace with the French Crown. Despite relative freedom from direct royal administration and the survival of somewhat larger powers of judicature than in other cities of France, Strasbourg gradually lost local autonomy under pressures from Paris.

[147] Babeau, Les Assemblées Générales des Communautés d'Habitants du XIII⁰ Siècle à la Révolution, 75–79.

to the Third Estate and drew up lists of grievances for their spokesmen to present.[148]

Some of the customs published in the sixteenth century took notice of these local assemblies. The question mainly dealt with was the relationship of the assemblies to the powers of the local lords. In two districts the published customs declared that local inhabitants could meet whenever they pleased and could make "statutes" on matters of common concern which would then bind all residents of the locality.[149] The customs of five other districts forbade such meetings without license of the local lord, though the lord's refusal to grant a license could be reviewed by a local royal judge or (in two districts) by his feudal superior.[150]

The aid of the local assemblies in collecting royal taxes and the relative unimportance of the matters they dealt with postponed any intervention by the central government.[151] It is true that the Parlement of Grenoble in 1544 punished the inhabitants of one neighborhood for meeting in the absence of the seignorial judge. The same Parlement in 1661 issue a general order that only the better citizens should be notified of meetings "in order to prevent confusion and in order that miserable persons with no interests at stake shall not prevail over the more notable." [152] Such sporadic supervision was no longer needed after the king issued a general edict in 1659, placing all the local rural assemblies under "administrative guardianship." This meant in fact that control was transferred to the royal intendants, who rapidly took over the directing role. Some local assemblies

---

[148] Babeau, 64 ff.; Babeau, *Le Village sous l'Ancien Régime* (Paris, 4th ed., 1891), 1–57; Chénon, *HDF*, II, 488–489. For the general comments in this paragraph the accounts by Babeau are the chief source. A shorter account appears in Lodge, "The Communal Movement, Especially in France," *Cambridge Medieval History*, V, 624.

[149] Customs of St. Sever and La Bourt (De Richebourg, *Nouveau Coutumier Général*, IV, 928, 977). The only expressed limitation on the validity of local legislation was that it be not contrary to "the common good" or prejudicial to the king.

[150] Customs of Bar (De Richebourg, II, 1021), La Marche (De Richebourg, IV, 1102), Auvergne (De Richebourg, IV, 1161), Nivernais (De Richebourg, III, 1124), and Bourbonnais (De Richebourg, III, 1232).

[151] This is especially suggested by the order issued by the Tax Court (*Cours des Aides*) of Paris in 1659, forbidding the ordinary judges of one locality to attend meetings of local inhabitants that were called to elect tax collectors and distribute locally the burden of the *taille*, in order that the meeting might be held freely. Brillon, *Dictionnaire des Arrests*, I, 167.

[152] Brillon, *Dictionnaire des Arrests*, I, 167.

continued to meet for years thereafter. The paralysis caused by "guardianship" did not come till the eighteenth century, when the local assemblies completely decayed.[153]

There was still need for regulations, despite the stream that issued from the king, his councils and intendants and all the other rule-making bodies. Someone needed to speak about obstructions to roads, harboring strangers, encroachments on commons, straying pigs, and other local matters. Such questions were bound to come up at the general meetings called assizes that were held by royal or seignorial officers in their travels through villages. One example was a meeting held in the *bailliage* of Vermandois in the early eighteenth century, where the following regulations were promulgated, among many others: no one shall dance during the time mass is held, no one shall get drunk, everyone shall be reverent to the local seigneurs, everyone shall carry a lantern when on the streets after 9 at night, no one shall carry a gun or let his pigs run at large, workmen shall not be idle on working days, and so on. These prohibitions and commands, enforceable with penalties, certainly seem laudable on the whole. The interesting point for present purposes is that the source of these regulations was not the assembled villagers but the judge of the local court-keeping lord.[154] Similarly in Brittany the judges of the seignorial courts issued regulations concerning weights and measures, the maintenance of essential public works, the sale of meat during Lent, and fixed the prices of food during times of scarcity.[155] In the region surrounding Paris which was governed by the Custom of Paris and contained a total of 460 court-keeping lords, there were at least some lords who exercised a "police" jurisdiction aimed at protection against fire and flood, cleaning and repairing streets, protection of public health and public morals and considerable economic regulation through supervision and control of the merchants' guilds. Included in "police" was a power to issue regulations, some of which merely repeated the terms of royal edicts though others were

[153] Babeau, *Les Assemblées Générales,* 206–259; Chénon, *HDF,* II, 488–490.
[154] Combier, *Les Justices Seigneuriales du Bailliage de Vermandois,* 150–156. Other examples of regulations issued by the *baillis* of "high" justice are referred to by the same author, 36–41.
[155] Giffard, *Les Justices Seigneuriales en Bretagne,* 129–134.

novel solutions of strictly local problems. In either case the power
to issue the regulations carried with it power to punish for
violations, and both powers were exercised by seignorial judges.[156]
From place to place, in different parts of France, there must
have been great variations in the extent of this seignorial "police."
It surely followed no general plan. In particular localities the
regulatory activities of seignorial judges must have been quite
sporadic. The point for present purposes is not the extent of
such regulation but the persons who undertook it. These powers
no longer resided in local assemblies or in descendants of the
scabini. They had passed to the crown and its numerous agents
or else to the seignorial judges, who were scarcely better than
employees of the owners of private courts.

One confronts at the end the puzzling question—why the
ancien régime failed to develop representative government, both
national and local. Its resources, institutions, and opportunities
were essentially the same as those of English society. For centuries the development of England and France proceeded on
parallel lines. For centuries the range of choices seemed equally
wide in both. The main lines of growth were determined, of
course, by actions and decisions of many individuals, at every
level of society and in every kind of human interchange. Court
organization and procedure were only one of the lines of traffic.
But the contention here is that the medieval courts were a central
highroad with feeders in all directions, so that the decisions concerning them that were made in the thirteenth century narrowed
immensely the range of other choices. By the fifteenth century
French government already showed a strong tendency to be-

[156] Lemercier, *Les Justices Seigneuriales de la Région Parisienne*, 154–181. In
an appendix (pp. 285-293) the author summarizes the records of assizes held by
the *bailli* of the Abbey of St. Germain des Prés in 1719 in two towns not far from
Paris. These assizes were the first such visitation by the *bailli* since 1648, but this
did not deter him from quite extensive regulations of local affairs.

The records of the Bailliage of Pontoise show similarly a wide range of "police"
ordinances, enforceable by the seignorial judges—regulating markets, fixing prices
of food supplies, ordering the maintenance of fences and the scouring of ditches,
forbidding masquerades and public dances, protecting public health by ordering
the killing of infected animals and forbidding butchers to leave offal exposed,
maintaining chimneys and preventing other fire hazards, licensing the settlement
of strangers, preventing drinking and games on Sundays and feastdays, ordering
parents to educate their children. Bataillon, *Les Justices Seigneuriales du Bailliage
de Pontoise à la Fin de l'Ancien Régime*, 96–115, 176–198.

come a government of "functionaries"; [157] already the channels for popular participation had been blocked off or diverted. In discussing the ultimate fate of the French monarchy attention is usually fixed on the failure of representative government at the national level through the national assembly of the Three Estates. But effective participation in the decision of great national issues required training and long experience for many people in the work of government that was close to home. The breakup of the medieval popular courts—the transfer of their powers to functionaries appointed by the crown and the feudal lords— had results for French society that could not have been foretold.

3. GERMANY

a. The Survival of the Schöffen

Evidence already presented suggests that France in the development of court organization and procedure was roughly 100 years behind England. Measured by similar tests, Germany was on the whole some 200 years behind France.

In court organization, most of the German states came through to the year 1200 A.D. with the Carolingian system basically intact. It is true that some territories like Saxony had departed somewhat from the basic plan. In other places there were personal exemptions for many of the nobility that withdrew them from the jurisdiction of the ordinary courts; grants of immunities had exempted whole districts from royal control; an increased power in the counts who presided made many of them loom larger as great landlords than as agents of central government. Yet the counts *were* agents of a central government that had by no means been dismembered. Law-finding and judgment-proposing were the functions still of the Carolingian *scabini* whose name had been Germanized to *Schöffen*. The *Schöffen* were permanent officers, free persons of good repute and local influence, required to be landowners and in fact very often large landowners. They sat in groups, sometimes the ancient number of seven but more often twelve or fifteen. In the general assemblies of local inhabitants that were held two or three times a year, the *Schöffen*,

---

[157] Dupont-Ferrier, *Les Officiers Royaux des Bailliages et Sénéchaussées*, 769–783.

as before, merely proposed judgments for assembly approval, though by now it was pretty clear that silence meant assent. In short the local courts that still functioned up to 1200 in most of the German territories were basically the ancient public courts, not yet feudalized.[158]

It was not until the thirteenth century that the disintegration of central authority and the expanding power of the local lordships transferred the public courts to private hands. Even before this time there had emerged strictly feudal courts, dealing with matters that directly affected the relations of lords and vassals and of vassals between themselves. As in France and in most of medieval Europe, the standard type of feudal court gave responsibility for judging to the vassals, subject to the concurrence of the lord who presided.[159] There were enough resemblances between the ancient community courts and the feudal assemblies, existing thus side by side, so that fusion could occur in particular places without any great disturbance. The judgment-proposers in the hundred courts—the Schöffen—were themselves landowners who were quite sure to be entangled somehow in the net of feudal relations as vassals of one or more lords. The count (Graf), whose representative presided in the hundred court and who supplied the executive power to carry out its decrees, was quite certain to be a feudal magnate, entitled to compel attendance from his vassals by virtue of their tenure. Grants by the crown of fiscal and judicial immunities had been frequent enough in earlier times, but after 1200 they became very common. In order to secure the support of the nobility in their great contest with the Papacy, the Hohenstaufen emperors showered their vassals with grants of immunity, thereby depriving local community courts of their tie with central authority. Prolonged civil war greatly weakened the powers of the crown; the process of destroying them was carried forward with what seemed almost perversity by Frederick II.[160] The dismantling of the Carolingian system, once begun, moved rapidly. In the records of thirteenth century Germany one can see openly at work the forces by which the

[158] Schroeder, *DRG*, 605–616; Hans A. Fehr, *Deutsche Rechtsgeschichte* (Berlin, 5th ed., 1952), 89–90.

[159] Schroeder, *DRG*, 632; Fehr, 90.

[160] Austin L. Poole, "Germany in the Reign of Frederick II," *Cambridge Medieval History* (Cambridge, Eng., 1929), VI, 80–109; Schroeder, *DRG*, 639–650.

community courts in France must have been feudalized in the general darkness that had prevailed in France some 200 years before.

For France the late thirteenth and early fourteenth centuries were a time of reconstruction, with rapid growth in the powers and institutions of royal government. During the same period in Germany, however, the forces of disintegration were very strongly at work. Church courts, feudal lordships, privileged cities and towns all struggled with the remnants of local community organization, and with each other, to extend or defend their powers. The result of this conflict was a great profusion of jurisdictions and a variety of types. In the towns existing forms of community organization were taken over and adapted, as in France, as agencies of self-government. Often it was the *Schöffen* of the ancient tribunals that expanded their functions as judgment-proposers, acquired rule-making and executive powers, and became the officers and governing councils of the free cities— some of them oligarchies who perpetuated themselves and some more or less elective.[161] Many of the community courts outside the towns were absorbed within the system of feudal relations, though retaining the broad competence and many of the features of the older public courts. Another major grouping centered in the manors and villages, where communal systems of land use required broader consultation and widened the range of participation by the poor and lowly.[162] In the general confusion and turbulence, courts could exist completely disconnected from the lines of feudal or royal authority. If a local ruler desired to organize his power or an existing community to maintain its cohesion, the suitable means was to have a court, for it was in courts that group decisions were made and force was made legitimate.

Despite this vast proliferation, much greater in Germany than in France, there was one aspect of the German development on which practice was consistent—that is, in preserving the idea and the forms of group participation in decision. It is true that in

[161] Schroeder, *DRG*, 678–706.
[162] Georg L. von Maurer, *Geschichte der Fronhöfe, der Bauernhöfe und der Hofverfassung in Deutschland* (Erlangen, 1862–1863), IV, 25–38, 63–69, 109–116. I regret greatly that the vast fund of information compiled in this work is handled in so pell-mell a fashion as to dates and places that I have been unable to make better use of it.

certain of the immunities, especially those administered by church authorities, judicial functions were assigned to appointed officials, who scrapped altogether the older forms of group decision.[163] On the whole this was rare. On the other hand, group decision certainly did not mean total democracy of the ancient Athenian type. The *Schöffen* represented a compromise between total conquest of the judicial function by political authority and popular self-government. The *Schöffen* were persons chosen from the community (sometimes even *by* the community) as specially worthy of trust and specially qualified to "find" the law. In the conditions of thirteenth and fourteenth century Germany there were reasons for their survival. The German lands were still governed, overwhelmingly, by customary law. The rules, which varied widely from place to place, persisted almost entirely in oral tradition. The French monarchy, confronted with similar problems in the thirteenth century, had adapted the Frankish group inquest and organized *ad hoc* juries to testify to the law. In Germany there was no longer a central power that could employ this device on a broad enough scale. Furthermore, with rules of custom that were orally transmitted and intensely localized there was real advantage in centering responsibility for maintaining community traditions. By choosing permanent groups of wiser men there was a better guarantee of continuity and some chance to develop expertise.

The procedure of the *Schöffen* courts in the thirteenth century preserved many archaic features. Trial by battle and ordeal still lingered on, though both forms of appeal to the supernatural were to disappear in the fourteenth century. A more common form of proof was by "witnesses" who were not much more than oath-helpers; they were not cross-examined and were seldom expected to testify to specific facts that they had observed.[164]

---

[163] Schroeder, *DRG*, 633–636.

[164] There has been some dispute as to whether the "witnesses" referred to in thirteenth-century sources were merely oath-helpers, supporting in general terms the assertions of the party who produced them, or were on the contrary expected and encouraged to disclose specific facts from their own direct observation. Planck, discussing Saxon procedure as described in the *Sachsenspiegel*, insisted that the "witnesses" were merely oath-helpers, even though they might in particular cases refer in detail to facts or events which showed that the claim they supported was just. Julius W. Planck, *Das deutsche Gerichtsverfahren im Mittelalter* (Braunschweig, 1878), II, 2–8, 76–81. The same conclusion was reached by Kleinfeller as

The court would designate which of the parties would be allowed to support his case in this manner and how many "witnesses" he would present. By meeting this quota he would win his case, so that for litigants proof by such means was not a burden; it was a privilege to be competed for. Proceedings were oral. Requirements of form, strictly enforced, regulated the oral statements of claim and defense made by the spokesmen for the parties and regulated also the oaths that the parties exchanged and the language used by the "witnesses." Attack on decisions was still by accusation of false judgment directed against the court itself.[165]

So long as this procedure survived, the conduct of trials imposed no heavy burden on the *Schöffen* in assembling and evaluating evidence. This initiative rested with the parties to persuade an essentially passive tribunal, whose primary task was to ensure compliance by the parties with an ancient and complex ritual. In most instances the *Schöffen* acted without independent knowledge of the facts. It is true that the *Schöffen* and their subordinate officers were allowed to testify to facts or events of which they had acquired knowledge in their official capacities; in the course of time this supplementary source of evidence became useful and important.[166] But to go outside their own membership and tap sources of information that might be available in their local communities required greater powers of coercion

---

to the practice in other districts of Germany in the fourteenth century. Georg Kleinfeller, *Die geschichtliche Entwicklung des Tatsacheneides in Deutschland* (Berlin, 1891), 14–26. However, a more recent author has argued at length that witnesses able to testify to facts or events within their own knowledge were used, indeed required, in many districts of Germany as early as the thirteenth century. The sources he quotes, however, are almost all concerned with criminal cases. Rudolf Ruth, *Zeugen und Eideshelfer in den deutschen Rechtsquellen des Mittelalters* (Breslau, 1922), 165.

[165] Schroeder, *DRG*, 844–856; Heinrich Brunner-Ernst Heymann, *Grundzüge der deutschen Rechtsgeschichte* (Munich-Leipzig, 7th ed., 1919), 175–177.

[166] Planck, *Das deutsche Gerichtsverfahren im Mittelalter*, II, 157–211; Schroeder, *DRG*, 851; Brunner-Heymann, 178. Originally "testimony by the court" related to events that had transpired before the court itself within sight and hearing of its members. Then court members or officials became competent to testify to events occurring outside court though in their presence. By this means there developed methods of certifying documents, often cast in the form of judgments in simulated law suits (as in the fine, common recovery, and recognizance of English law). Such court-authenticated documents came into widespread use in a variety of forms (transfers of land, acknowledgment of debts, etc.) and helped to establish the probative value of documentary evidence in general.

than most *Schöffen* courts could mobilize. The jury of trial, descendant of the Frankish royal group inquest, was used for limited purposes in a few districts.[167] Perhaps it could have been used more widely if political collapse had been arrested. Instead, one group of *Schöffen* courts abandoned their ancient passivity and developed a new kind of inquisition. These were the so-called *Vemgerichte* (penal courts), whose malignant growth was another symptom of the disorder in German society.

The *Vemgerichte* originated in western Germany in the general neighborhood of Cologne. Here there was lacking that kind of governing aristocracy that was conquering power through most of Germany during the late thirteenth century. In this situation the local courts continued to function, increasingly free of external control. In each case there was a presiding officer, the heir of the ancient *Graf* or count. Though often low in social rank and entirely outside the feudal hierarchy, the Westphalian counts began to act like owners of their court-keeping functions, to transfer and divide them and even to mortgage them to secure their own debts. Yet the ancient principle was still followed— the judgments were rendered by the *Schöffen*. Being essential parts of the courts themselves, the peasants who functioned as *Schöffen* and who met regularly over decades, began to conceive in themselves a kind of collective personality. In the universal warfare being conducted for control of the judicial function, the Westphalian courts eluded the grasp of rapacious neighbors and preserved their independence. They acquired the name of "free" courts, their presiding officer became a "free" count and the *Schöffen* became "free" *Schöffen*. Even as to their own internal relations there appeared an amazing fluidity. Though the administration of justice was more and more dispersed and localized, the "free" *Schöffen* moved from place to place and "many free counts had such a wandering existence that it is scarcely possible to determine to what free court they belonged."[168]

---

[167] Brunner-Heymann, 178. It should be noted also that in southern Germany group inquisitions ordered by the judge *ex officio*, analogous to the English presentment jury, put in an appearance in the fourteenth century in criminal cases, but the extremely summary procedure used caused it "to degenerate into formless arbitrariness." Brunner-Heymann, 73–74.

[168] Theodor Lindner, *Die Veme* (Paderborn, 2d ed., 1896), 2.

These developments were carried furthest in Westphalia and might have been localized there if central authority had not intervened. The feudal lordship of Westphalia was held by the Archbishop of Cologne, who as a high churchman refused to administer blood justice either directly or by delegation. The "free" counts, mostly small gentry and lower nobility, desired confirmation of their court-keeping rights, so they resorted to the king. The king responded by investing numbers of "free" counts with the royal ban, partly with the object of restoring his own much enfeebled authority. Later kings continued the practice, not only by direct grant of the royal ban to particular court-keepers, but by delegating to princes and cities the power to create "free" courts of the Westphalian type.

High political authority thus gave these local tribunals a support that was essential, but their immense popularity was due to the secrecy that surrounded them and to their inquisitorial procedure. They were intensely secret. The general public was rigorously excluded. Each member swore the most solemn oaths to disclose nothing that transpired; the penalty for breach was hanging, after extraction of the offending tongue. Each member assumed the duty to investigate and report offenses, to assist in compelling attendance of witnesses and accused persons, and to help in hanging offenders that the free court might convict. The courts acted on accusation by their own members, the accusers assuming the duty to apprehend accused persons and present proof of their guilt. In theory the free courts intervened only in criminal cases where other courts were powerless or unwilling to act. Since there was no effective control of their proceedings by way of appellate review, it is likely that they dealt with a considerable variety of offenses.[169] Indeed during the fifteenth century the *Vemgerichte* acquired a civil jurisdiction of some importance, though major crimes continued to be their main concern.[170]

---

[169] Ordinarily there was no appeal from *Vemgericht* decisions, though in Cologne, the "capital" of the free courts, there was set up a court of 28 persons which was authorized to hear appeals in cases arising in the neighborhood of Cologne. Lindner, *Die Veme*, 561–566. There also remained the ultimate power of the King or Emperor, on demand by the accused, to evoke cases for his own review—a power that was occasionally exercised during the period of royal sponsorship. Schroeder, *DRG*, 631.

[170] Lindner, 561–566. On the history of the *Vemgerichte* generally: Schroeder,

In the "free" courts, therefore, the law-finders of the community were made into secret inquisitors. This extraordinary transformation gives some measure of the alarm and terror produced by widespread social disorder. For this secret society attracted the very best people. In Westphalia itself the entire nobility and many prominent burghers of the towns were sworn in as "free" *Schöffen*. The Westphalian King Sigmund became a member. During the fourteenth century the order spread throughout the German territories. One great advantage of membership was that a member, after taking the oath in his own locality, could share the secrets and participate in meetings of "free" courts anywhere. There must have been many hangings whose authors no one could trace and no one in particular wished to trace, except the relatives of the victims. The brotherhood kept its secrets well. In the end it was so successful that it was overtaken by defiant pride. Some members built up the delusion that they were "the highest courts in the world" who could compel even an emperor to appear before them. Finally the Emperor who was thus summoned took alarm at the monster he had helped to create. There had been local examples of extortion and corruption, which helped mobilize opinion against them. The Emperor attacked the free courts, revoked imperial privileges previously granted, and stirred nobility and towns against them. By the end of the 1400's their power had been almost wholly destroyed, though remnants survived in Westphalia for centuries. The "free" courts and "free" *Schöffen* serve as a reminder of what terror can accomplish when it becomes a dominant motive and is organized under familiar forms with general social approval. The "free" *Schöffen* at their best, in the fourteenth century, were a respectable Ku Klux Klan.[171]

But the work of the *Schöffen,* viewed as a whole, should not be judged by the *Vemgerichte.* By no means all the *Schöffen* were "free." Many functioned in courts that were firmly anchored in local communities or were moored to the shifting lines of the

---

DRG, 625–632; Lindner, *Die Veme;* Johann F. von Schulte, *Lehrbuch der deutschen Reichs- und Rechtsgeschichte* (Stuttgart, 6th ed., 1892), 368–375.

[171] On the later phases of the *Vemgerichte:* Lindner, 432–434; Schroeder, *DRG,* 631–632; Eduard Kern, *Geschichte des Gerichtsverfassungsrechts* (Munich, 1954), 17.

feudal structure. Many *Schöffen* courts began in the fourteenth century to preserve their own records of decisions rendered and of rules pronounced. Very large numbers of these *Schöffen* "sayings," dating from the fourteenth and fifteenth centuries, have been published in modern times. Some came from village or manorial communities—reaffirmations of customary rules of private law or ordinances regulating economic relations and personal status. Many were decisions in litigated cases. Some were answers to questions submitted—advisory opinions, so to speak. In the larger towns the *Schöffen* acquired continuity of tenure and reputations for superior knowledge and wisdom; their "sayings" had influence outside the territories they directly served and helped to develop as well as to preserve the rules of their own districts. There was the usual intermixture of rule-making with adjudication. There were variations from place to place and from time to time in the methods of choosing the *Schöffen*, in their relations with their own communities, and the powers they exercised. But it is clear that as late as the fifteenth century there were many competent and responsible men, functioning all over Germany, not only "finding" law but applying it under established procedures in local public courts.[172]

The ultimate fate of the *Schöffen* courts is connected with the fate of the substantive law they applied. The *Schöffen* and most of the law they "found" were submerged in the reception of Roman law. The process began in the fifteenth century; by the end of the sixteenth the *Schöffen* had either been displaced or completely transformed, that is, Romanized. But for present purposes there is no need to enter far into the great debate as to the causes and consequences of the reception of Roman law. My object is merely to show how the position of the *Schöffen* became untenable through procedural changes that were similar, in both nature and results, to changes that had occurred in France some 200 years before.

[172] A general description of *Weistümer* derived from the peasant communities, dating mostly from the fourteenth and fifteenth centuries, appears in Otto Stobbe, *Geschichte der deutschen Rechtsquellen* (Leipzig, 1860), I, 585–593. There has been an enormous literature on the more renowned *Schöffen* courts located in important cities. The Brandenburg court is discussed in detail, with references to other leading examples, by Stölzel, *Rechtsprechung*, vol. I.

b. *The Progress of Roman-Canonist Procedure*

The introduction of Roman-canonist procedure was a gradual process occurring at different rates of speed in different sections of Germany, faster in the towns than in country districts, and with important differences between civil and criminal cases and between trial and appellate procedure. By way of general statement the most one can say is that around 1500 in many influential communities the oral trial and complaint of false judgment which were characteristic of German medieval procedure were displaced by the elaborate written system that the canonists had perfected.

The path had been prepared in the interval by the increased use of written records in trial courts. The most obvious need was for records of judgments rendered; some towns began as early as the thirteenth century to keep official court books for this purpose.[173] As was shown by the experience of England in the same period, records of this kind—even quite elaborate records—were entirely consistent with oral pleading and summary methods of fact-finding. But they meant as a minimum that there must be on hand at least one man, perhaps more, who had the exceptional ability to read and write, and such men were likely to have acquired at least a smattering of legal training. In the general history of the reception of Roman law, with which this study is only incidentally concerned, an important factor was the personal influence of court assessors and subordinate officials who were trained in canon or Roman law. In the course of the fourteenth and fifteenth centuries, most of the important towns hired such men, who were available not only to the courts but in general administration.[174] In the trial courts their presence made it possible to shift readily from oral to written pleadings as soon as there existed in the neighborhood enough lawyers who could draft written pleadings. From the point of view of the scribes, in fact, the use of written pleadings was more convenient, for it reduced their task to one of copying at leisure

---

[173] Stölzel, *Richterthum,* I, 176–179, referring to court books of the thirteenth through fifteenth centuries.

[174] Stölzel, *Richterthum,* I, 137–165.

instead of attempting to make their own digests of contentions made in open court.[175] The same practical reasons that led to the introduction of written pleadings in England during the fifteenth century [176] could operate in Germany when litigants and lawyers were ready to use them. The increased use of written documents in private transactions of any importance and the increased recognition of their probative value also helped, no doubt, to prepare the way.[177]

Since most of the *Schöffen* sat in courts of first instance, it was the transformation of pretrial and trial procedure that affected their functions most directly. But the progress of canonist methods of pleading and proof varied so greatly in different localities that detailed accounts require much local history. Such an account has been given by Helmut Coing, describing the course of events in Frankfurt-am-Main.[178] Here the *Schöffen*-court in the latter part of the fifteenth century was composed of fourteen persons, leading citizens who were mostly elderly merchants with wide experience in administrative and commercial affairs and with good education, though only a few had formal training in law.[179] Their sessions were ordinarily public, were held three times a week, and until late in the 1480's, were oral throughout. Proof was by "witnesses" who were first heard orally and then required to support the claim of the party who had presented them by making a general affirmation under oath. As in the medieval procedure that I have already briefly described, the party authorized to present proof would win the case if he succeeded in marshalling the required number of supporting oaths.[180]

It was not until the last two decades of the fifteenth century

---

[175] Stölzel, *Richterthum*, I, 179–186, develops this theme.

[176] Holdsworth, *HEL*, III, 639–653.

[177] The popularity of court-authenticated documents is referred to above, note 166.

[178] Helmut Coing, *Die Rezeption des römischen Rechts in Frankfurt-am-Main* (Frankfurt, 1939).

[179] Coing, 27–28, 173–175.

[180] Coing, 30–35. It should not be inferred that allocation of proof-presentation was determined by purely arbitrary tests. As Coing points out, and as was probably true to some extent in earlier procedure, the court was guided by its own view of the probabilities that lay behind each party's assertions. The survival in other districts in the fifteenth century of medieval forms of proof is discussed by Kleinfeller, *Die geschichtliche Entwicklung des Thatsacheneides in Deutschland* (1891), 26–49.

that the records of Frankfurt show cases presented on written pleadings. Interestingly enough, the earliest examples (in the 1480's) were disputes referred to arbitration. So far as they go these examples confirm the general observation of Stölzel that it was through references to arbitrators, among whom churchmen were often included, that canonist forms of written pleading were brought into general use in fifteenth century Germany;[181] it will be recalled that arbitration may have provided a similar port of entry in thirteenth-century France.[182] But this intermediate stage was brief in Frankfurt. In the 1490's there appeared a whole group of cases presented for formal decision by means of written pleadings, with positions, exceptions, duplic, etc. all the way to sextuplic, *litis contestatio,* and "articles" defining the facts to be proved by written interrogatories. For another decade the old oral procedures persisted side by side with the written. There was as yet no legislation or rule of court that compelled the parties or their lawyers to use one type of procedure rather than another; in the transition stage, at least, the choice of the new procedure seems to have been freely made by the litigants. But by 1505 the transition was accomplished. Canonist methods of pleading and proof became standard procedure thereafter; pleadings consisted of an exchange of papers, proof was by means of written interrogatories administered by the court or its delegates, with the answers of witnesses recorded in writing.[183]

Procedural changes of the kind that occurred so rapidly in Frankfurt were bound to change the role and the powers of the *Schöffen.* As compared with the older procedure, canonist methods compelled far closer analysis of the issues and the assembly and weighing of all the relevant evidence; this was no doubt the reason why litigants freely chose it. But the very refinement of these methods meant a greatly increased burden on the court. And worst of all, the material with which the *Schöffen* must work was now to be elaborately written. The Frankfurt *Schöffen* were able to read, unlike most of their counterparts in smaller towns and villages. But even the Frankfurt *Schöffen* were part-time

[181] Stölzel, *Richterthum,* I, 27–28.
[182] Above, sec. 2b.
[183] Coing, 106–118.

holders of their public office and few of them at this stage were lawyers. Concepts and rules taken from Roman law had been invoked in argument before them during the period before the advent of canonist procedure. After 1495 references to Roman law became much more common and it may well be, as Professor Coing thinks, that the closer analysis of issues that was now required helped to stimulate the use of Roman law conceptions by litigants and lawyers. Even without this to add to their troubles, the Frankfurt *Schöffen* felt compelled, as they tried to work through the mounds of papers, to seek advice from law-learned men. The Frankfurt city attorney was such a man. In his favor they abdicated, issuing judgments in their own names that had been actually drafted by their expert adviser.[184]

In most of the cities of Germany and still more in smaller towns the introduction of canonist procedure came somewhat later than it did in Frankfurt and by a more gradual process. Even without detailed studies of the kind that Coing has made, it seems safe to conclude that the adoption of the new procedure must have had similar results everywhere. Without education and indeed without some training in law, it was impossible for the judges to cope with the papers, to follow the procedure itself in all its complex stages, or to understand the strange new words that lawyers were using increasingly. It is true of course that for numerous reasons Roman law had acquired much influence well before 1500. Germans had studied Roman law in Italy and France. The analytical method, the vocabulary, and even specific rules of Roman law were borrowed for many purposes, often by persons who did not understand them too well. The *Schöffen* would have had in any event to come to terms with the learned experts and learn somehow to enlist their aid. But as a matter of timing, at least, it seems clear that the full-scale reception of Roman law by German courts was preceded by a shift to the canonist system of pleading and proof, which required "learned" or at least "half-learned" judges for its administration and drove the laymen away.[185]

[184] Coing, 115–118.
[185] Coing, 119, 180–183. This is of course a main thesis of Stölzel, *Richterthum*, whose remarkable book was published in 1872 and seems to me to have withstood exceedingly well the weathering of more than 80 years.

These tendencies in trial courts were much accelerated when an effective form of appellate review was organized. The old false judgment proceeding, aimed primarily at punishment of the erring court, was a very blunt weapon. Another device, more often used, was the request for legal advice, directed to feudal superiors or to the *Schöffen* courts of the larger cities. Neither provided a full-scale review, with power in the higher court to reverse or amend the judgment appealed from. Full-scale review was, of course, the purpose of the appeal in canonist procedure, which had been used in German church courts from an early time. Its use in secular matters was not well established until late in the fifteenth century, though the king's court began to use canonist forms of appellate review as early as the 1440's. Legislation in a few of the German principalities introduced the appeal in the ensuing decades,[186] but the principal model was the *Reichskammergericht,* created by imperial decree in 1495. The original decree required that one half of the membership of the new court must have doctorates in law; shortly this requirement was extended to the entire membership. The decree of 1495 also provided that its procedure should be "written." By a series of imperial decrees and then by action of the *Kammergericht* itself this general mandate was gradually rendered more specific. By the middle of the sixteenth century the court had succeeded in developing one of the most complex and dilatory systems of written pleading that had so far appeared on the continent of Europe. Coupled with this was the complete apparatus of written "positions" describing the facts to be proved by each party, written interrogatories, secret questioning of individual witnesses and written records of testimony.[187]

There has been much discussion as to how much the imperial *Kammergericht* contributed to the general reception of Roman substantive law. For present purposes it is enough to say that the feeble executive power of the imperial *Kammergericht* and the numerous grants of exemption from its jurisdiction faithfully reflected the weakness of the imperial authority on which it depended. An instrumentality far more powerful than this would

---

[186] Stölzel, *Richterthum,* I, 166–170.

[187] Wilhelm Endemann, *Die Entwicklung des Beweisverfahrens im deutschen Civilprozess seit 1495* (Bonn, 1895), 5–49.

have been needed to impose on a reluctant population the whole vast system of Roman public and private law.[188] But that does not mean that the *Kammergericht* was a negligible factor. Its decisions were reported and widely studied in the late sixteenth and subsequent centuries.[189] There are numerous traces of the pressure felt by lower courts to bring their procedure into conformity with *Kammergericht* procedure.[190] Still more important was the deliberate imitation of its structure and procedure by the lords of the principalities when they undertook, as they commonly did in the sixteenth century, to create appellate courts of their own.

Under the political conditions then prevailing in Germany, conquest of the judicial function and especially of the power of appellate review was a prize worth struggling for. Ambitious princelings set up chanceries, staffed with men that they had appointed, or expanded the powers and the membership of the feudal courts made up of their vassals. They then attempted to divert to their own courts the requests for legal advice that had previously been addressed to the courts of the towns, which were *Schöffen* courts of the ancient type though many by now were being Romanized. The canonist appeal, with its full rehearing on both law and facts, was an efficient instrument of direct control. The struggle over appellate powers, to extend or escape them as the case might be, went on all over Germany. There was great confusion until the new lines of authority were gradually settled in the course of the sixteenth century. Some of the courts in the larger towns succeeded for a time in maintaining their independence and *became* appellate courts. On the whole the main effect of the settlement was to confirm the political superiority of the territorial lords, which their appellate courts both symbolized and reinforced.[191]

It was inevitable that court-keepers in appointing personnel to the new appellate courts should show preference for men who

---

[188] Erich Döhring, *Geschichte der deutschen Rechtspflege seit 1500* (Berlin, 1953), 19–22; R. Stintzing, *Geschichte der deutschen Rechtswissenschaft* (Munich and Leipzig, 1880), I, 55–57.

[189] Stintzing, I, 485–502.

[190] Coing, 180; Daniel Waldmann, *Die Entstehung der Nürnberger Reformation von 1479* (Nurnberg, 1908), 19–20; Alfred Kühtmann, *Die Romanisierung des Civilprocesses in der Stadt Bremen* (Breslau, 1891), 44–46.

[191] Stölzel, *Richterthum*, I, 235–275.

were trained in the Roman-canonist system. By the end of the sixteenth century, doctors of law composed at least half the membership in nearly all appellate courts and usually a much higher fraction. Where lay members—nobles or knights—survived as heirs of the ancient feudal courts, they had lost most of their influence. This conquest of the territorial appellate courts by men who were expert in Roman law had effects that were of utmost importance, especially in promoting a general reception of the substantive doctrines of Roman law. But this is a subject we need not pursue. It is enough now to say that the movement of ideas was on the whole downward, with higher courts exerting constant pressure on lower courts to Romanize not only their procedure but also their doctrines and personnel.[192]

c. *The Surviving Mixture of Types*

By the seventeenth and eighteenth centuries certain patterns had imposed themselves in court organization and procedure, but the ancient profusion left much debris. The territorial appellate courts were predominantly staffed by "learned" judges. The older high courts that had not been drawn into the feudal hierarchy lost all influence or disappeared, except where staffed with doctors of law. In some university towns such as Leipzig and Jena the law faculties *became* the appellate courts and gave them much renown.[193] In the eighteenth century these courts lost leadership to other high courts, whose academic reputations were nevertheless high; these courts functioned often through voluntary submission by litigants and also did a considerable business in expert opinions.[194] Further down the scale the ancient titles and some of the functions of the *Schöffen* were retained in many places, though this was generally true only where Roman-law trained persons took over the office. Broadly, *Schöffen* survived in civil litigation only to the extent that they were Romanized.[195]

There was an important distinction, however, between civil and criminal proceedings. By an imperial decree of 1532 Charles V had required the concurrence of seven *Schöffen* in judgments

[192] Franz Wieacker, *Die Privatrechtsgeschichte der Neuzeit* (Göttingen, 1952), 92–101.
[193] Stölzel, *Richterthum*, I, 230–231; Schroeder, *DRG*, 949–950.
[194] Döhring, *Geschichte der deutschen Rechtspflege*, 26–28.
[195] Stölzel, *Richterthum*, I, 276–278, 332–336.

imposing the death penalty (four where the criminal penalty was less severe), and required also the presence of two *Schöffen* in criminal inquisitions, especially where torture was employed. This legislation, by direct effect and through imitation, served to maintain a principle of lay participation in criminal cases. It was much qualified in practice by requirements that "expert" opinions be secured in doubtful or difficult cases, yet the practice of using lay *Schöffen* in criminal cases lasted well into the eighteenth century, in some places into the nineteenth.[196] Its antiquity made it easy then to revive and extend the practice and provide a truly "German" alternative to the English type of jury.[197]

In addition to the *Schöffen* used in criminal cases, other ancient forms of community action also survived for some time. In the late Middle Ages, one feature of the public assembly courts had been the duty of accusation imposed on their members, usually for minor offenses. Decision on the matters so presented had been by the assemblies themselves on recommendation by the *Schöffen*. During the seventeenth century these practices fell into disuse but they were revived in the eighteenth century. In some places the assemblies were so enlarged by combinations of districts that the lay membership was reduced merely to a presentment function with adjudication of guilt or innocence transferred to the presiding officer. In other places the judicial powers of the assemblies lasted into the nineteenth century. Similarly, in many of the manors and small towns a police jurisdicton was retained by the local assemblies—for hair-pulling, ear-boxing and other violence that caused no open wound, for petty theft, false weights and measures, and so on. The line between major offenses, reserved for the territorial lords, and minor offenses, in which these local assembly-courts could act, was unclear and provoked constant dispute, but judicial powers of this limited kind survived in scattered communities. Perhaps more would have survived if Germany had not been convulsed by

[196] Kern, *Geschichte des Gerichtsverfassungsrechts*, 35–37; Döhring, 16; Schroeder, *DRG*, 950; Stölzel, 364–365.

[197] No attempt can be made here to describe the debates of the nineteenth century over the use of *Schöffen* as lay members of the courts. The solutions adopted in Germany in 1928, especially for commercial and criminal cases, are described in Fritz Stier-Somlo, *Handwörterbuch der Rechtswissenschaft* (Berlin-Leipzig, 1926–1937), V, 345–349.

the Thirty Years' War, which produced such disorder and insecurity during the seventeenth century that in many places the community courts did not meet for years and ancient practices were simply forgotten.[198]

It seems, therefore, that the triumph of the professionals was not as complete as it was in France. Yet if lay judges were not exterminated, they were brought to a state of subordination. The appellate courts were largely, sometimes exclusively, composed of doctors of Roman law. The procedure that they employed was elaborately written, not only as to pleadings, objections and arguments of counsel but in methods of taking and recording proof; though oral statement was used in the initiation of proceedings and in some lower courts orality was preserved in greater degree. Documentary proof played a large role and witness-proof was by court-conducted interrogation of individual witnesses.[199] The resulting complications brought heavy reliance, as in France, on the *rapporteur*, a member of the court itself who analyzed and organized the mass of papers and reduced them to manageable proportions by his summary and recommendations to his colleagues. Multi-judge courts were therefore common even at the lower ranges of the pyramid.[200]

It is impossible to say whether these basic conditions, so similar to those in France, brought a swarm of judges of comparable size. No census of judges was ever taken. The professionals appointed to the appellate courts were employees of the court-owners, who were mostly members of the medium and upper nobility. There was no national system of imperial courts reaching down to the trial level. The high imperial court, the *Reichskammergericht*, had 17 judges when first founded in 1495 and, after a series of gradual increases, 32 members by 1566. After the Peace of Westphalia in 1648 the high hopes for its future role led to a programed membership of 50 judges, but the shortage of funds in the imperial treasury permitted only 18 (later 25) to be appointed.[201] By English standards, these were

---

[198] Döhring, 14–15; Adalbert Erler, "Die Zentgerichtsordnung von Lutzelbach," ZSS (*germ.*), 66:528; Stölzel, *Richterthum*, I, 25, 366–385; von Maurer, *Geschichte der Fronhöfe*, IV, 510–515.

[199] Engelmann-Millar, *History of Continental Civil Procedure*, 544–565.

[200] Döhring, 198–258.

[201] Kern, 28–31; Schroeder, *DRG*, 914–915.

large totals, especially in view of the limited jurisdiction and feeble authority of the *Reichskammergericht*. In the high courts of the principalities it is probable that the totals were smaller. At lower levels, it is no doubt true that the displacement of *Schöffen* by professionals brought a net reduction in the number of persons engaged in judging. Yet the shift was from part-time unpaid persons (at most supplied with meals) to full-time professionals whose income was derived solely from their judicial duties. The transformation of *Schöffen* courts into multijudge professional courts therefore meant a real increase in the social burden and cost of the judicial system.

There are, again, no statistics to measure the cost. We only know that the professionals appointed by the private court-owners were very seldom paid by their employers and depended for their livelihood primarily on the fees and charges imposed on litigants. This was true even in high appellate courts. However, judgeships conferred an honorable status in the lower aristocracy, so there was competition for jobs. This honorable status had the drawback of imposing a style of living beyond the means of most incumbents. The price level rose in Germany, as in the rest of Europe, especially during the sixteenth century; as a result, tariffs of fees and charges and the occasional salary proved grossly insufficient as sources of revenue. The judges almost everywhere succumbed to the temptation to accept gifts from the litigants, using the justification that both parties were free to give. The resulting competition between litigants augmented the judges' income, but not enough to end the painful struggle of many judges to maintain a shabby gentility.[202]

d. *Political and Social Implications*

If the interpretations above suggested are valid, the substitution of functionaries for the laymen of the medieval courts not only promoted the reception of Roman law, but it marked a shift of political power and influence. The gain did not accrue to a central government, for the imperial ties that bound the German states together grew if anything weaker with the passage of time. Nor did all the gains accrue to the rulers of the states,

[202] Döhring, 75–105.

despite the steady increase in their authority and the attribution to them in political theory of the full composite of governmental powers. The structure that emerged was extraordinarily complex. In many states there survived after 1600 territorial assemblies, more or less representative, whose powers served as limitations on the rulers of the states and who engaged in contests to preserve their political influence and defend their special privileges. Court-keeping powers were distributed widely among the great and lesser nobility, though the reorganized systems of appellate review built pyramids everywhere.[203]

The clearest loss, which was also the first to occur, was at the lowest levels of the various pyramids, in the assembly courts of rural communities which had usually come to be labelled *Landgerichte*. Even at these levels it is difficult to generalize, since the results were not uniform throughout the German territories. It is difficult also to measure the loss, or the possibilities that were foreclosed. The contest here was mainly between the local communities and the lords with court-keeping rights in their immediate neighborhoods. The change in theory was simple enough—the judicial function, instead of being reserved for local assemblies or their representatives, became a subject of private ownership in the court-keeping lord. Not only the income but the authority invoked became the court-keeper's. The change was important not only in theory but in the daily lives of neighbors. It was important also because something more was involved than the decision of questions raised in formal litigation. As in France when a similar transformation had occurred, the more important question was whether means could be found to preserve and even to expand powers of local administration—what one can call self-government. Court records often disguised the gradual transfer of decisional powers to officials appointed by the lords, but the transfer was well completed by the end of the sixteenth century. The *Richter* was no longer merely the court's "director," but himself became the judge. The *Landgerichte*, the trial courts of the countryside, thereafter became throughout most of Germany the possession of local nobility, administered by their functionaries.[204]

[203] Schroeder, *DRG*, 940–956.
[204] Stölzel, 324–342; Schroeder, *DRG*, 950–951; Döhring, 51.

In the towns and at higher levels of the court systems the picture was less clear. Both the large cities and smaller towns retained through the sixteenth century an effective control of judicial functions and a power to choose their own judges.[205] This could be considered an application to the towns of the advancing notion of private ownership. On the whole there was a strong tendency to appoint "learned" professionals to judicial posts in the towns, but this specialization of function did not mean in itself a loss of broader powers of municipal self-government. This did not come until the seventeenth century, as a result of disorder and conflict during the Thirty Years' War and the growing power of the territorial rulers. Judicial functions in most of the municipalities were severely impaired as were other functions in local administration.[206] The shift of power and influence was to the territorial rulers and also to the nobility, who not only possessed personal exemptions from trial by ordinary courts, but also—in some of the states—a right to share in judicial functions at higher levels, either through having some lay nobles named as judges or else through a power to designate a percentage of the "learned" membership.[207]

In a society so multifarious one cannot trace the lines of influence except in the broadest terms. There was not in the German states, as there was in France, a national government to shake the scattered elements into a pattern and press the pattern on a whole society through the massive weight of a great bureaucracy. One can only say that judicial functions, dispersed and diffused like other functions of government, served on the whole to reinforce the position of the court-keepers. In the opinion of one recent writer on the subject, the judges of the seventeenth and early eighteenth centuries viewed government as an alliance between prince and aristocracy. The judges themselves were nobles, however shabby. They generally shared both the privileges and the prejudices of their employers. Despite efforts made to ensure technical training and competence in many of the courts, bias was almost inescapable in persons recruited

---

[205] Stölzel, 276–323.
[206] Schroeder, *DRG*, 957–960.
[207] Schroeder, *DRG*, 948–949; Döhring, 50.

and rewarded as most of the judges were.[208] And so it continued, with some reforms and improvements. The private ownership of courts was destroyed in France by one great stroke in 1789. The Germans had to wait longer, through long decades of piecemeal change that lasted well into the nineteenth century.

[208] Döhring, 46–48.

CHAPTER III

THE ENGLISH ROYAL COURTS

1. THE SURVIVAL OF THE ANCIENT ASSEMBLY COURTS

THE Norman Conquest worked a revolution in the upper strata of English society but it had little immediate effect on the ancient forms of community organization that governed the countryside. In the tenth and eleventh centuries Anglo-Saxon society had been converted from kindred groups into territorial communities; the liabilities of individuals and controls imposed by the group all came to be expressed through organized neighborhoods. These folk assemblies in shires, hundreds, and townships bore a strong resemblance to the Carolingian public courts. As in the Carolingian system a distinction was drawn between small assemblies meeting frequently—once a month or once every three weeks—and general meetings occurring usually twice a year. There also appeared in many places individuals with special influence and prestige who, like the Carolingian *scabini*, became spokesman for their communities and leaders in the assembly courts. Yet the courts retained their ancient quality. The judgment rendered was a judgment of the whole territorial community. All free and law-worthy men were privileged to attend. The executive power residing in the presiding officer—the earldorman or reeve—might be withheld if he did not concur in the decision but the judgment was by the doomsmen assembled in the court and the law they applied was folk-law.[1] Not long before the Conquest, Anglo-Saxon kings made some grants of judicial powers to private persons, but these could not compare in number or scope with the immunities already acquired, through grant and prescription, by the feudataries in France.[2] After the Conquest the smaller courts of the hundreds

---

[1] The standard histories of Anglo-Saxon institutions deal with these topics. The best recent statement I have found is that of John E. A. Jolliffe, *Constitutional History of Medieval England* (London, 3d ed., 1954), 56–64, 112–113, 151–152.

[2] Jolliffe, 64–71; Goebel, *Felony and Misdemeanor*, 339–378.

continued their slow drift into private ownership but even here the surrender by the crown was not complete. In 1066 and for a full century thereafter, the agencies that regulated the lives of most Englishmen were the ancient folk assemblies, organized now on territorial lines and only in small degree feudalized.

It will seem a paradox that the survival of these agencies, which produced so large a measure of self-government, was chiefly due to the continuing strength and stability of the English central government. This was indeed the great paradox, whose full implications would not unfold for centuries yet to come. But the experience of France and Germany confirms it. In France, as already suggested, the public courts were feudalized in the tenth and eleventh centuries and the completeness with which this was accomplished is a measure of the weakness of central authority.[3] In Germany the ancient folk assemblies survived into the 1200's and it was the weakness of the central government that permitted them thereafter to slip into private hands. In England the Anglo-Saxon monarchy, despite limited resources and limited ambitions, had maintained a uniform system of courts and administration, some fairly reliable sources of revenue, and ties of loyalty in the people that brought increasing success in the effort to maintain internal peace. There had been before 1066 no lasting or general dismemberment of central authority such as occurred in France in the sombre years from 900 to 1100.[4]

The Normans conquered England with an amazingly small army (perhaps 5,000 men) and for decades thereafter the barons who maintained the royal power were themselves very far from secure against internal revolt or foreign invasion.[5] Crown and barons

[3] Cam, "Suitors and Scabini," *Speculum*, 10:189 suggested three additional reasons for the survival of the English communal courts: (1) the influence of the Danes in preserving and fortifying the "democratic" institutions of the Anglo-Saxons and Jutes; (2) the high rank of Charlemagne's *scabini* which discouraged attendance by men of lesser rank in France, while in England the attaching of duty of attendance to land tenure might have kept a broader basis of participation; and (3) the fact that the feudal system was brought to England relatively late and fully formed, so that feudal courts could more readily retain a separate identity. These suggestions seem insufficient in themselves to explain such basic phenomena. In her own concluding comment Miss Cam argued that the most important factor was the relative strength of the English monarchy, both before and after the Conquest.

[4] Jolliffe, 98–138.

[5] Frank Stenton, *The First Century of English Feudalism* (Oxford, 1932), 190–

were tied together by self-interest and mutual dependence but until the death of William the Conqueror, at least, there was no doubt who was master. William's grants of land to his followers brought Norman feudalism to England and with full-scale feudal-ism there soon developed "courts" of lords and vassals reaching down the lines of tenure. These feudal courts, which dealt with disputes between lord and vassals or between the vassals them-selves, played an important part in bringing stability and order within the military tenures and greatly influenced the structure of English society in the twelfth century.[6] Yet the feudal courts were never permitted to fuse with and assimilate the shire courts. In the shire courts themselves, the royal reeve or sheriff became with the Conquest the king's agent and representative, usually a great feudal magnate and the most powerful man in the county. Yet the incipient dangers of usurpation were well under-stood by the Norman kings, who began early in the twelfth century the process, which was to go on for another 600 years, of diminishing the role of the sheriffs and reassigning their powers.[7] In only one English county, Cheshire, did a local magnate acquire an immunity for his court and even here the franchise of the earls of Chester was broken down in the thirteenth century.[8] The county courts and, to a lesser degree, the hundred courts were preserved as functioning agencies of government. The time soon came when powerful kings were able to reactivate them as instruments of national policy.

2. *The Introduction of the Jury*

The jury in its various forms entered the common law system from a very different direction. The early jury in England was, as Maitland said, in the widest sense "a body of neighbors sum-moned by some public officer to give upon oath a true answer to

192. The estimate of the size of the Conqueror's army is taken from William J. Corbett, "The Development of the Duchy of Normandy and the Norman Conquest of England," *Cambridge Medieval History* (Cambridge, Eng., 1926), V, 481. Ferdinand Lot, *L'Art Militaire et les Armées au Moyen Age* (Paris, 1946), I, 285 suggests 7,000 as an outside figure.
    [6] Stenton, 44.
    [7] William A. Morris, *The Medieval English Sheriff to 1300* (New York, 1927), 41–72.
    [8] Cam, "Suitors and Scabini," *Speculum*, 10:189, at 196.

some question." [9] This was the means employed by William the Conqueror in 1086 to extract from his conquered subjects the great fund of information compiled in Domesday Book. As the use of the jury was extended under William's successors, it clearly was not, as we consider the jury now to be, a major protection against oppression by government; it was, on the contrary, an oppressive exercise of the highest powers of government. The jurors were compelled to answer under oath and became subject to penalties for perjury. No preordained rules set limits to the kinds of questions that might be asked. In medieval societies, unaccustomed to large-scale intervention by central government, this kind of interrogation lay far outside the range of ordinary experience. Indeed, in our own society, if there were no limiting rules of relevance and no privilege against self-crimination, we would consider such roving commissions an intolerable intrusion. It must have been thus that many persons looked on the early jury in England.

As to the earlier history of the jury, some doubts persist. The classic account of Brunner achieved for some time an almost universal acceptance. By this account the jury was imported from Normandy by the Norman conquerors, who had inherited it as one of the powers of ducal government from the Carolingian crown. There is no doubt that the later Carolingians used the group inquest to secure information on matters of first importance to the central government. Brunner, of course, could not trace the lines of descent from generation to generation through the darkness of the ninth and tenth centuries. It was also perfectly possible that similar techniques could have been originated by strong political leadership in the twelfth, as readily as they were in the ninth century. But Brunner's view seemed for a time to be confirmed by evidence that the group inquest was made available to private litigants somewhat sooner in Normandy than it was in England. More recent studies indicate that the contrary may be true.[10] A more serious challenge to his thesis is the evidence, meager though it is, that juries were known in England

---

[9] Frederick Pollock and Frederick W. Maitland, *History of English Law Before the Time of Edward I* (Cambridge, Eng., 2d ed., 1898), I, 138 (cited hereafter as Pollock and Maitland, *HEL*).

[10] Charles H. Haskins, *Norman Institutions* (Cambridge, Mass., 1918), chap. VI, supplied what was believed to be the missing evidence of prior use in Nor-

before 1066. This is particularly true of the jury of presentment or accusation, as distinguished from the jury of trial. Group accusation of crime can be glimpsed in the Danelaw some seventy years before the Conquest. Somewhat later, but still before the Conquest, parties in dispute as to land boundaries can be found submitting, by consent, to the sworn verdict of a neighborhood jury.[11] It may be, therefore, that the jury was not simply a Norman importation and that it was more readily accepted in England because group testimony under oath was known in some localities. With time the folk assemblies in England might have added this new resource to their ancient modes of fact finding (oath-helping and ordeal). Voluntary submission to group verdicts by litigants might have prepared the way for a wider use of the jury in standard procedure, just as arbitration in France may have promoted the adoption of the canonist inquest. But this kind of gradual evolution did not occur. It still seems true, as Brunner contended, that the jury as it entered English law was in all essential respects a royal institution. It was used in England by royal officials in certain cases of private litigation during the eleventh and early twelfth centuries. Similar use in Normandy followed shortly if it did not precede these English adaptations. The authority on which these early juries depended was the authority of kings who, for their time, were extraordinarily

mandy. More recent doubts, with criticism of Haskins' evidence, appear in R. Besnier, " 'Inquisitiones' et 'Recognitiones,' " NRH, 1950, 183, at 199. Early instances of group inquests in England, ordered on royal authority, are collected and discussed by R. C. Van Caenegem, Royal Writs in England from the Conquest to Glanvill (Selden Society, London, 1959), 62–68.

[11] The evidence of a procedure for group accusation rests on the ordinance of Ethelred published about 997. That this was an antecedent of the presentment jury of the Assize of Clarendon is argued by Sir Paul Vinogradoff, English Society in the Eleventh Century (Oxford, 1908), 7–8; Sir Frank Stenton, Anglo-Saxon England (Oxford, 1943), 503, 643; G. O. Sayles, Medieval Foundations of England (Philadelphia, 1950), 334–336; and especially Naomi D. Hurnard, "The Assize of Clarendon," 56 Eng. Hist. Rev. 374 (1941). As to anything like direct derivation from Anglo-Saxon usages, the skepticism expressed by Plucknett, Concise Hist., 108–109, seems fully justified.

The evidence for a "popular jury" of trial, employed by consent of the litigants is presented by Caenegem, Royal Writs in England from the Conquest to Glanvill, 69–81. The argument rests chiefly on a single case, occurring about 1053–1055, but finds some support from the use of neighborhood juries in other boundary disputes and in various appraisals shortly after the Conquest. On the basis of this evidence, interesting as it is, it seems an exaggeration for the author to say (p. 81) that this kind of group verdict had "deep roots in the past."

powerful. This was still more clearly true of the decisions made by Henry II, which made the group inquest a standard feature of certain criminal and civil proceedings. The main steps were taken in 1166, the year of great decisions just a century after the Conquest.

It is not necessary for present purposes to describe in detail the innovations of Henry II except to repeat the familiar distinction between the two main types of jury he made available—the jury of presentment or accusation and the jury of trial. The jury of presentment was sketched in all its essential elements by the Assize of Clarendon, issued in 1166 and providing in its first clause that

for the preservation of the peace and the maintenance of justice inquiries be made through each county and hundred by twelve of the more lawful men of the hundred and four of the more lawful men of each vill, under oath that they will say truly whether in their hundred or vill there be any man who is accused or generally suspected of being a robber or murderer or thief or any man who is a receiver of robbers or murderers or thieves since the lord king was king.[12]

In the same year, and probably for similar motives, another assize undertook to provide royal protection to freehold land. It may be that the first stage was the use of the same kind of presentment jury as that provided by the Assize of Clarendon itself and that trial juries were not made available to private litigants for more than a decade thereafter. By 1179, at any rate, the remedy of novel disseisin was fully organized, with the jury of trial as its central feature. We need not follow the stages by which the possessory assizes, with the jury as fact-finding agency, were extended to other situations and the enlarged jury of the grand assize was made generally available in disputes over title to land. New forms of jury were rapidly manufactured for a great variety of civil and criminal proceedings during a period of innovation and experiment that lasted far into the thirteenth century. Then when the Lateran Council of 1215 threw the influence of the church very strongly against the use of judicial duels and ordeals,

[12] The Latin text is given by William Stubbs, *Select Charters and Other Illustrations of English Constitutional History* (9th ed., Oxford, 1921), 170–173. Caenegem, *Royal Writs*, etc., 285 has pointed out that the Assize of Clarendon was apparently conceived by Henry II as a temporary measure, but later confirmations had the effect of making it permanent.

the main recourse of royal officials was to persuade or induce the parties to consent to the use of juries. The superiority of neighborhood testimony over archaic modes of proof—through oath-helpers, ordeal or battle—made the jury itself attractive to litigants and brought popularity for the royal remedies of which it was rapidly becoming a standard feature.[13]

During the period of experiment with various sizes and forms of jury there was one central question that was not quite finally answered—should the jurors be treated as a group or as a mere aggregation of individual witnesses? From the first appearance of the royal jury in England the practice was to treat it as a group. But so it was also in Normandy, where the group inquest was highly developed, widely available, and very well known in both ducal and subordinate courts. Nevertheless the Norman jury could not compete with the new modes of proof by individual testimony that were organized by French royal courts during the thirteenth century and that gradually filtered across the borders into Normandy. For persons experienced in these modes of proof it was natural to inquire whether answers to questions came from persons with direct knowledge or were based merely on rumor or gossip. If rumor was the basis, this could be readily ascertained by experienced questioners. So the practice developed in Normandy of selecting out the well-informed jurors and examining them separately. Their answers were used at first merely to reinforce the collective verdict. Then the answers of jurors with direct knowledge came to be considered the only reliable source. The collective inquest or jury became optional; litigants who preferred to give "strict proof" could not be made to accept it. The jury became a last resort. Falling more and more into discredit and disuse, it was eliminated in Normandy by the provincial assembly of the three estates that reformed the customs of Normandy in 1583. The land that had exported the jury abolished it at home.[14]

---

[13] Pollock and Maitland, *HEL*, I, 144–150; Charles L. Wells, "The Origin of the Petty Jury," 27 *L.Q.R.* 347 (1911). Caenegem, *Royal Writs*, etc., 271–290 gives a most interesting account, with much new material, of the legislation that produced the assize of novel disseisin. It is his contention that private litigants were not permitted to purchase "recognitions" as of course until at least a decade after 1166.

[14] Brunner, *S.G.*, 450–457.

It is common to speak of the early English jury as a group of witnesses. As Maitland had said of this statement "for the purposes of a popular exposition it is true enough" but it is nevertheless inaccurate.[15] It was certainly never supposed that all the members of every jury would have been eye-witnesses of the events about which they spoke. Often the events would have occurred so far in the past that no living person could possibly have observed them or had more than a second or third hand report concerning them. In the records of royal court proceedings of the early thirteenth century the jurors are occasionally quoted as giving highly argumentative verdicts in which they disclosed the gaps in their own knowledge and the inferences they were forced to make from the scraps of knowledge they had.[16] In the period after elimination of the duel and ordeal had put new pressure on fact-finding machinery, the king's judges did not hesitate to examine the jurors, select the more credible among conflicting responses and draw their own conclusions as to the facts that had been proved.[17] Bracton, writing shortly after 1250, was quite explicit that the royal judge in a criminal case

[15] Pollock and Maitland, *HEL*, II, 622.

[16] *Pleas of the Crown for the County of Gloucester*, 1221 (ed. Maitland, London, 1884), no. 330. One Henry had been found dead with a knife nearby. John Miller was arrested because he was the last person seen with him. But John denied all association with Henry and denied that he had ever known him. John wished to defend himself by battle and was not willing to let the matter be decided by a jury. Twelve jurors, asked for their verdict nevertheless, said under oath that "because John denied any association with Henry or any knowledge of him, and the jurors know this to be false, and further because Henry went out in John's company but did not return and because John was unwilling to place himself on the jury, they understand that he is guilty." Three other groups of jurors rendered the same verdict, but the judges were not forced to decide so difficult a case since the master of the dead man gave the king 40 shillings to buy John the privilege of abjuring the kingdom.

[17] Plucknett, *Concise Hist.*, 121–124, gives deserved attention to a case from 1220 printed in the Selden Society volume, *Select Pleas of the Crown*, no. 192. In the particular instance four juries of eight persons each, drawn from separate vills, gave quite different answers to questions concerning the alleged theft of a horse. As Plucknett says (123–124): "The court examined the parties, and examined thirty-two jurors, and upon the evidence so obtained, itself decided upon the guilt of Elias. If this system had become permanently established, we should have had a regular inquisitorial procedure, such as that described on the continent by Beaumanoir, with a judge deciding questions of fact as well as law, and examining parties and groups of local representatives whose function was not to state facts, nor to decide the question of guilt or innocence, but merely to retail the gossip of the countryside."

Lady Stenton in her Introduction to the *Rolls of the Justices in Eyre for Gloucestershire, Worcestershire and Staffordshire*, 1221–1222 (Selden Society), lv–

should first inquire, if he has doubts of the case and the jury is suspected, from whence or from whom the twelve have derived what they offer in their verdict concerning the accused, and after their answers have been heard he will be able readily to determine whether there has been fraud or iniquity. If one or even a majority of the jurors should say that what they offer in their verdict was derived from one of the conjurors and each one when interrogated says that he derived it from another, thus the questions and answers may lead from one person to another till they come to a vile and abject person such that no credence whatever is to be placed in him. The judge should inquire in this manner so that his reputation and honor may be increased and so that it will not be said that Jesus was crucified and Barnabas set free.[18]

From the point of view of jurors also, it must have been painful to subscribe to collective assertions on subjects concerning which they were ignorant or had no reliable sources of knowl-

---

lvi, gives examples from the same period of interrogation by the justices to fill in gaps in jurors' verdicts. The indices of the *Curia Regis Rolls* so far published (up to 1230) refer to other instances—perhaps four or five a year on the average—in which the justices interrogated the jurors and secured collective answers on points left unclear or doubtful. This practice certainly persisted into the Year Book period —e.g., *Y.B. 21&22 Edw. I* (Rolls Series), 272 (1293); *Y.B. 30&31 Edw. I* (Rolls Series), 106, 110, 122, 128, 140, etc. (1302).

In *Curia Regis Rolls of the Reign of Henry III* (London, 1955), 529, no. 2644 (*anno* 1224), there is an example of interrogation and response by individual jurors. A Jew, Bonamy Motun, and his wife and two sons were appealed of homicide of a Christian who worked in Bonamy's household. Two juries of neighbors were assembled, one composed of 18 Christians and the other of 12 Jews. One group of the Christian jury responded that they suspected Bonamy's family but not Bonamy himself; others answered individually, to the same general effect but with variant forms of answer. Each of the Jewish jurors was recorded as answering separately, though they all concurred in the belief that Bonamy and his family were entirely innocent. The case has been printed also by H. G. Richardson and G. O. Sayles, *Select Cases of Procedure Without Writ under Henry III* (Selden Society, London, 1941), 3.

As late as 1321 the judges of the King's Bench were willing to intervene and interrogate individual witnesses where the jury was unable to render a verdict. In a case of that year, an action of trespass, defendant pleaded a deed of release and plaintiff denied that the deed was his. The jury interrogated four witnesses to the deed and found that they disagreed. The jury reported that it therefore could not say whether the deed was valid. The justices then examined the witnesses separately, found their statements to be directly in conflict, on many details of time, place, clothing worn, etc., so that the justices concluded the deed was void and gave judgment for the plaintiff. The case is itself a most instructive example of the difficulties that the judges would have encountered if they had undertaken generally to evaluate testimony, some of it plainly untrustworthy, that conflicted in many complicated and circumstantial details. *Select Cases in the King's Bench* (Selden Society), IV, 81.

[18] Bracton, fol. 143–143b, quoted and discussed in Holdsworth, *HEL,* I, 318.

edge. It is true that the jurors were often given advance notice of the questions they were to answer and freedom during the interval to inform themselves by making their own inquiries in the neighborhood.[19] But in some types of jury if the jurors spoke incorrectly they could be punished through the severe penalties of attaint (essentially a prosecution for perjury). Even where the attaint could not be used a conscientious person might dislike extremely the compulsion to swear on matters concerning which he was half informed or wholly ignorant. It is surprising that one does not find examples in royal courts of the sort of thing that occurred in the manorial court of King's Ripton in 1301, when the jury refused to speak concerning an event that none had seen. We can be fairly sure, however, that any jury assembled to answer the king's judges would be punished, as was the jury at King's Ripton, for such excessive scrupulosity.[20]

Through the first centuries of its history, in other words, the common law jury was a crude instrument, however superior it undoubtedly was to the modes of proof it supplanted. Its crudity was not due simply to a requirement of unanimity; indeed unanimity was not established as a firm requirement until the second half of the fourteenth century.[21] Whether the verdict

[19] Pollock and Maitland, HEL, II, 627–628.

[20] The incident is reported in the Selden Society volume, Select Pleas in Manorial Courts, 126. For refusing to answer and withdrawing from the room the jurors were declared to have committed "a great contempt" and each was fined 40 shillings for the use of the lord of the court.

C. T. Flower in his Introduction to the Curia Regis Rolls, 1199–1230 A.D. (Selden Society, London, 1944), 446–449, refers to several cases of the early 1200's where jurors disagreed or were allowed to confess partial or complete ignorance, without being penalized. In the event of dissent by a substantial minority, the usual course was to impanel another jury. But in a case recorded in the Curia Regis Rolls (London, 1931), V, 258 (anno 1208), a verdict was accepted in an action of novel disseisin and then the court proceeded to fine one of the jurors a half mark because "he said before taking oath that he knew nothing about it" (nichil inde scivit). On the other hand, in Curia Regis Rolls (London, 1926), III, 332 (anno 1205), an attaint of a jury in an action for novel disseisin was made effective only as to the eleven who concurred in the verdict; the twelfth, whose dissent had been recorded by the justices, was excused.

[21] James Thayer, Preliminary Treatise on Evidence (Boston, 1896), 86–90. That royal judges before that time were exerting pressure on jurors to agree appears in many sources. For example, in 1310 a jury that could not agree was ordered by the court to be "put in house" until Monday without food or drink; by vesper time the same day the jurors announced that they had agreed. Y.B. 3&4 Edw. II (Selden Society), 188. In a case in 1345 a jury verdict was challenged because taken out of court, but Scot, J., commented: "We can take a verdict by candle light if the jury will not agree, and if the court were to move we could take them in carts

was unanimous or by simple majority or by some intermediate fraction, the insistence on a collective or group verdict mingled indiscriminately the informed and the ignorant jurors. The remedy was simple and Bracton recommended it: let the judge interrogate the individual jurors and find out how much they really knew. If it then turned out that the jurors were ignorant or unreliable, it would not have been a very great step to assemble individual witnesses who were better informed; for in certain limited types of civil litigation proof by witnesses presented by the parties was quite well known to the thirteenth-century common law and there were also some examples of criminal proceedings begun by interrogation of individual witnesses rather than collective accusation by presentment jury. Suggestions like these were most seductive but there was only one direction in which they could lead—toward the adoption in England of the canonist inquest. It seems clear that the road was open, just as open in England as it was in France.[22] What was needed was extra zeal or sustained curiosity on the part of the English judges, inspired by a conviction that determination of the facts on which the judgment must rest was an essential part of the judge's task. But zeal and curiosity were both repressed. The whole drive was strongly in the other direction. Proof by individual witnesses was restricted, not expanded. Dissent by individual jurors, which had been both tolerated and recorded in early cases, was suppressed in the records and discouraged in fact. The pressure for unanimous verdicts grew constantly stronger. The judges in effect divested themselves of any duty to assemble or appraise the evidence. The fact-finding function was imposed instead on groups of laymen, whose ignorance was disguised by a group verdict and whose sources of knowledge the judges refused to examine.

We need not consider the long process by which methods of informing juries were slowly developed, documentary and witness proof were reinstated, and trial juries were finally transformed

---

with us, and so must justices of assize do." *Y.B. 19 Edw. III* (Rolls Series), 185. In 1346 a verdict of only eleven jurors was accepted, but the twelfth, who refused to agree to it, was sent to jail, *Y.B. 20 Edw. III*, vol. II (Rolls Series), 555.

[22] Pollock and Maitland, *HEL*, II, 638–639, 653–659.

into judges of the facts, so that their ignorance became a virtue. The final transformation came late. For a full 500 years from its organization in the thirteenth century the trial jury of the common law courts retained its mixture of elements. It was both source and judge of evidence, in proportions that were never completely defined and that changed gradually through the centuries.[23] So long as this confusion remained, a critic from the continent might well have described the common law jury as a twelve-headed monster, wholly uncanonized. To rely on it for establishing truth on disputed issues of fact and to leave it as free from judicial controls as the English did for centuries, would have seemed to a well-trained lawyer from Paris a judicial abdication.

Various reasons have been suggested to explain why the English royal judges followed the course they did. Their main choice was between the group inquest, with some form of collective verdict, and the Roman-canonist examination of individual witnesses conducted by the judge. The specific question, therefore, is why group verdicts were accepted and then insisted upon, instead of treating the jurors truly as witnesses and examining them individually. From Maitland comes the suggestion that group verdicts were accepted because the thirteenth-century trial jury was commonly used with the consent of the parties; since the parties had agreed to submit to a jury neither party could contest a result that he had in advance accepted.[24] But this seems to be less a statement of cause than rationalization of a result, since consent could be used, as it was in France, to confer on the judge a power to examine individual witnesses by means of the canonist inquest.[25] Another suggestion by Maitland seems again to do no more than describe a result, when he

[23] Holdsworth, *HEL,* I, 312–347.
[24] Pollock and Maitland, *HEL,* II, 623. It seems to have been even more plainly a rationalization for Maitland to say in the passage following that the verdict of the jurors contained "an element which we cannot but call quasi-judicial," in that questions were put to juries which they could not answer of their own direct knowledge and on which they needed to make such independent inquiries as they were able to make in the brief time allowed them. But the main problem is precisely that of determining why the jurors were thus compelled to speak on matters concerning which they were ignorant.
[25] Above, Chapter II, sec. 2b.

asserts that the verdict of a jury was a verdict of a neighborhood, "the voice of the countryside." [26] It is true that modern eyes cannot readily detect the spirit of community that pervaded these medieval societies. But even though it be true that the jurors were sometimes viewed as spokesmen for a larger group, the question remains why the English crown laid upon local neighborhoods so onerous a duty.

The answer seems to be that at the outset the crown had no choice. When large-scale use of juries began in 1166 there were scarcely enough experienced men merely to direct the new court system. If, where facts were disputed, the judges were to take on the fact-finding job and interrogate individual witnesses, whether the witnesses were members of juries or not would be relatively unimportant. The judges would have been drawn irresistibly, as they were in France, into examining the testimony, determining credibility and relative weight, and making the ultimate difficult findings on contradictory evidence. It is no wonder that the English royal judges in the twelfth and early thirteenth centuries resisted the temptation to start on this long road. Crude and clumsy as it was, the early common law jury was an essential means of conserving trained manpower in a government that had taken on new tasks of immense scope and complexity.[27]

In later developments there can be no doubt that if effective government had required a larger supply of men with legal training, they could have been produced. Men who had studied Roman and canon law had circulated in England from at least the middle of the twelfth century. In the thirteenth century the English universities gave lectures in Roman and canon law. Among the English clergy there were men with training and

---

[26] Pollock and Maitland, *HEL*, II, 626. This is not to say that the notion of the jury as spokesman for the community from which it was derived (e.g., hundred or county) was not at work or that it did not have some important specific consequences, as in localizing rules of venue. Plucknett, *Concise Hist.*, 127–128.

[27] The factor chiefly emphasized in the above passage is hinted at in Holdsworth, *HEL*, I, 312–321 and somewhat more strongly stated by Pollock and Maitland, *HEL*, II, 627:

"English judges find that a requirement of unanimity is the line of least resistance; it spares them so much trouble. . . . It saved the judges of the middle ages not only . . . moral responsibility, but also from enmities and feuds. Likewise it saved them from that as yet unattempted task, the dissection of testimony. An age which accepts every miracle and takes for sober history any tale of Brutus or Arthur that anyone invents must shrink from that task. If our judges had attempted it, they would soon have been hearing the evidence in secret."

experience; some could be described as men of learning. Of this group a considerable fraction were drawn into royal service and there proved to be extremely useful. Their total number was not large. But France certainly had no oversupply of such men when—decades later—the shift to canonist procedure began to create an insatiable demand. The clue to later developments, therefore, cannot be found in any lasting incapacity of Englishmen for law or administration. On the contrary, the need for specialists was restricted because means had been found by the Angevin kings to distribute widely through the population the burdens and responsibilities of government. Methods of delegation established so early were followed and extended as the workload continued to mount. This was true even of the central courts of common law, which were soon taken over by some extremely able specialists.

3. THE ADVENT OF PROFESSIONALS IN COMMON LAW COURTS

The new machinery of government introduced by Henry II produced an immediate need for personnel to administer it. It had long been common to send royal commissioners to tour the counties and inquire into matters—especially fiscal matters—in which the crown took special interest. After the innovations of 1166 this practice was regularized. The itinerant officials enforced royal rights of various kinds and dealt generally with malfeasance by local officers. They also clearly had a large and increasing volume of strictly judicial business, both civil and criminal. During a decade or so of experiment with different kinds of personnel, the number of persons assigned to these tasks grew rapidly—one report says that by 1178 it had reached a total of eighteen.[28] If this report is true, it would be most interesting to know what features in the procedure used or in the tasks assigned caused so rapid an increase, and to know also what reversals of policy enabled the king to reduce the total to five, as he did in this same year. For a time thereafter the number varied and it was not till the 1190's that the arrangements were stabilized and a specialized group of judges, normally five in number, were sitting regularly at Westminster, concerned mainly with civil cases. A permanent court of professionals, which was

[28] Plucknett, *Concise Hist.*, 147–148.

later to acquire the name of the Court of Common Pleas, thus assumed leadership and direction of the new royal system of remedies.[29] In comparison with the rest of western Europe, England reached this stage amazingly soon.

The judges of the Common Pleas retained for some time their tie with the king and council. Similarly, when another group of specialists emerged some decades later as judicial assistants of the king in cases reserved for royal decision, this second group— the King's Bench—retained for a much longer time its close connection with the lay barons and royal officers who surrounded the king in his Council. The survival of lay membership and influence within the central courts throws much light on contemporary attitudes toward the judicial power as an instrument of government. But the great barons and high crown officials were soon discouraged from regular attendance. They would have needed to spend most of their time on judicial business and they would surely have felt that most of this time was wasted. The records of the two central courts in the early thirteenth century reveal a great and increasing volume of very technical legal work. Attendance by nonspecialists was reserved for great matters and great occasions. For most purposes the specialists were in charge.

The rules applied by the royal judges were largely manufactured by the work of the judges themselves. There was therefore no question of finding men with formal preparation or training in English law. The judges appointed by Henry II and his sons were for the most part clergy, often very high clergy such as bishops and occasional archbishops. There is no reason to think that these early royal judges were close students of either canon or Roman law, though it is most probable that some were in a broad way familiar with canonist ideas and methods.[30] It is clear nevertheless that the thirteenth-century courts of Common Pleas and King's Bench were staffed by skilled, able and experienced men. In number they usually totalled seven or eight, four or five

[29] Pollock and Maitland, *HEL*, I, 153–156; Holdsworth, *HEL*, I, 47–53; Plucknett, *Concise Hist.*, 148–149, 232–233; G. O. Sayles, introduction to *Select Cases before the King's Bench* (Selden Society, London, 1936), I, xx–xxii, the latter modifying somewhat the earlier views as to the dates when the Court of Common Pleas was permanently organized.

[30] Pollock and Maitland, *HEL*, I, 131–135.

in the Common Pleas and three in the King's Bench, though variations in these numbers were frequent.[31]

It was entirely out of the question for seven or eight judges to handle the enormous and increasing volume of civil and criminal business that arose all over England. One partial solution has already been mentioned—detaching the fact-finding function and assigning it to neighborhood juries. But more than this was needed. The practice soon developed of pressing into service large numbers of local gentry to preside at trials, receive the verdicts of the juries, and enter judgments—to assume in effect a judge's role. No theoretical difficulty seemed to stand in the way. If the king's power to decide disputes between litigants or to punish crime could be delegated to his permanent judges, it could be distributed by special commission to any number of persons, in any place, as to any topic. The use of such special commissions began quite early and soon became one of the most remarkable features of English judicial administration. There were several types and great variations within each type. For criminal cases the most common commissions were *oyer* and *terminer* (giving general authority to "hear and determine" the classes of criminal cases specified) and gaol delivery (giving usually a narrower authority to hear accusations and render judgment against prisoners already confined in designated jails). In the thirteenth century commissions of gaol delivery were very common and were normally issued to knights of the shire— country gentry—sitting in groups of three or four.[32] In civil business the greatest volume of trial work was produced by the possessory assizes—mainly novel disseisin and mort d'ancestor— which had become immensely popular with litigants. Magna Carta had provided that the possessory assizes were to be held regularly in each county by two royal judges, with the assistance of four knights of the county chosen by the county court.[33] Cer-

---

[31] The lists given by Maitland in his Introduction to *Bracton's Notebook* (London, 1887), 139–145 cover the reign of Henry III. For the period from 1272 onward we have the lists of members of the two courts compiled by Sayles, *Select Cases in the Court of King's Bench* (Selden Society), I, cxxix–cxxxix.

[32] Pollock and Maitland, *HEL*, I, 200–201.

[33] Magna Carta (1215), c. 18 provided for the holding of assizes four times a year in each county, but the reissue of 1217 reduced this to once a year. In the 1217 charter, also, there appears no reference to election or choice by the county court. William S. McKechnie, *Magna Carta* (Glasgow, 2d ed., 1914), 269–278.

tainly practice was not hampered by this formula. Often a small group of persons was authorized by special commission to hear and decide a particular case then pending. Very large numbers of commissions were used; in the year 1273 alone some 2000 commissions of assize were issued.[34] Royal judges from Common Pleas or King's Bench were not always members, though it became very common for one judge to be associated with a small group of knights from the county in which the trial was held. The statute of 1285 which attempted to regularize the trial of the possessory assizes required that two central court judges be assigned to each commission, together with one or two of the "more discreet" knights of the locality.[35] But evidence collected by Maitland indicates that in 1305, at least, royal judges from the central courts provided a very small percentage of the judges employed.[36]

It was through their role as inquisitors on commission for general eyre that the central court judges had their greatest impact on thirteenth-century society. In theory a general eyre was a gathering of the whole court of the country in which the eyre was held; the king's justices merely presided, instead of the sheriff, over an ancient folk assembly. Included as members of the commission for the eyre would be a variety of local dignitaries—nobles, clergy, and other prominent persons. But the vigor and inquisitiveness expected of the commissioners meant that the royal judges took the initiative in this grand inquest into county affairs. Every crime committed, every infraction of royal rights, every deviation from duty by county, hundred, or township officers could be ground for money fine or other punishment. The presenting juries from all the smaller localities and the members of the county court itself were subject to punishment for slackness in informing the justices or for errors of fact in the information that they did supply. The frequent punishments meted out by the presiding judges made it clear that the great assemblies convoked for the general eyre were something more than the ancient county court. By sharpening the contrast be-

[34] Pollock and Maitland, HEL, I, 200–201.
[35] Westminster II (1285), c. 30.
[36] Maitland, Introduction to Memoranda de Parliamento, 1305 (London, 1893), xcix.

tween presiding officers and folk-moot they may well have helped to develop the conception of the "office" of royal judge.[37] The general eyre was also, as Plucknett has said, "a most impressive demonstration of the royal power over all sorts and conditions of men, from the baronial owners of great franchises and sheriffs down to the meanest villein." [38] It dramatized the extraordinary achievement of the English crown, in enlisting the active aid of Englishmen of every degree in the multiplied tasks of government.

To govern a nation as intensively as the Norman and Angevin kings were able to govern England it was necessary to rely on the unpaid amateur in many other ways than have been so far suggested. There was a vast amount of local administration in addition to that required to make the royal court system work. The frankpledge system of neighborhood security imposed the duty to maintain public order and control crime on local inhabitants down to the smallest vill; to administer this system it was necessary to have constant checks on performance and annual reviews of the frankpledge lists. Partly through the frankpledge system and partly by other means the duty to pursue and arrest malefactors was thrown on local inhabitants. Local courts were held regularly in county and hundred—once a month for the county courts and once every three weeks in the hundreds. Some of the king's business was done in these assemblies and attendance was a duty (not imposed on all, it is true) which the king's agents helped to enforce. When judgments rendered in local courts were subjected to attack, members of these courts were required to appear in person before the reviewing courts and even (until the early 1220's) to defend their judgments by judicial duel.[39] The heaviest share of all these burdens was laid on the country gentry, the knights of the shire, who also formed an essential element in most of the early juries. Thus the long tradition of "unpaid service by country gentlemen" was well established in the earliest times on which the common law records throw light.[40] Indeed this service extended beyond local law

[37] This suggestion appears in Plucknett, *Concise Hist.*, 233.
[38] Plucknett, 103.
[39] These matters will be discussed below, Chapter IV, section 8.
[40] C. S. Flower, *Introduction to the Curia Regis Rolls, 1199–1230*, 434–440;

enforcement and judicial administration into the collection of the king's revenue and most of the other subjects with which medieval government could deal. It is a key not only to thirteenth-century administration but to many events of later English history. The English crown, by attempting so early so ambitious a program of government, was forced to impose an enormous range of duties on unpaid nonprofessionals and thus trained English society, through its local leadership, in the skills and the practice of self-government.[41]

As to the work of the professional judges, the amazing thing is that so much could have been done by so few. In the thirteenth century and later the judicial power was one of the principal instruments in advancing crown authority and organizing English society. This was most plainly true as to the criminal liabilities whose enforcement was so rapidly transferred to agencies controlled by the crown and whose weight and impact were greatly increased in the process. Even in the administration of civil remedies it was a matter of first importance that delegates or commissioners acted in the name of the king, used royal procedure, and on the whole conformed to the rules and policies defined by the central government. With so large a share of government and general administration subsumed under judicial forms it was a remarkable thing that the main results could

---

Jolliffe, *Constitutional History of Medieval England* (3d ed.), 312–314. A fuller account of the role of the knightly class in local administration appears in Austin L. Poole, *The Obligations of Society in the XII and XIII Centuries* (Oxford, 1946), 53–56.

[41] This thesis is developed against a larger background in the illuminating sketch by Albert B. White, *Self Government at the King's Command* (London, 1933). A similar line of argument, directed mainly at the reasons for the growth in England of representative institutions will be found in C. H. McIlwain, "Medieval Estates," in *Cambridge Medieval History* (Cambridge, Eng., 1932), VII, 664, 691–693, 709–715.

In adopting the main thesis of White I have taken account of the contention of Sayles, *The Medieval Foundations of England,* 438, that it is "seriously misleading" for the reasons (1) that the monarchy acted primarily in its own interests and (2) that the large-scale participation by local gentry was the result of royal pressure and ultimately of royal sanction. It is true, of course, that the term "self-government" may mislead if it suggests that this unpaid service was spontaneous. But it is also true that the pressure exerted by the crown led the local gentry to perform, however reluctantly, manifold and essential duties, and as Professor Sayles says: "Thereby generation after generation of them learned to assume greater and greater responsibilities and received a severely practical training in methods of administration."

have been kept clear and consistent in a regime so decentralized.

In the fourteenth and later centuries the assignment of judicial duties was divided along two main lines that increasingly diverged. Royal commissions continued to be used—increasingly indeed—with the exception that the general eyre had become extremely unpopular and this particular form of royal scourge was abandoned during the fourteenth century.[42] But commissions of *oyer* and *terminer* and of gaol delivery were regularly used for criminal cases. Both of them became more and more concentrated on the more serious criminal offenses and acquired a larger percentage of trained lawyers in their membership. Similarly, the commissions of assize were more and more taken over by specialized professional lawyers, including in that term not only the royal judges of the central courts but serjeants at law and other prominent practitioners before the courts at Westminster.[43] Decentralization of trials was further promoted by the nisi prius system, which permitted any judge of any one of the central courts, when on circuit in any county, to conduct a local trial of all cases pending before any of the other central common law courts and ready for trial at the time of his visit. The statutes which authorized the nisi prius procedure continued to speak of a "substantial man" of the county, who was required to be associated with the judge from Westminster as a member of the bench. A lay element was thus deliberately preserved, at least in form. In fact the influence of these English *Schöffen* gradually faded as professional judges assumed the main leadership in trying major crimes and the standard civil actions of the common law.[44] The presence of the jury as fact-finder and the

[42] Holdsworth, *HEL*, I, 265–273.

[43] During the period 1327–1336 there were 57 justices of assize acting under general commissions of assize; of these 22 were judges of the King's Bench, Common Pleas or Exchequer or of the Irish Common Pleas. Seven others were lawyers who were subsequently (between 1336 and 1341) appointed as judges of one of these courts. Six others were active members of the bar. In short, 37 out of 57 were either judges or actively engaged in practice before the central courts. Mary M. Taylor, "The Justices of Assize," in *The English Government at Work*, 1327–1336 (ed. William H. Dunham, Cambridge, Mass., 1950), III, 219, 232–233.

[44] Holdsworth, *HEL*, I, 274–285; G. J. Turner, "Circuits and Assizes," *Encyc. of the Laws of England* (ed. A. W. Renton, London, 1897), III, 26; Bertha H. Putnam, *The Place in Legal History of Sir William Shareshull* (Cambridge, Eng., 1950), 60–61; Bertha H. Putnam, *Proceedings Before the Justices of the Peace in the Fourteenth and Fifteenth Centuries* (Ames Foundation, London, 1938), xlvii–liii.

absence of any effective modes of controlling the juries, meant during the earlier centuries that the judge's role was limited to maintaining courtroom order, framing the questions that the juries must answer, and ensuring compliance with the ground rules of the various forms of action. So far as the common law civil actions and prosecutions for major crime were concerned, this role was assumed as early as the fourteenth century by a specialized group of professional judges. And so it continued till modern times, through the long centuries which gradually brought enlargement of the judges' role in controlling juries and managing trials.

4. THE JUSTICES OF THE PEACE

The opposite course was followed for the minor crimes and police matters assigned to the justices of the peace. Here again the method of delegation was appointment by royal commission. The method itself goes back to the thirteenth century, when custodians of the peace, specially appointed by royal authority, were useful in local administration. Arrangements were not stabilized until the fourteenth century. Then the choice of personnel for commissions of the peace became a subject of political contest. High officials of the crown, including the common law judges, desired to ensure that there be at least a high percentage of trained lawyers among the justices of the peace. Their opposition came from the House of Commons, whose membership was largely composed of country gentry and merchants from the towns. They strongly desired that the commissions be controlled by men of their own kind. The kind of men they were appears in Strayer's description of the men whom the crown entrusted with collecting the royal revenues:

men who enjoyed financial independence, high social position, and considerable political influence in their communities. There were hundreds of them, closely bound together by ties of kinship, political association and business interests. The abbots and priors were often related to the leading laymen of the counties and the merchants of the towns were buying country estates and marrying their daughters into knightly families. They were loyal to the king and willing to make considerable efforts to satisfy his needs, but they were not dependent on the king for their income or for their political power. Such men could not be bullied into oppressing their neighbors for the benefit of the royal treasury; they could not be replaced by paid civil servants, not only because it would have been too expensive, but also because it would have contradicted one of the oldest traditions of the English monarchy. Unlike France, England had a centralized government before she had a bureaucracy, and the English centralized government had always depended on the unpaid services of the knights and law-abiding men of shires and hundreds. This tradition could not be reversed without wrecking the whole structure of English government, and as long as it continued it was an effective bar to absolutism.[45]

It was chiefly through Parliament that pressure was put on the crown to appoint local gentry to the commissions of the peace. The contest was particularly active in the years 1327–1344. The demands of the Commons were based in part on the obvious advantages of having men acquainted with local conditions in charge of affairs in the counties. To some extent the House of Commons was objecting to lawyers as such, though its objections partly rested on the association of the lawyers with the broad royal inquests, such as the general eyre, which imposed such heavy burdens on local officials and communities. The struggle was for control of a substantial segment of governmental power, a segment that was soon to grow larger as the powers of the justices of the peace were enlarged. But the importance of the issue was fully recognized at the time. There must have been many reasons why the crown decided to concede much to the Commons' demands. For all the work there was to do there was still a shortage of trained lawyers; the country gentry and their allies, the merchants, had already achieved political power and solidarity; there were advantages in having local affairs managed by local residents in matters that involved no real threat to the crown's supremacy. Whatever the reasons, the demands of the Commons were very largely met in compromise solutions that had permanent and profound effects on the structure of English government.[46]

The royal commissions appointing the justices of the peace

---

[45] Introduction by J. R. Strayer to *The English Government at Work, 1327–1336* (eds. James F. Willard and William A. Morris, Cambridge, Mass., 1940–1950), II, 12–13.

[46] Putnam, *Proceedings Before the Justices of the Peace in the Fourteenth and Fifteenth Centuries* (Ames Foundation), xl–lv; Putnam, *The Place in Legal History of Sir William Shareshull*, 65; and in more general terms Holdsworth, *HEL*, I, 286–298.

were annually renewed, so that both powers and personnel of the commissions could be changed from year to year. The crown retained considerable freedom to experiment and the ultimate appointing power. For the lawyers a beachhead was preserved by the *quorum* clause: among the long lists of local magnates and leading gentry would appear the names of certain common law judges or practitioners *quorum unum* (or two or three) any judgment rendered must include.[47] Often the requirement that a lawyer participate was limited to cases of serious crime. In fact the lay members became more, not less prominent, as statutes and annual commissions piled new powers on them. The justices of assize took over trials for major crime but the lay justices of the peace acquired the dominant role in all other phases of local government.[48]

As to the criminal law, which remained at all stages an important part of the work done by the justices of the peace, the combination of lay judges and presentment juries had effects of the greatest importance for criminal law administration. As Professor Plucknett has pointed out, the indictments presented by the juries expressed their own spontaneous reactions, relatively unhampered by technical legal learning. The lawyers were more profitably employed in civil litigation, especially the lucrative disputes over title to freehold land with which the central courts of common law were so largely concerned. They gave little attention to the problems or developing needs of the criminal law. With "an archaic list of felonies and an inadequate conception" of misdemeanor, the common lawyers had little to contribute and the controls of the central courts accomplished little more than obstruction. With such help as they could secure from likeminded persons in Parliament, the gentry in town and country worked out new conceptions of liability and brought the English criminal law to an "unstable equilibrium resulting from the forces of pedantry in the superior courts and the well-meant but unsystematic empiricism of the justices of the peace in sessions and in Parliament." [49]

---

[47] The first example of the quorum clause dates from 1343. Putnam, *Proceedings,* etc., 41. The form of the commission of the peace as standardized in 1590 is given by George W. Prothero, *Select Statutes and Other Documents Illustrative of the Reigns of Elizabeth and James I* (Oxford, 1906), I, 147.

[48] Putnam, *Proceedings,* etc., liv–lv, lxxxi–lxxxiii, cxxx.

[49] Plucknett, introduction to Putnam, *Proceedings,* etc., cxxxvi–cl.

Even in the fourteenth century, however, the powers of the justices went well beyond the limits that would be defined in a modern criminal code. The vast system of labor conscription and wage regulation inspired by the Black Death of 1348 was entrusted, after a brief period of indecision, to the justices of the peace. New statutes of the late fourteenth and fifteenth centuries extended their powers in such matters as the regulation of trade, the suppression of religious dissent, the maintenance of roads and bridges and the conservation of rivers. Through the troubled times of the fifteenth century these powers were exercised intermittently, but they did not lapse. The Tudors were quick to use them for the restoration of internal order and the reorganization of the national government. The justices became a primary element in that alliance between crown and propertied middle class which provided willing (though unpaid) servitors of an expanding national state while setting outside limits to Tudor despotism.[50]

No account of the Tudor system of local government can omit the justices of the peace. They were in truth the Tudor "men of all work." [51] New duties were rapidly piled on them by a House of Commons largely composed of men like them, merchants and gentry whose loyalty to the crown was inspired by similar motives. New tasks could also be imposed by altered terms in the royal commissions appointing them. As Holdworth has said, an enumeration of their powers "would involve a summary of the greater part of the legislation of the Tudor period." [52] For present purposes it is enough to note that the individual justices had very large powers of summary arrest or detention and extensive duties in supervising the work of subordinate local officers, but the main channel for official action in this period was a collective judgment of two or more justices sitting as a court of criminal law. It was through presentment and indictment by juries at Quarter Sessions, held four times a year, that wrongs, defaults and omissions of every kind were brought to the attention of the justices. For serious cases in which the facts were disputed, juries of trial could be empanelled. A verdict by a presentment

[50] David L. Keir, *Constitutional History of Modern Britain* (London, 4th ed., 1950), 1–18.
   [51] Holdsworth, *HEL*, IV, 137.
   [52] Holdsworth, *HEL*, IV, 137.

jury was often enough. The justices then would levy fines or order arrest or command affirmative action as the situation might seem to require. The remarkable thing was that so much government could be carried on through the forms of a criminal trial. These forms were used of course for individual offenses against the criminal law, but they were also used for the misdeeds of parish or manorial officers, for failure of parish or hundred to maintain roads or bridges or streams, and for levying assessments on local communities to pay the cost of poor relief or needed public improvements. As the Webbs have said of a later period, "the county, the hundred and the parish, together with most of the unpaid and compulsory serving officers, were, one or other of them, always in the dock as defendants to criminal indictments, on which they were perpetually being fined." [53]

These "rulers of the county," as Maitland called them,[54] were unpaid, part-time volunteers, though the powers conferred by the crown made them important public officials. In their rank in society they corresponded to many of the lesser nobility in France who were owners of seignorial courts. But it was surely a crucial difference that the criminal courts of the English justices of the peace were not privately owned. They were royal courts, working in aid of policies determined by the central government. They were theoretically subject to review and mandamus by the King's Bench at Westminster, though these controls were exerted sparingly. It was far more important that under the Tudors and first two Stuarts—until the Puritan Revolution—they were watched and controlled and prodded by a vigilant central government through a most active Privy Council. It is difficult to imagine what this strong control from the center might have done to the justices if the contest between king and Parliament had had a different outcome in the wars of the seventeenth century and the King's men had prevailed. As events transpired, the justices of the peace were too firmly rooted in their local com-

[53] Sidney and Beatrice Webb, *English Local Government from the Revolution to the Municipal Corporations Act* (London, 1906–1908), I, 308 (hereafter cited Webb, *ELG*). The work of the justices in the sixteenth century is described by Holdsworth, *HEL*, IV, 137–149. The use of the machinery of presentment in the seventeenth and eighteenth centuries is described by Holdsworth, *HEL*, X, 146–151.

[54] F. W. Maitland, *Justice and Police* (London, 1885), 80.

munties to yield very much to royal pressure. So it was that a medieval system of criminal courts, administered by laymen and functioning through local presentment juries, did the work of the paid functionaries that the French crown was developing as agents of its will. Acting under royal commission and exercising royal powers by delegation, the justices of the peace became a bulwark and an instrument of local self-government.

It is clear that the justices were mostly laymen. The commissions of the peace listed large numbers of superfluous persons, some of whom were trained lawyers. The Chancellor usually led the lists, being "a justice of the peace in every county of England." [55] He would be followed by lay nobility of the particular county and a miscellaneous group of judges and serjeants who might conduct trials of common law actions under commissions of *oyer* and *terminer* or gaol delivery. Many persons were named for purely honorary reasons and never bothered to qualify for active service in their counties. At times, no doubt, judges from Westminster sat in at Quarter Sessions, just as the justices of the peace could sit with judges commissioned for gaol delivery.[56] The listing of such large numbers made for flexibility in practice. But the records of the Quarter Sessions published by numerous county societies make it clear that in the sixteenth and seventeenth centuries the main burden had fallen on local gentry. By the end of the seventeenth century the quorum clause, as a device for ensuring the presence of some professional lawyers, had degenerated into a pure formality; all the justices listed were simply made part of the quorum.[57] To provide them with elementary knowledge of their powers and duties there were numerous treatises, some of which went through many editions.[58] Even more useful to the average justice, no doubt, was a small but permanent clerical staff appointed by the justices themselves.[59] As time went on the clerk of the sessions, who began to reimburse himself through fees charged to the

[55] The recital in the Chancery decree of 1588 reproduced in Cecil Monro, *Acta Cancellariae* (London, 1847), 575, at 580.
[56] Sir Thomas Smith, *De Republica Anglorum* (London, 1583), II, c. 23.
[57] Webb, *ELG*, I, 302–303.
[58] Some of the sixteenth-century literature is described by Holdsworth, *HEL*, IV, 134–145. For the later period Webb, *ELG*, I, 295 gives a short listing.
[59] Holdsworth, *HEL*, IV, 149–151.

litigants, became an important prop for the justices; in the eighteenth century the deputy clerk was often a local solicitor, on whom the justices depended heavily for legal advice.[60] In each of the fifty-two counties, therefore, there was likely to be at least one person who was technically proficient in law. In this later phase, furthermore, it was extremely rare for a justice once appointed to be removed by the appointing authorities.[61] Many decades of service by conscientious persons must have given them on-the-job training in legal technicalities. So it becomes almost a quibble to inquire whether such men should be called "professionals." Many were surely better informed than the thousands of paid employees who were hired to act as judges in the French seignorial courts. But however competent some might be and however permanent their tenure in fact, they were unpaid, very few had or pretended to have any formal training, and most of them worked very much part-time. They assumed these burdensome public duties as an inescapable consequence of their own wealth and social position. All this made quite a difference.

Neither the numbers nor the personal qualifications of the justices can be described with any precision. The Webbs have estimated that in 1689 there were about 3,000 justices commissioned, of whom perhaps 700 to 800 were active,[62] in a population of about 4,000,000. They were distributed over England quite unequally, according to no fixed plan. In the sparsely settled northern counties it was difficult to recruit men with the wealth and social standing that they were expected to have. Recruitment was even more difficult in the sprawling slums that the new industries produced in the eighteenth century. In the larger towns men of humble station managed to get themselves appointed and some of these employed their great powers for personal profit and extortion. Some of those who were socially acceptable and not corrupt were merely indolent; the degrees of their activity like the quality of their performance varied widely from place to place. The Webbs found evidence of a substantial rise in their personal qualifications and performance in the late eighteenth and early nineteenth centuries, but this

---

[60] Webb, *ELG*, I, 502–507.
[61] Webb, *ELG*, I, 379–382.
[62] Webb, *ELG*, I, 319–321.

improvement was paid for by the narrowing orbit within which they moved. Tory in politics, conventional in all matters of conduct and opinion, they held fast to the conception of government by the gentry that had inspired the institution from its late medieval beginnings. So it was nothing worse than anachronism for the justices of one county to go on strike in 1833 because a man had been appointed justice after owning a retail store in his earlier life. The justices who refused to serve were defended thus in a report to Parliament:

The refusal of the County Magistrates to act with a man who has been a grocer and is a Methodist is the dictate of genuine patriotism; the spirit of aristocracy in the county magistracy is the salt which alone preserves the whole mass from inevitable corruption. The power, which is almost irresponsible, could not have been endured if it were not controlled by the sense of private honour.[63]

This is not the place to discuss the work of the justices in local government generally or the "extra-legal constitution" through which they performed their vastly increased duties after 1700. As the Webbs have shown, the new procedures developed in the period after 1700 involved the creation of an administrative staff through various irregular devices and disguises, a specialization of functions through special committees among the justices themselves, and an increasing freedom to legislate through general orders applied county-wide. All this meant an increasing separation of administrative and judicial functions, greater freedom to transact business without observing the formalities of a public court and its apparatus of juries, and the weakening of restraints on their power—restraints arising either through controls by the central government or through the need for securing concurrence from local juries. As to the central government, direct supervision by the Privy Council had almost ceased after the restoration of 1660. And in general these freer modes of operation involved no real innovation but merely an extension of powers they had had from the outset. For the courts of the justices of the peace, like other medieval courts, had not drawn

[63] Webb, ELG, I, 385. The language quoted appeared in a report on the strike, made to Parliament in 1838.

The general comments made in the text on the numbers, distribution, and qualifications of the eighteenth- and nineteenth-century justices are a brief abstract of the account in Webb, ELG, I, 322–386.

sharp lines between adjudication, executive action and rule-making. The late medieval and Tudor statutes had thrust upon them extensive powers, with only the most generalized standards to guide them and few procedural limitations. In fixing wages, supervising poor relief, compelling communities to maintain their roads, licensing ale-houses and all their other diversified functions, it would have been impossible for the justices to adopt a purely passive role, merely registering the conclusions of the presenting juries. In great numbers of cases they had no choice but to issue commands, to persons and communities. If these commands were to be obeyed, it was the justices who must enforce them. Rule-making too was part of their duty; in some matters statutes expressly called for it (for example, wage regulation) and in others rule-making was implicit in any announcement of general policies they would follow in matters where discretion was wide. In the words of Sidney and Beatrice Webb: "As the Justices were themselves the tribunal that would deal with offenders, a public announcement by Quarter Sessions that any conduct of which the Justices chose to disapprove would be treated by them as a punishable offense amounted in effect—to all but the few who could pay for an appeal to a higher tribunal—to a legislative prohibition of such conduct." [64] The King's Bench might review their actions but the litigation required was too costly for many to undertake it. The cabinet and Parliament were most reluctant to intervene. All over England most of the important decisions affecting local government were made by "little knots of squires and parsons, acting on their own views of social expediency," meeting privately in their homes or in taverns without effective review by anyone.[65]

During the nineteenth century the powers of the justices in local government were pruned away by a series of statutes. Their courts as thus remodeled fitted more closely a twentieth-century image of a criminal court. But it is interesting to note that while judicial powers were thus detached and extracted from the previous intermixture, the tradition of unpaid service

[64] Webb, *ELG*, I, 538, with many illustrations for the period 1689 to 1835 given on pages 533–550; also Holdsworth, *HEL*, X, 152.
[65] Webb, *ELG*, I, 550–556. The "extra-legal constitution" is described by the same authors in chapter V, pp. 480–556.

by lay judges was not so easily abandoned. Even the radical reformers of 1832, it seems, preferred the country gentleman with all his biases to "the constant, artful yet specious operations of a pensioned servant of the Government, well skilled in the subtleties of the law." [66] Behind such opinions there lay not merely distrust of central governments but distrust of lawyers as such. Or perhaps it would be more generous to phrase it, as Maitland did in 1888, as a preference for laymen:

It is indeed very difficult to tell how much of the English respect for law . . . is centered in the amateur justice of the peace. If we have to name the institution which had most to do with its growth, we should long hesitate between the Commission of the Peace and Trial by Jury. Englishmen have trusted the law; it were hardly too much to say that they have loved the law; but they have not loved and do not love lawyers, and the law that they have loved they did not think of as lawyers' law. The most learned "barrister of seven years' standing" will find it hard to get so high a reputation among country folk for speaking with the voice of the law, as that which has been enjoyed by many a country squire whose only juristic attainment was the posses- sion of a clerk who could find the appropriate page in Burn's Justice.[67]

Perhaps Maitland was right. In matters of history he almost always was. At any rate, outside the large cities in England laymen still sit as justices of the peace—chosen from a much wider range of social types and reinforced by lawyers in certain more serious cases.[68] Perhaps this is another paradox, that the English respect for law is still partly due to the important share that laymen still have in administering it.

5. COURTS OF EQUITY

There would be some advantage in proceeding from the justices of the peace to other agencies of local government that operated under judicial forms—the courts of county, hundred, manor and town. But it seems better to examine first the courts of equity, especially the Chancery, which seem to have had very little to do with local government and to have been highly centralized in

[66] Webb, *ELG,* I, 606–607, quoting a statement in a newspaper of 1825.
[67] F. W. Maitland, "The Shadows and Silences of Real Life," *Collected Papers* (Cambridge, Eng., 1911), I, 476–477.
[68] Richard M. Jackson, *The Machinery of Justice in England* (Cambridge, Eng., 2d ed., 1953), 139–145; Lord Halsbury, *Laws of England* (London, 3d ed., 1954), IX, 452–454.

London. There were, it is true, some local courts of equity, such as the court in Wales and the court at York (for the five northernmost counties), but most civil litigation in equity was dealt with by the Chancery, with some useful help from the Court of Requests before it was abolished in 1641.[69] Both the Chancery and the Court of Requests sat only in London. Furthermore, the Chancery had only two judges—the Chancellor himself and the Master of the Rolls—until the nineteenth century. So the question arises—how could so much business have been dealt with by so few people?

The question seems especially puzzling because of the thesis that Dean Langdell has made popular—that the Chancery adopted the main elements of Roman-canonist procedure. If this were true, it would seem almost a miracle that two judges sitting in London could dispose of the hundreds, then thousands, of equity cases that poured in each year from most of England. It should be remembered that the Chancellor was a very busy holder of high political office. A Tudor or Stuart Chancellor would do well if he set aside half his time for purely judicial duties. The Roman-canonist procedure had long before proved on the continent its voracious appetite for judges. How could two judges (or one and a half) accomplish so much in England?

[69] The Council in the North was first organized in 1484 by Richard III and after a lapse under Henry VIII was reestablished in 1525. Then in 1537 it was placed on the basis that was to last until its abolition in 1640. Its jurisdiction covered the five northern counties of Northumberland, Cumberland, Westmoreland, Durham, and Yorkshire and included both common law and equitable remedies. In equity cases its procedure apparently imitated that of the Chancery in all essential respects. R. R. Reid, *The King's Council in the North* (London, 1921), 261–272.

The Council in Wales likewise was organized in the late fifteenth century and was considerably developed under Henry VIII. Its equitable jurisdiction was modeled in general on that of the Chancery, but there is little direct evidence as to its procedure now surviving. Caroline A. Skeel, *The Council in the Marches of Wales* (London, 1904), 217–234.

There were courts of equity also for the Cinque Ports, located in Dover, for the Duchy of Lancaster, and in the Mayor's Court in London. Plucknett, *Concise Hist.*, 676. But of the 40 English counties outside Wales it would be true in the main that 34 had to send their equity cases to London, either to the Chancery or to the Court of Requests; and these 34 were the most prosperous and heavily populated.

As to the Court of Requests more is known, chiefly through the *Select Cases in the Court of Requests* published by Leadam under the auspices of the Selden Society. In this volume there are numerous examples showing the court's reliance on examinations under written interrogatories through examining commissioners (pp. 22, 27, 72, 113, 185 and 191) and showing also the use of arbitration by "gentlemen in the country" (pp. xcviii, 71–80, 173–185).

Langdell himself gave a partial answer by showing that in the preparation of cases for trial the Chancery borrowed from the common law its machinery of pleading, including the demurrer.[70] This machinery, for which there is no real parallel in canonist procedure, obviously aimed to throw on the litigants, as far as possible, the burden of sifting out and simplifying issues. The pressure in this direction was mainly due to the presence of the jury, making it highly desirable to reduce issues of fact to the narrowest possible compass. Since the Chancery had no jury, it administered these borrowed pleading techniques with far less rigor than the common law courts. Freedom in allowing amendments reduced the penalties for incorrect allegations. Furthermore, as Langdell showed, the use of the defendant's answer as a mode of proof gave plaintiffs an incentive, which was altogether lacking in common law pleading, to extend and elaborate their allegations. The hybrid system of pleading that was thereby produced became overloaded in the course of time and eventually became a scandal. But in the sixteenth and seventeenth centuries this condition had by no means been reached. At that time the Chancery had avoided the excesses of common law issue-pleading and was able to use the common law techniques with reasonable efficiency, thereby saving the court much time and trouble in the initial framing of issues.

The main contention of Langdell was that the Chancery borrowed from the ecclesiastical courts the canonist methods of proof.[71] This is a crucial issue. In France the adoption of the canonist inquest in the thirteenth century had effects of enormous importance that have been described. Interrogation in secret of individual witnesses meant in France that there were written records, trained examiners, an increasingly complex written procedure and a transformation of the courts themselves, with major effects on the centers of power in French society. It is clear that the English Chancery did employ interrogation of individual witnesses under oath as its basic method of proof. Was this an importation from canon law, and if so, why did not more come with it?

[70] C. C. Langdell, *Summary of Equity Pleading* (Cambridge, Mass., 2d ed., 1883), sec. 53 and following.
[71] Langdell, sec. 47.

The early history of Chancery procedure is most obscure. Most of the records from which it could be reconstructed have disappeared beyond hope of recovery. In reading the records that do survive one faces the problem of determining when the infant court of equity was fully born and severed from its parent, the Council of the King. The birth process lasted for decades and through all this time the Chancery retained its intimate ties with the central administration. It is clear at least that long before a separate court of equity had emerged in the light of day, examination of individuals under oath was used as a method of investigation by various agencies of the crown—the King's Bench, Exchequer, Parliament, and certainly the Council.[72] Nor is there any evidence that church court procedures provided a model.[73] A royal government that had come to use juries—twelve-man inquests—on so enormous a scale would surely have had the power to interrogate individuals under oath, and this was an obvious recourse where questioning of individuals might elicit information that crown officers desired. On the other hand, the Council also informed itself by verdicts of local juries, taken under special commissions addressed to local officers.[74] Similarly, in that period of twilight sleep that preceded the birth of a court of equity, the Chancery (acting, it seems, on behalf of the Council) sometimes made its inquiries by special verdicts of local juries, convened under Chancery commissions addressed to justices of assize.[75]

[72] James F. Baldwin, The King's Council (Oxford, 1913), 296–300. In Select Cases Before the King's Council (Selden Society), 77–80, 33–34 and 103–104, appear examples of examinations conducted either before the full Council or by special commissions from its own membership.

[73] This point is made by Baldwin, Introduction to Select Cases Before the King's Council (Selden Society), xlii–xliii. The distinguished German historian, Professor Helmut Coing, has suggested an opposing view in his article "English Equity and the Denunciatio Evangelica of the Canon Law," 71 L.Q.R. 223 (1955). Even in the extremely guarded way in which the argument is presented, it seems to me unconvincing.

[74] Select Cases Before the King's Council (Selden Society), 39–41, 82–84.

[75] Select Cases in Chancery (Selden Society), case 10 (verdict of the jury taken by justices in 1393 concerning a charge of false arrest against a local court-keeping lord); cases 24–30 (eight commissions issued in 1397 to justices of assize to take verdicts from juries concerning charges of maladministration against the sheriff of Lincoln). The latter group of cases, authorized by 20 Edw. III c. 6, probably represented action taken on behalf of the Council. Baldwin, The King's Council, 243.

It is also worth noting that the petition of the Commons addressed to the King

When a separate court of equity began to emerge in the fifteenth century there is nothing to indicate a large-scale copying of canonist procedure. It is true that compulsion of the defendant to answer under oath was a standard feature; this was well known to be church court practice, alien to the common law.[76] But in the early cases there was none of the elaborate apparatus of the canonist inquest: the defendant was simply required to appear in person to be examined orally.[77] In one case in 1438 the Chancellor examined the defendant orally at the Chancellor's own manor in the country and secured a confession that a particular feoffment had been made in trust.[78] Then in the 1440's written answers by defendants began to appear in significant numbers; very soon thereafter the line of written pleadings was stretched to include plaintiffs' replications and even defendants' rejoinders.[79] But this shift to written pleadings can hardly be veiwed as a move toward canonist procedure. As Langdell pointed out, not only the names employed but the

---

in 1415 complained of the writs of subpena and *certis de causis* issued by the Chancery and Exchequer and addressed, among others, to the justices of the two Benches, so that the common law judges "when they should be hearing and taking inquests for the deliverance of your people are occupied with examinations under such writs to the great vexation, loss and expense of your subjects." *Rot. Parl.,* IV, 84 (1415).

[76] Among the grounds for complaint against the subpena that were voiced by the Commons in 1415 (referred to in preceding note) was that "these pleas cannot be ended except by examination under oath of the parties according to the civil law and the law of holy church, in subversion of your common law."

[77] *Select Cases in Chancery* (Selden Society), case 109 (1407–1409); *Calendar of Chancery Proceedings in the Reign of Queen Elizabeth* (Record Commission), I, xxxv (1443); I, xli (1436); I, xliv (1444–1450); I, xxx (Henry VI); II, xxi (1446). Oral examinations under oath were conducted by the Chancellor in *Select Cases,* case 95 (1408); *Calendar* (Record Commission), I, xxi (1429). Early cases in which defendants were ordered to appear *in propria persona*: *Select Cases* (Selden Society), case 2 (1386), case 7 (1388), case 9 (1389), case 11 (1394), case 14 (1395), case 35 (1398), case 48 (1402).

[78] *Calendar* (Record Commission), I, xliii (1438).

[79] Written answers: *Select Cases,* case 138 (1441); *Calendar* (Record Comm.), II, xxi (1446); I, xlix (1454).

Written answers and replications: *Calendar* (Record Comm.), II, xxvi (1449); II, xxxviii (1457); I, li (1459); II, xlviii (1465); II, lxv (1481).

Written answers, replications and rejoinders: *Calendar* (Record Comm.), I, lxviii (1466); II, xl (after 1460); II, lxvii (1482). Barbour stated that among all the numerous fifteenth-century pleadings that he examined he found no instance of equity pleadings extending beyond a rejoinder. Willard T. Barbour, *History of Contract in Early English Equity* (Oxford Studies in Social and Legal History, 1914), IV, 145–146.

whole apparatus of responsive pleadings represented a borrow-ing from common, not canon law.

When it came to examination of witnesses other than the defendant himself there was a greater problem. It was of course possible to bring witnesses into the Chancery for questioning and it seems that this was sometimes done.[80] But this was incon-venient and burdensome for witnesses living far from London. An alternative—the French solution—was to send judges or other officials from the court itself, armed with interrogatories, to the residence of the witnesses. There is no evidence that this solution was even seriously considered. A much more English compromise was adopted instead. Local gentry or dignitaries (abbots and occasionally even common law judges) were specially commissioned to examine witnesses under oath and report back in writing what the witnesses said. In the early cases, starting in the 1450's, the proceedings were most informal, as were the reports of their proceedings that the commissioners returned. No written interrogatories were prepared, so far as one can tell, to guide or limit the questioning.[81] The whole inquest procedure had almost nothing in common with the massive apparatus that the French had built around their *enquête*, except the result that both provided—a written record of sworn testimony by in-dividual witnesses taken in distant places.

The procedure could not remain as simple as this. If the taking and recording of testimony was to be thus decentralized and farmed out to laymen, the questioners could not be left with-

[80] *Select Cases in Chancery* (Selden Society), case 95 (1408); Barbour, *History of Contract in Early English Equity*, 215–219 (case of 1467–1468).

[81] *Calendar* (Record Comm.), II, xxxi (1454, commission to Thomas Reynold and Thomas Danyell, clerk); I, li (1458–1459, commission to Roger Keys and Sir Thomas Coke of Exeter); I, lxxii (1466, commission to the Abbot of Kenil-worth); II, xlviii (1464, commission to two gentry of Kent); I, lxviii and lxxxiii (1466 and 1467, commissions to Richard Choke, "one of the justices," and another to examine witnesses in Berkshire). Richard Choke was a Justice of the Common Pleas from 1461 to 1483. Edward Foss, *Lives of the Judges* (London, 1848–1864), IV, 486.

A still earlier example of an examining commission is that issued to the Bishop of Norwich in 1437 (*Calendar*, II, xvi), requesting him to examine the plaintiff's bill and report back. The Bishop examined both plaintiff and defendant under oath and reported their testimony to the Chancellor. But this may have been merely a variant of the commission to take the answer of a defendant unable to travel because of illness or age, which appeared later in the fifteenth century (*Calendar*, II, lxxxi (1481); I, cxxiv (1497)) and became very common in later Chancery practice.

out any guidance at all. The remedy was to prepare in advance, and in writing, a set of questions. The obvious persons to prepare the questions were the interested parties who had named the witnesses and asked to have them examined. The technique of examination by written interrogatories was used in the middle of the fifteenth century in an examination conducted by the Master of the Rolls in London.[82] It was an obvious solution for examinations conducted in the country by untrained laymen and, again, it required in itself no heavy draft on canonist ideas. The essential question was—how closely will the Chancellor or his subordinates review the questions in advance for relevance, for conformity to pleadings, for qualifications and competence of the witnesses addressed? If the English Chancellors had accepted full scale the assumptions of French proceduralists concerning the judge's responsibility, they would soon have been caught in the great machine of *intendits* and articles, checked and counterchecked through motions, objections and challenges, the delays and adjournments would have compelled them to keep a written record of interlocutory proceedings—all most precise and orderly but immensely voracious of time, effort and trained personnel. But was it really worth the effort to find and train the personnel? If the fifteenth-century Chancellors were mostly high churchmen, they were also very practical Englishmen, and if they were anything like their successors in the sixteenth century, they were willing that their justice be somewhat rough. They were certainly familiar with methods of delegating the work of government to responsible laymen all over the country, for the judicial commissions (including the commissions of the peace) and all sorts of other royal commissions were issued from the Chancery. So it is easy to guess some reasons why canonist methods, even if they were consciously copied, were also consciously modified to fit domestic needs.

It is not till the sixteenth century that one can extract from published records a clear picture of the Chancery's methods of investigation and proof. By that stage the Chancery had two examiners on its permanent staff, resident in London and available there year-round to examine witnesses. By a general order

[82] *Calendar* (Record Commission), I, lix (dated by the editors as of the reign of Henry VI, i.e., before 1461).

of 1545 the examiners were given in effect a monopoly of examinations conducted in or near London, the limit of nearness being later defined as twenty miles from the city.[83] For examinations conducted at a distance from London, a master in Chancery or one of the examiners could be sent out but this was extremely rare.[84] The normal solution was to appoint a commission of four lay persons, two named by each of the parties. The commissioners assembled at some place convenient for parties and witnesses, often a local tavern. Whether conducted in London by a Chancery examiner or in the country by special commission, the examination consisted of reading to the witnesses, separately and privately, questions prepared in writing by counsel for the parties. Objections to questions or to the methods by which the examination itself was conducted could be raised at a later stage after a written report of the examination had been returned and one or the other party moved for "publication." Then if no sufficient objection was raised, publication was ordered—that is, copies of the witnesses' answers were given to both parties and the information they contained was released from all restriction.[85]

[83] George W. Sanders, *Orders in Chancery* (London, 1845), I, 8, 11; Smith, *De Republica Anglorum*, II, c. 12. The 20-mile limit did not emerge until the seventeenth century, when the examiners complained to the Chancellor against the six clerks for arranging special commissions to examine witnesses in the city. The stakes in this contest, of course, were fees. The warfare went on for decades, the six clerks contending at one stage through their legal counsel, the Attorney General, that the general order of 1545 on the subject (quoted by Sanders, I, 8), which had been entered in the official Registrar's Book, was a forgery. Sanders, *Orders in Chancery*, I, 123, 164, 189–193. By an order of 1661 the 20-mile limit was reduced to 10 miles, so that the examiners' business was still further curtailed. Sanders, I, 304.

[84] Monro, *Acta Cancellariae*, 453 reports such a case in 1577. Sanders, *Orders in Chancery*, I, 326 refers to a case in 1668 in which one of the examiners was sent into the country. The Master in Chancery who wrote the "Treatise of the Maisters of the Chauncerie" in the period between 1596 and 1603 (Francis Hargrave, *Collection of Tracts Relative to the Law of England* (Dublin, 1787), 293) tells of a Master of Henry VII's time who was commissioned to examine some witnesses in Devonshire in a particular case. The author, a strong defender of the Masters, argued strongly that "this piece of service might be better performed by the masters of the court then by such commissioners as are now commonly chosen," but the fact that he could find only one such example in the sixteenth-century records suggests that there were not very many.

[85] A general account of Chancery methods of taking evidence, based mostly on eighteenth and nineteenth-century sources, appears in Holdsworth, *HEL*, IX, 353–358. On the whole this account is applicable also to the formative period, the sixteenth and early seventeenth centuries, to which attention is here primarily directed.

It is evident that this system shows certain analogies to canonist methods of investigation and proof. It is tempting to think that the civilians who served in the Chancery as Masters and in other posts deliberately cast its procedure in a canonist mold. This is the thesis that Langdell has made familiar. It is, however, suspect, not merely because of the lack of direct evidence but because the thesis was overstated by Langdell himself in order to promote his own theories about the nature of modern equity.[86] It is true that private examination of individual witnesses was a central element in most procedural systems derived from the Roman-canonist; preservation of secrecy until "publication" was also characteristic, though it is interesting to note that most French courts did not allow publication and kept the testimony secret to the end, even in criminal cases.[87] In determining the effects of publication (for example, whether it foreclosed submission of further proof), it was natural to look to the practices of courts that used this device and had rules on the subject.[88] In such details of practice there must have been

[86] Langdell, *Summary of Equity Pleading* (2d ed., 1883). The principal difficulty with Langdell's account is that he compares Chancery procedure of the sixteenth and seventeenth centuries with the perfected procedure of the English ecclesiastical courts in their last stage. The latter, as he says (sec. 48), provided that "every step in a cause takes place in open court, under the direction and supervision of the judge," with the hearing oral but a written record maintained by the court's own clerk. All this bears a much closer analogy to nineteenth-century reformed procedure of Germany or Italy than it does to late medieval or early modern systems that were inspired by the canonist model, and in any case none of this later experience was available to sixteenth-century Chancery officials. As he also says (sec. 46) of the procedure in the ecclesiastical courts, "in form it cannot be said that it was adopted at all, that is, the ecclesiastical procedure was never made *as such* the procedure of the court of chancery," which grew up in fact as an independent system. The theses promoted by Langdell's argument were of course his favorite notions that equity acts, unlike the common law, entirely *in personam* and that the court's power to command the litigant was the key not only to Chancery procedure but to substantive equity doctrines.

[87] Guilhiermoz, *Enquêtes et Procès*, 73–74. It was chiefly with reference to criminal cases, presumably, that Guilhiermoz here described this feature as "a truly monstrous iniquity."

[88] Monro, *Acta Cancellariae*, 32, reproduces a report to the Lord Keeper made in 1601 by Matthew Carew, Master in Chancery, on the two questions whether new evidence could be presented after publication and whether prior to publication witnesses once examined could be re-examined on new interrogatories. After stating that restrictions in such matters aimed to reduce the danger of subornation of perjury, he concluded that "the laws" permit re-examination, even after publication, if the questions relate to new matters. He therefore recommended that publication of the newly received testimony, with one exception, be permitted by the court. Sir John Haywarde, Master, confronted with a similar problem in 1617, concluded that where danger of subornation was eliminated "I take it to be agree-

much useful borrowing from the English ecclesiastical courts or the writings of the canonists. But when one looks beyond details to substance, the influences that seem to predominate are those derived from the English environment. Though pretrial procedure was organized to produce a written record of testimony, decisions were reached after an oral hearing in open court, at which the parties were represented by counsel. This alone is not decisive, for several procedural systems that were based on the canonist made provision for oral hearing *sine strepitu*. It is more important that the large-scale use of laymen as examiners set severe limits on inquiries and that the preparation of cases for trial was largely entrusted to the initiative of the parties.

For examinations conducted outside London, as has been said, the examiners were chosen by the parties, each side naming two. Their choice was free within certain outside limits on partisanship—they could not choose their own legal counsel or very close relatives.[89] But there was no systematic scrutiny of the lists. It was left to opposing counsel to object if undue partiality was to be expected and this was usually hard to show. Each pair of commissioners was labelled "plaintiff's" or "defendant's" commissioners and it was taken for granted that they would in some measure protect the interests of the parties that named them. At times this mild partisanship flared up into open animosity among the commissioners or between commissioners and witnesses.[90] On the whole they probably did not deserve the bad name

able to all laws and custom of courts wherein publication of witnesses is in use" to allow publication, and accordingly so recommended. Monro, *Acta Cancellariae*, 254.

[89] Counsel for one of the parties was excluded in Freeborne v. Lesieur (1618), digested by John Ritchie, *Reports of Cases Decided by Francis Bacon* (London, 1932), 117, and in Selwyn's Case, *Dickens*, 563 (1779). A son-in-law and cousin of one of the defendants were excluded in Tybott v. Lord St. John (1578), Monro, *Acta Cancellariae*, 460.

[90] Woodlye v. Grove (1573), Monro, *Acta Cancellariae*, 407, two of the commissioners certified that a third commissioner after "lewd and opprobrious words" drew a dagger and "very furiously did offer to smite them"; Deane v. Rolle (1620), Monro, 295, defendant's commissioner refused to attend any session with the plaintiff's commissioners; Love v. Love (1584), Monro, 537, witness for defendant, after being examined by defendant's commissioners, refused to answer interrogatories put by plaintiff's commissioners; Vaughan v. Morgan (1581), Monro, 502, plaintiff at a meeting of the commission drew his sword and attempted to assault the defendant's commissioners, with the result that they did not dare to sit with the commission and examine any witnesses for the defendant.

A sort of adversary principle is certainly suggested also by the strong reaction

they have been given by a Master in Chancery at the end of the sixteenth century who described them as "for the most part unlearned, inexpert, . . . and ever affectionate to one of the parties." [91] Unlearned they were for the most part and somewhat "affectionate" to one of the parties. This did not mean that they were corrupt or dishonorable men. Most of those of whom we have records were important men in their home communities— knights, esquires, and lesser clergy—the very types of people who were serving as justices of the peace and performing other important tasks of government. The office of examiner under Chancery commission was important enough that disturbance of their proceedings or disparagement of their persons was a contempt of the Chancery, punishable by arrest.[92] The trouble lay not with the ability or the status of the examiners themselves but with a system that was geared to the use of "unlearned" men, chosen by the parties, in judicial investigations calling for expertise.

The framing of the questions that would be addressed to the witnesses was likewise entrusted to the parties—that is, in practice to their legal counsel. As late as the sixteenth century, even perhaps the early seventeenth, it was possible for witnesses to be examined orally in open court, but this was certainly rare and was strongly disapproved later.[93] The basic reliance of the

---

of Lord Keeper Egerton in Thimblethrop v. Wood (1597), Monro, 700, where a commission had been appointed from names submitted by the plaintiff only, but Egerton considered this most improper even though the proceedings of the commissioners seemed in every other respect to be regular.

[91] "Treatise of the Maisters of the Chauncerie," in Hargrave, *Collection of Tracts Relative to the Law of England,* 304.

[92] Monro, *Acta Cancellariae,* 122, 295, 753 (cases of 1609, 1620 and 1600); Howard v. Ludlowe, *Reg. Lib. 1596A,* fol. 814a (April 28, 1597). In the last cited case the defendant was fined £20 and committed to the Fleet when it was proved that he "did very contemptuously behave himself against her Majestie in that he did not only offer abuse to some of the Comyssyoners in words and disturbed theyr proceedings in the examynacon of wytnesses which they were authorysed to doe by her Majestie's Com under the Greate Seale of England and lykewyse travayled with dyvers wytnesses which were served with her Majestie's proces of Spa to be examyned on the pls parte by vertue of that Com that some of them should not appeare upon the same proces and be examyned and that some others of them which had appeared should departe unexamyned in contempt of the same proces," but also insulted plaintiff's lawyer who attended the examination on plaintiff's behalf; "which severall Contempts and misdemeanors are in noe sort to be tollerated."

[93] In the manuscript Decree and Order Book for 1596–1597 there is a decree of May 26, 1597 in which the defendant, sued for rents collected from land owned by plaintiff, had previously been examined on written interrogatories. When Lord

Chancery for investigation and proof was on written interrogatories addressed to particular witnesses and administered
by the examiners in a separate proceeding. Over the content of
the questions the court's controls were minimal. In principle the
interrogatories were limited by the pleadings, but, again, there
was no check imposed in advance to ensure relevance or conformity to pleadings. Only when flagrant departures were called
to the court's attention by opposing counsel were special
measures taken.[94] Otherwise, the draft interrogatories were
simply filed with a Chancery clerk, along with the names of the
commissioners nominated by each party.[95] It may well be that in
the fifteenth and early sixteenth centuries the examiners were
left free to depart from the prepared questions. But there were

Keeper Egerton read defendant's answers "and upon his Lordship's further examynacon of the defendant now viva voce upon his oth towching the poynts aforesaid," the Lord Keeper decided there was no evidence that any sum remained due
from defendant and dismissed the bill. Gardyner v. Rieston, *Reg. Lib.* (1596A),
fol. 895b.

Hudson asserted that oral testimony in open court could also be used in the
Star Chamber, at the court's discretion, during the sixteenth and early seventeenth
centuries. William Hudson, "Treatise on the Star Chamber," in Francis Hargrave,
Collectanea Juridica (London, 1791–1792), II, 214.

The rule later developed, excluding oral testimony in the Chancery, is referred
to by Holdsworth, *HEL*, IX, 353–354. It should be noted, however, that the exclusion was not absolute, since oral testimony could be taken by the Chancellor in
summary proceedings, such as those investigating a breach of a suitor's privilege
against arrest (Moore v. Aylet, *Dickens*, 641, (1784)); and witnesses previously
examined on written interrogatories could be heard in open court to assert that
the written record of their answers was erroneous (Peacock v. Collins, *Cary*, 47,
(1560); Darling v. Staniford, *Dickens*, 358 (1763)).

It should be noted also that the standard methods of proof through written
interrogatories prepared by the parties could be supplemented by special interrogatories ordered by the court itself to "inform its conscience." The answers in these
cases were ordinarily not published and were kept for the court's own private information. Monro, *Acta Cancellariae*, 375 and 459 (cases of 1569 and 1578);
Bacon, *Orders* (1619), no. 74, in Sanders, *Orders in Chancery*, I, 119.

[94] In Rewse v. Tuthill (1566), Monro, *Acta Cancellariae*, 360, defendant's counsel informed the court that the plaintiff had called up witnesses to be examined on
matters not contained in the plaintiff's bill. The court did not verify this claim but
simply ordered that the witnesses were not to be examined on matters not contained in the bill and if any had been so examined their testimony was not to be
published.

A similar problem arose with witnesses' claims of privilege, as in Lee v. Mark-
ham, a case in 1569 reported by Monro, *Acta Cancellariae*, 375. Here a lawyer
informed the court that he was about to be examined concerning information he
had acquired as counsel for one of the parties. The court issued a special order
forbidding the examiners to ask for such information.

[95] Orders agreed on by the Six Clerks, probably 1596 or 1597: Sanders, *Orders
in Chancery*, I, 74–75.

dangers in this. The procedure had to be so organized that it could be operated by laymen who could not be expected to be completely impartial, who met at a distance without supervision by the court itself and who administered interrogatories that had not been reviewed in advance. All these factors pointed toward restriction rather than enlargement of the examiners' role. General orders issued in 1596, and confirmed by Francis Bacon as Chancellor in 1619, required that all interrogatories be prepared and filed with the court in advance, before issuance of commissions to examine, and strongly implied that questioning was to be confined to reading aloud of the written questions.[96] Actually it is likely that this was already the practice, for in very many cases the examiners would not have had the knowledge to wander far from the written text.

All these elements, taken in combination, meant that the court and its officials were relieved of time-consuming tasks in the collection of evidence. They also combined to produce one of the most irrational and inefficient systems of proof that Europe had known since duels and ordeals were abolished. Under this system the cross-examination of witnesses, both friendly and hostile, had to be undertaken before their testimony had been heard. This was not only difficult but often dangerous and was accordingly seldom attempted. All the lines of testimony that might develop had to be anticipated, as to witnesses presented by either side. No wonder the questions became prolix.[97] No

[96] Sanders, *Orders in Chancery*, I, 70, quotes a general order issued by Lord Keeper Puckering and Egerton, Master of the Rolls, in April, 1596: "All commissions to be awarded for examinacion of witnesses shall be *super interrogatoriis interclausis* onely and noe returne of deposicions shall be received unless the commissioners do either comprize the deposicions in one rolle subscribed with their hands or in diverse rolls where each one shall be soe subscribed." The substance of this order was repeated by Bacon in his general orders of 1619. Sanders, *Orders in Chancery*, I, 109, at 118.

The order of 1596 was not published till 1727 and its authenticity might be questioned if it were not for the fact that Hudson, "Treatise on the Star Chamber" (Hargrave, *Collectanea Juridica*, II, 202) ascribes to Egerton a similar regulation for interrogatories used in the Star Chamber. The reason stated by Hudson was that parties or their commissioners, after hearing testimony from particular witnessess, sought to cross-examine them by drawing new interrogatories "which he conceived to occasion much perjury." The order therefore provided that examinations should be only on the basis of interrogatories filed in advance and that parties or commissioners "cannot add to or alter any of those interrogatories."

[97] The recitals in the general order of 1635 are persuasive. Sanders, *Orders in Chancery*, I, 176.

help could be had from the examiners, whose role became that of recording and reporting the answers of the witnesses. For the court itself, this system meant that the Chancellor's view of an equity case had horizons determined by the imagination of legal counsel, exercised while counsel themselves were still in the dark and without possibility of effective cross-examination.

It was to avoid the hazards of this crude system that litigants resorted increasingly to the pleadings as a substitute form of proof. Actually the Chancellors' willingness to permit this misuse of the pleadings marks another main point of divergence from canonist procedure. The canonist systems elsewhere were careful to distinguish the two functions of allegation and discovery. They required the parties, after the pleadings were completed, to prepare *positions* or *articles* defining the facts they intended to prove; each party was then required to swear to the truth of the facts summarized in his own *articles* and also to state under oath whether the facts asserted by his adversary were or were not true.[98] There is nothing to indicate that the English Chancery ever imported this machinery. Instead, from the very beginning, the defendant in Chancery was required to answer directly the plaintiff's bill—orally at first and then by written answer. Since the answer was under oath in either case, it was a short step to the conclusion that it could be used as evidence. Then as equity pleadings grew more elaborate and the common law bar took over their preparation, counsel for plaintiffs had every incentive to extend recitals of fact, to repeat them in different versions, and even to join additional parties from whom evidence might be extracted. The defendant, in order to squeeze evidence from the plaintiff, could file a cross-bill and if he did so would have similar incentives to repeat, elaborate and extend his allegations. During the seventeenth and later

[98] Robert W. Millar, "The Mechanism of Fact-Discovery: A Study in Comparative Civil Procedure," 32 *Ill. L. Rev.* 261, 424 (1937), esp. 266–294 and 437–442; Guilhiermoz, *Enquêtes et Procès*, 53–66. The confusion of allegation and discovery in equity pleading had been pointed out first by Langdell, *Summary of Equity Pleading* (2d ed.), sec. 68, with the comment: "There is no reason to suppose that this flagrant departure from principle was intentional." This comment presupposes, of course, that in its organization of pre-trial procedure the Chancery at the outset imitated directly the canonist model. The argument I have presented in the text rejects this assumption and presupposes instead that from the beginning the Chancellors' streamlined methods reflected an extreme reluctance to commit sufficient numbers of trained personnel.

centuries equity pleadings thus became an exercise in artful probing and still more artful evasion, complicated still further by motions and amendments as instruments of delay. These abuses were not the worst feature of Chancery procedure during its later phase of full-scale degeneration. But for present purposes it is important to note that this massive jungle growth of equity pleadings was primarily due to the breakdown of the Chancery's ordinary modes of proof.[99] And this breakdown occurred because whatever canonist procedure was copied by the Chancery was so thoroughly Anglicized. Like other agencies of English government, the Chancery preferred to pre-empt laymen and streamline their duties, rather than build its own bureaucracy and do the whole job itself.

The Chancery did possess a large and avaricious staff of clerk-copyists and record keepers, and also a small bureaucracy of semijudicial officers, the twelve Masters in Chancery. The Masters were clearly a group of paid, well-trained professionals. Most of them were trained in civil law, though there were common lawyers among them.[100] Their status originally had been quite exalted. They were descended from those high officials of the Chancery, receivers of petitions, whose role in the Parliament of 1305 was so extensive that Maitland called them "under-secretaries of state." [101] If the English Chancery had continued to play as large a part in general administration as the Chancery in France, the Masters in Chancery might have developed functions as extensive as their French counterparts, who under the name of *intendants* played so large a part in governing France under the last two centuries of the Old Regime.[102] In England the growth of competing agencies of government, more directly subject to the king's personal control, served to diminish the role

[99] Holdsworth, *HEL*, IX, 357–358.

[100] For example, the learned author and antiquary William Lambard who served as a Master in Chancery from 1592–1601, was called to the bar in 1567 and became a bencher of Lincoln's Inn in 1578–1579. Holdsworth, *HEL*, IV, 117.

[101] Maitland, *Memoranda de Parliamento*, 1305, xxxvii.

[102] The intendants had the title of "Masters of Requests of the King's House," which goes back to the fourteenth century at least. It then described those active and useful agents of the King, usually numbering six in the fourteenth century, who received and acted on petitions, held their own court for limited classes of cases, and served the Great Seal and the Chancellor, presiding at the Seal in the Chancellor's absence. Their work prior to 1350 is described by André Guillois, *Recherches sur les Maîtres des Requêtes de l'Hôtel* (Paris, 1909).

of the Chancery and reduced correspondingly the range of duties assigned to the Masters in Chancery.[103] Nevertheless the Masters remained, for some time, dignitaries of considerable rank. As late as the sixteenth century they were entitled to sit, and for a time to speak, in Parliament.[104] Within the Chancery they had a large responsibility for certifying form and content of the important documents still issuing under the Great Seal and for supervising the work of the Chancery staff. They also assisted and advised the Chancellor in his judicial work. They were often asked to summarize and evaluate the evidence produced by interrogatories, to report on the sufficiency of bill or answer, to determine whether Chancery orders had been disobeyed or whether contempts had been sufficiently purged. They could be called on, in short, to render an opinion on any matter that the Chancellor chose to refer to them. They were very useful indeed.[105] They were the nearest English equivalent to the French *rapporteur*, who assembled and organized the documents produced by the *enquête* and who then recommended conclusions on both facts and law to the assembled bench, of which the *rapporteur* was a full member.

It would have been quite possible to expand the functions of the Masters and give them a real and permanent share in decision-making in equity. In fact, for brief periods this experiment was tried. On several occasions during the sixteenth century, when vacancies occurred in the office of Chancellor or Master of the Rolls, joint commissions were issued to common law judges and Masters in Chancery, authorizing them to hear and decide equity cases. The longest experience with such interim arrangements was during the first seven years of Egerton's tenure (1596 to 1603); in the absence of the Lord Keeper the Chancery bench then consisted of one common law judge

[103] Bertie Wilkinson, *The Chancery under Edward III* (Manchester, 1929), 64–72, 187–188, describes the varied services rendered to the central government by the Masters in Chancery during the fourteenth century and their diminishing role as Chancery functions in general administration were taken over by other agencies.

[104] Holdsworth, *HEL*, I, 417–418.

[105] Monro, *Acta Cancellariae* provides the best evidence, in sources presently published, as to the range of activity of the Masters in judicial matters. The first half of his volume is a collection of Masters' reports to the Chancellor for the period 1589–1625. The second portion, reproducing selected decrees taken from the Chancery Decree and Order Book, confirms the picture from another direction.

and three or four masters, deciding as a group. This arrangement seems to have worked quite well and to have had no
noticeable effect on the grounds or the acceptability of Chancery
decrees.[106] One can only guess the reasons why it was not made
permanent, producing in the Chancery a collegiate bench of the
type so common on the continent. We know it was not rendered
permanent. Instead it became increasingly clear that the authority exercised in the Chancellor's court was that of the
Chancellor alone.[107] So far as the twelve Masters themselves
were concerned, their role remained strictly subordinate. Particular cases might be referred to a Master for final decision,
without further review by the court.[108] A Chancellor who felt
unsure of himself might adorn the bench with a group of
Masters to give him advice.[109] But unless empowered by special
commission they were advisers only and their powers in cases
referred to them were fixed by the order of reference. Highly
qualified and useful though they were, they were there to help
when called on. In the late seventeenth and eighteenth centuries
there is some doubt as to how much they really helped—whether

[106] The commission was issued in May, 1596 to Justices Clench, Gawdy, Beau-
mont and Owen and certain Masters in Chancery "to hear the causes in the absence of the Lord Keeper until a Master of the Rolls be appointed." Francis Bacon,
Letters and Life (ed. James Spedding, London, 1862–1878), II, 32–33. There
were apparently six Masters named to the commission, for this is the number of
different Masters' names appearing in the Decree and Order Book as members of
the bench. One of them was Carew, the author of Cary's Reports, and another was
William Lambard. This composite bench, composed of one common law judge
and three or occasionally four Masters, sat regularly on Wednesdays and Fridays,
when the Lord Keeper was himself presiding in the Star Chamber, and occasionally
on other days.
    Similar commissions had been issued in 1529, four months before Wolsey's dis-
grace, to 20 persons including the Chief Baron, Justice Fitzherbert, and six Masters in Chancery (Foss, *Lives of the Judges*, V, 85); in 1558 during the illness of
Lord Keeper Bacon (*Reg. Lib. B*, 5 P. & M. and 1 & 2 Eliz., fol. 232a); and on
the death of Sir Christopher Hatton in 1591 (Foss, *Lives of the Judges*, V, 397).
[107] Coke, *Fourth Institute*, 84; Bacon, inaugural speech on being sworn in as
Chancellor: "I know well the judicature resides wholly in myself." (Bacon, *Letters and Life* (ed. Spedding), VI, 187).
[108] Examples of such orders appear in Monro, *Acta Cancellariae*, 71 (1607) and
112 (1608).
[109] Sir Christopher Hatton declared in an order of April 18, 1588 that the dignity
of the court of late years had been "in some part blemished and the same destitute
of such assistance and advice of theires as were meete and necessary" because of
the failure of the Masters to attend hearings. He ordered that four of them should
sit regularly on the bench during hearings in court and two should attend him at
his home on Mondays, Tuesdays and Thursdays in the afternoon to advise him on
the hearing of cases. Sanders, *Orders in Chancery*, 60.

references to Masters contributed more to expedition than to confusion, expense and delay.[110]

The question then arises why the Chancellors did not make fuller use of their expert staff in the actual decision of equity cases. Even after it had been settled that the Chancery would rely mainly on the initiative of the parties in pleading and in framing interrogatories and would delegate examinations for the most part to lay examiners, it might have been possible to share more fully with the Masters the responsibility for final decision. It may well be that the Masters were kept in the background because the wide departures from established law achieved through the Chancery's remedies would have been harder to maintain and defend if the authority invoked had been that of a collegiate bench, largely civilian-trained. But this line of argument cannot be pressed very far, for it assumes an unpopularity of Chancery doctrines and remedies that did not exist for substantial periods of time. Certainly Parliament, inspired by the common lawyers, resisted the growth of the Chancery in its earliest stages, but the need for some of the Chancellor's reforms was clearly felt, even at times by the Parliament itself,[111] and it would be too much to say that they were generally unpopular. As to the common lawyers, the history of their relations with the Chancery has been greatly distorted by Coke's sudden attack on the Chancery in 1616. This was merely a brief eruption, important more for the possibilities it foreclosed than as a symptom of deep-rooted antagonism on the part of the common lawyers.[112] Indeed, for many decades before 1616 the working relations of Chancellor and common lawyers had been intimate and harmonious. It has already been noted that for brief periods in the sixteenth century common law judges sat with Masters in Chancery on the Chancery bench issuing equity decrees and administering equity remedies in the usual way. The judges were constantly consulted in matters arising in equity cases. Practice in the Chancery was entirely in the hands of the common law practitioners, the most active being the serjeants and other

[110] Holdsworth, *HEL*, IX, 360–365.
[111] As in cases of breach of trust by feoffees in trust, as to which the Commons in 1402 petitioned the Council to provide some remedy. Plucknett, *Concise Hist.*, 578.
[112] J. P. Dawson, "Coke and Ellesmere Disinterred," 36 *Ill. L. Rev.* 127 (1941).

leaders of the common law bar. The introduction of a bench of expert civilians might have impaired these good working relations, but this would have been more for personal and practical reasons than because of opposition to the Chancery's policies and program.

The subordination of the Masters in Tudor and Stuart times seems to be explained less by opposition to the Chancery's reforms than by the vagueness and imprecision of the equity doctrines employed, limiting the contribution that an expert staff could make. A major clue here is the widespread use of arbitration in disposing of equity cases. The importance of arbitration at this formative stage has almost escaped attention. The early reports of equity decisions are much too cryptic to do more than suggest it. Only in unpublished manuscript records is it fully revealed.[113] We do have published registers of the work of the Privy Council, which included among its manifold duties a considerable jurisdiction over private disputes in the period before 1640. I have pointed out elsewhere that the Privy Council used arbitration on a very large scale, not merely to save the time of the Council for more important tasks but through what seems to have been a conscious preference for solutions through arbitration.[114] In the Chancery the same motive was strongly at work. It was so important a feature that we should pause to consider some of the reasons why arbitration was so much used, since they are relevant to this study.

In the first place, the large-scale use of laymen to conduct examinations of witnesses outside London opened opportunities for mediation through spontaneous suggestions from the ex-

[113] The frequency with which arbitration was used was noted by George Spence, *The Equitable Jurisdiction of the Court of Chancery* (London, 1846), I, 384–386 and the collection of cases taken from the Chancery Decree and Order Book and published by Monro, *Acta Cancellariae* also includes some examples, which will be referred to below. Otherwise the account that follows will depend on the series of manuscript Decree and Order Books, usually cited *Reg. Lib.*, which begins in 1545. Each ordinarily contains the decrees and orders of a single year, and after the first few at the beginning of the series there are two for each year, identified as (A) or (B) and duplicating each other except for variations in the order of the entries. I have examined on a sampling basis a number of the books for the second half of the sixteenth century but have given particular attention to the year 1596–1597, the first year of Egerton's Lord Keepership, and most of the references given here will be for that year.

[114] Dawson, "The Privy Council and Private Law in the Tudor and Stuart Periods," 48 *Mich. L. Rev.* 392, 423–428 (1950).

aminers themselves. The examiners were usually persons with prestige in their local communities so that suggestions from them would carry weight. If the opposing parties lived some distance from London, settlements achieved in this way would not only save the expense of travelling to and lingering on in London but would have some assurance of fairness because of the personal reputations of the examiners themselves. This function of examining commissions in promoting private settlement appeared as early as the fifteenth century.[115] It was a natural development which did not necessarily reflect any particular bias on the part of the court itself, except for a general readiness to accept the results of such mediation. From this it was a very short step to a form of examining commission which expressly conferred authority on the examiners to "hear and end" if they could. In the Court of Requests this type of order was used in the early sixteenth century. After 1545, when the Chancery began to keep a systematic record of decrees and orders, this type of combined commission was fairly common—not standard procedure but quite often used.[116]

A clearer indication of attitudes was the commission to "hear and end" which provided for simple arbitration without any provision for formal examination of witnesses. This could be, like the commission of oyer and terminer issued to decentralize trials at common law, a formal commission issued under the Great Seal. But unlike the common law commission of oyer and terminer as it had developed by the sixteenth century, the equity commission to "hear and end" was normally addressed not to common law judges and serjeants but to lay persons in the locality. Being issued in cases that originated in equity it carried

[115] The Calendar of Chancery Proceedings published by the Record Commission refers (I, lxxii) to a case in 1466 in which the Abbot of Kenilworth, commissioned to examine witnesses in a dispute between two brothers, succeeded in bringing about a settlement between the parties, which he then reported to the Chancellor. Lovet v. Chamberlen, *Choyce Cases* 164 (1583) is a reported case of this type.

[116] Court of Requests Decree and Order Book, III, 21a (1502); III, 127a (1503); III, 167a (1504). Examples of such combined commissions in the Chancery in the year 1596–1597: Norrys v. Kinge, *Reg. Lib. 1596(A)*, fol. 74a; Cowper v. Phillips, *Reg. Lib. 1596(A)*, fol. 714b; Pawlyn v. Keyme, *Reg. Lib. 1596(A)*, 857b; Kinge v. Reydon, *Reg. Lib. 1597(A)*, fol. 25b; Lawrence v. Sackvyle, *Reg. Lib. 1597(A)*, fol. 197b. An earlier example is Principal of Brasenose College v. Lord Williams, *Reg. Lib. 1558(A)*, fol. 5b. William West, *Symboleography* (London, 1615), vol. II, sec. 58, p. 191b gives an example of a combined examining and arbitral commission among the standard forms for Chancery procedure that he supplies.

authority to "hear and end according to equity and good conscience." This type of commission was very common in the Court of Requests before 1500 and in the records of Chancery decrees when they began in 1545.[117] It was usual to provide that if the referees could not end the case, they were to report their proceedings and opinions to the Chancellor. But the court was prepared, in some cases, to use its own process to compel attendance and often the parties were placed under stronger pressure by persuading them to execute penal bonds or recognizances in substantial sums to conform to any award the referees might make.[118] As with the Privy Council, which freely used this same device,[119] the liabilities thereby assumed constituted something more than an empty threat. The strict and technical attitudes of common law courts in enforcing penal bonds exposed nonconforming parties to serious risks and thus, by a strange inversion, added a useful sanction for equity courts in accomplishing their own purposes.

References to arbitration could also be ordered without formal commission or reinforcing penal bonds. An oral request to "hear and end" made by the Chancellor might suffice or the Chancellor might volunteer to write his own private letter to one or more persons, "entreating" him or them to hear and end the case. It was enough for one of the parties or his counsel to suggest that there was some chance of settlement through mediation by outsiders.[120] Often the Chancellor or Lord Keeper

[117] The first volume of manuscript Decree and Order Books for the Court of Requests begins with entries dated 1497. Commissions to hear and end, usually addressed to country gentlemen, are among the earliest entries: I, 19a, 19b, 26a, 31b, 47b, 51a(2), 56b, 57b, 58a, 59b, 63a, 63b (to the Chief Justice of the King's Bench), 64b, etc. C. J. Bayne, Introduction to *Select Cases in the Council of Henry VII* (Selden Society, 1958), cv–cvi, discusses the matter further.

The first volume of the Chancery Decree and Order Book (*Reg. Lib. 1545*) shows 43 such commissions during the first year.

[118] In Web v. Barnes, *Reg. Lib. 1596(A)*, fol. 125a, the court threatened to attach the defendant for failing to appear before an arbitral commission. In the Decree and Order Book for 1558–1559, the first year of Elizabeth, there appear 48 orders referring cases to arbitration in the period of 13½ months between Oct. 13, 1558 and Dec. 2, 1559. In ten of these penal bonds were secured from the parties, undertaking to perform the awards made by the arbitrators.

[119] I have discussed the use of penal bonds and recognizances by the Tudor and Stuart Privy Council in 48 *Mich. L. Rev.* 627, 636–637 (1950).

[120] As in Worsopp v. Barnes, *Reg. Lib. 1596(A)*, fol. 663b, where the order recites that the court "forbeareth to gyve nowe any Judiciall order" because of a suggestion made by defendant's counsel that one of the Masters and Thomas Spencer, esquire, were familiar with the case and might succeed with arbitration.

himself persuaded the parties to submit to his own mediation, to avoid a judicial hearing and bring the dispute to an "arbytrable and frendly end." [121] The aid of the most varied types of people was enlisted in this way. The Masters in Chancery were often called on, especially in cases they had already investigated and reported on.[122] The common law judges, including the chief justices of the two Benches, were similarly asked to "hear and end"; serjeants and other common lawyers were joined with judges or Masters or local gentry.[123] In 1596 Edward Coke and Francis Bacon were asked to join as arbitrators to end a Chancery case in which they were counsel for the opposing parties.[124] Indeed Coke showed himself to be a persistent and effective negotiator, earning the Lord Keeper's gratitude for

[121] For example, in Longe v. May, *Reg. Lib. 1597(A)*, fol. 503a, Lord Keeper Egerton after full hearing had concluded that the 99 year lease, title to which was in dispute in the case, should pass on the death of one Henry May to three nieces of his (daughters of his brother), but Egerton "forbore" to enter a judicial order to this effect because the result would be to leave nothing for the daughter and heir apparent of Henry May. The decree recites that the Lord Keeper thought it meet "to make some mocions for an arbytrable and frendly end betweene them whereunto both the sayd partyes and theyre councell humbly submytted themselves." As a result it was ordered with the assent of the parties that the parties prevailing should pay an annuity to the daughter of Henry May for her life to avoid her disinheritance. Similar intervention by the Lord Keeper, persuading an uncle to pay his nephew 300 marks, to which the nephew was not otherwise entitled, appears in Bussey v. Topclyef, *Reg. Lib. 1596(A)*, fol. 419a. Again in Ragland v. Wilgosse, *Reg. Lib. 1596(A)*, fol. 58a and 367a, the plaintiff was suing to enforce a trust in land against a purchaser, allegedly with notice of the trust. After the case had been heard for two whole days by the Lord Keeper, assisted by the Chief Baron of the Exchequer, it was "moved" by them that the parties submit to arbitration by the Lord Keeper and Chief Baron. In this case the attempt failed, for Coke, counsel for the plaintiff, insisted on a "judicial" hearing (*Reg. Lib. 1597(A)*, fol. 22a).

[122] In the Decree and Order Book for 1596 cases of this type appear on fols. 33a, 93b, 100b, 107b, 124b, 179b, 202a, 238b, 252a, 295a, 297b, 399b, 446b, 535a, 548a, 663b, 720a, 723b. In Munro, *Acta Cancellariae*, references to Masters as arbitrators appear in cases on pp. 20, 49, 468 and 622.

[123] To common law judges: *Reg. Lib. 1596(A)*, fol. 100b, 189a, 194b, 312a, 548a, 746a; to a Baron of the Exchequer and the Solicitor-General: fol. 253a; to the Solicitor-General alone: fol. 196a and 297b; to common law serjeants: 135a, 299b, 396b, 518b; to other common lawyers: fol. 61a and 124b; to a common lawyer and a Master: fol. 193b; to Edward Coke and a Master: fol. 121a. Arbitral commissions addressed to common law judges appear in Monro, *Acta Cancellariae*, 53 and 752, and in the earlier Decree and Order Books: *Reg. Lib. 1545*, fol. 158b (to the Chief Justice of the King's Bench); *Reg. Lib. 1552*, fol. 249a (same).

[124] Warde v. Fulwood, *Reg. Lib. 1596(A)*, fol. 370a and 786a. The irony of this case, in the light of Coke's attack on the Chancery 20 years later, was that Coke was counsel for a plaintiff who sought relief after a judgment against him at common law.

his success in settling another troublesome case.[125] But it was not only the common law judges and practitioners who served in this way. Still more important and more characteristic were the references to "gentlemen in the country"—the holders of offices in the towns, knights and esquires, the ubiquitous landed gentry who keep reappearing in every account of Tudor and Stuart government.[126]

In searching for reasons why the Chancery took these affirmative measures to organize arbitration, one finds only two classes of cases in which special reasons appear. One class is the dispute between near relatives—father and son, brother and brother—which were viewed with dislike as "unnatural" and shipped out of court wherever possible.[127] Then there were merchants' cases in considerable numbers, some of which involved complex accounts for which special accounting skills were needed. The inadequacy of the common law rules regulating mercantile transactions, the technicalities of common law

[125] Wentworth v. Knightley, *Reg. Lib. 1596(A)*, fol. 268a (June 29, 1596). The case involved an assignment of a lease for years to four persons in trust for the assignor, whose equitable interest passed first by will to his son and then by sale to Sir Henry Vuton, who assigned it to trustees for the payment of his debts. Of the four original trustees of the leasehold, two had died in the meantime and the contest was mainly with an heir of one of the deceased trustees. A full day was required merely to hear the testimony presented by only one of six or seven parties, so Coke (then Attorney General) was asked by Egerton to join with Croke, the Recorder of London (the author of Croke's Reports), to persuade the parties to a "generall peace" (fol. 579a). After fruitless attempts by Coke and Croke to mediate (fol. 624a), the case was heard at length by the Lord Keeper, assisted by the two Chief Justices. "Forasmuch as the said Lord Keeper and the said two Lords Chyef Justics beinge nowe presente in Cowrt did nowe declare that they fynde the Cawse of some dyffyculty," they asked Coke and Croke to renew their efforts at mediation (fol. 691a). Finally two months later, on Apr. 13, 1597 (fol. 735b), Coke was able to report that he and Croke had brought all the parties to "a frendlye perfect and fynall agreement" and the court was able to direct that a decree be drawn to give effect to the agreement.

[126] *Reg. Lib. 1596(A)*, fol. 39a, 44a, 46a (to the Earl of Bath), 55a, 64a, 67a, 74a, 109b, 120b, 128a, 154a, 231b, 252a, etc.: Monro, *Acta Cancellariae*, 51, 256 (the latter being a decree of Lord Chancellor Bacon in 1618); Sanders, *Orders in Chancery*, I, 79a (decree of 1598 by which Robert Sackville, Esq. and Sir Nicholas Parker were to be "entreated eftzoones to heare and ende the same yf they soe pleased and could soe do").

[127] Vysey v. Walton, *Reg. Lib. 1596(A)*, fol. 650b (since the suit is between brothers, the court "wysheth a frendly and quyet end," so if two knights to whom the case is referred cannot end it the suit is wholly dismissed from the Chancery); Starky v. Starky, fol. 34b; Fyshe v. Fyshe, fol. 454a (referred so as to end "these unnaturall controversyes" between father and son); Monro, *Acta Cancellariae*, 721 and 722 (cases of 1598).

procedure and the ignorance and bias of juries created a general need for more efficient and more expert tribunals, a need to which both the Chancery and the Privy Council responded by organizing arbitration commissions of merchants to deal with merchants' cases.[128] But apart from the motives appearing in such specific types of case there was one general theme that constantly recurred—the desirability of settlement by consent as a means of avoiding strife and promoting peace. The recitals in a decree of 1596 are characteristic:

It was moved and thought meete by this cowrt that some indifferent gentlemen who are of understanding and dwell in the county where the controversy groweth and may thereby knowe the partyes and credytt of the wytnesses. . . .

should be asked to call the parties and bring them to a "frendly and quyett end." [129] The color provided by such adjectives as "frendly and quyett" is a significant clue to main attitudes. Often the preference for arbitration was expressed still more positively.[130] It seems that even after the firm government of the Tudors had established general order and security, the settlement of individual disputes by consent had advantages that made it worth pursuing.

At this intermediate stage of the Chancery's development there was one further reason for organizing and promoting arbitration—the lack of formulated rules as guides to decision. The Chancery in the sixteenth century had of course certain main policies that were well known—strict control over the penal bond, hostility to other kinds of forfeiture, enforcement of trusts and of promises to sell land, and so on. But main policies did not decide concrete cases—the immensely varied, tangled knots of human problems that were tossed out at random by the remorse-

---

[128] References to merchants: *Reg. Lib. 1596(A)*, fol. 76a, 95a, 150b, 163a, 224b, 239a, 245b, 250a, 485b, 538b, 648a, 818a, 893b; Monro, *Acta Cancellariae*, 427, 484, 520. Parallel action by the Privy Council is described by Dawson, "The Privy Council and Private Law," 48 *Mich. L. Rev.* 393, 408–410 (1950).

[129] Horton v. May, *Reg. Lib. 1596(A)*, fol. 278b.

[130] Elton v. Denton, *Reg. Lib. 1599(A)*, fol. 143a: "This Cowrte is desyrous that the matter should rather take end by conference and agreement betweene the partyes then bye judiciall sentence"; Pelham v. Seymour, *Reg. Lib. 1596(A)*, fol. 106a: "It seemeth that the matter hath not taken that frendly corse for an end as was moved by the nowe Lord Keeper beinge then Master of the Rolls and by Mr. Justyce Walmesley" at the last hearing, so two Masters are asked to join with Sir Robert Dormer and renew the effort to achieve a "frendly and quiet end."

less machine of the common law. They were very hard to classify and in detail they were hard to deal with. Sometimes the Chancellor was perfectly candid—after prolonged judicial hearing he might say that he found the case very "difficult" and would therefore prefer that it be ended by consent of the parties.[131] Or, in a case where a mortgagor's default had been long and quite unexcused so that it would be hard to relieve him, the Chancellor might find enough elements of "extremyty" so that he would request the parties to name "some indyfferent citizens" to whom the case could be referred. In cases like this a fair and practical solution could be just as well reached, perhaps better reached, through the persuasion of local merchants or gentry, respected neighbors, who were leaders in their communities.[132]

The pervasiveness of arbitration in Tudor and early Stuart equity was a symptom, in short, of a general condition. The remedies of the Chancery at this stage were a response to an immense and scattered range of particularized injustices produced by the common law. In manufacturing correctives the Chancellors could not find much help in Roman or canon law. The problems were English, created by an English law that had walled itself off for centuries from the developing needs and values of English society. The results produced were an outrage to common sense and no lawyers' logic was needed to prove it. The same common sense, inspired by a morality that did not need to be highly refined, could dictate practical solutions; it seems indeed, though this is not the place to present the proof, that

---

[131] An example is given above, note 125.

[132] Hopkyns v. Hoddyho, *Reg. Lib. 1591(A)*, fol. 187b and 314a. The case was one in which the plaintiff in return for £100 had mortgaged land in 1571 to secure the payment of a £16 annuity to defendant's father for life. Payments by plaintiff ceased in 1578, so that "in law" the whole right in the mortgaged land was vested in the mortgagee and passed on his death to his infant heir, the defendant. The court's order recites, however, that the mortgagee in his lifetime indicated that he would not take advantage of the plaintiff's default, that the land was "of good valewe," that plaintiff had been paid only £100 and also was liable on a bond for £200 guaranteeing payment of the annuity. The court declared that it "forbeareth to geve nowe a judiciall order" and asked the parties to name "some indyfferent citizens of London" to whom the case could be wholly referred. The second entry (fol. 314a) summarizes the report of the arbitrators, who declared it to be their opinion that it would be "very extreme" for plaintiff to lose land worth about £50 a year for nonpayment of £16 a year. The arbitrators pressed the defendant either to pay £300 to the plaintiff to buy out his interest or else to give the land back on plaintiff's payment of £200. The final result in the case does not appear.

the Chancellors themselves did not aim for much more during the Chancery's first 300 years. Whether this be true of the Chancellors or not, it should at least be evident that the device of arbitral commission brought powerful help to the Chancellors in effectuating their reforms. Common lawyers, judges, merchants, gentry—the whole network of social and political leadership in English communities—were enlisted in the effort to find specific solutions that were acceptable to the parties themselves and that conformed to the ethical standards prevailing in English society. Included among the manifold services they were called on to render was that of helping the courts of equity to restore sense and decency in private law.

Unfortunately for the subsequent reputation of the Chancery it was not abolished in 1641, along with the Star Chamber, the Court of Requests and the other subordinate courts of equity. Even before that date there were premonitions of things to come —delays and complications in Chancery procedure, the piling up of unfinished business.[133] We cannot tell from records so far published when the large-scale use of arbitration was abandoned. It was probably a gradual process, coinciding with the steady increase of the Chancery's business, the elaboration of pleadings and the growing dissatisfaction with the Chancery's modes of proof. It was not until the eighteenth and nineteenth centuries that the Chancery's "monstrous system of procedure" produced "its decaying houses and its blighted lands in every shire, its worn out lunatic in every madhouse, and its dead in every churchyard." [134]

There were many reasons for the final collapse. The main difficulty, shortly stated, was that the Chancery undertook to do too much with insufficient means. From the very beginning it had rejected the common law mode of fact finding—neighborhood juries operating under few controls through a brief, collective verdict. For this time-saving device the Chancery had its own inadequate substitute: evidence was collected, so far as

---

[133] Holdsworth, *HEL*, I, 423–424, refers to the debates in Parliament in 1623 concerning delays in the Chancery. During the debates the statement was made that 35,000 subpoenas were issued in one year, though Holdsworth considers 20,000 to be a better guess as the annual rate for this period.

[134] The phrase "monstrous system of procedure" is Holdsworth's and the rest is quoted by him from Dickens' "Bleak House." Holdsworth, *HEL*, IX, 375.

possible, by lay examiners using questions framed on the initiative of counsel. Though these methods were crude and increasingly ineffective, it should be remembered that their object was to assemble all the evidence and present it to the court, in writing but wholly unprocessed. Confronted thus with the whole case, so far as the examiners could discover it, the court must then decide disputed issues of fact, construct its own picture of each case from the raw data presented, and then go on to search out some ground for decision. For some time arbitration and mediation provided avenues of escape from this responsibility, but settlements founded essentially on consent of the parties could not deal with the expanding work load. During the seventeenth and later centuries the coverage of equitable remedies steadily expanded; isolated instances of equitable relief grew into types; "grounds" emerged as ideas previously obscure became explicit. It was not till late in the seventeenth century that the common lawyers, by then fully in charge, began self-consciously to formulate equity doctrine.[135] During the interval and indeed even after the process was well begun, the very vagueness of equity's leading ideas required all the more a close and careful appraisal of each case. The Chancery aimed more and more at refined results, though hampered by its modes of proof, distracted by the maze of pleadings, and obstructed by many roadblocks from its avaricious staff. Firmer controls over the staff and better internal administration could have prevented the worst abuses. But with the transformation of equity the need was for a considerable group of professionals to take active charge of a busy court. Instead two men, the Chancellor and the Master of the Rolls, struggled to do it all alone, with little help from an experienced group of professionals, the Masters in Chancery, whom they had never learned to put to good use.

The calamities of the Chancery in the eighteenth century can be traced to decisions made in the fifteenth. The most important decision was negative—not to recruit and employ the

---

[135] The edition of Nottingham's Chancery Cases, vol. I, published by the Selden Society in 1957 under the editorship of D. E. C. Yale, gives a fascinating internal view of Nottingham's motivations during his nine years of service in the Chancery (1673–1682). Though not a treatise, his notes on the cases reveal on every page the difficulty of expressing in general terms the accumulated traditions of the Chancery.

trained personnel that were eventually to be needed. The reluctance to employ them was deep-rooted and very English. A court that was highly centralized in form distributed to laymen all the functions it could. In this it followed the pattern of government that had been established in England centuries before. In the Chancery for two centuries, at least, the pattern worked remarkably well. If the growth of equity had been arrested or if equity doctrines had been more rapidly absorbed by the common law, this would have seemed in retrospect a successful adaptation. As the equity system expanded, the use of laymen as fact-collectors and as arbitral-judges proved harmful or at best ineffective. But the modes of action that had been organized around them were carried forward into the eighteenth century when this peculiar hybrid system, so English in its main elements, broke down of its own weight.

6. OTHER ROYAL COURTS

The Tudor expansion of the crown's governing powers brought with it and was aided by a luxuriant growth of royal courts. Most of them did not survive the Puritan Revolution. Some were highly specialized, like the "courts" that were mainly concerned with administering the royal domain and collecting royal revenue (the Court of Augmentations and the Court of Wards and Liveries) [136] and that early form of court martial, the Court of the Constable and Marshal.[137] The Court of Requests was a small-scale model of the Chancery. The Councils in Wales and in the North had both common law and equitable jurisdiction; in neither apparently did they introduce any important new elements. But there were others that had some lasting effect, either because they survived much later than 1641 or because in lives that were short they contributed in specific ways.

Of the short-lived group the most important by far was the Star Chamber, a high prerogative court of criminal law. It rendered great service to English society until it was embroiled in political and religious contests, so that for later history it

[136] Walter C. Richardson, *Tudor Chamber Administration, 1485–1547* (Baton Rouge, La., 1952), 310–374, describes these and other courts that were primarily concerned with administration but became involved in dispute-settlement incidentally.

[137] Holdsworth, *HEL,* I, 573–580.

became a symbol of tyranny. The Star Chamber had a membership mainly composed of laymen, though they were the highest laymen in the land, the king's chief ministers who sat in the Star Chamber because they were members of the king's Privy Council. But it was chaired by the Lord Chancellor and bolstered by a group of common law judges. Its procedure coincided closely with that of the Chancery—perhaps the influences at work were reciprocal. On issues of fact it relied not on juries but on testimony under oath by individual witnesses, collected as a rule by examining commissions of lay gentry. During the 150 years of its active life it contributed much to the public peace and also new and needed content to the substantive criminal law.[138] Like the Chancery it was a hybrid. Unlike the Chancery it bloomed too fast.

The Privy Council itself, not specially organized as a judicial tribunal, was also a court with an extensive jurisdiction. Much of its intervention was limited; for example, it issued many orders for the stay of proceedings pending in lower courts, arranged changes of venue, gave litigants aid in collecting evidence, and so on. But in a considerable group of cases, the Privy Council in effect displaced the established courts and itself undertook to hear and decide. Even more commonly it refrained from full-scale adjudication and remitted disputes to arbitration by arbitrators of its own choice. In such cases, however, the terms of its orders often expressed views on issues of private law; in particular the Council lent its great prestige to support the main lines of reform that the equity courts were promoting. In its wide-ranging activities in private disputes the Council was seldom assisted by legal advice from judges or the crown's law officers, though some may have come from the Chancellor who normally presided. Except for its judicial branch, meeting formally as the Court of Star Chamber, the Privy Council did not organize a judicial committee or develop a special procedure. Its work in private controversies—what can be called civil litigation—was intermingled with the multifarious actions and decisions required for general government. For the busy men who comprised the Privy Council the jurisdiction over private disputes was a distraction and nuisance of which

[138] Holdsworth, *HEL*, I, 492–516; V, 167–214.

they tried to relieve themselves. There is a question, however, whether further growth in the powers of the central government would not have brought in due course a judicial branch, formally organized and broadly competent. For the narrower purpose of deciding appeals from overseas such a branch was organized after the Puritan Revolution, was taken over gradually by professional lawyers, and survived as a special court of appeal into modern times. But with this one exception the Privy Council was abruptly excluded from judicial activities by the Parliament of 1641. Together with the Star Chamber, the Council's jurisdiction in private disputes was swept away as a prelude to revolution.[139]

The court of Admiralty proved in the end to be hardier. After the reorganization of the Admiralty under Henry VIII it was regularly staffed by civilian-trained professionals. The juries that had been used earlier in criminal cases soon fell into disuse and in any event the need disappeared when the whole jurisdiction over maritime crimes was transferred to common law judges.[140] The procedure used for the residue, civil cases including cases of prize, seems to have been quite elaborately written, and fact-finding depended, again, on examination of individual witnesses with much reliance on examining commissions.[141] How directly the procedure and court structure of the Admiralty was actually copied from canonist models we shall not know until more evidence is assembled. It may well be that the civilians gathered in this small enclave drew heavily on the systems in which they were trained, as they clearly did for much substantive law. Despite the assaults of the common lawyers the Admiralty survived as a port of entry for ideas derived from that larger world that existed across the narrow seas.

The ecclesiastical courts should also be briefly mentioned. They have been grievously neglected by historians of English law

[139] These matters are discussed by Dawson, "The Privy Council and Private Law in the Tudor and Stuart Periods," 48 *Mich. L. Rev.* 393, 627 (1950).

[140] Holdsworth, *HEL,* I, 550–551. The use of a jury of trial appears in the fifteenth century in *Select Pleas in the Court of Admiralty* (Selden Society), I, liv. A jury of presentment, however, could still report to the Admiralty nuisances and affrays that had some maritime element. I, 35 (1528–1530).

[141] This appears in numerous cases partially reproduced in the two Selden Society volumes of *Select Pleas in the Court of Admiralty,* but unfortunately the editor chose to eliminate from most of his cases the important procedural issues. A brief account of Admiralty procedure is given by John Godolphin, *A View of the Admiral Jurisdiction* (London, 2d ed., 1685), 43.

and I will now follow their example. For centuries the church courts exerted on the daily lives and opinions of English people a continuing influence, not merely at the supreme moments of birth, marriage, and death. Their structure and functions have been described in general terms, but on details that are of interest here not enough is known for useful comment.

The ecclesiastical courts present some insoluble problems of classification. The Court of High Commission, organized under the Tudors, can properly be called a royal court, for it was a servant of Tudor and Stuart policy and its membership and activities were under firm royal control.[142] The High Court of Delegates was not truly a court, but a method provided by statute in 1533 for creating *ad hoc* royal commissions, in which common lawyers and civilians were intermingled, to act as boards of appeal from the ordinary courts of the church. If not *a* court, the Delegates could be called a series of courts whose members had royal appointment.[143] But the search for labels becomes almost fruitless when one looks to the complex network of church courts that existed below this level. They had an ancient history, a moral authority which they believed to transcend the state, and a large jurisdiction long before acquired. They were not "private" and not quite "public." They must simply be called the courts of the church.[144]

The courts of the church were probably staffed with civilian-trained persons, as is commonly said. Their procedure and structure were probably derived by direct imitation of canonist models. They left for modern times a lasting legacy in the law of marriage, the administration of decedents' estates and the law of intestate succession, all heavily stamped with Roman-canonist ideas. Until someone has really studied them we can only take it for granted that the courts of the church (adding perhaps also the Admiralty) were the only courts in England that from start to finish measured up to the standards that were developing on the continent—standards that require the judge to be at least

[142] The details are given fully by Roland G. Usher, *The Rise and Fall of the High Commission* (Oxford, 1913), and summarized by Holdsworth, *HEL*, I, 605–611.

[143] Holdsworth, *HEL*, I, 605–611.

[144] The ecclesiastical courts and the scope of their jurisdiction in general are described by Holdsworth, *HEL*, I, 598–632.

somewhat trained for his task, to devote substantial time to it, and to retain full command and responsibility so long as the case is before him. Until we know more we can only surmise that the judges in church courts were protected against the impulse that worked so strongly on royal judges, to split off parts of the judicial function and distribute them widely to laymen.[145]

Among the specialized jurisdictions, it is the House of Lords, which became the highest court of all, that seems strangest to modern eyes. By medieval standards, it is true, there was nothing strange in judicial functions exercised by laymen who also engaged in legislation. The "suitors" in the House of Lords differed from the suitors in other courts chiefly through their exalted rank—they were the highest nobility in the land and were suitors to the king himself.[146] But as time went on it must have seemed anomalous—perhaps also a diversion of energies— for the House of Lords to compete directly with established courts in matters that these courts were equipped to handle. Whatever the reasons, the original jurisdiction of the House of Lords fell into disuse during the fourteenth and fifteenth centuries, to be revived under the Commonwealth but almost wholly abandoned after 1670.[147] One fragment of original jurisdiction that still survives is the "trial by peers" in its narrowest sense— the original jurisdiction to try charges of treason or felony against peers from the Lords' own membership.[148] But at the very times when the original jurisdiction was thus being largely abandoned, an appellate jurisdiction was revived and expanded. The Lords'

[145] This is certainly the impression left by the illuminating study of Brian L. Woodcock, *Medieval Ecclesiastical Courts in the Diocese of Canterbury* (London, 1952), 37–49, 50–71. Though the study is limited to the Diocese of Canterbury, it seems likely that the special position of the Diocese in relations with the Archbishop did not greatly affect the kind of personnel and procedure employed. By the fifteenth century, at any rate, the records show trained personnel, working within a quite well organized career service and using for contested cases a written procedure with court-directed examination of witnesses. The summary disposition that characterized a large percentage of both "instance" and ex officio cases would not seem to be at all inconsistent with canonist precepts.

[146] Plucknett, *Concise Hist.*, 232–234, suggests the analogy between the House of Lords in its functions as a trial court and the suitors in ancient community courts.

[147] Holdsworth, *HEL*, I, 365–368.

[148] Holdsworth, *HEL*, I, 379–390, discussing both the trial of peers for treason or felony and the similar procedures on impeachment, the last example of which in England was in 1805.

jurisdiction in common law cases through writs of error had seemingly been headed toward disuse before 1600, but was reasserted in the seventeenth century. Then after the restoration, despite much opposition, the House of Lords succeeded in establishing its power to hear appeals from the Chancery.[149] This revived jurisdiction, until the nineteenth century, was often exercised by a vote of the entire membership, lay as well as professional. The result was a spectacle that seems strange indeed —an assembly that time had transformed into the upper branch of a legislature, deciding by vote of untrained laymen issues of law of the most technical kind. On the whole their votes in appellate cases did not alter main directions for either common law or equity. The lords on most occasions accepted the advice of the professional judges who were by then fully in charge in the Chancery, as they had been for centuries in common law courts. The views of the judges were overruled only in special cases where the lords' own interests were seriously involved, though there was some fairly sordid lobbying on behalf of friends or relations. It was not until 1844 that the right to vote in appellate cases was declared to be reserved for "learned" lords. Finally in 1883 one lonely lay lord made history by raising his hand to vote in an appellate case and by being politely ignored.[150] In this brief moment he symbolized for all the time we can now foresee the triumph of professionals in royal courts. It was a triumph achieved in the common law system as early as the thirteenth century, in equity much later. The triumph was partial, a compromise which left much room for laymen in administering the system. But it was too ancient and well established to be seriously jeopardized, even by laymen of exalted rank who intruded themselves belatedly at the summit of royal justice.

[149] Holdsworth, *HEL*, I, 370–375.

[150] Holdsworth, *HEL*, I, 376–377; Thomas Beven, "The Appellate Jurisdiction of the House of Lords," 17 *L.Q.R.* 357, 365–369 (1901). The latter author gives further details as to lobbying activities, especially those of Charles II "upon the solicitation of any of the ladies in favour."

CHAPTER IV

THE ENGLISH LOCAL COURTS

1. THE COURTS OF COUNTY AND HUNDRED

W<small>ITH</small> the county and hundred courts we return to those ancient forms of community organization that reach far back of the Norman Conquest. Unlike the royal courts so far considered, they did not originate through an exercise of royal authority, though their usefulness as agencies of government and the preservation of their "public" character were primarily due to the continuing strength of the English crown.

The county courts of the thirteenth century have been fully described by Maitland.[1] As in the Carolingian system, their presiding officer was a representative of the central government—called sheriff (*viscount*) rather than count. The sheriff was at once a representative of the central government and the executive officer of the court itself, with a duty to carry out its decisions. Judgments were made by the suitors, though the presence and authority of the sheriff were indispensable—neither the sheriff nor the suitors could act without the other. Throughout most of England the county courts met once a month, with augmented assemblies twice a year. The place of meeting was usually a castle or manor house in the county town, though there are hints that some courts were still held in forest or field as in ancient times.[2] Attendance was a duty attached in most cases to the tenure of land, comparable to the duty to supply knights or fight-

---

[1] Pollock and Maitland, *HEL*, I, 532–556. Maitland's materials were reworked by William A. Morris, "The Early English County Court," *University of California Publications in History* (Berkeley, Cal., 1926), XIV, 89.

[2] *Hengham Magna*, c.4 (ed. William H. Dunham, Cambridge, Eng., 1932), cited by Pollock and Maitland, *HEL*, I, 555. In the *Casus Placitorum* (ed. William H. Dunham, Selden Society, 1952), a set of notes prepared by a lawyer shortly before 1272, there appears a case (p. 35) in which a buyer of a stolen ox, brought before a county court, suddenly spied "going along the king's highway" the man who had sold him the ox, and pointed him out to the sheriff. The editor of the volume, Professor Dunham, points out the implication that the court was "a wayside assembly held within sight of the highroad."

ing men or render other kinds of feudal service. It seems unlikely that decisions by those attending conformed to modern notions of democracy; hierarchies of wealth, status and experience were known within the county courts and produced some analogues to the Carolingian *scabini*.[3] But these gradations of prestige and influence were not magnified or formalized by any action of the crown itself. The county court spoke as a body, for the county as a whole. For its mistakes the whole county was liable. It *was* the county, personified.

During the thirteenth century, the period of their greatest usefulness, the county courts dealt with the most multifarious business—financial, military, administrative as well as judicial. The machinery of presentment by local juries that was organized by Henry II in 1166 had opened avenues for large-scale intrusion in local affairs by the crown, which used not only the sheriffs and royal justices but subordinate officials of various kinds that were chosen by or reported to the county courts. The beginning of a national system of taxation focused attention on the county courts as agencies for collection and also for mediation between the crown and taxable individuals. Common action in fiscal matters helped to reinforce the growing sense of common interest and internal cohesion, so that when the demands of the crown for revenue led to the convening of national assemblies—the Parliaments—it was natural that representatives from the counties should be chosen by the county courts.[4] This political role lasted late and gave the county courts a significant place in the building of the English constitution. As Maitland wrote in 1885: "The statute book authorizes the modern county voter to believe, if he can, that when in strictest secrecy he is dropping his voting paper into the ballot box, he is attending a county court of the old type held by the sheriff."[5]

A great range of duties was thrust on the thirteenth-century county courts, but there was clearly no intention on the part of the central government to confer large powers on assemblies that were recruited thus, somewhat at random, from local owners of land. Concurrently with the increased use of county court

[3] G. Lapsley, "Buzones," 47 *Eng. Hist. Rev.* 177, 545 (1932).
[4] Jolliffe, *Constitutional History of England* (3d ed.), 304–314.
[5] *Justice and Police*, 22–23.

machinery there was a counter movement to withdraw important classes of cases from the jurisdiction of the county courts. Criminal cases rapidly disappeared from them after 1215, when Magna Carta prohibited sheriffs from hearing pleas of the crown.[6] Actions for land lingered longer but the county courts soon became not much more than a way station at which land actions might pause on their way to the royal courts. The most important limitation on their powers was that introduced by an inverted reading of a statute of 1278, a reading that limited the ordinary jurisdiction of the county courts to cases in which the value in controversy did not exceed 40 shillings.[7] This limitation was soon generalized to cover not only the county courts but hundred courts and local courts of every description. For this reason it is important, and we must return to it later. For the present it will suffice to say that in the thirteenth century 40 shillings was a considerable sum of money; it was the later decline in the value of money that made this restriction severe.

Written records of county court proceedings were seldom kept, apparently, during most of the thirteenth century and those that were kept have mostly been lost in family archives. It is therefore impossible to give a clear picture of the judicial work of the county courts. We can only guess that it was important in the thirteenth century and diminished only gradually thereafter. Actions were begun without writ, by simple plaint, so that remedies could be awarded outside the scope of the common law forms of action.[8] Actions to collect money debts, for injury to or detention of animals, and for unaggravated trespass to land seem to have been the principal types, but it seems that informal promises could be enforced or damages given for defamation.[9] A court roll for the county of Bedford for 1332–1333 shows 74 actions pending during a seven-month period, 67 of these being started by simple plaint to the sheriff.[10] By special writ of *justicies* a

---

[6] Holdsworth, *HEL*, I, 71–72.

[7] 6 Edw. I, c. 8, discussed by Pollock and Maitland, *HEL*, I, 554.

[8] Rolls from the Office of the Sheriff of Beds. and Bucks, 1332–1334, in *Bedfordshire Historical Record Society* (ed. G. H. Fowler, London, 1929), III, 51; Sir Henry Finch, *Nomotexnia* (London, 1613), 114b.

[9] T. F. T. Plucknett, "New Light on the Old County Court," 42 *Harv. L. Rev.* 639 (1929), at 664–669.

[10] Bedford County Roll, cited note 8 above, p. 50. Of the 67 cases 38 were actions to collect money debts.

county court could be authorized to entertain cases involving values in excess of 40 shillings.[11] It was a serious disadvantage that in some counties the archaic mode of proof through wager of law could be insisted on by the defendant, but it was also possible for a common law jury to be empanelled if both parties requested it.[12]

In their later history, from the sixteenth century onward, the county courts declined steadily in importance. Their functions in general county government were usurped by the justices of the peace and other subordinate officers under the justices' control. As to the less serious crimes the justices of the peace had displaced them earlier. Their civil jurisdiction was steadily drained off either by the common law courts or by other local courts. Yet for brief times in particular places the ancient forms were revived and the county courts, still meeting regularly, rendered useful service as small claims courts. Even where this did not occur, the forms were preserved throughout England. It was only in 1846 that the suitors and other antique trappings were stripped away and modernized county courts were set up to replace them.[13]

A similar fate overtook the courts held in the hundreds. The antiquity of the hundred courts is equally clear, though their origins are doubtful and there was much rearrangement of boundaries before their geographical divisions were stabilized.

[11] Three examples appear in the Bedford County Roll for 1332–1333, no. 84, 212 and 213 (III, 58, 63, 64). In the early seventeenth century 115 gentry of Chester signed a statement that frequent grants of the writ of *justicies* had permitted the county court in Chester to dispose cheaply and efficiently of much litigation, in a manner very satisfactory to the signers. Cyrus H. Karraker, *The Seventeenth Century Sheriff* (Philadelphia, 1930), 50.

[12] Bedford County Roll, no. 270 (1933) is a case in which the defendant waged his law, but in the same series entry no. 100 is a case in which a jury of 18 was empanelled to determine whether two charters, detained by defendant, had been deposited with him by way of pledge, as defendant claimed. *Bedfordshire Historical Record Society*, III, 66 and 59.

Finch, *Nomotexnia*, p. 117a, asserted that "the suitors are the judges" but then also said that trial in county courts was by wager of law except in some where by "prescription" trial was through juries. He does not explain how the use of wager of law or jury was reconciled with the principle that the suitors were the judges. It seems likely that Sir Matthew Hale gave a more accurate picture when he said that in his own time, some county courts used juries, some used wager of law, and others used majority vote of the suitors. Matthew Hale, "Considerations Touching the Amendment or Alteration of the Laws" in Hargrave, *Law Tracts*, 253, at 283.

[13] Webb, *ELG*, I, 290–291, gives references for the period after 1689.

In Anglo-Saxon England shortly before the Conquest the hundred court, far more than the county court, was the agency of government that loomed largest to most people.[14] The size of the hundreds varied widely in different sections of England; a county might have as few as six or as many as sixty hundreds.[15] In the thirteenth century meetings were held every three weeks, though in the west country where the hundreds were larger the intervals were longer.[16] Twice a year the hundred court was visited by the sheriff and at these meetings for the sheriff's "tourn" it took on special attributes as a royal court for police and minor crime. Apart from this semiannual transformation, the hundred court in its normal functioning was a duplicate model of the county court. Its jurisdiction was extensive, covering miscellaneous matters affecting the local community—fiscal, police and judicial. The actions and decisions of the hundred court likewise bound the community. A bailiff presided instead of the sheriff; the judgments were "made" by the suitors.[17]

In one respect, however, there was an important difference. Quite unlike the county courts, the hundred courts were slowly drifting into various forms of private ownership. The process had begun in Anglo-Saxon times and by the Conquest perhaps a sixth of the hundred courts had reached private hands through royal grant or prescription. After the Conquest there were more royal grants. Miss Cam has estimated that by 1272 there were 628 hundreds altogether in England and that 358 of these (about 57 per cent) had been transferred in some degree to private ownership.[18] There were variations in degree. The owner might merely be given a right to the income from the court, to be paid to him directly or else kept by a bailiff whom the owner had appointed and who had perhaps purchased the office. Or the transfer might come close to creating a true immunity in the court-owning lord, excluding the sheriff and giving power to the

---

[14] Vinogradoff, English Society in the Eleventh Century, 97–104. Recent literature on the origins of the hundreds is summarized by S. B. Chrimes, Introduction to Holdsworth, History of English Law (7th ed.), I, 7*–9*.

[15] Pollock and Maitland, HEL, I, 556, summarizing results of the Domesday survey.

[16] Pollock and Maitland, HEL, I, 557; Helen M. Cam, The Hundred and the Hundred Rolls (London, 1930), 168–169.

[17] Pollock and Maitland, HEL, I, 556–560.

[18] Cam, The Hundred and the Hundred Rolls, 55–57, 137–139, with analysis by counties in the appendix, 260–285.

immunist to serve royal writs through his own officials. There were great variations in these arrangements, but it seems that the crown was quite content at this level of administration to share with private owners both the profits and the responsibilities of these ancient "public" courts.[19]

This shift to private ownership did not necessarily imply any change in structure or function of the hundred courts themselves. They continued to meet, the suitors continued to render the judgments, and so far as one can tell from scanty evidence the matters considered were much the same.[20] In civil matters they were subject to the same limitations as the county courts, including the 40 shilling ceiling on the values that could be sued for. In criminal matters the sheriff's tourn became the model for small criminal courts, the courts leet, that were soon scattered all over England. This meant that the hundred courts no longer possessed any special features that required their survival. Many of them simply disappeared, a few survived for centuries. Some became town governments, as in the case of Birkenhead; others kept the more modest role of local small claims court. In the late 1830's there were still 56, most of them quite inactive.[21]

The courts of both county and hundred, then, were preserved and reactivated by the central government in the twelfth and thirteenth centures but their life was gradually drained away in the centuries thereafter. The future lay with new agencies like the justices of the peace, which the crown chose from the leadership that the community courts had trained. It was nevertheless a major achievement for the Norman and Angevin kings to adapt these ancient institutions to the needs and purposes of a strong national government. As Miss Cam observed:

Without extinguishing local self-expression in the shire court they made the knights of the shire and the men of the hundred do the work of the central government, creating new traditions which were in their

[19] Cam, 126–127, 144–145.

[20] One of the few early hundred rolls published is that for Whorwelsdown in 1262, after the sheriff's rights had been purchased by the Abbess of Ramsey. *Manorial Courts* (S.S.), 177–182. *The Court Rolls of the Abbey of Ramsey* (ed. Warren O. Ault, New Haven, 1928), contain hundred rolls for the hundred of Walsoken for 1284 (147–169). This was an ordinary court, meeting on the average every three weeks and without view of frankpledge. Cam, *The Hundred and the Hundred Rolls*, 181–183, discusses the civil jurisdiction of the hundred courts generally.

[21] Holdsworth, *HEL*, I, 134; Webb, *ELG*, II, 50–63.

turn to become sacred with well-established use and wont. Not with any conscious aim of statesmanship, but to serve their own purposes, the kings preserved the vitality of these local courts, and so left the countryside an articulate voice, which was, in the course of time, to be heard in the colloquies and parliaments of his own central council.[22]

And it was not only through their large and lasting effects on political organization that these ancient courts left an imprint on English society. The patterns they developed, particularly in the hundred courts, became a type that was reproduced all over England in the courts of the manors.

Before considering the manor courts we should glance at the seignorial courts maintained by the great lordships, to see how their growth was arrested.

2. THE SEIGNORIAL COURTS

The greatly sharpened conceptions of feudal relationships that were introduced by the Norman Conquest had as their first effect the multiplication of private courts. For in England, as on the continent, it was taken for granted that each lord had a right to hold court for his vassals if he wished and to compel their attendance when duly summoned.[23] Enforcement of the duty to attend and participate was undertaken not by royal officials but by the lord and fellow vassals. The courts so assembled were agencies for consultation on all matters of common interest, but they were also empowered to decide disputes between lord and vassals and between the vassals themselves. They appeared at every level of the feudal hierarchy and rendered important services in stabilizing the new order during its first one hundred years.[24]

There were in addition some private courts whose powers extended well beyond the range of these small feudal assemblies. Some rested on express royal grants of jurisdiction by the late Anglo-Saxon kings. Such grants, which continued after the Con-

---

[22] Cam, *The Hundred and the Hundred Rolls*, 20.

[23] *Leges Henrici*, 55, 1: "Omni domino licet submonere hominem suum, ut ei sit ad rectum in curia sua. Et si residens est ad remocius manerium eiusdem manoris unde tenet, ibit ad placitum, si dominus suus submoneat eum." Felix Liebermann, *Die Gesetze der Angelsachsen* (Halle, 1903), I, 575.

[24] Jolliffe, *Constitutional History of England* (3d ed.), 165–167. Also Holdsworth, *HEL*, I, 24–26; George B. Adams, *Council and Courts in Anglo-Norman England* (New Haven, 1926), 157–158.

quest, occasionally carried immunity from royal writs and excluded royal officials.[25] As the powers of the Norman government were mobilized, this dismemberment of public authority was arrested and efforts were made to restrict by interpretation the court-keeping rights already conferred. The great *quo warranto* inquiries under Edward I, beginning in 1274, put the claimants of court-keeping rights to the strictest proof, though in the end Edward himself admitted prescription as well as royal charter as a sufficient title. It seems unlikely that Edward had any settled purpose to destroy the great franchises entirely. If frontal assault was intended, it was soon abandoned.[26]

It was through several kinds of flank attack that the seignorial jurisdictions were reduced. Some of these attacks, though indirect, were extremely bold. In retrospect it seems that the boldest came first, in the measures adopted by Henry II in 1166 and later. Disputes over title to or possession of land were swept within royal control by the writ of novel disseisin and its derivatives which gave royal protection to possession; also by the principle successfully asserted that no man need answer for his freehold without a royal writ, and by the grant of the right to a royal jury (the grand assize) in proprietary actions.[27] The rapidly lengthening list of crown pleas, over which royal courts asserted a monopoly, meant that the punishment of major crime was withdrawn from private courts that could not prove an unmistakable title. In civil remedies generally royal justice was more speedy and efficient and had the special attraction of jury trial; the ability of the private courts to use jury trial was somewhat impaired by legislation in 1259 and 1267 which forbade private court-

[25] Jolliffe, 64–71; Stenton, *Anglo-Saxon England*, 485–495. The discussions inspired by Goebel's contention that such grants carried only the profits of justice, without power to adjudicate, are summarized by Chrimes, Introduction to Holdsworth, *History of English Law* (7th ed.), I, 16*–18*.

[26] Cam, *The Hundred and the Hundred Rolls*, 233–239; T. F. T. Plucknett, *The Legislation of Edward I* (Oxford, 1949), 40–49; Helen M. Cam, "The Quo Warranto Proceeding under Edward I," *Liberties and Communities in Medieval England* (Cambridge, England, 1944), 173; G. O. Sayles, Introduction to *Select Cases in the Court of King's Bench* (Selden Society, London, 1938), II, liv–lviii.

[27] *Manorial Courts* (S.S.), liv–lvi. Plucknett, *The Legislation of Edward I*, 25–28, argues that the privilege of freemen not to answer for their freeholds without royal writ was not the product of legislation by Henry II, as Maitland suggested, but goes back to the earlier twelfth century. R. C. Van Caenegem, *Royal Writs in England from the Conquest to Glanvill* (Selden Society, London, 1959), 223–225, gives a more detailed argument to similar effect.

keepers to coerce freeholders into swearing against their will, [28] though as will be seen this restriction did not seriously hamper the manor courts. The duty of vassals to attend their lords' courts was not a matter of direct royal concern, but it was questioned by at least one royal lawyer, Bracton, and by statute in 1267 it was denied unless established by the terms of the tenant's own charter or by usage antedating 1230.[29] The 40 shilling limit on values in controversy was extended from county and hundred to private courts, apparently without contest and without express legislation.

The most telling blow of all was the elimination of successive appeals up the lines of feudal tenure. This was accomplished by legislation in 1259 and 1267 which gave a monopoly over claims of false judgment to the royal judges. There is reason to think, though the evidence is negative, that claims of false judgment had previously proceeded from vassal's court to lord's court as feudal principle required.[30] It is indeed remarkable that the change occurred during a period when baronial revolt had weakened the power of the crown. The lesser nobility may have provided the main support for the change in order to free themselves from subjection to their feudal superiors. The practical consequence of this measure was to destroy one of the principal reasons for keeping fully staffed courts in the greater lordships. As Maitland said, for a feudal magnate "a court merely for his great freehold tenants, some dozen or half-dozen knights, was hardly worth having and became less and less worth having as time went on." [31] More than this, each feudal court was now

---

[28] *Manorial Courts* (S.S.), lvii. The use of civil juries in manor courts will be discussed below.

[29] *Manorial Courts* (S.S.), xlvii–l. The important social implications of this provision are discussed by Plucknett, *The Legislation of Edward I*, 63–75.

[30] This view is contended for in the unpublished thesis of S. F. C. Milsom, *The Origins and Early History of Judicial Review in England*, chaps. I and II. He argues from the fact that Bracton's Notebook and the Curia Regis Rolls so far published contain very few examples of writs of false judgment bringing to royal judges any cases from private courts; those that do appear were mostly concerned with royal manors or the courts of greater liberties. Since the number of private courts was so large, the author concludes that before the middle of the thirteenth century complaints of false judgment must have proceeded ordinarily from the courts of inferior lords to the courts of their superiors.

[31] *Manorial Courts* (S.S.), lviii–lix.

exposed to direct review of its actions by royal judges. The levelling out of the hierarchy of feudal courts meant a major assertion of royal power. Combined with the other means adopted to weaken and contain the seignorial jurisdictions, it meant that by 1300 England had already moved a long way in a direction directly opposite from that followed in France and Germany.

It is true that some seignorial courts survived, the most important being in the west and north—Chester, Lancashire, Durham, and Yorkshire. Scattered over England there were other smaller enclaves of private jurisdiction, civil and criminal.[32] The courts of some honors and liberties survived into the nineteenth century, a few covering areas of hundreds of square miles.[33] But they were merely rarities, silent testimony to what might have been. It was at another level, chiefly in the manors, that feudal principles were combined with royal franchise to preserve the ancient modes of community decision, in ways that profoundly affected the structure of English society.

To explain how this happened it is necessary to consider first the court leet.

3. THE ORIGINS OF THE COURT LEET

The term "leet" (Latin, *leta*) originated in East Anglian dialect and probably meant no more at first than "land" or "landed property." It came into general use to describe a particular form of court in the early part of the fourteenth century.[34] The phenomenon it describes, however, is considerably older—the judicial and administrative activity of the sheriff in his semiannual "tourn" through the hundreds. The sheriff's tourn goes back at least to the time of Henry I (1100–1135) but the key element in its machinery, the jury of presentment, was not added until Henry II's Assize of Clarendon in 1166. That legislation ordered inquiries to be made through twelve of "the more lawful men" of each hundred and four of "the more lawful men" of each vill into

---

[32] Pollock and Maitland, *HEL*, I, 582–585; Warren O. Ault, *Private Jurisdiction in England* (New Haven, 1923), chap. II (discussing the honour courts of the Abbey of Ramsey); *Court Rolls of the Abbey of Ramsey* (ed. Ault, 1928), 1–104, giving the court roll of the Honour of Clare; Holdsworth, *HEL*, I, 108–132.

[33] Webb, *ELG*, II, 62–63.

[34] F. J. C. Hearnshaw, *Leet Jurisdiction in England* (Southampton, 1908), 14–16.

robberies, murders, and thefts that had recently been committed. The inquest so provided for was clearly a royal procedure, administered in the king's name by the sheriff.[35]

One of the chief duties of the sheriff on his tourn was to review and fill up the frankpledge lists. Frankpledge was an ancient system of neighborhood security, originating in Anglo-Saxon times and maintained after the Conquest throughout southern and central England. By it the men of each neighborhood were enrolled in groups, nominally comprising ten though actually the numbers varied from four to more than twenty. The members of each group of ten (tithing) were collectively responsible for the good conduct of other members and were bound to produce those accused of any offense.[36] Each tithing was represented by its "chief pledge" and as the machinery of the sheriff's tourn was organized it was natural that a duty to respond to the sheriff's questions should be cast on them. The chief pledges had a continuing responsibility for the maintenance of order and could properly be asked to disclose offenses they knew about, for which their tithing might perhaps be liable. The "view of frankpledge" thus became something more than a routine scrutiny of the frankpledge lists. The chief pledges became a source of informal presentments, competing with and often hostile to the presentment juries which had official responsibility for assembling information from all sources and laying their accusations before the sheriff.

For a time there was a real overlap and confusion of functions as between the presentment juries and the chief pledges of the frankpledge groups. The confusion lasted late in the records of many town and manorial courts, where the presentment juries were often described as "chief pledges" and the court itself was labelled, not as a leet, but as a court, "with view of frankpledge." From the fifteenth century onward this confusion was more apparent than real; the functions were merged and the procedures described were identical. Decay of the frankpledge system after 1300 had the effect of eliminating real duplication. In some communities the chief pledges, remaining active, *became* the present-

[35] Maitland, *Manorial Courts* (S.S.), xxvii–xxviii.
[36] William A. Morris, *The Frankpledge System* (N.Y., 1910), describes the system at length.

ment juries of the leet; in others they were demoted in effect to the rank of village constables and the function of presentment was fully assumed by presentment juries assembled *ad hoc* for each leet. In inquiries into the origins of the leet juries it is tempting to think that they were directly descended from the ancient folk assemblies, coming by way of the frankpledge system.[37] But Maitland argued convincingly that despite the overlap and confusion of the thirteenth century, the presentment juries of the sheriff's tourn originated in the legislation of Henry II in 1166. They were royal juries, making accusations on behalf of the crown, and were merely aided and reinforced by more ancient forms of neighborhood security.[38]

The sheriff's tourn after 1166 expanded its inquiries far beyond the three types of major crime—robbery, murder, and theft— that were listed in the Assize of Clarendon. All sorts of minor violence and antisocial conduct began to appear in the articles that were read to the juries and on which they were forced to speak. After 1215, when the sheriffs were forbidden to try pleas of the crown, persons accused of major crime were bound over for trial by common law judges, by trial commissions such as commissions for gaol delivery or, later, by justices of the peace. But in minor matters—the sale of diseased food, dishonest weights and measures, failure to maintain bridges or scour ditches, overburdening common pasture land—the sheriffs dealt summarily, taking the juries' accusations as equivalent to proof. Fining offenders in such cases brought income to the court-keeper and some satisfaction to the communities whose spokesmen had complained. In other words, the list of minor offenses was treated as expansible—expansible to some extent by the sheriffs themselves and much more by the spontaneous action of the presenting juries.

The central government had no strong incentive to cling to this class of judicial business. The crown's willingness to surrender

[37] William Stubbs, *Constitutional History of England* (Oxford, 1874), I, 618: "The leet juries of the small local courts do not draw their origin from any legal enactment and bear every mark of the utmost antiquity." Quoted by Maitland, *Manorial Courts* (S.S.), xxxvii.

[38] Maitland, *Manorial Courts* (S.S.), xxviii–xxxiv; Hearnshaw, *Leet Jurisdiction in England*, 51–73. The latter author gives the argument for a double origin of the leet juries and carries somewhat further the analysis of Maitland.

it had already been shown by the continuing transfer into private hands of the hundred courts themselves. The jurisdiction of the sheriff's tourn was merely a special, semiannual phase of a hundred court. There were many hands ready to grasp it. First of all, it was profitable through the amercements it assessed. Even more valuable than the income was the control it gave over conduct. For the owners of manors, administering their lands together with lands of their tenants as economic units, there were great advantages in having the presentments made at assemblies of their tenants. Perhaps for the tenants also there was some advantage; "they could manage their own affairs without the interference of 'foreigners.' " [39] Not only in the manors but also in the towns the police-court jurisdiction of the sheriff's tourn gave important opportunities for self-regulation through the machinery of presentment; as early as 1278 a full-scale "court-leet" in Norwich was fining local citizens for obstructing and polluting streets and ditches, selling defective merchandise, charging excessive prices, committing assaults and petty theft—all the minor misdeeds of a growing urban settlement.[40] Without resistance from the crown, usually without even the formality of a royal grant, the lords of manors and officers of the towns began, through their stewards and bailiffs, to administer the articles of the sheriff's tourn to local presentment juries.[41]

This, then, was the court leet. It was not so much a court as it was a model procedure of a "public" type that could be fused with going institutions, ancient or recent. It attached itself readily to the courts of the manors. It was equally available to the towns as their markets and manufactures expanded and urban life was organized. The geographical divisions from which the jurors were drawn did not need to follow the ancient boundaries of hundred and vill. What was needed was simply a natural grouping, whose leadership could be assumed by an important local landowner or a group of town officials. Not every manor or town had a court leet, and in the larger boroughs there were

[39] Pollock and Maitland, *HEL*, I, 581.

[40] *Leet Jurisdiction of Norwich* (Selden Society, ed. William Hudson, London, 1892).

[41] Morris, *The Frankpledge System*, 138, comments on the few instances in which efforts were made in the *quo warranto* proceedings under Edward I to recover the view of frankpledge from private lords, but they were very few.

courts with civil and criminal jurisdiction that developed from ancient charter or liberty along other lines.[42] But the court leet became a standard pattern, reproduced in its essential elements all over England in thousands of small farming and urban communities.

Thus in the late thirteenth and early fourteenth centuries the procedures organized for the sheriff's tourn were broadcast all over England. There was no strong interest that stood opposed. If anyone might have been opposed, it would have been the officers of the crown itself. But the franchise courts of the greater lordships were already under firm control. For major crime the trial of offenders was now safely reserved for the crown's own appointees. As for the rest, "it was for the good of the peace that there be as much presenting of offenders as possible"[43] and trials of minor offenses could well be summary if a sworn jury of neighbors was willing to testify. A central government that relied so much on unpaid help must have viewed this adoption of its procedure, not as a usurpation, but as a welcome addition to its own resources in matters too unimportant for courts of higher rank.

The courts leet, like the sheriff's tourn, met normally twice a year. In the theories of the lawyers—most of it developed much later—the decisions in courts leet were not made by the suitors but by the presiding officers, heirs of the sheriff.[44] The procedure still rested essentially on presentments by the leet juries. By the statute of Westminster II in 1285 a minimum jury of twelve was required, but in many communities it was difficult to assemble as many as twelve; in practice this requirement was probably enforced only as to presentments for major crime. For most of the minor offenses on which courts leet acted, the statute probably had the effect merely of making indictments traversable in a common law court if the jury comprised less than twelve.[45] After unanimity was established as a requirement for other kinds

[42] Below, section 7.
[43] Maitland, *Manorial Courts* (S.S.), xxxvi.
[44] Below, section 6a.
[45] Hearnshaw, *Leet Jurisdiction in England*, 86–87. In *Y.B. 45 Edw. III 26* (1372), a leet presentment by only four persons was held to be no defense in an action of replevin against a distraining bailiff where the plaintiff, whose property had been distrained, denied the charge asserted in the presentment (harboring a stranger who was not enrolled in the frankpledge lists).

of verdict, it was probably extended to the verdicts of leet juries, though this matter too is obscure. All one can say is that the early entries uniformly make it appear that the verdicts were unanimous.[46]

The normal sanction for a court leet's decisions was an amercement expressed in money and collectible by distraint of the offender's chattels. As to the size of amercements there were two limitations: (1) the 40 shilling limitation on the values that might be sued for was in practice assumed to apply as well to the amercements that could be assessed, though this amount was sometimes exceeded; (2) by Magna Carta, c. 20, amercements of freemen, merchants and villeins were required to be assessed through the oaths of "honest men of the neighborhood." [47] This limitation applied to courts leet generally and was usually enforced by appointing a separate group of "affeerors" who reviewed amercements for reasonableness. A broad conformity with community opinion was thus ensured, not only by the fact that action was initiated by a jury of local residents but by a post-audit of verdicts by a small group or persons who were specially chosen and specially sworn for the purpose.

4. THE ORIGINS OF THE MANOR COURTS

Numerous ingredients entered into the making of the manor courts. Most of these ingredients were not peculiar to England. Throughout France and Germany in the late Middle Ages, similar methods of land use and similar forms of social stratification brought a clustering of the rural population around local lords of the land, exercising a similar kind of "low" justice in their *seigneuries* and *Fronhöfe*. But in France and Germany the surviving superstructure of feudal jurisdictions, built on an ascending

[46] John Kitchin, *Le Court Leet et Court Baron* (London, 1587), 7, said that a verdict of 12 was needed in the court leet but that when the number of leet jurors exceeded 12, a verdict in which 12 concurred was good even though the others disagreed. (This work will be cited hereafter as Kitchin, *Court Leet*.)

An example of a jury divided 7 to 5 is mentioned below, p. 238, but this was an unusual case and involved "homage" rather than leet jury. As late as 1893 Charles Elton and H. J. H. Mackay, *Law of Copyholds* (London, 2d ed., 1893), 308, expressed uncertainty as to whether the jurors of the homage were required to be unanimous, though concluding that probably they were not.

[47] This provision of Magna Carta is discussed with background by McKechnie, *Magna Carta* (2d ed., 1914), 284–294, and is referred to again in section 6g below, especially in notes 183 and 184.

scale, distracted attention from the special forms of economic and social organization that existed at the base. In England the crumbling of the superstructure left the manors as the chief—in most places the only—surviving repository of private jurisdiction. The enormous importance that the manors came to have in the ordering of English rural life brought them eventually under the spotlight of the lawyers. But this did not occur until the sixteenth century and the spotlight used by the lawyers gave a somewhat distorted view.

The manor had only gradually acquired its central place in the organization of the farming economy. Long before the Norman Conquest there had been powerful forces pressing toward the concentration of the rural population in villages, grouped around miltary leaders who gave protection in return for maintenance and labor services. The policies of the Conqueror laid on the local military aristocracy responsibility for the feudal dues and military service extracted from their communities. This sharpened the lines of social stratification and increased the power and authority of the larger land owners.[48] This increased power and authority worked within complex patterns of land ownership and land use, usually described as the open field system, whose origins were ancient and which appeared in essentially the same forms through most of northern Europe. By the thirteenth century probably two thirds of the land of England was regulated by it. The open field system involved a division of the arable land into long, narrow strips of about a half acre each, whose ownership was distributed among the different householders of each rural settlement. To till these strips it was necessary for the various owners to cooperate not only in the use of their plowing animals but in the timing of sowing and harvesting and in the rotation of crops. Pasture for animals was ensured not only by common land permanently reserved for pasture but by periodic reversion of arable land to pasture, to be grazed over and fertilized by the animals of the entire settlement. These arrangements, which have been so

[48] Sir Paul Vinogradoff, *The Growth of the Manor* (London, 1911), is devoted throughout to an account of origins, the discussion on pages 332–365 being concerned more directly with the effects of the Conquest on social stratification. These issues have of course been much discussed by others. For the Anglo-Saxon period Stenton, *Anglo-Saxon England,* 463–474, is extremely valuable.

often and so fully described, required a high degree of cooperation and collective decisions in every phase of husbandry.[49]

Sir Paul Vinogradoff argued that the joint use of arable lands,
pasture, woods and waste through the changing seasons required
a large degree of community control, and social institutions
through which control could be exerted. Though evidence for
the pre-Conquest period is extremely scanty, he pointed to early
examples of village officials appointed to oversee the use of
pasture lands, to impound trespassing cattle and otherwise to
protect the interests of the farming communities. Reeves chosen
at village meetings not only had responsibility for reporting and
maintaining local customs but represented their villages before
higher authorities. He claimed, in short, that there was a rudi-
mentary local government in Anglo-Saxon times, existing independently of incipient feudal relationships connected with
land tenure.[50] Some indirect support for his argument may be
found in the "archaic communities" described by Maitland and
surviving as late as the seventeenth century—villages that lay
outside any manor or that were contained within several different
manors. In these communities, which had decisions to make that
no one manorial court could validate, land was assigned for till-
age to different farmers by rotation, regulations governing land
use and the maintenance of gates and bridges were made by
chosen representatives, and these representatives had power to
impose penalties on individuals for infractions of their rules.[51]

[49] Vinogradoff, *Growth of the Manor*, 165–185. It would be impossible to summarize here the voluminous literature on the subject. A convenient and interesting
account is that of Charles S. Orwin, *The Open Fields* (Oxford, 1938), which de-
votes considerable space to the history and functioning of the village of Laxton,
where the open field system was in full scale use at the time of publication in
1938. Particularly useful is his estimate (pp. 59–66) of the extent to which open
field methods were actually practiced in England, the estimate in the text (two
thirds of English farmland in the thirteenth century) being taken from this passage.

[50] Vinogradoff, *Growth of the Manor*, 185–196.

[51] Frederick W. Maitland, "The Survival of Archaic Communities," *Collected
Papers*, II, 313. At the end of his argument, however, Maitland in this essay returned to the contention that a large degree of "communalism" was not required
by the open field system and that the customary course of argiculture could in
general be maintained by common law rules of trespass. In Pollock and Maitland,
HEL, I, 617–620, there is further discussion of the problems arising in villages
that lay outside any manor or were included within several manors. In this passage Maitland made the concession that "cultivation of the common fields implies
a system of agriculture which must in some degree be communal." The issue in

That there was need for such arrangements is suggested by the late survival in France of village assemblies exercising similar powers though detached from any "court." [52]

The evidence of Vinogradoff for large-scale community regulation comes mainly from manorial records of the fourteenth century, when manorial courts throughout England had already been molded into a well-known stereotype. These manorial records have many examples of "by-laws" or "ordinances" promulgated by common consent of the assembled tenants, regulating the use of common fields and pasture, defining the rights of tenants to cut wood or other fuel, fixing the dates for the seasonal transition from one type of land use to another. As he conceded, these regulations were usually quite general in character and did not deal with all the minute details on which daily decisions were needed.[53] Furthermore, the evidence from manorial records comes from a much later time and provides at most some argumentative support.[54]

Maitland, in his account of origins, had set himself firmly against the idea that English institutions in the thirteenth century preserved any large elements of "communalism." He sought to minimize the degree of community regulation or cooperation that was necessary in administering the open field system and asserted that "once it had been started" it maintained itself by the force of custom, reinforced by the common law of trespass. Rights of common, at least in the freeholders, he explained as individual rights—"individualism *in excelsis*"—which were to be fully equated with the right to the freehold itself. He questioned the power of manorial courts to bind freeholders by their ordinances or "by-laws." It was only among the non-free, villein tenants that he was willing to recognize the elements of true community, but he asserted that whatever measures they took to protect the interests of the group as a whole were subject to

---

his mind seems to have been whether this rural communalism left a deposit in permanent institutions or in the rules of the common law itself.

[52] Above, p. 90.

[53] *Growth of the Manor*, 196, suggesting that the hundred courts could not "look after the endless and minute incidents of agrarian practice" and (in the footnote) that "this is the solution of the difficulty suggested by Professor Maitland."

[54] *Growth of the Manor*, 268–270.

the overriding power of the manorial lord, who delegated to them a share of his power but who remained, as to his rightless villeins, a "constitutional king." [55] He explained the manorial court itself, when it emerged to our view in the thirteenth century, as an expression merely of the feudal principle that the lord may hold court for his vassals.[56] On this analysis the manorial court was merely an extension of the feudalism that was organized in England by the Norman conquerors, with no important deposit from Anglo-Saxon times.

For present purposes, fortunately, it is not necessary to take sides in this contest or to decide whether the manorial courts of the thirteenth and later centuries were direct descendants of Anglo-Saxon village communities. What is perfectly clear is that their internal organization followed the patterns that had been long before established both in the "public" courts of county and hundred and in the feudal courts of lords and vassals. The suitors were the judges. The stewards who presided on behalf of the manorial lords possessed the executive power, but in rendering judgments it was the suitors who spoke. The methods of voting are most obscure, as in other courts of this type in early times. Divisions of opinion were seldom reported; if any source was mentioned it was the whole court that purported to speak.[57] For a medieval court so organized, the possession of a mixture of powers, including the power to legislate, called for no special explanation. This was a common feature. The county courts, for example, could lay down "provisions" that would control within the particular county or in their judgments in particular cases could lay down general rules.[58] It is therefore quite conceivable

[55] Pollock and Maitland, *HEL,* I, 620–633; Frederick W. Maitland, *Township and Borough* (Cambridge, Eng., 1898), 25.

[56] *Manorial Courts* (S.S.), xxxviii–xliii. It should be pointed out, however, that Maitland's argument here was addressed to the question whether a "feudal" principle was to be preferred to the notion that possession of a manor itself gave jurisdiction, this notion being approved by common lawyers at a later stage when the composite powers of manorial courts had been fully recognized.

[57] *Manorial Courts* (S.S.), lxv–lxix; Henry S. Bennett, *Life on the English Manor* (Cambridge, Eng., 1937), 207–209.

[58] Plucknett, "New Light on the Old County Court," 42 *Harvard L. Rev.* 639, 652–657, referring especially to the prohibition of subinfeudation by the Chester county court 25 years before the statute Quia Emptores. The full text of this "provision" is quoted by Plucknett, *The Legislation of Edward I,* 108.

Goebel, *Felony and Misdemeanor,* 229–233, gives other instances of what

that the thirteenth century saw nothing more than a transfer to the manors of organizational forms that both public and feudal courts had made completely familiar. For present purposes it is more important that, located now in the manors, the ancient forms survived.

On the question of origins, however, it is significant that there is scarcely a trace at any time of a division between freeholders and villeins within the manorial courts. In defining landholders' rights under the common law this distinction was to be crucial for centuries to come. By the early thirteenth century the freehold tenant had already been given access to the whole battery of remedies by which common law courts protected interests in land and goods, not only in contests with other claimants but in contests with his own manorial lord. Since the villein was rightless by the common law and held "at the will of the lord," any protection he might have in the thirteenth century must come from the court of the manor. The distinction between freeholder and villein was therefore vital to individual status and security, but on the internal structure and functioning of the manorial courts its influence was slight. As Maitland conceded, freeholders and villeins were mingled indistinguishably in the whole body of suitors. No different personnel or procedure was employed for cases in which freeholders or villeins were personally involved.[59] The same was true for the semiannual transformations in which manorial courts became courts leet, purporting to act through a jury of presentment; villeins were free to serve on the juries without distinction of status.[60] At a somewhat later stage when

---

amounted to legislation as early as the tenth century, especially in laying down new standards in the law of wrongs.

[59] *Manorial Courts* (S.S.), lxix–lxxiii. Scattered cases have been found, it is true, in which distinctions of status were insisted upon. George C. Homans, *The English Villager in the Thirteenth Century* (Cambridge, Mass., 1941), 239–240 refers to two cases in 1297 in the manor of Alsowen. In one there was a special jury composed entirely of freeholders who declared that one William, another freeholder, was not bound to contribute to amercements laid on some villein jurors for false presentments and for concealment. The other case involved the same William, who was distrained to take oath as a juror and who claimed that he was not bound to serve in that or any other office to which he was elected by villeins. On this issue William put himself "on the judgment of his peers." When the villeins who had proposed him were asked whether they would insist that William serve, they replied that "those who are of better condition" were all away serving the king. Decision of the issue was postponed to the next court.

[60] *The Court Baron* (Selden Society, London, 1891), 110. Some rare exceptions

"by-laws" and "ordinances" were regularly recorded, it seems quite clear in principle that they were equally binding on all inhabitants of the district, though freeholders might have greater powers of resistance to any encroachment on their ownership or any increase in their services and dues.[61] In the later theories of the common lawyers, distinctions of status were emphasized by a requirement of at least two freeholders to constitute a manorial court, but there were thirteenth-century manors in which no freeholders appear [62] and this supposed requirement seems nothing more than an artificial product of lawyers' logic, exercised much later in retrospect. Despite the differences in status, wealth and influence that no doubt existed among their membership, when they met for the transaction of common business they acted as a group. This degree of solidarity would strongly suggest that if manorial courts were merely a form of consultation between feudal lords and their vassals, the forms thus provided became a channel for forces already powerful, in small peasant communities whose land and people were intermingled on the open fields.

5. SOME THIRTEENTH CENTURY MANOR COURTS

The earliest record so far published of an English manor court dates from 1237. Toward the end of the thirteenth century such records became fairly numerous, in the fourteenth century abundant. Their styles were not uniform, for the forms of procedure were not standardized at first and the clerks employed by the lords to compile them found different matters to be worth recording. In substance, however, they give very similar accounts of the kinds of business transacted.

A considerable number of the entries are concerned with ordinary civil litigation between residents of the neighborhood. Actions were brought to collect money debts, for trespass to land,

---

can be found. For example, in the *Court Rolls of the Manor of Ingoldmells* (Lincolnshire, ed. W. O. Massingberd, London, 1902), the rolls, which start in 1291, do not distinguish between free and bond tenants until the reign of Richard II; but during that reign and later presentments were often made separately by juries of freemen and juries of bondmen. (Introduction, xvi and entries on pages 180, 185, 190, 194, 204, etc.)

[61] Vinogradoff, *Growth of the Manor*, 187–188; Holdsworth, *HEL*, II, 313–314.
[62] Pollock and Maitland, *HEL*, I, 600–601. An attempted justification of the common lawyers' positions appears in Holdsworth, *HEL*, I, 179–184.

for destruction of or injury to animals and crops, for personal assault and defamation (all subject in general to the 40 shilling limit). Since actions were begun informally, by oral statement of claim, remedies were awarded without regard to the limitations of the common law writ system. Informal contracts were freely enforced and damages given for defamation some centuries in advance of the common law.[63] In a case in 1270 a manorial court of the Abbey of Ramsey enforced payment of a legacy in an action against executors.[64] There were numerous disputes between villein tenants as to rights to occupy villein land which the lord (in common law theory the owner) had assigned to occupancy by his tenants.[65] The atmosphere in which civil litigation in general was conducted is well suggested by a case of 1247, which is interesting as an example of early and somewhat crude specific performance of contract and also for the rare feature that dissenting suitors were mentioned (and indeed were punished for their dissent):

The whole vill of Norton and also that of Newham with the exception of William the reeve, Alexander the son of Emma, and Stephen Boveton say that it was agreed between William Thomas and Walter the son of Robert under the ashtree in the court of St. Albans that the same William would give his daughter to Walter together with that fourth furlong of land that was in dispute between them in order that Walter marry her and also so that the same Walter would remain in the custody of the same William and serve and obey him and provide for his needs. And they say that the same William took him and they kissed and it was agreed that Walter would remain with him until his daughter reached the age when she might marry. And afterward the same William drove away the said Walter and failed to carry out his agreement (*deficiebat ei in conventione*). And of this the same Walter complains. The cellarer [steward of the Abbot] by the judgment of the hall-moot placed the same Walter in seisin of the aforesaid fourth furlong of land together with the aforesaid daughter of the same William. William the reeve, Alexander the son of Emma, and Stephen the son of John are in mercy (12 pence each) because they contradicted the whole vill in its verdict.[66]

[63] Maitland in *The Court Baron* (Selden Society), 115–118; Plucknett, *Concise Hist.*, 98–99, both relying on evidence of the early fourteenth century.
[64] *Court Rolls of the Abbey of Ramsey* (ed. Ault), 260.
[65] Examples are cited below, note 68.
[66] Court Rolls of St. Albans Abbey, published by Ada E. Levett, *Studies in Manorial History* (Oxford, 1938), 329–330.

Meeting often (supposedly every three weeks, like the hundred courts) the manorial courts by 1300 were clearly providing an immensely useful forum for the settlement of private disputes of every type, using a procedure of the utmost simplicity.[67]

It is worth noting that though the archaic wager of law appears as the mode of proof in many of the earliest records, it soon became the practice for disputes as to possession or "prior right" to villein land to be settled by the verdicts of trial juries, after sale by the lord to one or the other of the adverse claimants of this special privilege.[68] As time went on specially empanelled trial juries were employed for other purposes also, where information was needed to supplement the suitors' own knowledge.[69] Looking

[67] The general observations in the above paragraph are based primarily on the thirteenth century records published by Maitland in *Manorial Courts* (S.S.), 6–47; Ault, *Court Rolls of the Abbey of Ramsey*, 173 ff.; Levett, *Studies in Manorial History*, 300–337; *Court Rolls of the Manor of Wakefield* (ed. William P. Baildon and John Lister, Yorkshire Archaeological Society, vols. 36 and 57, 1906 and 1916); *Manor Rolls of the Convent of Durham* (ed. W. N. Landor, vol. 82, Surtees Society, 1889); *Alrewas Court Rolls*, 1259–1261, 1268–1269, and 1272–1273 (Staffordshire Historical Collections, X (n.s.) 258–293, and 1910 volume, 93–137, London, 1907 and 1910); *Court Roll of Chalgrave Manor*, 1278–1313 (Bedfordshire Historical Record Society, vol. 28, Streatley, 1948); *Court Rolls of the Manor of Ingoldmells* (ed. Massingberd, 1902).

[68] In the records of the manors of the Abbey of Bec, which start with entries of 1246, there are eight references between 1247 and 1249 to special juries of trial (usually 12) authorized to render verdicts in disputes over rights of occupancy or in some cases over boundaries (*Manorial Courts* (S.S.), 9, 13, 14, 15, 17, 18, 20, 21). Similarly in the year 1275 there were four (pp. 22, 24, 25, 26) and in 1290–1291 there were three (pp. 39, 40, 41).

In the records of the St. Albans manors, from which selections have been published by Miss Levett, the entries begin in 1237. The device first referred to in disputes over interests in land is a payment by one of the litigants to the lord for the privilege of having "the judgment of the hall-moot" (*considerationem halimoti*) and there are five such entries between 1241 and 1249 (Levett, *Studies in Manorial History*, 302, 303, 307, 310, 313, 326). Presumably the same thing was meant by grant of the privilege to have "the verdict of the vill" (Levett, 307, 308, 313, 323, 325, 326, 327, 332). But concurrently with these there were requests made and granted for juries, usually of 12 but in one case of 24 (304, 306, 307, 321, 325, 326, 327, 331, all being entries between 1243 and 1250); and in another case what looks like a jury of attaint, composed of 24, was secured to reverse a verdict already rendered by a jury of 12 (p. 325).

It was also possible for the steward himself, as presiding officer, to direct an inquest on his own initiative, without request of an adverse claimant, where he suspected an occupant to be in without right (Levett, 316).

In manorial records of the late thirteenth and fourteenth centuries juries of trial, especially in disputes over interests in land, become so common that listing of instances seems fruitless.

[69] Action to enforce a "contract" (Levett, 317—*anno* 1244); personal assault (*Manorial Courts* (S.S.), 36—*anno* 1290); action for rent (*Manorial Courts* (S.S.), 38—*anno* 1290); action to collect a legacy (*Court Rolls of the Abbey of*

forward to the probable effects that the use of the royal jury
would have, Maitland surmised from thirteenth and fourteenth
century evidence that in the course of time the use of the jury
might reduce the role of the suitors to that of mere fact-finders
and correspondingly elevate the steward into judge of "the law." [70]
There seems to be no early evidence in support of this suggestion,[71] and, as we shall see, in later times the role of the suitors
was fully maintained. The introduction of a trial jury in civil
cases, in this limited way, merely added a new and more efficient
resource and increased the usefulness of the manorial courts in
small-claims litigation. As in the case of the court leet presentment
jury, the model provided by the central government served to
strengthen, not to weaken, local machinery.

Apart from the settlement of private disputes the early manorial
courts took on another main task, which in the records was not
sharply distinguished—the enforcement of services due to the
lord and protection generally for his interests. This included the
imposition of money fines on tenants who trespassed on the land
of the lord, who ploughed it badly, who stole his wood or corn or
animals, who failed to appear to help in harvesting his crop or
washing his sheep, who ground their corn at a mill owned by
another, or who married a female villein without the lord's consent. Insofar as discipline of the labor force was involved, it can
be assumed that the commands and penalties were addressed to
villeins. The same assumption can be made as to other kinds of
drastic control over personal affairs such as the order given in
1294 to Sarah Bishop, a young widow, who was directed to find
herself a new husband before the next court met.[72] But the lord's
interests required protection against encroachments by freeholders also, and so far as the records reveal the duty to report all kinds
of encroachment was laid on the suitors as a group. From the point

Ramsey, 260—anno 1270); assault and defamation (Court Rolls of Wakefield,
I, 5—anno 1274); wrongful detention of goods (Court Rolls of Wakefield, 18—
anno 1274); actions for damages for trespass (Court Rolls of Wakefield, 32, 37,
60—all in 1275).

[70] Manorial Courts (S.S.), lxvii–lxxiii.

[71] Ault, Private Jurisdiction in England, 165–172 discusses this issue in connection with evidence from the manor courts of the Abbey of Ramsey and concludes
adversely to Maitland's suggestion.

[72] The unfortunate Sarah's case is mentioned in the Court Rolls of the Abbey
of Ramsey (ed. Ault), 211.

of view of the court-keeping lords this function of the manorial courts must have given a strong incentive to strengthen and encourage them. Not only did the court-keeper derive money income from amercements but he could secure the support of the local residents in defending his rights and maintaining the accustomed course of cultivation.[73]

For the manorial courts, as has been suggested, it was an easy transition from commands or penalties addressed to particular individuals to the announcement of general rules. If the decision of a particular problem could be expressed as a result of established custom, the assembled tenants who made up the court did not hesitate to declare what the custom was.[74] But some of the rules were new legislation. Sometimes they have almost the appearance of a multilateral contract of the tenants between themselves, but more often the language used shows a conscious assumption of legislative power—"it is ordered" or "provided" by an "ordinance" or "statute." [75] Without challenge from crown or

[73] The kind of activity described in this paragraph is sufficiently illustrated by the records of the Abbey of Bec, published in *Manorial Courts* (S.S.), 6–47, all dating from the thirteenth century. Even in records that are so far published there are hundreds of such entries. It might perhaps be noticed that in most cases the action seems to be in the form of verdict by presentment jury, though at times the court itself is not formally constituted as a court leet (as in the "domanial courts without view" quoted by Ault, *Court Rolls of the Abbey of Ramsey*, 239–280).

[74] *Manorial Courts* (S.S.), 24–25 (*anno* 1275): "The full court declares that in case any woman shall have altogether quitted the lord's domain and shall marry a free man, she may return and recover whatever right and claim she has in any land; but if she shall be joined to a serf, then she cannot do this during the serf's lifetime, but after his death she may."

Manorial Courts (S.S.) 29 (*anno* 1281): "It is presented by unanimous verdict of the whole court" that if any woman who has a right in land by the custom of the manor marries, and then surrenders the land to the lord who re-grants it to her new husband, the heirs of the woman are barred and the land goes to the new husband and his heirs. "Therefore let William Wood, whose case this is, hold his land in the manner aforesaid." (William paid 6 shillings 8 pence for this inquest).

Manorial Courts (S.S.), 44 (*anno* 1296), where a widow, claiming as dower the right to occupy all the land owned by her deceased husband during their marriage, paid the lord sixpence for a verdict of the court, which replied that such was the custom, so that the widow remained in possession as against the claim of her husband's brother.

Levett, *Studies in Manorial History*, 313 (*anno* 1250): "Walter King offered the lord 12 pence for an inquest by the hall-moot as to whether a serf can bequeath his chattels to someone other than his heir or not."

[75] Leet of Walsoken (*anno* 1295): "The jurors say that [six named persons] sell fish outside the vill. Therefore they are in mercy and it is provided by common consent that none of the aforesaid fishermen and no other fisherman whatever shall in future sell any fish outside the vill without first bringing the fish to the church for sale if anyone in the parish wishes to buy it and whoever in future is

lords' officials, the gatherings brought together in these small communities assumed (or perhaps reasserted) a power to regulate their own affairs, by legislation which they themselves enforced.

Regulation of conduct was carried much further in another way, without prior announcement of rules, through the court leet machinery of presenting jury. There is no discernible limit to the types of conduct that could be made the subject of a presentment. Very often this method was used to report infringements of the rights of the lord or failure to render services due him. It was also used to punish conduct injurious to individual inhabitants and for which they themselves might perhaps have sued—trespass to land, personal assault, theft or wrongful detention of goods, even breach of contract. But the injuries could be more general, to the farming settlement as a whole—obstructing pathways, stopping up water courses or drainage ditches, overburdening pasture lands with excessive numbers of grazing animals. John Wardeboys, serving as cattle warden in 1307, no doubt deserved to be fined for losing cattle of the lord *in fornicando cum pluribus mulieribus*.[76] One John Hale in 1294 was similarly fined when a verdict established that "he was accustomed to beat his wife at night because of which she raised the hue and cry to the terror of the neighbors." [77] As one reads over the many hundreds of entries in the records so far published, it seems that amercements could be ordered for any conduct injurious to the economic interests of the farming communities as a whole, for any acts that were

convicted of this shall be amerced a half mark." *Court Rolls of the Abbey of Ramsey* (ed. Ault), 179.

Manorial Court of Broughton (*anno* 1310): "Because it appears that in a court of the Lord Abbot [held in 1291] . . . all the customary tenants submitted and obligated themselves under penalty of sixpence to be paid to the lord that no one of them would enter on the pasture of another to cut grass" and they all now confess that they have done so "contrary to the aforesaid ordinance and statute," each one of 78 tenants is ordered to pay sixpence. *Court Rolls of the Abbey of Ramsey*, 254, a further entry in the same matter appearing on p. 259.

In the Alrewas Court Rolls (*Staffordshire Historical Collections*, 1910, 103) there is an entry for the year 1272 by which *concessum est in plena curia* that Aldersal moor should not be used by horses and cattle that their owners had sold and later courts proceeded to enforce this regulation against several offenders.

Numerous other thirteenth-century examples are described by W. O. Ault, "Some Early Village By-Laws," 45 *Eng. Hist. Rev.* 208 (1930). By-laws and ordinances of the fourteenth century are referred to by Vinogradoff, *Growth of the Manor*, 270–275.

[76] *Court Rolls of the Abbey of Ramsey*, 243 (*anno* 1307).
[77] *Court Rolls of the Abbey of Ramsey*, 223 (*anno* 1294).

likely to disturb peace and order or were offensive to widely held moral convictions. The top of the list of offenses was firmly closed, in the sense that the king's officials dealt with the trial of major crimes. At the bottom the list was open and there was no one who wished to close it. The money proceeds went to the lord. Who should object if the community wished to use public condemnation and money fines to protect and to purge itself?

Even in the thirteenth century there was one more function whose dimensions were to grow far more in the future. This was the function of protecting the interests of copyhold tenants in the land assigned to them. The issues here are much too large to be dealt with fully, for they involve the whole meaning of servile status and the protection accorded the laboring class against oppression by their lords. For present purposes it is perhaps enough to quote from Sir Paul Vinogradoff:

The very root of villainage lay in the impossibility for owners and lords to work their dependents at their will and pleasure. Feudal law could lay as much stress as possible on the idea that everything a villain acquired is acquired for his lord, and that there is nothing to prevent any extractions whatsoever on the part of a lord: villains were in the ordinary course of things peacefully possessed of their lands, moveables and money, and the exactions of the lord assumed a fixed customary character in amount and in kind. . . . Whatever violence and oppression may have existed in single cases, the daily life of the peasantry followed a steady and orderly course. . . . The medium between the privileged and seemingly autocratic position of the military class and the claims of the working class to a tolerable existence is found for a time in the reign of custom, which appropriates a good deal of the labourers' work for the benefit of the master, but still leaves a sufficient margin for their exertions in their own behalf. Villains are not admitted to prosecute in the king's courts, but their standing in the manorial courts is anything but an abject and rightless one: a body of customary law is evolved in all these local tribunals which keeps in close touch with the development of the common law, and paves the way towards the ultimate recognition of the binding character of customs.[78]

The recording of transactions between lord and villein was only gradually developed. But even the earliest manorial rolls suggest

[78] Vinogradoff, *Growth of the Manor,* 348–349. Particular instances of disputes between lords and tenants in manorial courts of the thirteenth and early fourteenth centuries, in which the interests of tenants were defended, are described by Homans, *English Villagers in the Thirteenth Century,* 319–323, with similar conclusions.

the part that manorial courts already played in the structuring of English village life. When the records begin they open a door for us into the past—at least a recent if not distant past. For the village assemblies they describe were no sudden inventions. They were held with some regularity under a well-understood procedure that was similar in them all. The meetings were public and dealt with a great range of local business. Even without a record kept by the lord, decisions in such assemblies were apt to carry weight and be remembered, for memories then were long. After records began, the decisions recorded must have had powerful effects in defining usage more sharply and providing fixed points around which new rules might grow. This would be true even of transactions between lord and villein that had the outward form of special bargain, such as the payment of 5 shillings by one Ralph Strode in 1237 "that he remain without a wife for the space of a year," [79] or the promise of John Wallrich in 1271 to give his lord two chickens a year "during the time he remained away from the land of the lord." [80] Many of the transactions fixing rights in land also had at first the outward form of special bargain—both where the object was an initial grant to an occupant and where the lord exacted a price for permitting a transfer of a tenant's interest, on the tenant's death or by grant in his lifetime. But such transactions occurred in a "court" and therefore before a good many observers, even though their shelter was merely an ash-tree. Where a transfer was necessary because of a tenant's death a court composed of neighbors would know well and could testify what heir should be admitted. Where a tenant wished to convey his interest, by way of gift or sale, both the lord and the neighbors would have some interest in the terms of the transfer and the identity of the transferee. In the earliest records there is evidence of a practice of "surrendering" the tenant's interest to the lord before the court, followed by re-grant to the designated transferee.[81] But "surrenders" made before such assemblies of neighbors, on terms

[79] Levett, *Studies in Manorial History*, 302.
[80] *Court Rolls of the Abbey of Ramsey*, 263.
[81] Numerous examples, commencing with the earliest entries in 1237, appear in Levett, *Studies in Manorial History*, 300 ff. Also Alrewas Court Rolls (*Staff. Hist. Coll.* X, n.s.), 258–293, give examples for the period 1259–1261. Later instances, in 1289–1296, appear in *Manorial Courts* (S.S.), 32, 34, 40, 46; and numerous cases from 1278–1313 in the Court Roll of Chalgrave Manor (*Bedfordshire Historical Record Society*).

proposed by the tenants, could soon become a familiar and approved type of alienation, subject to rules that took form through reiteration and became just as binding as the customs which fixed duties between the tenants themselves. The suitors would quickly learn these rules and know them at least as well as the steward or others of the lord's officials. The suitors would also know quite well what defaults on the part of a tenant would ordinarily justify the lord in cancelling his grant to the tenant and it would not be long before "the court" would be calmly telling the lord that he might now treat certain land as escheated and was therefore free to grant it to whomever he wished.[82]

Some of the earliest entries we have show the manorial court performing functions that were later to be organized nation-wide into the institution of copyhold tenure. The development of copyhold tenure—tenure "by copy of court roll"—was only one phase of a social revolution, the emancipation of the villein class accompanied by the commutation of labor services into money rents. Many forces worked for centuries to produce this vast transformation of English society. Copyhold tenure itself was the product of many minds and "slow-growing wisdom," [83] insistent demands and stubborn refusals, conflicts and settlements which were more and more fully recorded in thousands of manors scattered all over England. It was not till much later (perhaps in the fifteenth but certainly by the sixteenth century) that the Chancery intervened to give protection to the copyhold tenant against his lord. It was not till the late sixteenth century that the common law courts followed the Chancery's example and began to award legal remedies.[84] Through all this long time, protection of the

---

[82] Levett, 335 (*anno* 1280).

[83] The phrase is that of Karl N. Llewellyn, *The Bramble Bush* (New York, 1951), 38: ". . . as fine a deposit of slow-growing wisdom as ever has been laid down through the centuries by the unthinking social sea." The difficulty in applying these phrases, far out of their context, to the phenomenon of copyhold comes from the adjective "unthinking." There is the same difficulty with Professor Plucknett's description of the growth of copyhold as a "social revolution, which in England was effected without an insurrection, without legislation and almost without deliberate thought." Introduction to *Y.B. 13 Rich. II* (Ames Foundation, vol. VII, Cambridge, Mass., 1929), xliii. The absence of deliberate thought was on the side of royal government, statisticians and social philosophers; but the vast number of small people who shared these experiences must have deliberated much.

[84] Holdsworth, *HEL*, III, 206–213; VII, 296–308; Plucknett, cited in the previous note, xxxv–xliv, gives an illuminating glimpse of the whole problem from the perspective of the late fourteenth century.

villeins who were becoming copyholders was left to local manorial courts, "owned" by the lords, presided over by their stewards,
but controlled by the farming tenants who voted and decided
collectively, as they had in the thirteenth century.

There was nothing peculiar to England in having matters of
such moment decided by rules of local custom in strictly local
courts. The problems of England were presented in what seemed
a sharper contrast because England had so early a national common law, enforced by judges of the central government and giving so much protection to a substantial segment of the population,
the freehold tenants of land. Neither France nor Germany had a
national common law in this sense until modern times; almost
all their law was custom—custom augmented and organized
through help from Roman law. Neither France nor Germany
therefore had reason to distinguish so sweepingly between free
and servile tenants. But both France and Germany had servile
classes, whose status was likewise rising through the late Middle
Ages, though in Germany the rise was arrested. Both France and
Germany also had community courts, some of which were located
in manors, were presided over by lords' officials, but acted by vote
of the suitors. It seems extremely probable that grants and transfers of farming land were for a time reported and recorded at
meetings of these manorial courts, just as they were in England.[85]

The real peculiarity of England was that English manorial
courts at the critical time—in the thirteenth century—were left
with an immense amount of important and useful work to do,
under procedures that unlearned men could well understand.
They were not meddled with and bewildered by the central
government or by great feudal lords. We need not decide whether
the English manorial courts, as they move on past 1300, were a
remodeled form of Anglo-Saxon village community, or a downward extension of Norman feudalism, or a spontaneous growth
through institutional forms that took shape in the thirteenth century—probably all three of these were combined. The main point
is that once they had been organized, the manorial courts were
left alone. They were equipped with juries, borrowed from the
royal courts; they were stripped of any functions that might
threaten the supremacy of the central government or might prej-

[85] Von Maurer, *Geschichte der Fronhöfe*, IV, 143.

udice its interests; they were surrendered to private owners, the lords of the manors, with whom the local farmers must make peace by their own means. And then, in substance, they were left alone.

For most of the people then living in England what went on within the manors was what mattered most. From the Domesday survey in 1086 for something like 500 years, nine tenths of the English population were engaged in farming or depended directly on farming for their livelihood. Most of these were gathered in small settlements, containing after the Black Death perhaps 50 to 200 inhabitants. The total English population grew steadily from its low point of about two million around 1400. But the growth of the towns was at no faster rate than the growth of the farming population, and may have been somewhat slower. Until the middle of the sixteenth century, at least, the ratio was still roughly nine to one.[86] Most of the active farmers, whether living in villages or in isolated cottages, were probably subject in some degree to manorial jurisdiction. In the north and west of England it seems that manorial organization was primitive or, in places, non-existent. But by the fourteenth century through most of the heavily populated areas of England the manors had become much more than centers of administration for the farming economy. They were jurisdictional units, possessing a wide range of powers. They were also organized communities, largely self-contained and already experienced in self-government. Their success or failure could greatly affect the main course of English society.

6. A SUFFOLK MANOR IN THE SIXTEENTH AND EARLY SEVENTEENTH CENTURIES

In trying to discover the stage that the manorial courts had reached by the sixteenth and seventeenth centuries, one soon discovers the main problem to be an oversupply of information. Excerpts from many court rolls of this period have already been published. Manuscript records, both in public and private collections, survive by the wagon load. The only remedy seems to

[86] These estimates are taken from J. C. Russell, *British Medieval Population*, 54 (Domesday survey), 304–305 (the estimate of urban population as 10 per cent in 1377), 305–306 (the similar estimate for 1545), 269 (estimate of 2,100,000 as the total population of England in 1400), 309 (size of rural settlements, the estimates here being based on a very small sample).

be to concentrate on a single manor, and I have fallen on Redgrave, a manor of the eastern midlands forty miles northeast of Cambridge.

The court rolls of Redgrave, for the period up to 1711, are now located at the University of Chicago. They form part of the large collection known as the Bacon papers, for Redgrave was purchased from the crown by Sir Nicholas Bacon, Elizabeth's first Lord Keeper (1558–1579) and the father of Sir Francis Bacon. Redgrave had previously been owned for centuries by the Abbot of Bury St. Edmunds and had been acquired by the crown on the dissolution of the monasteries under Henry VIII. In 1703 it passed with other Bacon manors to the ownership of Lord Chief Justice Holt, and it has remained in the ownership of his descendants until the present time. Since the rolls have not yet been published it will not be useful to give detailed citations, but they have the great advantage of being well-kept and complete. Unlike many of the manorial records so far published, which mainly emphasize the court leet phase, the Bacon rolls give all the entries that relate to copyhold transfers and private litigation. The court rolls of Redgrave begin in 1260 and continue with a few gaps till at least 1711.[87] In all essential respects Redgrave and its rolls seem typical of what would be found in thousands of manors all over England in the sixteenth and seventeenth centuries.

The court rolls for Redgrave alone are so voluminous that I have undertaken only a sampling—the first ten years of Edward IV (1461–1470), the first ten years of Elizabeth (1558–1567), the first ten years of James I (1603–1612), and the last seven years (1705–1711) of the series preserved in Chicago. I have examined other portions of the Redgrave series on particular questions and the published records of other manors have been checked in order to be sure that the Redgrave samples are representative. Chief emphasis will be placed in the discussion that follows on Redgrave manor in the first ten years of Elizabeth and the first ten years of James I, though other periods and other manors will be mentioned incidentally.

[87] I have not discovered the whereabouts of the Redgrave rolls for the period from 1711 to 1836. They are presumably in a local museum. By the kindness of John Holt Wilson, Esq., the present lord of Redgrave Manor, I have been permitted to examine the records of the "court baron," covering copyhold transactions only, which continue from 1836 until the 1920's.

a. *Court Baron and Court Leet*

The scribes who compiled the Redgrave records were evidently conscious of a distinction between the "court baron" and court leet. The order of entries, in particular, showed a rough kind of classification. The entries regularly start with a list of absent suitors, giving a record of excuses accepted (essoins) and amercements imposed on those who failed to attend. They then give lists of lawsuits between the tenants, followed by quite elaborate records of transfers of copyhold land. The next series is regularly introduced by the heading "Now as to the leet" (*Nunc de leta*). Under this heading are recorded the actions appropriate for a small manorial police court, using juries of presentment. The distinction between court baron and leet is further emphasized by the terms describing the membership. In the "court baron" phase the jurors are usually described as "the homage" (*homagium*). In the court leet phase the presentments are made by "jurors" (*jurati*). Where homage and jurors were separately listed (often they were combined), the transformation into a small royal court was often marked by a marginal note which labelled the *jurati* as "the twelve for the lord king" (*xii pro domino rege*). This latter phrase was not peculiar to Redgrave, but common in other courts leet.[88]

In the legal theory of the sixteenth century the distinction between court baron and court leet had come to seem crucial. According to this theory the court baron had nothing to do with regalities but was a private court, held as a matter of common right. As Coke was to say, "court barons are incident unto every manor so that every Lord of a Manor may keep a Court Baron." [89] The suitors were the judges and the lord's steward merely presided.[90] The court leet, on the other hand, was a royal franchise

[88] *Extracts from the Court Rolls of the Manor of Wimbledon* (Wimbledon Common Committee, London, 1866), and *Court Rolls of the Manor of Preston* (Sussex Record Society, vol. 27, 1921), give numerous examples. The same phrase appears in the *Modus Tenendi Cur' Baron'* of 1510 (published by the Manorial Society, London, 1915), 19.

[89] *Complete Copyholder* (London, 1641), sec. 31 (p. 61 in 1641 ed.).

[90] Coke, first part of the *Institutes of the Laws of England* (London, 1817), 58a and *Complete Copyholder*, sec. 31; Kitchin, *Court Leet*, 41b; Jentleman's Case, 6 *Coke Rep.* 11a (1583); Rowleston v. Alman, *Croke Eliz.* 748 (1600); Pill v. Towers, *Croke Eliz.* 791 (1600); Readings on the Statute of Merton, *Readings*

which could be exercised only by those manor courts that had acquired the power by royal grant or prescription. It was technically a court of record whose judgments were reviewable by common law courts through writ of error or certiorari. In legal doctrine, often repeated, the steward who presided was sole judge in the leet.[91]

Coke gave wide circulation to another refinement. He asserted that the court baron itself was "of two natures," one a court of freeholders in which the suitors were judges and the other a court of copyholders in which the lord or his steward was judge.[92] Despite its repetition by legal writers, it seems quite clear that this distinction was ignored in practice and in the court rolls of Redgrave no trace of it has been found. Indeed, in many parts of England any attempt to enforce it would have encountered great difficulties. By the reign of Elizabeth the personal disabilities of servile tenure had been so nearly eliminated that it was possible and perfectly respectable for a knight or gentleman to purchase copyhold land and many copyholders owned freehold land.[93] But the essential unity of the manorial population, meeting in manorial courts, did not depend merely on the practical difficulties of enforcing segregation. As has been suggested, it had its roots in the distant past, in the ancient methods of open field cultivation that still prevailed through most of England—it was rooted, one might say, in the land itself. The effort of the lawyers was to ra-

---

and Moots at the Inns of Court in the Fifteenth Century (ed. S. E. Thorne for the Selden Society, London, 1954), cxii–cxiii.

In Armyn v. Appletoft, *Croke Jac.* 582 (1621), the plaintiff sued in debt to collect a 10 shilling amercement laid on the defendant in what plaintiff alleged to be a court baron held "before his steward," the privilege of holding such a court being alleged to arise by prescription. The court held the declaration to be bad, not because a "court before his steward" could not arise by prescription but because a court baron must be *coram sectatoribus.*

[91] Coke, *Complete Copyholder,* sec. 31; Kitchin, *Court Leet,* 41b; Jentleman's Case, 6 *Coke Rep.* 11a (1583); *Viner's Abridgement,* VI, 586 ff.

[92] Coke, *First Institute,* 58a; Melwych v. Luter, 4 *Coke Rep.* 26a. It had already been suggested by Kitchin in his first edition which appeared in 1585, that in a court baron composed only of copyholders the steward must be the judge because of the "base condition" of copyholders. Kitchin, *Court Leet* (1585 ed.), 59.

[93] R. H. Tawney, *The Agrarian Problem in the Sixteenth Century,* 55–56; Mildred Campbell, *The English Yeoman under Elizabeth and the Early Stuarts* (New Haven, 1942), 118–119. In the published court rolls one can find numerous entries like that for 1584 in the *Court Rolls of Great Cressingham,* Norfolk (ed. Henry W. Chandler, London, 1885, p. 103) where the homage reported that William Methwold, "gentleman," was a copyholder who owed suit of court.

tionalize and explain these ancient institutions, without any real attempt to impose on them the forms deduced by legal analysis. To impose these forms effectively would have required control and intervention by the central government, whose whole policy still was to abstain.

There was a channel, however, through which legal doctrine could reach manorial officials. Practical handbooks or guides for court-keepers had begun to appear as early as the thirteenth century. At first they were fairly empty of common law doctrine and aimed at not much more than description of local practices.[94] The demand for such literature must have been large, for the guides were widely circulated in manuscript. The printed series of court-keeping guides began with an edition of 1510, entitled *The Manner of Holding a Court Baron With View of Frank-pledge*.[95] It ran through several editions. In the late sixteenth and early seventeenth centuries more elaborate treatises began to appear, Coke's own *Complete Copyholder* being published in 1630 shortly before his death.[96] Despite the numerous references to Yearbook learning that some of them included, the guides still aimed for the most part at very practical instruction. They gave the stewards, as presiding officers, extensive lists of the subjects into which they might inquire, quoting appropriate language for their charges to homage and jury. They also suggested, with numerous examples, the proper form of court roll entries for all the miscellaneous business that might come before a manorial court. Being drawn up in a uniform style and largely copied from each other, the sample entries in the court-keeping guides clearly had great influence in standardizing the work of the scribes who prepared the court rolls and must also have helped to standardize court procedure.

Undoubtedly one effect of this enormously popular literature was to stress for stewards and scribes the distinction between the court baron and court leet. Especially was this true in a neg-

---

[94] Three such guides were published by Maitland in *The Court Baron* (Selden Society), the earliest being surmised by him (p. 7) to date from about 1268.

[95] Reprinted in 1915 by the Manorial Society of London. A later edition of the same treatise, issued in 1650, has also been published by the Manorial Society.

[96] The literature of this and later periods is described by Hearnshaw, *Leet Jurisdiction in England*, 30–42, and Webb, *ELG*, II, 10–11.

ative sense. A manorial court that was not a court leet found the range of its work restricted. This appears, for example, in Redgrave manor. As was true also in other neighborhoods, the principal court of Redgrave met in conjunction with the courts of other manors that were owned by the same lord. There were two sub-manors connected with Redgrave, Botisdale and Gislingham. Of these Botisdale possessed a court leet while Gislingham did not. The entries for Gislingham do not refer to presentment juries and are almost entirely restricted to copyhold transactions and breaches of the duties owned by the tenants to the lord.

This kind of limitation, generalized over England, must have had real importance. It is difficult to say how much importance, since the total number of manor courts, with or without courts leet, is quite unknown. No nation-wide census of manors was undertaken after the Domesday survey itself. It is certain only that the total number of manors was very large. A clue is given by Warwickshire, which apparently had in the sixteenth century a total of about 400 manors.[97] One cannot simply multiply this figure by 52, the number of English and Welsh counties, and thus raise the total beyond 20,000. In some of the less populous counties in the north and west the number of manors per county must have been far fewer. In Warwickshire itself it is clear that the land area and the number of persons included in some holdings that were described as "manors" were quite small. If they had no leet and no copyhold land their courts may have disappeared quite early. It is therefore quite impossible to give more than a guess as to how many manor courts survived in England as late as the sixteenth century and, of those that did, how many were also courts leet. All one can say is that most of the farm land of England was assumed to be in some kind of manor and that the court "with leet" was a standard type, the type described

---

[97] A total of 403 appears in the *Victoria History of the Counties of England: Warwickshire* (London, 1945–1951), vols. III–VI. These volumes provide a detailed survey of the settlements, roads, buildings and principal land holdings of the county. The "manors" are separately analyzed and followed through the changes of ownership and place names from earliest records, often into the nineteenth and twentieth centuries. I have tabulated only those manors described as entities recognized in the sixteenth century. Many of this group lasted much later, of course. The survey of Warwickshire gives little direct evidence as to how many of the manors described had courts of one or another type.

by most of the court-keeping guides. There must have been several thousand.

For those manors that had the leet franchise, the assimilation of courts baron and leet was promoted by the reduction in the frequency of manorial assemblies. The great economic changes of the fourteenth and fifteenth centuries, marked especially by the transmutation of labor services into money rents, had reduced very greatly the need for internal economic regulation. Regular meetings every three weeks, which were the normal expectation in the thirteenth century, were a burden for tenants and indeed for manorial officials also. Since the enforcement of attendance at the lord's own court was a matter between lord and tenants, royal officials were not concerned. The only requirement imposed by law was that leets should assemble twice a year and this was not strictly enforced. So in many places by the sixteenth century meetings of the "court baron" for strictly manorial business tended to coincide with meetings of the court leet. This transition had already occurred in Redgrave manor by 1461, and by the time of Elizabeth the meetings of the leet itself were normally held but once a year, in September or October. There remained in other places some exceptional manor courts that met every three weeks, as late as the seventeenth century.[98] But much the more common pattern was that of Redgrave, where the "court baron" could meet in special sessions but most of the time met once a year as "the general court with leet." In fact if not in legal theory the two had largely coalesced.

The connection between the two phases went far beyond simple co-existence or coincidence in time. The business dealt with in these annual assemblies covered the whole range of matters that troubled the manorial community. The verdicts of leet presentment juries mingled indiscriminately various failures of duty by copyhold tenants (as in not repairing their dwellings), injuries to the community (as in overburdening pasture land or obstructing common pathways), personal assaults, and various other kinds of misconduct such as haunting taverns or harboring strangers. In reproducing this medley the court rolls followed the

[98] Hugh A. W. Leconfield, *Petworth Manor in the Seventeenth Century* (London, 1954), 3, describes a Sussex manor whose court met in the seventeenth century every three weeks "with commendable but not absolute regularity," a general or "capital" court being held once a year in the neighborhood of Michaelmas.

models provided in the published court keepers' guides.[99] There was no real reason to draw sharp lines between the types of accusations that the jurors of the leet brought against their neighbors. The only distinction the scribes tried to draw was between private lawsuits and copyhold business, which were dealt with by the "homage," and everything else, which was dealt with by the leet jury—"the twelve for the king."

And so the question arises whether this distinction—relating both to procedure and substance—marked a real division in membership, splitting the court in two.

b. *The Redgrave Juries*

The Redgrave court rolls do not disclose the names of all who attended. They merely list the names of those assigned to the two kinds of jury—the homage and the leet presentment jury. Otherwise only absentees are noted, some being excused and others amerced. It is therefore quite impossible to state precisely the total in attendance at the annual meetings or to determine whether they all sat through all stages of the proceedings.

It can be assumed that in most manors the duty to attend the "court baron" was a normal feature of copyhold tenure. But it could also be a service due from particular holdings of freehold land.[100] As to attendance by freeholders, the widest variations must have existed in different manors, since the duty of freeholders would normally result from usages stabilized in the distant

[99] As in the *Modus Tenendi Cur' Baron'* published in 1510 and Kitchin, *Court Leet,* 8b–13b. Kitchin's sample charge to the jury starts with major crimes, then goes on to injuries to the lord's rights and then miscellaneous injuries to communal interests mixed in with personal affrays, scolders and brawlers, eavesdroppers, keepers of bawdy houses, vagabonds "who walk by night and sleep by day," false weights and measures, etc.

[100] The distinction between "suit service" owed to courts baron and "suit real" owed to courts leet by virtue of residence is drawn in the reading quoted in *Readings and Moots in the Inns of Court in the Fifteenth Century* (Selden Society), cxii–cxiii. The learning on the subject is developed at length in *Y.B. 12 Henry VII,* 15. "Suit service," an incident of tenure, must be the explanation of amercements for nonattendance that appear so commonly as to persons who were evidently freeholders, such as the amercements in 1560 at Tey Magna (another Bacon manor) of the Earl of Oxford, Sir William Woodhowse, and William Walgrave, "gentleman." The court book of Lymington, a port town near Southampton, is preserved in manuscript at the University of Chicago. It shows the jurors regularly amercing for nonattendance the Earl of Southampton, the Warden of the College of Winton, several knights and other gentlemen, *"liberi sectatores et liberi tenentes huius manerii."*

past but not immutable, for particular individuals might purchase special exemptions.[101]

As to the court leet, however, legal theory laid down a rule that was more clear-cut: the duty to attend the court leet was supposed to fall on all residents of the locality, by virtue of their residence. Women, earls, barons, and higher clergy were exempted by statute; every other resident between the ages of twelve and sixty was supposedly bound to attend.[102] But since enforcement rested with the lord of the leet, there is no way of telling the extent of compliance without knowing how complete a census of residents was maintained by each court leet. At least it seems that this framework of theory gave a mixed court like Redgrave a large cross section of eligible persons from which leet jurors might be chosen.

In the light of the lawyers' attempt to distinguish courts leet and baron, it is interesting that from time to time at Redgrave the "homage" and leet jury were fused into a single composite body. This was especially true from 1558 to 1567. Throughout this period the individuals in the membership changed from year to year, but in a general court that was held in the early fall a single mixed body was used for all purposes; when dealing with transfers of copyhold they were called the "homage" and for most other entries they were called "jurors" or "chief pledges," but the persons were the same. Their numbers varied from 12 to 19, with an average of 15.[103] In the period 1603–1612 a similar

---

[101] For example, the Redgrave roll of Oct. 11, 1609 has an entry to the effect that "Thomas Buckenham, gentleman" and John Buckenham will pay fourpence a year "for relief from suit of court." Such entries are fairly frequent.

[102] Hearnshaw, *Leet Jurisdiction in England*, 84–85; Reading on the Statute of Merton in *Readings and Moots at the Inns of Court in the Fifteenth Century* (Selden Society), I, cxii–cxiii. In *Y.B. 6 & 7 Ed. II* (S.S.), 112 (1313), the question was raised whether the lord of a manor could discharge a tenant of the duty to attend court leet. Inge, J. was inclined to think he could not since "leet is ordained for the maintenance of law and the peace." But it was decided that, since the lord's release of the duty to attend had been by deed in the particular case, he could not act contrary to his own grant so that the lord's distraint for failure to attend was ineffective. I have found no later discussion of this question.

[103] These figures are for Redgrave itself. The somewhat smaller manor of Botisdale had fewer persons listed but showed the same intermixture of homage and leet. At two special sessions convened at Redgrave in April 1562 and March 1568 for the transaction of copyhold business only, there was no intermixture of juries; the jury was described only as the "homage."

Composite juries appear in other manors. *Court Rolls of Great Cressingham*, 53 (*anno* 1489), 67 (*anno* 1490), 85 (*anno* 1584); and in the sixteenth century

phenomenon appeared, but irregularly—only in five of the fourteen meetings. On the five occasions when composite bodies were
used their numbers were large—from 16 to 24 members. Of the
nine other meetings a few were special sessions called to record
strictly copyhold business. In the others, which dealt both with
copyhold transfers and the general business of the leet, the "homage" and "chief pledges" were separately listed with no overlap of
membership. These shifts in practice occurred irregularly through
the succeeding years and nothing in the subjects discussed will
serve to explain them. One can only conclude that the alternate
use of composite and separate bodies reflected no more than the
convenience of the moment.[104]

In looking more closely at who these men were, one finds
certain veterans reappearing frequently. In the period 1558–1567,
for example, there were 33 persons listed on eleven juries. Of
these 3 appear on all eleven juries, 2 on ten, 2 on nine, and 2 on
eight; but the remaining 24 persons are very much scattered and
more than half of the total of 33 appear only five times or less.
A similar picture emerges after 1603, though with a considerably wider scattering. For the meetings between 1603 and 1610
there were fifteen juries, some combined and some separated. On
these one person served eleven times, 2 served ten, one served
nine and 3 served eight, but of the total of 65 jurors 16 served but
twice and 20 once.[105] And it seems impossible to find any pattern

---

entries in the *Court Rolls of the Manor of Wimbledon* (published by the Wimbledon Common Committee, 1866).

[104] The years in which a single composite jury was used were 1603, 1605, 1606,
1609, and 1611. For Botisdale in the same years composite bodies were used,
though with somewhat smaller numbers.

The practice at Redgrave showed variations in other periods than the two decades here chiefly considered. Under Henry VIII the use of combined juries was
frequent, but in the later years of Elizabeth (the 1580's and 1590's) the lists
of homage and leet jurors were carefully kept separate. For none of these changes
in practice is there any explanation stated in the rolls themselves.

[105] The attendance lists for Botisdale, both in 1558–1567 and 1603–1610 give a
similar picture. Gislingham, whose jurors are throughout described only as the
"homage," shows in the period 1603–1610 that on eight juries there were 2 who
served 7 times, 1 who served 6 times, and 3 who served 5 times, but of the total
of 16 appearing on the homage lists 10 served 4 times or fewer.

A tabulation for Redgrave in 1461–1470 shows a somewhat greater regularity of
service by relatively few, but I hesitate to conclude from this small sample that
the intervening 150 years had brought a wider distribution of jury service.

I have also made similar tabulations for another Bacon manor, Hindercley,
during 1558–1567 and 1603–1612 and derived almost the same results, though

dividing those who were "homagers" from those who were called to serve in the leet. A few names can be found that appear only on the lists for the leet, either in separate or composite bodies. But in the lists that distinguish between leet jury and homage, almost all of those who served several times will have moved in successive meetings from one list to the other. There may have been grounds for choice that do not appear in the lists themselves, but in the absence of other evidence it seems that jury service at Redgrave was distributed widely among a large group of "law-worthy" men, without any clear distinction between different types of juries.

Whether or not all the jurors of Redgrave were freely trans-ferable from one group to another, the attendance figures them-selves suggest a major change that centuries had brought. The court of the manor in the non-leet phase no longer purported to comprise the whole manorial population owing suit of court. The "homage" was now a selected group, specially sworn—another form of jury. The principle of collective decision was still pre-served, but the group that decided was very much smaller than the total group of eligibles and probably smaller (though this cannot be proved) than the number actually attending.[106]

It seems that this transformation of the manorial court into another form of manorial jury was not peculiar to Redgrave and

---

with a somewhat greater distribution of jury service over a large group in the period 1603–1612.

[106] Since there was no attempt to list attendances other than those empanelled on the juries, it is impossible, as has been said, to estimate total attendance. The only clue comes from the relatively small number of absentees. At the opening of the court the jurors were required to report the names of "tenants and suitors" who were absent. In the two periods chiefly considered, the highest number of ab-sentees was 18 (on Oct. 22, 1603). Usually the number was in the range of 3 to 6. In view of the much larger numbers of persons whose names appeared from time to time on the jury lists, it seems likely, though wholly unprovable, that per-sons were present who were not empanelled.

Manorial records from other manors that have been published so far are equally inconclusive on this question. However, the Harvard Law Library has a manu-script copy of the court book of Sir Thomas Smith for the Manor of Ashford in Kent during the period 1581–1600. This series is unusual in providing lists of the persons attending as well as those absent and those serving in the homage. The numbers attending were regularly much larger than the numbers listed in the homage, often more than twice as large. For example, on Oct. 12, 1581, there were 36 in attendance and 13 in the homage; on April 7, 1586, there were 24 in at-tendance and 12 in the homage; on Sept. 30, 1586, there were 38 in attendance and 16 in the homage. Of course, the practices in Ashford, Kent, do not prove much about Redgrave, Suffolk.

that it was probably completed in many English manors well before 1500. Court rolls of the fourteenth and fifteenth centuries reveal an increasing resort to special juries, convened by the stewards, to secure information on matters concerning the interests of the lord, such as failures of copyholders to repair their buildings or render customary services and attempted alienations of copyhold land on which no fines had been paid. The title commonly used to describe such juries was "inquest of the steward ex officio" (*inquisitio ex officio seneschalli*). They were in effect presentment juries, required to disclose under oath any conduct or neglect that might prejudice the rights of the lord. At times it appeared that the work of the "steward's jury" was done in the presence of a larger group of homagers, but often it carried on throughout the session as the only group referred to.[107] The phrase was used at Redgrave as early as 1391 and became a standard description of the Redgrave homage in sixteenth-century entries. In other manors also there is evidence that the inquest ex officio was identified with the homage and became in effect the manor court.[108]

The "homage" of the sixteenth-century manors thus had a close resemblance to the leet presentment jury. Both were sworn in by the steward; both spent much (not all) of their courtroom time making accusations against their neighbors; the size of both was limited, so that selection by some means was needed. The same question arises for both, therefore—whom did they represent?

This question is given added interest by the traces found in

[107] In the *Court Rolls of Great Cressingham*, Norfolk, for example, entries for 1328 (p. 21) show the *inquisitio* reporting the death of a copyhold tenant without any known heir and at the same meeting "the whole homage" proceeds to elect a reeve. But in the rolls of the same court for 1490 (p. 65), the "jury presents" that copyhold has been sold to a transferee who has not done fealty and then proceeds to deal with the usual conveyances of copyholds. In the Oxfordshire manors whose rolls are partially reproduced by Nathaniel J. Hone, *The Manor and Manorial Records* (London, 1912), 168–202, there are numerous fifteenth-century examples of the homage (identified often as quite separate from the "frankpledges" of the leet) making presentments on matters affecting the lord's interests and going on to deal with other "court baron" business. Similarly in the *Court Rolls of Wimbledon* (Wimbledon Common Committee), where the "homage" is usually called the "*inquisitio ex officio*."

[108] *Modus Tenendi Cur' Baron'* (1510), 12–19 (edition of Manorial Record Society); *Court Rolls of Wimbledon* (cited previous note). In the manors of Crowland Abbey the jury *ex officio* is first mentioned in 1391 and the phrase became common at Crowland thereafter. Frances M. Page, *The Estates of Crowland Abbey* (Cambridge, Eng., 1934), 36, 413ff.

other manors, in earlier times, of a "manorial bureaucracy," assuming leadership in their local communities and exerting influence through membership in the juries.[109] This was of course quite possible, for the manorial juries, like the *scabini* and other "law-finders" of the continent, could reflect the social structure of the communities that employed them—oligarchy, wide diffusion of power and responsibility, or anything in between. By the sixteenth century there had developed within the English manors an active land and small loan market; superior energy and ability had enabled many farmers, among them many copyholders, to become relatively wealthy by purchases from their neighbors. In place of the rough equality in holdings that characterized the medieval farm settlements, new patterns of inequality were being manufactured by the advance of small-holders' capitalism.[110] The question is whether these inequalities were reflected in the juries and affected the work of the manor courts.

A crude measure of wealth at Redgrave was the series of by-laws issued by the court, fixing the number of "great beasts" that particular individuals were allowed to pasture on the common. At the Redgrave court held October 19, 1603, for example, a by-law named 25 persons who had the right to pasture "great beasts," in numbers ranging between five and eight beasts per person. All other "ancient tenants" (not named) were entitled to pasture four, and all "new tenants" two. If these 25 persons can be taken as being the larger capitalists of Redgrave, we can then examine the jury lists to see how closely the lists coincided. The results are inconclusive. Of the 25 persons with special pasturing privileges, three were hardly perennials on the jury lists for 1603–1610, serving either ten or eleven times on various juries. But three of the 25 (not counting the Widow Bugge, who was disqualified by sex) did not appear at all, and five only once or twice. Conversely, of the 65 jurors in this period (both homage and leet) a large majority are not named as having special "great beast" privileges. The same picture emerges for the satellite manor of Botisdale, whose

[109] Bennett, *Life on the English Manor*, 212, giving a summary of thirteenth-century jury lists that reveal regularity of service by relatively few. Homans, *The English Villager in the Thirteenth Century*, 312, speaks of "an aristocracy of jurymen" in some villages, though he found "no general uniformity . . . in the composition of manorial juries."

[110] Tawney, *Agrarian Problem*, 57–97.

"great beast" lists were even more detailed and comprehensive; some of the larger owners served quite regularly on juries but many did not serve at all and at any particular meeting the juries were predominantly made up of persons not named in the privileged group.[111]

It would be interesting to pursue this question with other data as to wealth and status which could be extracted from manorial extents. But at least a tentative conclusion seems justified—that some of the substantial citizens of the neighborhood were active on juries but that on the whole jury service was widely distributed under no discernible plan. The method by which the choices were made is not disclosed and remains for the present a mystery. The steward, presiding, must have played some part. How far he consulted the suitors in the manor hall might have been left for his own decision. I have found no trace, on the other hand, of anything like election by the suitors themselves. All one can say is that in net result, with frequent changes from year to year, the jury lists seem to provide a broad cross-section of the manorial population, not merely its upper crust.

Partial answers have already been given to the question first raised—whether the Redgrave court, responding to lawyers' pressure, divided itself in two or three. Certainly not three, for no trace was found at Redgrave of Coke's distinction between freehold and copyhold tenants. As to homage and leet jury there was a distinction in the names of the juries and an attempt was made to distinguish types of business appropriate for each; but from time to time, irregularly, personnel of the homage and leet jury were completely fused. Even when the leet jury was separately listed, it acted throughout as guardian for the interests of the whole community, reserving for the homage—which had now become another small jury—those matters that directly concerned the relations of lord and copyhold tenants or involved civil litigation between the tenants themselves. Redgrave surely gives some

---

[111] The tabulations I have made for Botisdale are based on the "great beast" by-laws issued by the Botisdale court on Oct. 19, 1603 and Sept. 19, 1558. In 1603 there were 45 persons in Botisdale manor entitled to graze from 2 to 5 animals apiece. Of these 17 did not serve as jurors at all from 1603 through 1610, 13 served 4 times or less, and 5 were regulars serving 8 or 9 times. In 1558 there were 26 persons on the pasturing lists. Omitting 4 women as disqualified, one finds 12 of the remaining 22 who were called for no jury service at all, 6 who served 4 times or less, and 5 who served as often as 8 or 9 times.

support for the general thesis urged by Hearnshaw, that on English manors there was "a single undifferentiated court" performing different functions; "whatever differences there may have been as to times of meeting, order of procedure or constitutions, they were not differences of essence, nor yet differences of form radical enough to split up the one court into several." [112]

c. *The Lord and His Steward*

If the right to the money profits of a court were proof of private ownership, the Redgrave court like other manor courts was clearly owned by its lord. The account books of Sir Nicholas Bacon (both Lord Keeper Bacon under Elizabeth and his son of the same name under James) record the fines and amercements of the Bacon manors as current income. In the court-rolls themselves the amercements for nonattendance by suitors, for violation of by-laws and other miscellaneous offenses are described in innumerable entries as payable to the lord, and it was the lord or steward who remitted them whenever they were remitted. Even more plainly the fines assessed on admission of copyhold tenants to their holdings were a tax on transfers, paid to the lord. It was the latter form of revenue that bulked much the largest. This was partly because the amercements were often very small—threepence was a common figure. Amercements were not only small but very numerous and their collection must have been a burdensome nuisance. The sanction for their collection was distraint of goods, other powers of coercion (especially by arrest) having been lost in the limbo of time to the extent they ever existed.[113]

---

[112] Hearnshaw, *Leet Jurisdiction in England*, 77. The same conclusions had been reached by Maitland as to thirteenth century manor courts: "The court which had been enforcing the customs of the manor did not become some other court when it turned to punish breaches of the peace or to adjudicate upon actions of debt between the tenants; a lawyer might analyze its powers, might insist that some were royal franchises while others were not, but all its powers, whatever they might be, were used in the mass and apparently with little thought as to the various titles by which they had been acquired." *Manorial Courts* (S.S.), xviii.

Webb, *ELG*, II, 64–89, describes for the period after 1689 the variety of forms among manor courts, some with composite juries, and the various means for differentiating between the classes of business handled. But basically still, in the opinion of the Webbs, the manor court was an "undifferentiated court."

[113] As to the power to arrest, there are numerous examples of arrests ordered, presumably of villein tenants, in manorial courts of the thirteenth and fourteenth centuries. Among many others: Levett, *Studies in Manorial History*, 334 (*anno* 1280); *Court Rolls of the Abbey of Ramsey* (ed. Ault), 262 (*anno* 1271); *Manor Rolls of the Convent of Durham* (Surtees Soc., vol. 82), 20, 36 (*anno* 1358 and

But some of the amercements were certainly collected and the revenues of a manorial court, added together, represented sums that were worth the attention of prudent managers.[114]

The control and direction of court proceedings had long before been surrendered to a steward named by the lord. There seems to have been no rule of the common law that required this delegation and it may be that in some individual manors the lords still claimed the right to preside. But the use of a steward as presiding officer had become common practice as early as the thirteenth century and certainly was by the sixteenth. The steward's decisions might perhaps be reversed through an informal appeal to the lord, but there is not much evidence that this recourse was used.[115]

In the courts of France and Germany that were held under private authority, judges and court staffs were mainly paid by the fees and fines of litigants. The incentive this gave to judges, clerks and process-servers to multiply their exactions was a major source of complaint and did much to debase the quality and performance of court personnel.[116] For popular confidence in English manorial courts it was important, therefore, that a statute passed in 1604 forbade profit-sharing arrangements. The statute recited that the profits of manorial courts had so greatly increased in recent times that stewards had secured grants from their lords of the profits from courts leet and courts baron, and this in turn had led to excessive amercements of litigants. The statute forbade stewards from taking any of the profits from such courts, on pain of £40 fine and disability to serve as steward in any court.[117]

---

anno 1365); *Court Rolls of Great Cressingham,* 27. It was Coke who was chiefly responsible for the view that manorial courts had no power of arrest and could only distrain, and his view became standard doctrine. Webb, *ELG,* II, 24. I have found no traces in Redgrave records of arrest being ordered, or of the use of pillory or ducking stool.

[114] For example, the Redgrave account rolls for 1618 show the proceeds received from the Redgrave-Botisdale court of Oct. 22, 1618 to be £32.15.5 of which £21.2.11 were for fines on alienation of copyhold estates, 1 shilling was for fines for nonattendance, and 8 shillings 4 pence for amercements. For 1567 the account rolls show receipts of £8.1.

[115] *Choyce Cases in Chancery,* 105 refers to a Chancery case in 1605 in which relief in the Chancery was refused to persons suing for copyhold land, with the comment that "no writ of false judgment lay of a copyhold case from a manor" but from the steward the claimants could appeal to the lord "as a Chancellor."

[116] Above, Chapter III, secs. 2e and 3d.

[117] 2 James I, c. 5.

There is no direct evidence whether the prohibition was fully enforced, but the absence of complaints against self-enriching stewards suggests that it had some effect.

The office of steward was an honorable and responsible one, suitable for a gentleman. In the first ten years of James I the steward of Redgrave and of other Bacon manors was Sir Edward Bacon, brother of Sir Nicholas, the lord of the manor.[118] In the important manor of Manchester the chief steward in the Elizabethan period was the Earl of Derby, and he actually presided at some sessions, being replaced in his absence by an understeward—John Gregory, gentleman.[119] Prominent lawyers were willing to serve. We find, for example, that in 1538 Edward Montague, recently appointed serjeant at law and shortly to become Chief Justice of the King's Bench, presided as steward in the court of John Mulsho, whose battles with his tenants were carried before the Chancery and Star Chamber.[120] In the seventeenth century men like James Whitelocke and Sir Francis North, who were later to become prominent judges, started their careers by serving as stewards in manorial courts and Roger North strongly recommended this course of training for young men as a valuable introduction to a career at the common law bar.[121]

It is an entirely different question whether the office of steward required of its incumbents an extensive knowledge of the common law. Holdsworth has said that "from the end of the thirteenth century [the steward] was generally a professional lawyer; and it is clear from the very technical books which were written to instruct these stewards in their duties that a professional lawyer

---

[118] Edward Bacon was admitted to Gray's Inn on April 27, 1570 (*Pension Book of Gray's Inn,* 5), became an ancient of Gray's Inn on Nov. 21, 1576, was later a member of Parliament and sheriff of Suffolk in 1601, and was knighted by James I in 1603. *Dictionary of National Biography,* II, 371. The first entry I could find mentioning him as steward of Redgrave was in 1598 and his name appears frequently thereafter until 1622, presumably the year of his death (though the D.N.B. gives Sept. 6, 1618 as the date of his death). Edward Bacon's predecessor was William Horneby, whom I have not been able to identify. But the steward under Lord Keeper Bacon, serving at least until 1584, was John Ashfield, who was admitted to the Middle Temple in 1561 and who maintained chambers there into the 1580's. *Middle Temple Records* (London, 1903), I, 131, 243, 248.

[119] *Court Leet Records of the Manor of Manchester,* 12 vols. (Manchester, 1884–1890), I, 85ff.

[120] *Select Cases in the Court of Star Chamber* (ed. I. S. Leadam, Selden Society, London, 1911), II, 65. The biographical data as to Montague are given by Edward Foss, *Lives of the Judges* (London, 1848–1864), V, 309–313.

[121] Holdsworth, *HEL,* I, 185–187.

was needed." [122] It is true, as has just been pointed out, that the experience was useful for young lawyers with ambition. It is also true that some older men, like Sir Edward Bacon who presided at Redgrave, were at least exposed to legal training through attendance at one of the Inns of Court. Diligent authors of court-keeping guides, like John Kitchin, supplied their readers with great masses of legal jargon and citations to Yearbooks, but Kitchin himself explained that his book was written precisely because many stewards in courts baron and leet were wholly ignorant of law. He considered the abuse sufficiently great so that *quo warranto* proceedings should be used to forfeit court-keeping privileges where ignorant stewards were used.[123] But it seems that Coke expressed more correctly the attitudes of the common lawyers. He considered that the range of matters dealt with in courts leet made it "requisite" that stewards be learned in the law. But he also said that "the law is not very curious in examining the imperfections of the Steward's Person, nor the unlawfulness of his authority" for even if he was an infant, an idiot, or an outlaw whatever he does as an incident to his office is valid "because he performeth them as a Judge, or at least as Custom's Instrument." [124]

The question involved is crucial for this inquiry. Rephrased, the question is whether in English manorial courts, as in French and German seignorial courts, the problems encountered had reached such a stage of complexity that effective power and responsibility had been transferred to a group of professional judges. In German terminology, was the *Richter* no longer a mere "director" of the court and on his way to becoming a "judge"? The question can only be answered by describing the work of the courts themselves and their mode of operation. But it is not too soon to suggest a conclusion—that reliance on juries with collective verdicts set narrow limits on the steward's powers. For the "court baron" phase this conclusion would hardly have startled sixteenth century common lawyers; this was in effect what they meant when they said that in the "court baron" the suitors decided. For the "court leet" phase there might be a ques-

---

[122] Holdsworth, *HEL*, I, 185.
[123] Kitchin, *Court Leet*, preface.
[124] Coke, *Fourth Institute*, 265; *Complete Copyholder*, sec. 45.

tion since the lawyers said that in the court leet the steward was judge. But from the earliest beginning of court leet procedure, the central feature was the presentment jury whose verdicts named the offenders and commenced the court's action against them. The steward was usually a stranger to the events of the neighborhood, a visitor for a day. Disobedience or disorder that happened in court he could know about, for he had his own eyes and ears. But for offenses occurring outside the court he had in theory and in practice no sources of knowledge, "and therefore [said Coke] the power of presenting them, and imposing punishments for them, belongeth unto the Jurors of the Leet, and not unto the Steward." [125] After the presentments were brought in, the stewards might have had an important share in decision-making if the ordinary business of manorial courts had raised complex issues of law or interpretation. But as we shall see, they seldom did.

The ultimate settlement, which reduced the steward to a passive role, was certainly not inevitable. The stewards were often vigorous men, with social status of their own and important interests of their masters to serve. In earlier records one finds hints of the kind of conflicts that must have flared up—the suitor fined sixpence "for talking too much," the suitor fined a half mark "for his contempt and disrespect before the steward in full court and because he wished to contradict the steward's command," the steward who called armed men, barred the doors of the manor hall, and killed three suitors who had opposed him.[126] And when it came to issuing commands, some of the early "by-laws" were plainly marked as the product of common consent but others in the same series were "precepts" or "orders" that were at least ambiguous—perhaps they expressed the wishes of the suitors but they read like steward's commands.[127] It was through conflict

[125] Coke, *Complete Copyholder*, sec. 25 (p. 41 in 1641 ed.).

[126] Ault, *Private Jurisdiction in England,* 175 mentions this thirteenth century incident and on pages 172–176 discusses more generally the active role that stewards often took in early manor courts.

[127] There are many examples, but perhaps the *Manor Rolls of the Convent of Durham* (Surtees Society, vol. 82), will suffice. In a court of 1366–1367 it is recorded (p. 61) that *"injunctum est"* to all tenants that they come to the lord's mill and then immediately following is the entry: *ordinatum est ex communi assensu tam liberi quam alii ten' domini* that no one should allow his animals to leave home without a guardian. In 1375 *ordinatum est ex communi assensu* that no one was to "speak ill of any other person" (p. 129). But in numerous other

and adjustment in small local assemblies, over several centuries, that the powers of the stewards were reduced. It was certainly not the work of the central government for the king's officials did not intervene until the main issues had been decided. In particular places it must have been all too often that nonconforming individuals were summarily repressed by strong-willed stewards. Even whole communities must have found it wiser, for the sake of peace, to submit to petty tyranny.

Yet one should not underestimate the long-term effects of court procedure in shaping basic attitudes. It was extremely convenient for lords and their stewards to rely on local juries to supply information, to name offenders, and even to define the offences themselves. This meant for manorial officials, just as it had for the thirteenth-century common law courts, a tremendous saving of time and trouble. But it also meant, as in the common law system, that effective powers of decision were in large measure transferred to juries of the neighborhoods, whose motives and sources of knowledge were submerged in collective verdicts. Even if the stewards appointed the members of manorial juries, as they may often have done, the juries were drawn from farming communities that worked together in the open fields, who had known each other from childhood, and were fully aware of their common interests. If their sense of outrage grew strong enough the whole group had the means to retaliate, as John Mulsho discovered in 1538 when his embattled farmers refused to enter any verdicts whatever, paralyzed his manorial court and compelled Mulsho to appeal to the Star Chamber to overcome their collective resistance.[128] It was seldom, no doubt, that matters went this far.

---

entries *preceptum* or *injunctum est* in such a way that the lord or his steward seems to be speaking—the tenants are not to transfer their land without the court's license (p. 25), they are to attend the next court *ad tractandum de communibus negotiis* (p. 70), and so on. In 1366 (p. 55) one Adam was fined for allowing John Lolles to stay in his home "contrary to the command of the lord at the last halimote."

[128] *Select Cases in the Court of Star Chamber* (Selden Society), II, 57–67, esp. 66–67. Equally instructive is the 1544 case of Foreacre and others v. Frauncys, reproduced at length in *Select Cases in the Court of Requests* (Selden Society, London, 1898), 101–172. The proceeding in this case was brought by the tenants against joint owners of the manor, Frauncys and Warre. The tenants claimed that the lords refused to give effect to several customs of the manor, the one chiefly in issue being a custom allowing the widow of any deceased copyholder a life estate in all the copyhold land held by her husband. The contest arose on the death of Richard Rousewell, when his widow Alice appeared and asked to be ad-

But it must have been quite often that exasperated stewards found themselves helpless before stubborn yeomen who refused to swear collectively to what they did not believe. The Norman device of the jury, which left such a mark on the common law, was surely a major factor in reducing the stewards to not much more than presiding officers and preserving for farm communities effective control of their own affairs.

d. *Civil Litigation and the 40 Shilling Limit*

Proceeding now to examine the main business dealt with by the Redgrave court, we should consider first the role it played as a small claims court in civil litigation. With this is connected the question of the 40 shilling limit, but the importance of the 40 shilling limit reaches beyond its restrictive effects on the intake of private lawsuits. For it was assumed for most purposes that the 40 shilling (£2) limit was also a ceiling on the amercements that manor courts in general could impose—a limit therefore on the courts' own powers.

In the thirteenth century, when the limit was invented, 40 shillings was a lot of money. A first rate farm worker in the thirteenth century—a ploughman or carter—could work for a year and earn only 35 shillings. If his wife worked also for 100 days the 8 shillings she might earn would carry them 3 shillings over the £2 limit. In the fourteenth century, Rogers estimated, £3 would pay for the housing, food and essential supplies for a year of a farm family of four, living on a twenty-acre farm; or if one measures money in livestock, 40 shillings in the fourteenth century might buy three healthy live cattle or twelve grown up pigs.[129] The price rises of the fifteenth century were gradual and interrupted. It was

---

mitted as tenant for life of his lands. The steward refused to admit her, whereupon the whole homage refused to make any further presentments and walked out of court. A week later the steward assembled another court and the tenants again refused to render any verdict and "departed." The Court of Requests proceeded to appoint an examining commission, which interrogated numerous tenants, the lords, steward and others on written interrogatories, took extensive excerpts from the court rolls of the manor, and examined various written statements of its ancient customs. The final result was adverse to the widow and as to other customs asserted by the tenants was adverse to them also, though the lords were directed not to punish the tenants for their failure of duty in refusing to be sworn and to render verdicts in the court.

[129] James E. Thorold Rogers, *History of Agriculture and Prices in England* (Oxford, 1866–1902), I, 289–290, 682–686.

the flood of new world silver in the sixteenth century that brought something like a tripling of most English prices in the last two thirds of the sixteenth century. It is difficult to learn the effects on the farming population of these catastrophic changes, beyond the broad impression that wages lagged well behind other prices. As to wages, one general source is the series of wage regulations issued by the sixteenth century justices of the peace, fixing ceilings on wages for various classes of laborers. The rates were not uniform in the different counties and were no doubt often exceeded in fact, but they represent at least the targets set for official action. In the county of Rutland in 1563 the proclaimed maximum wage for one year was 38 shillings and fourpence for "a common servant in husbandry, which can mow, sow, thrash, and load a cart and cannot expertly make a rick, hedge and thatch the same." But for "a mean servant in husbandry" the same regulations fixed an annual wage of 29 shillings, and for women of course still less.[130] The levelling upward of both prices and wages continued through the rest of the sixteenth century, but in its last decade 40 shillings was more than the maximum annual wage of most unskilled farm workers and women, and this sum would buy 4 sheep or possibly half of a full grown cow.[131] It seems safe to conclude that for the farming population—about 90 per cent of the people of England—the 40 shilling limit had by no means destroyed the coercive powers of manorial courts, and it left them still accessible in a considerable share of private disputes between residents of the manors.

Yet the sample taken at Redgrave shows a sharp decline after 1600 in the volume of civil litigation. In the decade 1461–1470 the Redgrave roll shows 23 cases of debt commenced, 12 of trespass, and one "plea of broken agreement" (*placitum conventionis fractae*). Of this whole group of 36 cases, 15 were settled by compromise, 7 were decided by verdicts of special juries, in one there

[130] Rogers, IV, 120–121. As to women, a "chief woman servant" who could cook, bake, brew and oversee other servants was supposed to get 26 shillings a year, while "a mean or simple woman servant, which can do but outworks and drudgery" was limited to 16 shillings a year. Ephraim Lipson, *Economic History of England* (New York, 1929–1931), II, 386–389 discusses similar wage regulations of the Elizabethan period.

[131] Campbell, *The English Yeoman under Elizabeth and the Early Stuarts*, 398; *Hertford County Records*, 1581–1698 (Hertford, 1905), I, 8–12. The estimates as to the cost of livestock come from Rogers, VI, 249–256.

was a confession of judgment, and no disposition was recorded of the remaining 13. In the decade 1558–1567 there were 40 actions commenced—22 for trespass, 9 for debt, and 9 cases of "trespass on the case"; but of the total of 40 cases, final decisions are recorded in only two. In the decade 1603–1612 only four civil actions were started, of which two were labelled "trespass" and two were actions by widows of copyholders for assignment of dower; no disposition is recorded for any of the four. The Redgrave rolls for the rest of the seventeenth century give a similar picture—civil litigation for practical purposes disappears, except for an occasional contest between adverse claimants of copyhold land. This decline, which had commenced in fact in the 1580's and 1590's, cannot be explained by the effects of inflation in lowering the 40 shilling ceiling. It may have been due in part to dissatisfaction of litigants with delays in the disposition of cases—postponements were frequent and in two cases actions brought were still pending four and six years later. The drift of private litigants away from the Redgrave manor court seems to have been acquiesced in, for the period after 1600 shows no effort to preserve jurisdiction over private disputes by punishing tenants who sued elsewhere as was done in earlier periods.[132]

Apart from the common use of special juries, one can find few clues to procedure. Decisions could be very prompt—on the day the claim was first presented—though postponement from court to court seems to have grown more common. Written pleadings sometimes appear; attorneys (other local residents) could be used but seldom were.[133] The grounds of decision are seldom stated and

---

[132] In the Redgrave court roll for March 17, 1565 there is an entry stating that "day is given to the homage" to inquire whether John Foster impleaded John Lynne in the court of the hundred of Haslemere in a matter determinable in the Redgrave manor court *contra ordinacionem in ea parte factam*, so that he had forfeited the penalty of 40 shillings. The ordinance in question is evidently that issued in Oct. 1530, while Redgrave still belonged to the Abbot of Bury St. Edmunds: *Constitutio facta est per omnes tenentes huius manerii quod deinceps nullus tenens implitabit alium tenentem domini huius manerii extra curiam domini sine licencia domini subpoena* [40 shillings].

[133] The Redgrave roll for 1567 records the filing of a written bill, to which the defendants were ordered to respond by written answer (Bull and wife v. Sewell, 10 Eliz.). The Hindercley roll for Sept. 18, 1558 gives another example of a written bill in an action brought to recover copyhold land, and the Hindercley roll for Oct. 11, 1606 gives still another. The latter case was an action to collect a debt of 30 shillings. After reading the plaintiff's written bill the defendant "ac-

the issues in the "debt" and "trespass" actions were probably of the simplest kind.

A case in the nearby Bacon manor of Hindercley indicates that in situations of somewhat greater complexity these farmer courts could use "equity" powers. The case in question was first introduced (in the court for October 7, 1564) not as a private suit but through presentment by the leet jury. Along with reports that the nearby river was insufficiently scoured, that three houses had fallen into decay, and so on, the jurors brought in a verdict that the heirs of John Smallwood refused to care for and maintain Katherine Biggelye, contrary to an agreement made between John and Katherine. At the next court, held September 3, 1565, the full story emerged. By an indenture of May 19, 1552, John had agreed to supply Katherine with necessaries in return for her surrendering certain copyhold land in his favor. John had since died and his heirs refused to support her.

Therefore it is adjudged by the court that the said Katherine shall take back her copyhold tenement and two acres with their appurtenances to her use and the use of her heirs.

The steward on the spot admitted Katherine as copyhold tenant and "with the court still sitting" she surrendered the lands to the use of Robert Goodwyn. The steward then admitted Robert as tenant "on condition that he and his heirs care for and honestly and sufficiently maintain the said Katherine and supply every necessary for her sustenance and clothing during her natural life." A further clause was then inserted that if Katherine should die within five years Robert Goodwyn would pay to one Alice (evidently a younger relative of Katherine) the sum of four marks

---

cording to the custom of the manor" immediately responded "that he does not owe the money *et de hoc ponit se super patriam*" and the plaintiff did likewise. The steward, Sir Edward Bacon, ordered that a jury be at once empanelled and the bailiff responded by naming 12 persons, who promptly rendered a verdict that the defendant owed the 30 shillings to the plaintiff. Judgment for plaintiff was then immediately given by the steward "with the consent of John Fale, gent., and Gregory Carter, free tenants and suitors of the said court." Why the free tenants in question were brought into the argument is not indicated.

The Redgrave roll for 1466 has a case in which a friend was permitted to appear on behalf of one of the litigants, and other examples from earlier records are referred to by Bennett, *Life on an English Manor*, 221. See also *Court Rolls of the Abbey of Ramsey* (ed. Ault), 102 (*anno* 1309).

when she reached eighteen, with a proviso that if he failed to do
so the land would revert to Katherine's heirs. The court roll for
1571 shows the proviso was effective, for Alice acknowledged re-
ceipt from Goodwyn of the sum reserved for her.

At least for the reign of Elizabeth, the comments of Sir Thomas
Smith seem apposite. In his Commonwealth of England, first published in 1583, he commented on how strange it might seem that
all lawsuits in England were drawn to Westminster, to be heard
during terms that lasted only a fourth of each year. "And one
would thinke that there should be much lacke of Justice and
right, and much wrong taken without redresse. But it is not so."
Smith pointed to the courts of the counties and hundreds and then
to the court baron that the lord of every manor could hold with
his tenants.

They make orders and lawes amongest themselves, the paine of
them if they be after broken, commeth to the Lorde. And if anie small
matter be in controversie, it is put to them, and commonly they doe
ende it. But these courtes doe serve rather for men that can be content to be ordered by their neighbors, and which love their quiet and
profit in their husbandrie, more than to be busie in the lawe.[134]

In the period after 1600 it seems likely that the volume of civil
litigation declined in manorial courts generally. But there were
some exceptions, as there were with the courts of county and hundred. Some of these exceptional manor courts lasted as late as the
nineteenth century. A survey in 1841 showed more than fifty
"courts baron" in Northumberland, more than twenty in Durham,
and others scattered over the country, some handling hundreds of
small claims a year.[135] But it would seem that court owners had
no strong incentive in most places to preserve their jurisdiction
over small debt and damage claims. One class of cases survived
somewhat longer, contests over title to copyhold land between
adverse claimants other than the lord himself. The courts of the
manors remained the primary tribunals for this type of case and
where money judgments were incidentally required (as for the
value of possession wrongfully withheld) the 40 shilling limit did
not operate.[136] But even here the extension of common law

---

[134] Sir Thomas Smith, De Republica Anglorum, II, c. 17.
[135] Webb, ELG, II, 119–120.
[136] Shaw v. Thompson, 4 Coke Rep. 30b (1595).

remedies gradually reduced the importance and independence of manor courts.

It was in earlier centuries, at least till the reign of Elizabeth, that the manor courts rendered an important service in English private law. They provided the great bulk of the English people with justice that was cheap and could be speedy, through the judgment of neighbors very close to home. But their contribution was not only to England, for the early English colonists transplanted to America the rules of law and procedure that they had learned in these community courts. What Goebel has said of the Plymouth colony surely applies to many of the other North American settlements:

> Except what these humble men may have known of the ecclesiastical courts, with their sompnours spying upon their amours, and the apparitors to take them to jail if they worshipped heretically, the workings of the county, manorial or borough tribunals were the length and breadth of their knowledge of the administration of justice, the local customs the sum of their law.[137]

With few if any lawyers to guide or hamper them, the settlers in North America created societies that in many ways were new. But the law that they brought with them was "a curious mixture of religious ideas and of half-remembered customs from other lands." [138] Since most of the English population still lived in farming communities when the migration began, we must search primarily in the English manor courts for the law, the procedure and the aspirations that molded the new societies as they spread out into the wilderness.

e. Copyhold Transactions

The story of copyhold is longer and very much more complex. Copyhold tenure, in form at least, lasted in England until 1925. For the purpose of administering it manorial courts had to be

---

[137] Julius Goebel, "King's Law and Local Custom in Seventeenth Century New England," 31 *Col. L. Rev.* 416, 420–421 (1931).

[138] George Haskins, "A Problem in the Reception of the Common Law in the Colonial Period," 97 *U. of Pa. L. Rev.* 842, 852 (1949). The influence of copyhold on the early recording system in Massachusetts is discussed by the same author in "The Beginnings of the Recording System in Massachusetts," 21 *Boston Univ. L. Rev.* 281, 298–300 (1941).

maintained over a large part of England until the middle of the
nineteenth century. How important was copyhold?

Coke made the statement, and also attributed to others the
statement, that estates by copy of court roll were "a great part
of the kingdom." [139] When one seeks to be more precise, difficulties arise. The relative numbers of freeholders, customary tenants,
and leaseholders varied greatly from county to county and from
manor to manor. In particular, in Suffolk (where Redgrave is located) the percentage of freeholders was abnormally high, comprising perhaps half of all occupants of land in the county. Classification is hampered by the mixture of holdings (freeholders
owning copyhold and vice versa), and by the looseness of contemporary terminology, which described copyholders as "customary" tenants but lumped in with them various kinds of tenants
at will, some of whom had no "copies." But the term "customary"
tenants was at least quite sure to *include* the copyholders. Tawney's analysis showed that in the sixteenth century the proportion
of landholders who were "customary" tenants was in Northumberland 91 per cent, in Suffolk and Norfolk together 54 per cent,
in a group of southern counties 77 per cent. For 118 manors located in various parts of England the average proportion of "customary" tenants was 61 per cent.[140] And from other sources it
seems clear that a very large fraction of the "customary" tenants
had copies of court rolls and held by the custom of their manors.[141] They were indeed "a great part"—they were much the
largest single group in the sixteenth century and they were probably more than half the farming population in a land mainly devoted to farming.

By the sixteenth century the methods of transferring copyhold
interests were well organized and well understood. Whether the
transfer was by sale or mortgage, by lifetime gift or through succession at death, it had no effect until the transferee was admitted
by the manorial steward in open court after certification by the
homage. Normally the transferee must appear in person to render

[139] Coke, *Complete Copyholder*, sec. 57 (p. 167 in 1641 ed.). Similar language
was attributed to Wray, C. J. in Kite's Case, 4 *Coke Rep.* 25a (1589), and to the
whole King's Bench in Hobart's case, 4 *Coke Rep.* 27b (1600).

[140] Richard H. Tawney, *The Agrarian Problem in the Sixteenth Century* (London, 1912), 25. The work will be cited hereafter as Tawney, *Agrarian Problem*.

[141] Tawney, 48–49.

fealty. But no other formalities were required. Where the transferor was alive and able, he too could appear in court, but this
was not required. On the contrary, in a very large share of the
transactions recorded on the Redgrave rolls the transfer was initiated by action occurring out of court, in the presence of two
or more residents of the manor. There are occasional references
to the handing over by the transferor of a rod (the "verge") as
a symbol of ownership, a practice that was usual enough in other
places so that in common speech copyhold tenants were often
described as "tenants by the verge." [142] It is clear in some of the
Redgrave out-of-court surrenders that the transferor prepared
beforehand an elaborate written statement of his intentions, either
an indenture of gift or sale or a testamentary document. But it
seems also clear that oral directions would suffice, provided there
were at least two trustworthy persons present, the transferor's
intent was clearly expressed and the two witnesses could persuade
the homage at the next court to accept their testimony.

Copyhold is remembered as a maze of technicalities which
taxed the ingenuity of the conveyancing profession. This recollec-
tion may be justified by the trouble that came in receiving within
English property law the tangled growth of local customs expressed in copyhold. But from the point of view of the copyhold
tenants it was totally otherwise. It is true that for copyholders
exclusion from the common law system had been on the whole
a great disadvantage since it meant they had no royal protection
in contests with their lords. But the reverse of this was freedom
from the restrictive rules of the common law. In determining the
course of intestate succession, the rights of surviving husband
and wife, the types of estates that could be created, the power to
convey to a living spouse or to a grantee yet unborn—in all these
and related matters there could be special rules of local custom
deviating from the common law.[143] The glimpses one gets from
the court rolls and custumals of medieval manors suggest that
deviant rules existed in great profusion, though over the course

[142] Coke, *Complete Copyholder*, sec. 39 (p. 104 in 1641 ed.), pointing out that
in some manors, straw or a glove was used instead of a rod. On the formalities for
transfer of copyhold, a good statement appears in William Greenwood, *The
Authority, Jurisdiction and Method of Keeping County Courts, Courts Leet and
Court Baron* (London, 9th ed., 1730), 324–327.
[143] Holdsworth, *HEL*, VII, 296–304.

of centuries the weight of the common law system pressed toward greater conformity. Just as the manorial courts were surely far in advance of the common law in enforcing informal contract and extending liability in tort, there were some manors that led the way in enlarging powers of disposition. An example is the power to dispose by will. Despite the incredulity of Maitland, it seems that by local custom in many manors villeins could make wills of villein land some 200 years before the Statute of Wills gave this power for freehold land.[144]

Even more important in practice was the cheapness and efficiency of the transfer process itself. It is true that the newly admitted copyhold tenant would normally have to pay the lord a "fine" for his admission; if fines for the particular holding were "uncertain" he would have to bargain with steward or bursar and in times of rising prices he might have to pay quite high. But apart from this disability, to which much copyhold land was subject, the process was cheap and easy. The grantor could declare his intent before two trusted neighbors. He did not even need to appear in court. The manor court roll gave a continuous record, a registry of title, that was enormously more reliable than indentures laid away in chests. The court rolls were not the only safeguard, either, for they were nothing more than a record of proceedings conducted in open court before neighbors who could remember what was said. As Tawney pointed out, it was the security and simplicity of this system that so greatly promoted the active market in copyhold land in the fifteenth and sixteenth centuries.[145]

One interesting thing to discover at Redgrave was the large-scale use of mortgages. Mortgages of copyhold at Redgrave were frequent in the 1460's and no doubt go back earlier. In the sixteenth and seventeenth centuries they were very numerous; the same phenomenon has been noted elsewhere.[146] Mortgages took the usual form—a surrender to the lord "to the use" of the trans-

---

[144] Levett, *Studies in Manorial History*, 208.

[145] Tawney, *Agrarian Problem*, 86.

[146] Leconfield, *Petworth Manor in the Seventeenth Century*, 11–13, calculating that between 1628 and 1717 the copyholders of Petworth raised a total of £16,750 by mortgages on their lands. Published records of other manors contain numerous examples of similar transactions—e.g. *Court Rolls of Great Cressingham*, Norfolk, 57–59, 65, 75.

feree—but with a condition added that the surrender would be void if a named sum was repaid on or before a certain day. A considerable number of mortgage debts were paid on time, satisfaction being acknowledged in court by the mortgagees and noted on the court rolls. Where the mortgagee reported, and the homage agreed, that the mortgagor was in default, foreclosure was accomplished, in effect, by the steward's second admission of the mortgagee as a tenant, this time without condition. But it was possible for the steward to act as a Chancellor and relieve from forfeiture. In a case in 1611, Sir Edward Bacon, steward, learned from the homage that the mortgagor had died leaving a widow who had not paid the mortgage debt, though the land was worth more than the balance due. Bacon agreed to remit the lord's share of the fine for admission and "in consideration" of this the mortgagee stated that he was "contented and well pleased and doth promis in full court" that the widow have nine years' occupancy of the dwelling located on the mortgaged land; also that if he sold the land in the meantime he would pay the widow 15 shillings yearly for the balance of the nine year term. It seems that this tempering of the wind for the widow would have been approved by Coke, for Coke asserted that in disputes between adverse claimants of copyhold land the lord (and presumably his steward) "is not tied to the strict forme of the common law, for he is a Chancellor in his court." [147]

In presenting the facts on which the stewards took action the role of the homage was an equivocal one. In the court-keepers' guides and at Redgrave itself, the standard introduction to entries recording transfers of copyhold was "It is ascertained through the homage" (*Compertum est per homagium*). In the body of the entries there often appear such statements as "the homage say" or "the homage present," and it seems clear in general that whatever they said was under oath. Yet in innumerable instances it is still more clear that most of the homage could not possibly be informed through their own direct knowledge of the events that they described, especially in those numerous cases where they reported surrenders made outside of court through a copyholder's delivering a wand or a document to two manorial residents who were not even members of the homage that day.

[147] Coke, *Complete Copyholder*, sec. 43 (p. 122 in 1641 ed.).

This practice of using hearsay as the basis for verdicts was of course not peculiar to manorial juries. The trial juries of the common law had been compelled from very early times to answer questions on which they were partially or wholly uninformed, without much aid (for centuries at least) from documents or witnesses that were brought before them. But in the conveyancing business of manorial courts this feature meant that the homage was not so much a direct source of knowledge as it was a validating agent, certifying to the steward that the transaction conformed to manorial custom and the facts reported were credible.

In one Bacon manor in 1603 some jurors of the homage refused to accept this dubious role. This occurred, not at Redgrave, but at the nearby manor of Hindercley. The steward in his charge to the jury had specially requested a report of any conditional surrenders of copyhold land and "whether the conditions in them were performed or not." In response to this charge "Robert Lock, one of the Jury, confessed in full court before the steward, homage, and other there" that he had acted as an intermediary in a surrender of certain copyhold land by one Strangman to John Onge on condition of payment of £3.10 by May 1 last past. Lock stated further that the money was not paid by that day but John Onge "took his [the mortgagor's] promis for the money and held himself satisfied and said he would not medle with the land which confession to that effecte the Steward requested [them] to bring in as parcell of their verdict." However, five members of the jury refused to join, the other seven agreeing to have it "parcell of their verdict." George Person, in particular, "made answere directlie that he wold not make it parcell of his verdict." All this was recorded in the court roll and there the matter rested.

The interesting feature of this entry is the dependence of the steward on securing a verdict from the manorial jury, even a divided verdict, as a basis for any entry in the rolls. No similar case was discovered in which a division within the jury was reported. But from the regularity with which the entries recite that "it has been ascertained through the homage," and from the automatic acceptance these certifications received, one finds some support for the conclusion already suggested—that in matters on which the custom was clear the role of the steward had become routine. Coke was explicit on this point too (and as owner of some sixty manors he ought to have known).[148] In his *Complete Copy-holder* he stated the familiar theory that since the lord had originally been free to keep the land or dispose of it as he wished, he "might be reputed absolute owner; yet because in disposing of it he is bound to observe the custom precisely in every point, and can neither in estate or tenure bring in any alteration, in this respect the law accounts him custom's instrument." [149] By the early seventeenth century the common law had reached the position that the terms for any transfer that were imposed by the copyholder transferor must be accepted by the steward if the terms were consistent with the custom of the manor, so that any attempt by the steward to introduce new or different terms was simply ineffective.[150]

Behind all this lies the much larger question whether the developing rules of copyhold tenure gave copyholders protection against the powerful economic forces at work in the sixteenth and seventeenth centuries. One thoughtful student of manorial history has referred to the "disastrous decay of English manorial courts which deprived the small landholder of his main line of defence and his only method of corporate self-expression, leaving him inarticulate in the midst of a predatory world." [151] If this is meant to suggest that the safeguards to copyhold tenure developed by manorial courts were suddenly and dramatically swept away, it is surely incorrect. The difficulty was rather that the walls of protection built around the small holders had major gaps through which the "predatory" elements could all too readily infiltrate.

One problem, for example, was the enclosure or appropriation of common lands, which deprived the tenants of pasture for their animals. Pasture of animals was an essential feature of the open field system of land husbandry, "a linch pin the removal of which brought the whole structure of village society tumbling down." [152] Rights of pasture were a constant concern and inspired much regulation in manorial courts. They were as vital for most of

---

[148] Catherine D. Bowen, *The Lion and the Throne* (Boston, 1956), 527, with a list of 30 of his holdings quoted pp. 552–553.
[149] Coke, *Complete Copyholder*, sec. 41.
[150] Holdsworth, *HEL*, VII, 305–306.
[151] Levett, *Studies in Manorial History*, 20.
[152] Tawney, *Agrarian Problem*, 239.

the free-holders as they were for copyholders. But for both types of tenants, rights to the use of common lands were considered not primary objects of ownership, but merely "appendant" or "appurtenant," and they depended on proof of immemorial usage which satisfied common law tests for prescription. This was often difficult under the limitations of common law procedure, in unequal contests between tenants and lord.[153] An even more serious difficulty was that copyhold tenures took many forms other than outright estates of inheritance. But it was only the full estate of inheritance, transferable for "certain" fines, that gave long-term security. In surveys of 142 sixteenth-century manors Tawney found that slightly fewer than half of the tenants had estates of inheritance or the equivalent. Most of the rest had estates for one or more (sometimes three or four) lives; here manorial managers were free, at the end of lives in being, to reassign the holding on different terms or adopt the form of simple lease to free it from copyhold restrictions. In the same surveys it appeared that in nearly two-thirds of the holdings fines on alienation were "uncertain," so that the lord could capture the increased capital value of the holding through a greatly increased fine—perhaps driving the new tenant away altogether by excessive demands.[154]

Copyhold tenure itself could not give a bulwark against the pressures and expedients of manorial lords animated by the profit motive. Some of the lords desired, through more efficient methods of land use, to increase the productivity of the land itself; some sought, by shifting from crops to sheep-raising, to share in the profits of the wool trade; and many merely aimed to correct in their own favor the vast distortions in domestic prices and rents that had been caused by large-scale inflation. The population actually displaced by enclosures in the sixteenth century was apparently not large, but the effects on English society were multiplied in many directions, both at the time and later.[155] The en-

[153] Tawney, 237–253.

[154] Tawney, 287–301, esp. p. 300.

[155] Tawney, 403–404, summarized some of the later consequences in language worth quotation. After indicating that even by 1642 the main course of events had been determined, he said: "By that time the expansion of the woollen industry has made it certain that England will be a considerable manufacturing nation, and consequently that the ancient stable routine of subsistence farming will gradually give place to agricultural methods which swing this way and that, according to

closure movement continued through the seventeenth century and was greatly accelerated in the eighteenth; at the same time there occurred a shift from copyhold to other forms of land tenure. Some of the later shifts were initiated, like most of the earlier ones, by the lords in their own interest but from the point of view of the tenants there was often much to be gained by "enfranchising" the land from the ancient restrictions. Legislation of the middle nineteenth century gave further aid to enfranchisement.[156] The elimination of copyhold proceeded thus by gradual stages, both through powerful economic pressure and through voluntary action, and was well on the way to completion when copyhold tenure was finally abolished by the Real Property Act of 1925. But enough copyhold survived so that meetings of the "homage" were frequently held in many places in England, at least until the middle of the nineteenth century.[157] At Redgrave itself the meetings of the "court baron," to record transfers of copyhold interests, continued until the 1920's, though during the previous eighty years the homage was reduced to only two members, their role was evidently nominal, and the court book itself was nothing more than a convenient register of local land titles.[158]

the fluctuations of the market. It is certain that, sooner or later, the new and more profitable economy of enclosure will triumph. It is certain that the small holder will have a hard struggle to hold his own against the capitalist farmer. It is certain that, owing to the substitution of variable for fixed fines on admission to copyholds, and the conversion of many copyholds into leases for years, a great part of the fruits of economic progress will no longer be retained, as in the fifteenth century, by the mass of peasants, but will pass, in the shape of increased payments for land, into the pockets of the great landed proprietors. It is almost certain that to any new development which may be detrimental to them the peasants will be able to offer a much less effective resistance than they have in the past. For the security of many of their class has been undermined; the gulf which separates them from the landed gentry, though still bridged by the existence of many prosperous free-holders, has been widened; and above all, the destruction of the absolute monarchy has entrenched the great landlords inexpugnably at the heart of government, both central and local, and has made their power as great as their ambitions. Both from below and from above they are unassailable. For a century and a half after the Revolution they have what power a Government can have to make and ruin England as they please."

[156] Holdsworth, HEL, VII, 311–312.

[157] Elton and Mackay, Law of Copyholds (2d ed., 1893), 304–323, give an extensive account of the procedure for assembling a manorial court, following ancient practice closely. The Copyhold Act of 1841 had dispensed with the assembling of the homage for the mere recording of transfers of copyhold, so that by 1893 the most frequent reason for assembling a manorial court was to secure the assent of the tenants to surrender or limitation of their rights of common.

[158] The court book of Redgrave manor for the period 1836 to 1935 is in the

The problems of the small holder had been given peculiar sharpness and urgency in England by the premature growth and precocity of the English common law. In view of the immense tasks that confronted the royal judges in England during the thirteenth century, one can understand their reluctance to give remedies to that very large class of servile tenants—then much more than half the population—whose status had been debased after the Conquest, whose labor services took so many forms and whose tenure was still precarious. But the lines of classification that were adopted by the common law cut sharply across the farming population and ignored the similarities in activities, interests, and personal condition that might exist within individual settlements.

In France, on the other hand, the whole process of definition was much longer postponed, until the transmutation of labor services into money rents had stripped away most of the marks of servitude. So in the sixteenth century, when the analysis of French lawyers began to be applied to the classification of property rights in their relation to status, the tenure of small holders had the outward marks of full-scale ownership. It may even be, as Bloch has suggested, that the very abstractness and plenitude of Roman law conceptions of ownership worked to the advantage of the smaller tenants, by eliminating restrictions and disabilities that did not readily fit within the simplified Roman system.[159] In any case, the peasant tenures were assimilated and protection for them was extended with far less commotion than there was in England. This could happen, it seems, because the unfree peasants in France had not been cast much earlier into an outer darkness from which they had to be rescued. Their absorption into French private law could be peaceful and orderly since in this, as in other matters, French law was not brought prematurely to sharp definition and rigidity, excluding or deflecting new forces of growth.[160]

---

possession of Thomas Wilson, Esq., of Bury St. Edmunds, solicitor for the present lord of the manor, John Holt Wilson, Esq.

[159] Marc Bloch, *Les Caractères Originaux de l'Histoire Rurale Française* (Cambridge, Mass., 1931), 132–135.

[160] This general question is discussed by Dawson, "The Equitable Remedies of the French Chancery Before 1789," *Festschrift für Ernst Rabel* (Tübingen, 1954), I, 99.

The French were not so fortunate in the methods they used to register land titles within the French manors. The Hundred Years' War destroyed many of the records of land titles. When a great reconstruction of manorial records was undertaken in the fifteenth century, the seignorial courts had already lost their lay personnel—the tenants had faded away. Having no local assemblies to confirm and validate surveys, the lords felt the need for some higher sanction and commonly secured it by special royal letters issued from the royal Chancery. The documents produced in this manner, commonly called *terriers,* included much more than current conveyancing business. They were comprehensive statements of rights and duties, of both lords and tenants, and included much material that in England would have been recorded in manorial extents rather than in standard court rolls. It may be that in the earlier centuries a *terrier* could be made or "renovated" by a local seigneur acting on his own authority, but royal sanction was resorted to increasingly and by the eighteenth century was felt to be indispensable. Decrees of some of the Parlements rejected as void any provisions in manorial documents that had been written down without securing royal authority. Royal decrees were issued declaring it unlawful for the lord to assemble his tenants for this purpose without specific royal approval. Within the notarial profession there appeared a branch that was specially trained in the renovation of *terriers.* They acted under royal commission. Armed thus with royal authority, they moved through the *seigneuries,* calling assemblies of local inhabitants and compelling them to testify.[161]

One eighteenth century author, de Fréminville, who was himself active as a royal commissioner for *terriers,* gave a vivid account of the difficulties encountered in these visitations. The functions of the commissioners were conceived to be quasi-judicial, but many of them showed considerable zeal in unearthing ancient burdens of the inhabitants that had lapsed with time and in promoting generally the interests of the lords who arranged for their employment. Since "renovations" occurred every twenty or thirty years, they were a prolific source of conflict and trouble. The

[161] The subject matter of this paragraph is more fully developed by Bloch, *Les Caractères Originaux de l'Histoire Rurale Française,* 135–136 and Edmé de la Poix de Fréminville, *Pratique Universelle pour la Rénovation des Terriers* (2d ed., 1752), I, 51–64.

local communities often refused to send any spokesmen and were then cited before royal judges for their disobedience, with litigation that lasted years. There were riots in some places when the commissioners arrived. Individuals locked their doors and refused to admit them. De Fréminville complained that it was almost impossible to find truthful witnesses and recommended that the few who could be found should be interviewed secretly by night, in order to avoid reprisals by their neighbors. In conducting his own land surveys he said that he himself had often had to work by moonlight, though the results were less satisfactory than they would have been if he could have worked in the daylight.[162] Altogether it seems that a complex procedure, increasingly dependent on royal authority and administered by functionaries, sharpened class divisions and deprived most Frenchmen, in one more way, of a voice in their own affairs.

In England, on the other hand, the copyhold system of land transfer and title registry was part of a much larger pattern of manorial self-government. Through verdicts of the homage a substantial segment of each manorial community, meeting at regular intervals, was given a primary share in organizing the whole set of tenure relationships, so vital to the welfare and security of most of the inhabitants. It is impossible to measure the gains in self-respect and self-reliance, in training for concerted action and in the sense of responsibility, that came from this long experience. The gains would have been great even if manorial courts had concerned themselves only with copyhold business. But copyhold business was only a core—a central, vital and continuing core around which other functions could cluster.

f. Powers of Self-Government

The range of the matters dealt with by Tudor and Stuart manorial courts was immense. They employed various modes of action that we would now try to distinguish—rule making through by-laws and ordinances, commands addressed to individuals and directing them to desist from conduct that was disapproved, or conviction for past misconduct with the penalty an amercement. But in the sixteenth and seventeenth centuries such distinctions would have seemed artificial. Modes of action were intermingled

[162] De Fréminville, I, 76–100.

and limits of action were left undefined. The manorial juries acted in the confident belief that they had a general mandate to serve community interests in the ways that seemed best to them.

Redgrave again provides a series of samples that seem entirely typical. We can start with a particular day; October 2, 1607 will do as well as any. Most of the entries will be merely summarized. Where they are directly quoted, the Latin of the original roll will be translated; the English that occasionally filters into the original roll can be readily identified by the Jacobean spelling. Under the general heading *Ex Parte Cur' de Redgrave*, the entries for October 2, 1607 start with a list of jurors and some copyhold business and then proceed:

Ordinatum est ad hanc curiam that every man take out theire sheepe and great cattel and stoppe uppe theire gappes next the fennes always before St. Faythes daye uppon payne of every one that shall breake this Constitution—3s. 4d.

Whereas William Sheppard has a newly erected house "which ought not to comon" and yet he has commoned, he is directed (*preceptum est ei*) not to repeat on pain (subpoena) of 39s.

Whereas four persons "have sett uppe Chymnyes in their barnes and stables" and are thereby become commoners, they are in mercy for 12 pence and are directed not to repeat their commoning on pain of 39s.

William Jasper has commoned "contrary to a Bylawe made at the laste Courte." He is in mercy 12 pence and directed not to repeat on pain of 39s.

William Jasper has taken furze on the common "contrary to an order made at the last Courte." He forfeits to the lord of the manor 3s. 4d.

Ex Parte Lete de Redgrave

[A list of jurors]

"Qui dicant quod . . . William Martyn dothe Brewe and Bake without licence." In mercy 12d.

Thomas Kynge wrongfully commoned with a colt. He forfeits "the pain (*penam*) imposed on him at the last court" of 3s. 5d.

Michael Clarke, gentleman, commons where he has no right to do so. He is in mercy 10s.

Samuel Ware has not lopped his trees "overdreepinge the highewaye called Buggs Lane." In mercy 3d. "He is directed to cut the said trees" (*arbores praedictas loppare*) before March 15 next on pain of 3s. 4d.

The same for Robert Harte.

Item wee ordayne at this leete until the next be holden for the towne-shipp of Redgrave that all olde tenants maye take uppon the Common three score furre fagotts, and newe tenants but fourty in one Yeare,

Neyther shall they make them unreasonable and shall not carry awaye any at any tyme until he hath made twenty together and wee appoynt Launcellot Jasper and Thomas Howell and Robert Welles to consider the reasonableness of them, and to viewe them, and that they or one of them be called to see them before they carry them in payne of every offender 10s.

"Item ordinatum" that if two dwell under one roof they shall take no more furze than one ought to do. Subpoena 6s. 8d.

[Then follows a general revision of the "great beast" by-law, passed at an earlier court, regulating the number of cattle and horses that particular tenants were entitled to pasture on the common.]

"Wee ordayne at this Courte and leete" that every man who is allowed to keep two or more great beasts on the common shall for every two beasts do one day's work "in the common rivers of Redgrave" and shall forfeit 12 pence for each day's work not done. "And wee appoint for sewers of Redgrave" Thomas Cage, and Thomas Cooke.

"Wee ordayne that" no one shall cut on the common more thatching stuff than he can cut in one day.

"Wee doe appoynte dryvers of the Commons" two persons.

"Wee ordayne" that no one shall put sheep on the common to feed.

No one shall keep on the common more than one brood goose and one gander, with 6s. 8d. to be forfeited to the lord in the event of breach.

As these entries indicate, a constant concern of the Redgrave court was protection of the commons of pasture from direct physical injury and from overgrazing. Regulations of the use of the commons were frequently repeated, with many variations in detail. One menace to the commons, perhaps the greatest, is omitted from the above-quoted list of offenders and that is the unringed pig. Indeed the problem of the pig at Redgrave, as in other medieval and early modern communities, far transcended the damage it could do by uprooting pasture land. The pig was an important element in the food supply, the chief source of meat, since pork could be readily salted and the shortage of fodder limited the number of other meat animals that could survive the winters. One gets the impression that in medieval settlements, and indeed far into the seventeenth century, roving pigs were a universal scourge. There was no by-law so often repeated at Redgrave as the prohibition of "unringled" pigs. Amercements and "pains" were constantly assessed for failure to ring them or for merely letting them run at large. Among English manors of the time, Redgrave was certainly not unique in this respect.[163]

[163] Unringed pigs were a problem at Petworth in Sussex (Leconfield, *Petworth*

The entries quoted also indicate that another main subject of concern was drainage. Probably the chief purpose was improved sanitation, for there is no reason to think that Redgrave was ahead of other Tudor and Stuart communities in the disposal of its refuse. But the cleaning of the river and the scouring of watercourses and ditches could also prevent floods at high water. Redgrave, again, was not alone in facing these problems.[164] They were met at Redgrave for the most part without legislation, by commands to individuals "under pain" (*subpena*) or by amercements for past defaults. But there was some legislation, taking the form of by-laws that laid the duty of clearing watercourses on persons whose land was contiguous or required the inhabitants to contribute a specified number of workdays per year, sometimes with a flat rate per inhabitant and sometimes with a progressive rate that increased the number of workdays in proportion to the number of beasts that the individual had the right to pasture on the common.

Another method of conserving the assets of the community was to prevent immigration by strangers. The power to control immigration had been expressly conferred upon the courts leet by a statute of 1589 and conformed to the general policies of Elizabethan poor laws restricting new settlements.[165] These policies were supported enthusiastically at Redgrave. By-laws were passed repeatedly, forbidding any person to harbor "inmates." Sometimes the prohibition was absolute and sometimes the housing of strangers was allowed with the approval of five or six "principal men" of the vill.[166] Violations of these by-laws led as usual to amercements and then to the forfeiture of larger "pains" if specific commands to desist were disobeyed. Another sanction, invoked

---

Manor in the Seventeenth Century, 27), Taynton in Oxfordshire (Hone, *The Manor and Manorial Records,* 175), Gnossall in Staffordshire (Hone, 201), and Preston in Sussex (*Court Rolls of the Manor of Preston,* in Sussex Record Society, XXVI, 35, 36, 38, 39, 40, 42, 43, 47, 50 and so on, each reference being to one of the repeated prohibitions, which then go on in an almost uninterrupted series, against unringed pigs).

[164] G. Eland, *At the Courts of Great Canfield, Essex* (1949), 39–45, describes the maintenance of drainage as the chief problem at Great Canfield, though the author gives an interesting description of other business of the leet.

[165] 31 Eliz., c. 7, providing (with numerous exceptions for towns, mining areas, etc.) that no building should be built or converted for habitation unless provided with at least four acres of land and forbidding more than one family in each "cottage." "Every lord within the precinct of his leet" was authorized to inquire into and punish violations.

[166] This latter provision appeared in a by-law passed in the court of 1603.

in a by-law of 1605, was the forfeiture of all rights of common by persons who harbored strangers without license.

These were the principal subjects of express legislation at Redgrave during the early years of Elizabeth and James I. But there were others. In 1558, for example, there is the following entry:

It is ordered by the tenants and chief pledges aforesaid . . . that henceforward no inhabitant within the precinct of this leet shall procure or cause to be procured any defamation or false declaration concerning any neighbor of his. And if anyone shall offend in this respect after warning given to him by the bailiff of the lord and with proof by two sufficient witnesses, that then he shall forfeit for each offense 10 shillings to the lord of this manor.

And in 1560 appear the following entries:

It is ordered by the homage and chief pledges aforesaid that in future no tenant or occupant of any house shall take into his house any persons suspected of vagrancy or known to be of evil conversation (*peioris conversacionis*).

It is likewise ordered by the whole homage that no one intentionally or knowingly shall engage in evil conduct (*male gesture utentur*) or frequent houses or places that are suspect or of ill fame, by night or at other unsuitable times [on penalty after warning from the bailiff of 10 shillings "pain"].

That this legislation was not thought to be needed in order to confer power is suggested, however, by the entry immediately following:

Likewise the homage say that John Marten and his wife and Richard Chapman and his wife are of ill fame and bad conversation and lead their neighbors into obloquy and humiliation by their suspect conduct [so that they are in mercy 3 pence and are ordered to leave the vill by the feast of St. Edmund next on pain of £3.6.8].

It seems quite clear from the language used in the Redgrave by-laws that the legislative will expressed is that of the homage or leet jury. This appears in some of the quotations already given. It is true that the introductory language of most of the by-laws is neutral—"It is ordered" (*ordinatum est*)—but quite often the phrase is filled in—*ordinatum est per homagium, constitutum et conventum est per capitales et tenentes predictos, jurati predicti ordinaverunt,* or simply in English: "wee ordayne." And entries quoting by-laws are mixed in no particular order with presentments of individuals that obviously originated with one of the juries.

It may be that there was some kind of veto power in the lord or his steward. After examining many rolls of the fourteenth and fifteenth centuries, Professor Ault has found one case in which such a veto was exercised, the by-law in question being one that attempted to restrict directly the pasturing rights of the lord himself.[167] I have found no others. It may well be that an indirect veto existed in the sense that the scribe employed by the lord might be instructed not to enroll by-laws of which the lord disapproved, so that they would be lost to later history whatever their status might be in the interval. Nevertheless, if a power of veto existed, either directly or by censorship of the rolls, there is no sign in thousands of entries that the power was exercised. On the contrary, there is much affirmative evidence that in the matters that chiefly concerned the manorial community, the jurors were left free to make their own rules, which they themselves enforced. This was a most convenient solution, for enforcement of the common will would add cash to the coffers of the lord.

As an incident to rule-making through by-laws the jurors could choose local officers to help in their administration. Examples of this have already been mentioned—pasture wardens charged with policing the commons to check on the number of geese and "great beasts" brought in, officers specially elected to examine the loads of furze that were taken for fuel by the tenants. Another example was a by-law issued in 1605:

Item the Jury aforesaid do constitute Jeromy Kempe, Nicholas Hawsted and old Greenwood to look to those swine that be unringled on the commons And eny hogg or shott that they fynde unringled they do dryve them whome to the owners and to give them warning thereof and the owners to give them for their Labor every hogg a penny that is unringled And if eny shall refuse so to do they forfeit to the Lord of the Mannor 3s. 4d.

In addition to these special officers, constituted *ad hoc*, there were the regular officials, elected to their offices for one-year terms. Those most commonly mentioned were the constables,

---

[167] *Court Rolls of Great Cressingham* (Norfolk), 67 (*anno* 1490). In the margin of the roll appears: *Vacat quia dominus nolluit affirmare.* The entry is referred to by Professor Ault in his article, "Some Early Village By-Laws," 45 *Eng. Hist. Rev.* 208, at 230 (1930).

the policemen of the settlement. Often the rolls mention the election of tasters of bread and ale, sealers of leather, "searchers" of leather, and "sewers" to check on drainage. These offices were passed around among the inhabitants. We can safely assume that they were unpaid, except for special instances like the retrievers of "unringled" pigs who were given one pence per pig for their labor. This type of conscripted, unpaid service by inhabitants of manorial communities goes back at least to the thirteenth century and is reported in some of the earliest rolls. Both in earlier times and at Redgrave in the sixteenth and seventeenth centuries, the method of choice was usually described by a neutral term such as *electi sunt* which could include choice by the steward.[168] But in occasional entries it becomes very clear that the election was done by the jurors. There is every reason to conclude that this was the common practice.

For control over conduct generally, neither ordinance nor administrative action by special officers was anything like as important as the specific commands issued to individuals and the penalties for specific misconduct. As the quoted entries indicate, these two types of sanction were often combined; after the jurors had reported some misdeed in the past, for which an amercement was assessed, the offender would be directed (*preceptum est ei*) to desist on pain of a much larger sum, perhaps 10 or 20 or 30 shillings to be forfeited to the lord of the manor. Then at the next court if the offender had not complied, the jury would present that the "pain" had been forfeited and was now collectible. This double technique was most commonly used in matters of primary concern like protection of the commons, but it was a useful form of discipline for many other offenses—insufficient fencing, failure to repair the common fountain (used against the whole vill of Botisdale), maintaining chimneys that were fire hazards for the neighbors, "annoying the street" with an overflowing gutter, encroaching on the street or obstructing pathways, selling bread or ale above the price ceilings, placing a mangy horse on the common, or throwing the entrails of animals into a front yard *ad nocumentum ligeorum domini Regis ibidem transeundum*. Local

---

[168] This point is made by Professor Ault, 224, in the course of his discussion of manorial officers. Homans, *The English Villager in the Thirteenth Century*, 290–302, also discusses the election of early manorial officers.

brawls could lead to amercements, as in the case in 1603 of Francis Farrowe who *percassit Thomas Howlet et de eo trahabat sanguinem contra pacem domini Regis*. Perhaps this Francis Farrowe does not deserve much sympathy, but it is hard to suppress all fellow feeling for Alexander Rayson and Gyles Sidon who are named (after several owners of "unringled" pigs) in the following entries of 1613:

Item presentant, That Alexander Rayson hath byne and still is, a common player at cards and tables in Alehouses, *Ideo est in misericordia* 3d. *Preceptum est ei quod imposterum ne ita faciat subpena* 10s.

Item presentant that Gyles Sidon is a common night walker and an alehouse haunter. *Ideo in misericordia* 3d. *Perceptum est ei imposterum ne ita faciat subpena forisfactura* 10s.

As will be pointed out later, various Elizabethan statutes expressly authorized courts leet to present some of the offenses with which Redgrave juries were concerned. And it should be remembered that the presentment jury of the court leet included within its responsibilities the reporting of major crimes—felonies—that occurred in the neighborhood, even though their trial must occur before royal judges on circuit or before justices of the peace at Quarter Sessions.[169] The court leet was, as the lawyers said, a court of the king, operating through a jury that was sworn to do the king's business. Yet through various modes of action—rule-making, administration by its officers, and coercion of individuals—the court leet of the sixteenth and early seventeenth centuries was above all an agency of local government, working through judicial forms. Redgrave, again, was in no way peculiar in this respect. Other manor courts of the same period that have been studied show the same freedom and vigor, being "both a focus of community life and an active agency of government." [170] No doubt, also, the powers possessed by manor courts fell more

[169] Examples of this are rare in the Redgrave rolls for the periods I have chiefly studied, since the presentment of major felonies had presumably been taken over by the juries at Quarter Sessions. There is one example, however, in the court of September 26, 1562, where the jurors *dicunt* that one Richard Pereson, a horse-thief, had brought the stolen horse into the precincts of the manor and was there captured. Pereson had already been turned over by the constables to the Queen's justices and was in jail at Bury St. Edmunds.

[170] Especially valuable is the account of William B. Willcox, *Gloucestershire, A Study in Local Government, 1590–1640* (New Haven, 1940), 267–305, the language quoted being taken from page 267.

rapidly into disuse in some than in others. An extreme example of their survival is Laxton in Nottingham, where manorial juries were still assembled in the twentieth century, for Laxton retained its open field system of agriculture at least until 1938. But in the thorough study of Laxton by Orwin, published in 1938, there are comments that equally apply to Redgrave in the sixteenth and early seventeenth centuries and surely describe many other communities of that earlier time:

Whatever may have been the practice in other places, the Laxton court leet and court baron from 1651 onwards has been no mere formal institution. There has been no dictation to the people by their lord. The records of essoigns, the fealties, the election of officers, were matters of routine, and they were recorded year by year in the same forms of words by the lord's steward. But the jury elected from the people was a living institution, intervening to regulate the economic and social life of the community by a system which required personal service from each man at frequent intervals. The administrative officers were drawn from the community, and the various offices rotated amongst its members. The decisions of the jury recorded by the Court were no mere stereotyped forms or repetitions; they made their presentments in their own hand and phrase, with vividness and spontaneity; they assessed the appropriate fines without fear or favour. The flexibility of the administrative machine was ensured by the powers of the Court to make new by-laws, year by year, and to vary the old ones, to a degree that is impossible in an agricultural community controlled, instead, by ancient customs and laggard statutes. A custom is not a custom until the "memory of man runneth not to the contrary," and a statute never reaches the Statute Book until long after the need for it has arisen. The by-laws of the Laxton Court could be, and they often were made and varied every twelve months. They extended to questions of agricultural policy affecting the whole community, as well as to matters of detail in which only individuals were concerned, and the emphasis was always changing to meet changing needs.[171]

By the early eighteenth century, however, the vigor and activity of the Redgrave court had certainly diminished. It still met regularly once a year and sometimes oftener on special call when there were copyhold transfers to record.[172] By-laws were still

[171] Orwin, *The Open Fields,* 171. The manor of Laxton is not so unusual in its late preservation of the open field system as the Orwins believed. John Holt Wilson, Esq., the present lord of Redgrave and Hindercley Manors has found an example near Redgrave where the ancient methods were still used in 1957 on an extensive tract. There may well be other examples in Suffolk and southern Norfolk.

[172] One of the special meetings was on Jan. 13, 1710–1711, where a lawsuit,

issued and renewed, but there were fewer signs of experiment and innovation. At the meeting for 1705, for example, the by-laws almost seem like a code, compiled as a summary of the well-tried rules that had accumulated for centuries. Thirteen were sworn as the "inquest" for Redgrave and these jurors "say that they have ordered" (*dicunt quod ordinaverunt*) that

no one shall pasture sheep on the common
no one shall put unringed hogs on the common
no one shall sell outside the vill any thatch cut on the common
each inhabitant shall work one day during the forthcoming year cleaning the river known as "the swimming ditch"
no one shall pasture more beasts on the common than are fixed in the "rate"—and so on.

Then "the said jurors present" Roger Salter and two others for pasturing more beasts on the common than are permitted them in the "rate" and the jurors "have mulcted" (*mulctabant*) them each 6s. 8d. The jurors present that "they elect" (*eligent*) two persons as constables. The entries of this type continue at least till 1711 and possibly somewhat later, but the activity of the court was steadily diminishing and the entries had become routine.

In their studies of English local government after 1689 the Webbs have described other manors that functioned very actively until the latter part of the eighteenth century, issuing elaborate by-laws that were often revised, electing local officers, amercing individuals for nuisance, and various other offenses.[173] The most remarkable instance was the manor of Manchester, whose court leet became the government of the great industrial city of Manchester which grew up within its precincts. "Year by year the Court went on appointing its officers, making its presentments and imposing its fines with unslackened zeal, and doing an un-

---

evidently collusive, was brought for copyhold land with the object of extinguishing a possible claim of one Robert Symonds, who appeared and then defaulted, so that final judgment was entered against him. Common recoveries were apparently much resorted to in manorial courts to perfect titles to copyhold land; enough so that when the Chancery in 1685–1686 was asked to set one aside the Master of the Rolls refused to do so, pointing to the dangers of upsetting "a multitude of settlements" made in manorial courts by this means. Ash v. Rogle, 2 *Chan. Rep.* 387.

[173] Webb, *ELG*, II, 71–98. Hearnshaw in his survey found 220 courts leet still meeting in 1835 and gave a list of 44 that were still meeting in 1908 when his own book was published. *Leet Jurisdiction in England*, 6, 248–321.

diminished amount of work right down to the nineteenth century." Finally in 1846 the town council bought the lordship rights from Sir Oswald Moseley, the lord of the Manor of Manchester, for the enormous sum of £200,000 and the court with all the apparatus it had developed was allowed to disappear.[174]

Long before 1800 effective power in local government through most of England had been gradually drifting to other agencies. The symptoms of decline were numerous in records of the manorial courts; the contracting circle of topics dealt with, reduced attendance, the decline of presentments into mere repetition, sometimes to a mere *omnia bene* or "all well but the pigs." [175] The agencies that displaced the manorial courts were the justices of the peace and their subordinate officials and, at the local level, the parishes. This is not the place to describe the growth of the church parish as an expanding center of secular local government. The core of its functions, though not the earliest, was administration of poor relief, which was assigned to the parish by Elizabethan legislation. Empowered to distribute the costs of poor relief through local assessments and developing a kind of executive staff (controlled, it is true, by the justices of the peace), the parishes were a natural magnet for new powers and functions as needs developed. The parish officials operated on the whole without the trappings of a court, though they were often brought into contact with the justices of the peace in the court of Quarter Sessions, where they received advice and discipline. The parishes became the main centers of local administration, outwardly new and employing officials with new titles. But they absorbed and adapted for new purposes, not only some ancient offices like that of constable, but the whole complex of attitudes that were built so deeply into English neighborhood communities. The parish officials, like other English local officials, were most of the time unpaid. Service was compulsory, though many succeeded in evading it and there were certain exemptions recognized for such persons as peers, clergy, soldiers, and lawyers. The duty of service was passed around, "by house-row in rotation." As the Webbs have said, the predominant principles of eighteenth-cen-

---

[174] Webb, *ELG*, II, 99–113. The language quoted in the text appears in Webb, II, 108.

[175] Webb, II, 122, the latter quotation coming from a presentment in a Welsh manor in 1804.

tury local government—common consent and local autonomy—
were derived from an ancient heritage, the heritage of the manors.[176]

This free growth of local institutions did not necessarily mean
the greatest good for the greatest number. There were no firm
controls from any outside source. The central government was
blandly indifferent. So the thousands of small parish communities
were free to adapt themselves—to anything from impregnable
little oligarchies or corrupt misrule by the unfit to well run little
democracies in which decisions were made by common consent.
On the whole it is difficult to feel much regret for the English
eighteenth-century institutions that were swept away in the nineteenth. But they preserved the main elements of an ancient experience, widely shared and fully recorded. They preserved the
freedom of English people to govern, or misgovern, themselves
in the ways that they preferred.

g. *The Trial and Review of Presentments*

Before finally leaving the manor courts we should take one last
look at court leet procedure, to observe the seamy side. The sanctions of the court leet were mild. They all ended up in a money
judgment, enforced by distress of goods. The amount of the judgment was normally small, at least for those who had some money
to pay—seldom more than 40 shillings and usually very much
less. So perhaps it was not such a serious matter that court leet
procedure in general made no real provision for a trial at all.

This was the meaning of the statement by the common lawyers
that a presentment in a court leet was not "traversable." The discussions of the common lawyers related to the court leet, but the
proposition was equally true of the "court baron" insofar as it
undertook, as it often did, to punish specific misdeeds or prevent
them in the future. Many thousands of entries simply record that
"the jurors present" (*presentant*) or "the jurors say" (*dicant*),
followed by the name of the offender, the nature of his offense,
and the price he must pay. In none of them is there the slightest

---

[176] Webb, II, 19. The history of the parish is described by Holdsworth, *HEL*, IV,
155–163 and X, 128ff., with numerous comments on the continuity of the traditions inherited from medieval local government. The development of parish government after 1689 is described in detail by Webb, *ELG*, I, 9–145. The comments
in this and the succeeding paragraph depend entirely on the account of the Webbs.

suggestion that witnesses were called, that arguments were heard, or that the presentments were followed by a separate trial. In other words, accusation by the jury equalled guilt. As Lord Mansfield put it, the jury of the leet "accuses and punishes at the same instant." [177]

It may not have been quite as bad as it seems. The manorial juries were made up of neighbors assembled in the manor hall or some other local building. Their verdicts must have been preceded by at least a brief period of discussion, and at this point it might well be that the accused could speak up for himself. In these discussions feelings must often have risen high, for neighbors were reporting each other's misdeeds—indeed, this was their duty. Two incidents at Redgrave will give the mood. At the session held in the fall of 1610, Robert Welles, a juror, "was telling the court certain matters that should be looked into" (*fuit demonstrans Cur' quasdam materias ad tunc inquirend'*) when Edward Fyssher, another juror, used "contemptuous and opprobrious words in open Court," namely that "thou (*predictum Robertum Welles innuendo*) art a foole and an asse"; Edward was fined for this, 40 shillings. At another session the following year four members of the jury were fined 20 shillings each because they "did misdemean themselves in disturbing Andrew Flack, wrighter of their verditt, casting acres at him and using other unseemelie usages whereby he could not effecte the same verdytt" ["acres" were apparently "acrestaffs," poles used to clean plows]. In neither instance is there any clue as to the cause of these outbreaks, but it may be that the persons using these strong means were repelling accusations against themselves. The means they used proved somewhat costly and were no doubt unwise. But if the jurors could not be dissuaded before their verdicts were filed, it is hard to see what other recourse there was in the manor court. In many cases there was no harm done. Many offenses presented were manifest; everyone in the village knew whether Samuel Ware let his trees "overdreep" the highway or left his chimney in disrepair, and he could

[177] Colebrooke v. Elliott, 3 *Burr.* 1859 (1766). In this case one of the questions was whether a statute defining a misdemeanor should be construed as conferring jurisdiction on courts leet. Lord Mansfield, for the court, concluded it should not, in particular because the statute in question required that the defendant "shall be summoned and have an opportunity of making his defence," and such a hearing could not be given in a court leet which "accuses and punishes at the same instant."

hardly deny the charge. But it could well be that the person accused *had* scoured his ditches and ringed his pigs, that he did *not* haunt alehouses or rail at the constables or beat his wife. For such victims of gossip or neighbors' vengeance, the remedy must be sought elsewhere.

If a remedy was sought in a common law court, there were at least four means by which a review might be secured. After the amercement or "pain" had been duly recorded, the lord's bailiff could collect it by distraint of goods and the victim of the amercement could then challenge the bailiff's seizure by a common law action of trespass or replevin. Or, if the person amerced had no goods within reach of the bailiff, the lord might bring an action of debt on the manor court judgment; a defense to this action might be interposed. Or, the person amerced could sue out a writ of certiorari and seek to have the whole case removed to the King's Bench for trial there on the merits. Or, if he wished to take a very long chance and if the amercement was imposed in a court leet rather than in the "court baron" phase, he could sue out a writ of error to reverse the manor court's judgment.

A writ of error was clearly not available to challenge the *amount* of the amercement. In a case decided in 1610, a writ of error was used to attack an amercement as "unreasonable." Noy, counsel for the lord of the manor, argued: "After that this amerciament is once affeered, you shall not afterwards have a writ of error that this amerciament was unreasonable, and you shall never have a *moderata misericordia* in such a case; the whole court agreed clearly in this, that this is no error now to be assigned, and therefore by the rule of the court, the same [that is, the manor court's judgment] was affirmed." [178] The implications of this firm negative went beyond the immediate issue decided and gave little encouragement for the use of writs of error. In litigation in common law courts less direct means of attack were usually employed.

In a case decided in 1505 the line of attack was trespass against a distraining bailiff for the taking of a horse. The bailiff justified the taking by alleging that the plaintiff had been amerced three pence in a court leet for failure to scour a ditch, the duty to scour being attached by immemorial usage to a tract of land of which the plaintiff was owner. Plaintiff denied the ownership of any

[178] Stubbs v. Flower, 1 *Bulstrode* 125 (1610).

land to which was attached a duty to scour the ditch in question, and in order to open an avenue for the introduction of this issue, claimed that the presentment "touched" freehold and therefore was traversable. But the reporter quoted Frowicke, C. J., for the statement that "a presentment in a leet is to be taken as gospel and this is said in these very words in our books." In order to justify this conclusion Frowicke pointed out that the presentment must be by a jury of 12 persons at least and that a leet presentment must relate to events that had occurred within a very small area and that would be fresh in memory, since they must have occurred since the last leet was held. "For all these reasons the party will be condemned by the presentment itself, so that he will have no means of responding by this presentment unless the matter touches freehold or a man's life. *Quod fuit concessum.*" Frowicke added that there was in the Register a writ of false presentment which might possibly give a remedy against the jurors themselves for their false presentment but the comment is added (apparently from the reporter, Keilwey): "But I have never seen this writ used." The discussion then went on, raising some interesting questions as to leet presentments against non-residents for failure to render suit of court or for conduct occurring outside the precincts of the leet; here Frowicke was willing to concede that the presentment "is void in itself and *coram non Judice.*" But in the case before him Frowicke indicated that if the ditch in question was located within the precincts of the leet the plea was bad; and even though it concerned freehold, the remedy lay through removal to the King's Bench and not by an action of trespass against the distraining bailiff.[179]

The doctrine that a verdict by a jury of 12 or more was conclu-

---

[179] *Keilwey* 66 (1505). Similar issues were raised in *Y.B. 41 Edw. III 26*, where one John was amerced in a court leet for "harboring" a servant for a year and a day without enrolling him on the frankpledge lists. John denied that the servant had resided within the precincts of the leet for a year and a day and his counsel argued that since presentments in the King's Bench could be traversed, "a presentment in a lower court (*en court pluis base*) will not be more conclusive." When the judges found this argument unacceptable, counsel for the plaintiff shifted to the contention that the denial went to the jurisdiction of the court, referring to another case, claimed to be analogous, where "it has been adjudged" that a presentment for stopping a roadway was successfully traversed by showing that the roadway lay outside the precincts of the leet. Two of the Justices expressed their opinion that the issue as to the servant's residence could be raised since it went to "jurisdiction." The case was adjourned without decision.

sive of guilt was standard doctrine among sixteenth and seventeenth century courts and authors; the only exceptions were the unlikely case of jeopardy to life and the case in which freehold was involved; here the remedy was removal to the King's Bench by certiorari, not a traverse of the indictment in the leet court itself.[180] This extraordinary doctrine, confirmed though it was by frequent repetition, began to produce some restlessness toward the end of the seventeenth century. In a case in 1688, for example, trespass was brought against a distraining bailiff by a resident of Westminster, who had been presented and amerced £5 for a nuisance in melting stinking tallow. To the bailiff's justification the plaintiff replied by denying that he had melted any tallow. At the first hearing of the case Powell, J., repeated the standard comment that a leet presentment was not traversable unless it affected freehold. At a second hearing Holt, C. J., suggested that if the action had been replevin the plaintiff's denial would have been admissible, though Holt said he was reluctant to hold the officer in an action for damages for trespass. "Afterwards the Court inclined, that the traverse in the principal case was well taken, for they held that presentments in the Quarter-Sessions of the Peace and even in the King's Bench are traversable; and if 'tis so in courts superior to the leet, a fortiori it must be so in presentments at the leet. Besides, if this presentment should be removed by certiorari into the King's Bench, 'tis clear that 'tis traversable." In the end the court was able to give judgment for the plaintiff on the technical ground that the defendant had not set forth any warrant from the steward to justify his distraint.[181]

It was not till the time of Lord Mansfield that the remedy of removal into the King's Bench by certiorari became available in all types of cases. The case confronting Lord Mansfield was a distressing one, though no more distressing than many thousands of others that must have occurred in the past. The defendant in the court leet had been amerced £50 for keeping a disorderly house, without any notice of the proceeding or any opportunity to be heard. The King's Bench granted certiorari, after an ad-

---

[180] *Dyer* 13b (1536); 1 *Freeman* 340 (1673); Kitchin, *Court Leet*, 41; Hearnshaw, *Leet Jurisdiction in England*, 136–139. Joseph Ritson, *The Jurisdiction of the Court Leet* (3d ed., London, 1816), 129–146, collects numerous other authorities.

[181] Matthews v. Cary, *Comberbach* 76 and *Carthew* 74 (1688).

journment of the court for review of all the precedents. Lord Mansfield was clear that no traverse of the presentment was available in the court leet, but stated that certiorari should be granted since "it would not be just that he should be fined and condemned unheard." His colleague, Justice Aston, added the comment that if removal to the King's Bench were not granted, "this would give a court leet power superior to that of any other jurisdiction in the kingdom." [182] Yet it seems that this was precisely what courts leet possessed for centuries, until indirect controls were thus tardily imposed. And it should be noted also that removal by certiorari to the King's Bench at Westminster required money to pay expensive lawyers and much time and trouble. For most of the population, assessed small sums for minor offenses, it was a remedy not to be thought of.

There remains the question whether the post-audit of amercements, by the process known as "affeerment," gave a measure of protection within the manor courts themselves. Affeerment was required by Magna Carta, but it antedates 1215, for Glanvill declared that persons in the king's mercy should be amerced "through the oath of lawful men of the neighborhood . . . lest they lose their honorable contenement." [183] Magna Carta, sec. 20 provided that amercements of freemen, merchants and villeins must be "in accordance with the gravity of the offense" and must preserve for the offender his essential means of livelihood; the amercement was to be in every case "through the oaths of honest men of the neighborhood" (*per sacramentum proborum hominum de visneto*).[184] This provision applied only to offenders who had fallen into the king's own mercy, so that it is at least doubtful whether it could apply to local courts generally. But courts leet were sufficiently royal courts so that when the court leet pattern was de-

[182] Rex v. Roupell, 2 *Cowp.* 458 (1776).
[183] Glanvill, *De Legibus et Consuetudinibus Regni Angliae* (ed. George E. Woodbine, New Haven, 1932), IX, 11.
[184] McKechnie, *Magna Carta,* 334–346, gives the text of the 1215 charter with commentary. The exemption for freemen was their "contenement," for merchants their "merchandise," and for villeins their "wainage," but the central idea in each case was to preserve the essential means of livelihood.
Parallel to section 20 was the provision of section 21, that earls and barons were to be amerced only by their "peers." The latter provision could be satisfied through assessment by Exchequer barons, who were "peers" for this purpose at least. McKechnie, *Magna Carta,* 346–349; Keeney, *Judgment by Peers,* 165 (esp. his note 138).

veloped in the later thirteenth century, manor court rolls regularly recorded the names of "affeerors" (usually two) who were separately appointed. Their function was not to review the truth or falsity of the original accusation but the fairness of the penalty that was to be imposed on the offender.

Magna Carta, sec. 20, did not require any particular number of "honest men" or prescribe that they be separate from the jury of the leet. From an early stage it must have occurred to some persons that the leet jurors were also presumably "honest men," and they were usually from the neighborhood.[185] Why not combine the two functions? Even in the early rolls the names of affeerors are sometimes omitted, though this is not strong evidence since the scribes were not systematic in recording the names of officials chosen in the manorial courts. But as time went on the references to separate affeerors became so rare that the negative evidence is persuasive. At Redgrave, as at other manors, it seems extremely likely that by the sixteenth century the function of affeering became fused with the presentment function and had passed to the manorial juries. The language of many entries, some of which have already been quoted, strongly suggests that homage and leet juries included in their verdicts not only their findings of liability but the precise sums that the offenders should pay.

The reaction of the common lawyers to this development was somewhat indecisive. In his report of a decision in 1588 Coke threw in the incidental comment that affeerment by the verdict of a leet jury would be sufficient and no separate affeerors were needed.[186] Hobart in the early seventeenth century expressed precisely the opposite view—that the offices of jurors and affeerors "cannot be confounded." [187] But in a case in 1688 the whole King's

[185] Though the duty of attending courts leet was imposed by virtue of residence, it seems that residence in the neighborhood was not a requirement for membership in a leet jury. There was a comment by counsel in a Yearbook case of 1429 that was widely quoted: "It has been said that if a person is riding by a place where a leet is held, the steward for want of others may compel him to be sworn." Y.B. 7 Henry VI, 12. Later authors also stated that strangers could be forced to serve if the numbers already present were insufficient. Kitchin, Court Leet, 7; Coke, Complete Copyholder, sec. 31.

[186] Griesley's Case, 8 Coke Rep. 38a, at 40b.

[187] Hobart, 129 (1617). His view was followed in Evelin v. Davies, 3 Lev. 206 (1684), an action of debt to collect a court leet amercement that was alleged to have been affeered by the leet jury. A demurrer to the declaration was sustained on two grounds, one of them being that affeerment must be by persons chosen by the steward and could not be by the jury.

Bench was reported as agreeing that "Antiently two were sworn to affeere; now the same jury do both"; and Lord Holt on this as well as another occasion stated his own view that "If the jury amerce to a particular sum, there is no need of an affeerment." [188] A later author indicates that this practice extended to courts baron as well when the homage voted amercements for copyholders' failures of duty.[189]

A different question was presented by fines imposed on the steward's authority for offensive language or disturbances during the sessions of the court itself. Despite the qualms expressed in Yearbook cases over the steward's acting as judge "in his own case," [190] the common lawyers conceded a power to punish for this class of offenses, free from review by any kind of affeerment. The power resided in the steward himself, as the holder of a judicial office. The requirement of affeerment in Magna Carta was easily skirted; penalties of this class were not amercements, but fines used to maintain judicial authority, so Magna Carta did not apply.[191]

Most of the misdeeds and omissions that were reported by manorial juries occurred, of course, outside of court. For a large share of the money penalties imposed by manorial courts, therefore, Magna Carta required some affeerment. But in the minds of common lawyers of the seventeenth century, for whom Magna Carta had become the Great Charter of Liberties, its provision

---

[188] Matthews v. Cary, 1 *Show.* 62 (1688). Actually the discussion as reported was more wandering and confused than the brief summary in the text would indicate. Holt, C. J., and Eyres, J., were first quoted for the opinion that amercement "ought to be the act of the Court and the affeering to be by the jury; the jury cannot amerce." But Dobbin, J., said: "The jury do amerce, and there are affeerors for that purpose appointed." Holt had the last word: "If the jury amerce to a particular sum, then there is no need for an affeerment." In a later case in 1707 (after he had acquired Redgrave), Holt was quoted in dicta: "The jury may amerce in a certain sum if they will and then there needs not an affeerment; though the proper way is 'ideo sit in misericordia', and then an affeerment."

[189] Charles Watkins, *A Treatise on Copyholds* (London, 4th ed., 1825), II, 384. The author here pointed out that amercements could not be sued for in common law courts until they were affeered, but that the usual practice was merely for the homage to declare on oath "what penalty they in their conscience think the offender deserves."

[190] *Y.B. 7 Henry VI,* 12; *10 Henry VI,* 7. The arguments in both cases are translated by S. E. Thorne, "Courts of Record and Sir Edward Coke," 2 *Toronto L.J.* 24, 42–43.

[191] Coke, *Complete Copyholder,* sec. 26; Griesley's Case, 8 *Coke Rep.* 38a (1588).

for affeerment of amercements fell into a larger pattern; it was a form of judgment "by peers." [192] Then if judgment by peers meant jury trial, as many people had come to think, it was consistent with Magna Carta, and might seem to promote its purposes, to entrust to the same jury both the finding of guilt and the fixing of punishment. And so we have the paradox that Magna Carta itself may have helped to remove the last restraint on manorial juries, which could convict without trial and now could determine without review how much the victims must pay.

Before condemning outright this summary procedure, one should recall that the manorial juries were groups of unlearned men, with constantly changing membership. Elaborate rules of trial procedure would have baffled and bewildered them. Indeed at the outset, when manorial courts were first organized, it would have been hard to find a source from which such rules could be borrowed, for the common law itself had not yet developed rules of evidence, judge's instructions or the other means of controlling juries with which we are now familiar. As rules of trial procedure were slowly organized by the common law, their transfer to manorial courts would surely have paralyzed initiative and driven the suitors away; France and Germany showed what could happen. If one views the problem from the point of view of the central government, including the central courts, there were great difficulties in responding to such appeals as that sent to Parliament in 1314 by the commonalty of Suffolk, that some remedy be provided against "the chief pledges of the leets and the sheriff's tourn [who] falsely present men as guilty under the articles of the leet and sheriff's tourn when they are guilty of nothing." [193] To intrude in such matters, in thousands of manors, would have multiplied enormously the tasks of the central government and the

---

[192] Coke, *Complete Copyholder*, sec. 26.

[193] *Rotuli Parliamentorum* (London, 1767), I, 293, quoted Hearnshaw, 89 and 151. The reply was merely: "If anyone wishes to pursue false indictors or the procurers of false indictments, let him follow them in the Chancery and he will have competent remedy." An indirect remedy was later provided by statute in 1483 (1 Richard III, c. 4), which recited that persons of no substance serving on juries of the sheriffs' tourns often turned in false presentments. It required that no one should be empanelled who was not of good repute and who did not own freehold land of a yearly value of at least 20 shillings or else copyhold land of a yearly value of 26 shillings 8 pence. I have seen no suggestion anywhere that this property qualification was extended beyond the sheriff's tourn to include manorial juries.

personnel it employed. The presentment jury, acting by collective verdict, was already firmly fixed as a central feature of manor court procedure. To the men who governed England it must have seemed immensely easier to accept this voice of the neighborhood and hope that each community would work out its own correctives for falsehood and private vengeance. This was the hope that Coke expressed in his benign old age:

And so I conclude with Copyholders, wishing that there may ever be a perfect union betwixt them and their Lords, that they may have a feeling of each others wrongs and injuries; that their so little Commonwealth, having all his members knit together in complete order, may flourish to the end.[194]

Simplification of procedure was part of the price that had to be paid if such ideals were to be realized and effective powers of decision were to be preserved in manorial juries. Yet it seems that the price actually paid was higher than it needed to be. It should have been possible for manorial courts to empanel special juries of trial on the demand of accused persons; trial juries were normal in civil cases. Common law courts could have stepped in much sooner, extending both the review of judgments by writ of error and the removal jurisdiction, even though both were too cumbersome and costly for constant use by small-farmer litigants. It is amazing that a procedure contradicting the most elementary notions of fairness could have been tolerated so long without protest. Perhaps the absence of protest is negative evidence that on the whole these "little Commonwealths" managed their business well.

7. BOROUGH AND TOWN COURTS

At every stage of their history until the nineteenth century the English boroughs and towns used governmental forms that were extremely diversified. They originated at different times and under pressures that differed from place to place. With the growth of trade in the twelfth and thirteenth centuries, the people who had clustered around fortifications and market places took on new importance, though for centuries they were to remain, as has been said, no more than a tenth of the whole population.[195] Their demands for special privileges and larger powers of self-

[194] Coke, *Complete Copyholder*, sec. 62.
[195] The estimates of Russell, *British Medieval Population* have been summarized

government met resistance from the crown and also from neighboring lords, but the resistance gave way from time to time in concessions that were not uniform. Since the future in the end was to lie with the towns, their struggles for self-government have exceptional interest. A large modern literature has developed but the evidence is scattered and difficult to interpret. Disputes, especially over origins, have complicated the subject further.

It seems safe to say that in their earliest forms most of the towns were not sharply distinguished from the settlements in which the farming population was mainly gathered. In the century before the Norman Conquest many places that called themselves burghs had farming land within or immediately beyond their walls and some of their residents engaged in farming. The more important settlements had courts, but in form and structure they strongly resembled the hundred courts that have already been described and that were cast in a standard pattern over most of England. Whether the larger boroughs had courts of their own, detached from the hundred courts of the surrounding neighborhoods, is a disputed question. In most the separation probably came after 1066. But the hundred courts were at least a most convenient forum for resolving the new problems of the trading communities and giving effect to their new needs. Professor Tait has said:

It was mainly in these hundredal courts adapted to the needs of the burgesses that their aspirations to greater liberty and self-government first woke to life and found in them an instrument which, powerfully aided by merchant gilds, ultimately secured the realization of those aspirations and became the sovereign body, the *communitas*, of the fully developed municipality.[196]

For the full development of municipal self-government much more than courts was needed. After the Conquest had sent cascades of power down the new lines of feudal tenure, it was nec-

---

earlier, in Chapter 5, section 5. For Russell's purposes a town was taken to be a settlement of 400 persons or more, though some places with the title of "borough" had less than this number (Russell, 283).

[196] James Tait, *The Medieval English Borough* (Manchester, 1936), 62. The various theories on these complex subjects are well summarized by Professor Tait (pp. 30–66) and I have relied chiefly on his work. The views that he chiefly aimed to refute were those of Professor Carl Stephenson, *Borough and Town* (Cambridge, Mass., 1933), which minimize the growth of the towns before the Conquest and in the words of Tait would view the Anglo-Saxon borough as "merely a walled microcosm of the rural world without" (Tait, 68). Tait concedes only part of Stephenson's contention that the late Anglo-Saxon town settlements included a substantial amount of farming land (Tait, 68–77).

essary first of all to oppose the pretensions of local lords of the land. For individual residents this meant a release from the duties of labor service and their commutation into money rents, an essential of free burgage tenure. This process began early, long before a similar movement was well started in rural areas. For the town communities themselves the aim was to secure freedom from tolls and other exactions of neighboring lords and especially to exclude the lords from control over town courts—the type of control they were acquiring in rural manors. Quite apart from the struggles with local feudal lords—struggles that were occurring all over Europe—there were special problems in England because of the power and vigilance of the central government. As its power advanced, the growth of local government in the towns came to depend more and more on persuading the crown to relax its vigilance and grant concessions to the towns.

The most important of the privileges granted by the crown had no direct connection with court organization—the privilege of collecting royal taxes due from the town's inhabitants and remitting the proceeds directly. Though such grants had been made in earlier times, Richard I and John were led by financial needs to make them on a much larger scale. Then under John began a series of grants in more general terms, giving privileges of "free boroughs." These privileges were sometimes defined by specific enumeration or by cross-reference to other boroughs, but often the meaning was left at large. The difficulties caused by the absence of common standards were then greatly increased by the flood of concessions made by feudal lords in the late thirteenth and fourteenth centuries.[197] The "seignorial boroughs" thus created might acquire a large measure of internal self-government and with the vicissitudes of time might outstrip in wealth and population some boroughs possessed of royal charters.

In the boroughs of the thirteenth century a separate borough court was a standard feature. It would almost always carry a civil jurisdiction, with varying limits of value, and a criminal jurisdiction at least as wide as that of courts leet. As in the manors, there was freedom to develop rules of private law that diverged in important respects from the common law. The greater needs for regulation in densely populated areas produced local legislation

[197] Tait, chaps. VII and VIII, discusses the subjects of this paragraph.

in great variety.[198] But this energetic response to newly acquired liberties created its own problems. The volume of business to be transacted required frequent meetings, time and thought, and some continuity in personnel. Even if no other pressures had been at work, there would have been need to concentrate responsibility on those ready to assume it. And there were other pressures that in England, as on the continent, were producing major divisions among the town-dwellers themselves.

There soon appeared in some of the towns a phenomenon that no one has yet detected in the rural manors—a continuing group or council that was clearly distinguished from the general body of citizens who met in the community court. As early as 1193 the citizens of London took an oath to be obedient to "the mayor of London and to the skivins (*skivini*) . . . and to follow and maintain the decisions of the mayor and skivins and other good men" associated with them. In thirteenth-century records there appear councils, usually made up of 12 or 24 persons, who were "elected" to serve not only in judicial matters but in general management of town affairs. By the end of the thirteenth century such arrangements had become quite common.[199] As to their origins, Maitland threw out the suggestion which acquired for a time a wide following, that the councils grew out of the older borough courts by a gradual restriction of membership.[200] To some extent this did occur. On the other hand, the contacts with Europe maintained by the trading communities make it seem at least plausible that the town councils of northern France and the Low Countries, some of them derived from the Carolingian *scabini*, provided stimulus if not specific example.[201] The towns with sea borne commerce were exposed to influences that could scarcely reach the farming population.

With expanding powers of government now centered in fewer hands, the methods of choosing the councilors took on crucial importance. It seems that in the beginning the town community

[198] *Borough Customs* (ed. Mary Bateson, Selden Society, London, 1904–1906); Holdsworth, *HEL*, II, 386–394.

[199] Tait, 266–290; Pollock and Maitland, *HEL*, I, 658–659; Bateson, Introduction to *Borough Customs* (Selden Society), II, cxlvii–cxlviii.

[200] "The Origin of the Borough," *Collected Essays* (1911), III, 31, 42.

[201] This is the conclusion of Tait, 285–301, disagreeing somewhat with Stephenson, *Borough and Town*, 183–185.

as a whole took part in some kind of informal election.[202] But the wealthy and prominent citizens on whom responsibility had been cast tended to remain on in office or if they withdrew, to influence the choice of their successors. In some places, quite early, the councilors acquired life tenure. The growth of "oligarchy" in the towns was rapid and has been much discussed. Protests against the rule of the *potentiores* brought bitter conflicts in many places and required at times that the king or Parliament intervene. To secure a wider base of representation, a two-council system was much used in the late fourteenth and fifteenth centuries; a "common council" was added and given a voice in such matters as taxation, the choice of officials, and often more. But in the words of Professor Tait:

Unfortunately, inadequate systems of election and more generally the use of nomination soon put the common councils out of touch with the mass of the commonalty, and in the end they did no more than broaden the base of civic oligarchy.[203]

The growth of town councils did not at first involve a separation of the judicial function from other functions of local government; the same men performed them all.[204] But as municipal administration grew more complex it was clearly necessary to relieve the councilors as to a great range of matters—private disputes and individual misconduct—that could be dealt with under judicial forms. It is impossible to describe in general terms the immensely varied solutions that were adopted. But there is one theme that constantly recurs, the use of juries—especially the type of presentment jury developed in the courts leet. Even as late as 1689 most of the organized towns still employed the presentment jury as standard equipment.[205] Transferred to the towns with the full panoply of intermingled powers, the leet-type juries were in a sense competitors for a share in government. The methods of choosing the jurors are as obscure as in the manor courts, though sometimes it is clear that the choice was by the governing councils or by subordinate officials whom the councils con-

---

[202] Tait, 281–282.
[203] Tait, 303. The question is further discussed by him on pp. 302–338 and by Charles W. Colby, "The Growth of Oligarchy in the English Towns," 5 *Eng. Hist. Rev.* 633 (1890).
[204] Tait, 288.
[205] Webb, *ELG*, II, 344–345.

trolled.[206] There were questions as to the jurors' power to legislate, a power which was usually exercised with the utmost freedom but which in some places like Coventry was controlled by a requirement of prior approval by the mayor and council.[207] Since the executive power was usually held by the council and the officers it appointed, their refusal to collect the amercements and "pains" that were voted by the jurors could reduce the jurors to frustrated impotence.[208]

However controlled or hampered by the governing councils, the presentment juries of the sixteenth and seventeenth century towns appear in town records as extremely active agencies. As on the manors they acted through ordinances cast in general terms and also through commands and punishments directed to individuals.[209] The subjects of their concern included many that troubled manorial juries. Some communities still had common lands whose use for farming or pasture required regulation. The town juries struggled to maintain water supply and drainage, to clear the streets of obstructions and filth, to eliminate fire hazards. In closely settled areas pigs were an even greater blight than in the countryside. Rules against roving pigs were constantly repeated. The jurors in Southampton were exasperated when they discovered that the mayor himself had a pig in his backyard; at

[206] Hearnshaw, *Leet Jurisdiction in England,* 191 and the *Coventry Leet Book* (London, 1907–1913), xxii, refer to the cases of Southampton and Coventry. In Southampton the jurors were chosen by the town clerk and sheriff, in Coventry by the mayor and council. In King v. Joliffe, 2 *Barn. & Cress.* 54 (1823), it was asserted by the judges that normally the bailiff chose the jurors, but this left at large the question, who chose the bailiff?

[207] *Coventry Leet Book,* xx–xxii.

[208] Hearnshaw, *Leet Jurisdiction in England,* 196–197, discussing the records of Southampton. The frustration of the jurors appears in many entries in the *Southampton Court Leet Records* (ed. Hearnshaw, Southampton, 1905–1907), covering the period 1550–1623. For example, in 1550 the jurors recorded that in 1545 the governing council of Southampton had agreed that no men from Jersey and Guernsey would be made burgesses of Southampton. The jurors declared this agreement had not been carried out and demanded that it should be, "and yf you refuse this to do, we will stryke all our names owt of yor bookes and so comyt all the chargs of the towne into you hands" (I, 18).

[209] The comments that follow are based on the *Southampton Court Leet Records* in 3 vols. (1550–1623); *Coventry Leet Book* (1420–1555); *Court Leet Records of the Manor of Manchester,* 12 vols. (1552–1846); *Liverpool Town Books* (Liverpool, 1935), vol. II (1571–1603); *Preston Court Leet Records* (ed. Hewitson, covering 1653–1813); and the court book of Lymington, a manuscript volume in the Bacon papers at the University of Chicago which gives the entries from 1609 into the 1680's. In all these the sixteenth and early seventeenth centuries are the period I have chiefly studied.

one point in despair they declared that if something was not done about pigs "we thinck yt mete" that every man in town should keep pigs "so that when the thinge is at the worste shame may redresse yt." [210] Almost next to pigs were foreigners, who used the town's assets, crowded the buildings, and encroached on the trading privileges of the native burgesses. The jurors at Preston in Lancashire declared in 1653 that "wee find there are great number of forrayners crept into this Towne"; they amerced them all, particularly named ten foreigners who were to leave at once, and added another group who were "unfitt members to abide or inhabit within this Towne" and were to leave within five months.[211] Beside these matters, defective materials, bad meat, false weights and measures led to frequent amercements and commands to desist.

If there was any difference between towns and rural manors in the impact of presentment machinery, it lay in the more intensive control over conduct that resulted in the towns. With dwellings close and daily contacts frequent, friction and tension were multiplied. Many brawls and "tusles" brought amercements on all participants. There was the problem of the "evedropp" who "stands under mens windows lisoning and carrieing stories betwixt neighbour and neighbour, to the great disquietnes of neighbours and to the evill example of others." [212] Some of the commands and punishments reflected local standards of morality. Individuals were told to go to church "as every well dysposed person ought to do." [213] Unmarried women, who might be tempted into

[210] *Southampton Court Leet Records*, I, 7 and 17 (1550). In 1604, however, the jurors presented that the orders for pigs were still unobserved and "we finde this abuse daylie more and more encreaseth tendinge to the greate disgrace of the government." The Webbs, *ELG*, II, 104, quote the editor of the Manchester court leet records as follows: "Pigs, as the most perverse animals, required the firmest and most rigorous handling; and hundreds of folio pages of Jury orders relate to swine alone and their numerous misdeeds and nuisances, their eating corn in the market and desecrating the churchyard."

[211] *Preston Court Leet Records*, 10 and 13.

[212] *Preston Court Leet Records*, 92 (1661), recording an amercement of Thomas Sidcocke for offending in this way. But it seems that self-help measures against eavesdroppers were discouraged. On Oct. 20, 1654 amercements were assessed both against Margaret, wife of George Berchall, "for lookinge and herkinnge at the window of William Dobson" and also against William Dobson himself "for a Chamber pott emptied and throwne out his windowe into ye backside of Geo. Berchall, to ye great Annoyance of ye said George" (Preston Records, 39).

[213] *Southampton Court Leet Records*, I, 119 (1575).

evil ways, were ordered to go into service or take residence with "an honest person." [214] These "non-traversable" presentments brought money penalties, usually small, but they also brought public censure. The pressure to conformity must have born down hard on eccentric persons. Who can say whether justice was done when there was no standard for measuring justice but the opinion of the community expressed through juries of changing membership? At least it can be said for the presentment machinery that it preserved a large sector in which community opinion could make itself felt, even after the primary powers of local government had been captured by exclusive groups of *potentiores,* largely self-selected.

The later history of the courts in the towns is merely a part, though a vital part, of the whole history of municipal self-government in England. As the Webbs have said, "the administration of justice in its various branches . . . more than any other [function] determined the evolution of the working constitution of the Municipal Corporation and its relation to the local inhabitants." [215] In thousands of growing communities new powers of administration grew out of manor courts—courts leet or court baron or both combined. These communities achieved varying degrees of independence (some of them, complete independence) from their manorial lords.[216] A reference has already been made to one large community, Manchester, that developed an elaborate machinery, lasting until 1846, under the forms of a court leet. The homage jury of the court baron could also be adapted and expanded for the administering of common assets and managing common affairs, and for a time this pattern was widely used.[217] The other main line of growth, especially for the newer communities, was grant by royal charter. Such grants continued, though the powers granted varied widely from place to place.

[214] *Coventry Leet Book,* xxviii.
[215] Webb, *ELG,* II, 278.
[216] Webb, II, 148–185 discusses the complex differences of degree between what the authors call "the lordless court," "the lord's borough," and "the enfranchised manorial borough."
[217] Webb, *ELG,* II, 200–211, describes the growth and decay of many incipient communities, originating in courts baron that lacked court leet powers. In the end most of those without court leet powers could not survive the competition of parish officers, the justices of the peace, and other officials with administrative powers.

In the development of court structures there was an increasingly sharp distinction between criminal and civil jurisdictions. As to criminal jurisdiction the courts leet of the towns had carried the main load but the justices of the peace became powerful rivals. One of the chief objectives of the men who managed town affairs was to secure their own justices of the peace, either by acquiring the power to name appointees or by a requirement that town officers be included in the commissions. Some fortunate boroughs, more than forty in number, also succeeded in excluding the jurisdiction of the justices named for counties. Resident justices were more convenient for the townspeople. The rulers of the towns, from whom the justices were chosen, were enabled through their royal office to expand their control over local affairs.[218] The wider powers of the justices of the peace, their personal prestige and their continuity in office brought a transfer to them, in many places, of the powers of the courts leet. Sometimes the two courts were actually fused; more often the courts leet simply disappeared or were reduced to routine functions. During the late seventeenth and eighteenth century, in the organized towns as on rural manors, the court leet generally fell into disuse. The place of lay juries, chosen somewhat at random, was taken by lay gentry, chosen with foresight from a governing group.[219]

As to courts of civil jurisdiction the forms were more varied. The town communities that grew out of manors would normally inherit a "court baron" that could deal with civil cases. A bewildering profusion of such courts, under strange names, appeared in the seventeenth and eighteenth centuries.[220] Most of the larger boroughs had ancient civil courts based on royal charter or prescription. London's court of hustings, a specialized court for civil cases, was a very old example that was widely known and somewhat imitated. By 1602 and for some time before, Northampton, for example, had a court of hustings whose judges were the mayor, two bailiffs and two coroners.[221] The use of permanent town officials as judges was in fact very common. Sometimes the civil court was in theory composed of all the aldermen

[218] Webb, II, 279–284.
[219] Webb, II, 344–358.
[220] Webb, II, 339–342.
[221] J. Charles Cox, *The Records of the Borough of Northampton* (London, 1898), II, 118–119.

or all the "close body" that governed the town,[222] though it seems unlikely that all the *honoratiores* would have found it worth while to attend all the time.

For the present study an important question is whether this concentration of judicial powers in fewer persons brought an infiltration of "learned" men, trained for and specialized in judicial duties. Until this question has been closely studied it is dangerous to generalize. It is clear at least that from the sixteenth century onward most of the larger boroughs had a "recorder" who was usually a professional lawyer, available to give legal advice on all problems of municipal government; common lawyers who later achieved high distinction held this office midway in their careers. There were scattered instances in which the town recorder was a member, even the presiding officer, of the borough's civil court.[223] But it seems that this was extremely rare. As to criminal cases, the boroughs that had their own justices of the peace sometimes arranged that the recorder be appointed as one of the justices and the bench at Quarter Sessions would thus be provided with at least one learned member.[224] Then in the nineteenth century, especially through the reform legislation of 1835, provision was made for professional lawyers as the judges at Quarter Sessions in the larger towns.[225] So there were means by which persons with legal training could influence the work of the borough and town courts, either by direct participation or more commonly by advice. Furthermore, one should not underestimate the experience accumulated by permanent town officials, even though not formally trained, who handled specialized classes of litigation in busy courts over extended periods of time. All one can say with confidence is that judging in borough and town courts in general showed no signs of becoming a vocation. Most of the men who engaged in it were also occupied with other tasks in municipal administration. Then with the decline of the civil jurisdictions in the late eighteenth century— through defects in their procedure and limitations on their powers —further growth was largely foreclosed. Though some of the ancient city courts survived much longer, most were eliminated

---

[222] Webb, *ELG*, II, 337–343.
[223] Webb, II, 321–323.
[224] Webb, II, 356–357.
[225] Holdsworth, *HEL*, I, 145.

in the great reforms of the nineteenth century or else fell into disuse.[226]

8. ATTITUDES OF THE CENTRAL GOVERNMENT

It has been necessary to refer many times to the general policy of abstention adopted by the English central government toward local institutions. It seems desirable now to view the scene from the vantage point of Westminster and examine certain specific issues that the central government had to decide.

The first issue lies in the field of procedure—the problem of appellate review. In an earlier chapter I have contended that the transformation of the French court system was primarily caused by the introduction of canonist methods of investigation and proof, whose growing complications brought specialists in to administer them and drove the laymen away. In the introduction of the canonist inquest French royal courts provided the main leadership, not only by example but by constant pressure on lower courts exerted through appellate review. The mode of review was of course the canonist appeal—a full-scale rehearing on law and facts. Some 200 years later, in Germany, the adoption of the canonist appeal was part of the whole process of importing Roman law and Roman-canonist procedure. In Germany I have contended that the new procedure had similar results in transforming the ancient *Schöffen* courts. French and German experience suggests that appellate procedure in England could have opened some channels of influence or control. It is instructive to follow the stages by which English royal judges devised their truncated version of an appellate proceeding, the writ of error.

In Anglo-Saxon and early Norman times England, like the rest of northern Europe, used the complaint of false judgment as the mode of attack on a judgment already rendered. Like its analogues on the continent, this archaic procedure was punitive and was aimed at the falsely-judging court. The burden of defending it fell on the court itself. Bracton's Notebook gives examples of such proceedings directed against county courts. In these cases four knights, sent from the county, came before the royal judges and

[226] Webb, II, 342–343; Holdsworth, *HEL*, I, 150–151.

"made record." If the complaining party challenged the record and the knights maintained that it was correct, the solution was a duel between the complaining party and one of the knights, or between their hired champions. As Maitland pointed out, the justices managed in the cases in question to prevent an actual resort to the duel.[227] After the 1220's when judicial duels had fallen into disfavor, witnesses could be used instead. It was clear, however, that successful attack on the judgment led not only to reversal but to amercement of the offending court.[228]

In France the canonist appeal was grafted on the ancient false judgment proceeding in the late thirteenth century but the punishment of "false" judges survived late as a vestige in French procedure.[229] The writ of error which emerged in England at almost the same time very soon lost the feature of direct punishment of the erring judge. But this dilution of the punitive element was intimately connected with a change in the nature of the "record" employed.

In false judgment proceedings of the early thirteenth century it seems clear that the "record" was reported orally by spokesmen who appeared in person.[230] If this report disclosed a fault in the challenged court's procedure, reversal and punishment might follow. Otherwise the contest was limited to the correctness of the report itself; the issue was whether the men who "made record" gave a truthful account of what the court did. Their story could be disproved, at first by duel and later by witnesses. Even the gradual shift to written reports did not mean for some decades that the reports were conclusive. This possibility of controverting the record did not mean, however, that false judgment proceedings

---

[227] Pollock and Maitland, HEL, II, 667–668. Cases of interest in Bracton's Notebook are nos. 40 (1219), 995 (1224), 1019 (1224), 1412 (1220) and 1672 (1225). Another example appears in the Rolls of the Justices in Eyre for Lincolnshire and Worcestershire (Selden Society, London, 1934), 523.

[228] Glanvill, De Legibus et Consuetudinibus Angliae, VIII, 9; Pollock and Maitland, HEL, II, 667.

[229] Above Ch. II, 2c.

[230] Thorne, "Courts of Record and Sir Edward Coke," 2 Univ. of Toronto L.J. 229 (1935), describes this stage and the main lines of later development. The controversies that developed in the 1930's over whether the county court was a court of record are also referred to by Professor Thorne, though they can be laid aside in this discussion despite the interest of the subject and the distinction of the participants.

brought full-scale review, for if the procedural steps taken by the challenged court were strictly correct, it was seldom that the grounds of decision were reviewed or even disclosed.[231]

New techniques which carried the inquiry somewhat further were mainly developed, it seems, because of the need to control the lay gentry, acting under special commissions, who were assigned to preside at common law trials. It has been pointed out earlier (Chapter III, sec. 3), that this form of delegation was extremely common in the thirteenth century. As Maitland said, speaking of the commissions of assize which were composed as a rule of four knights of the shire:

These justices of assize, while acting under royal commission, are royal justices; but they are not professional lawyers. The central court seems to hesitate in its dealings with them. On the one hand, they cannot be accused of false judgment; on the other hand, they can be directed to bear records of their doings before the central court; they can be amerced for their errors and their errors can be corrected.[232]

A more recent author, S. F. Milsom, has developed this thesis in a manuscript study that is as yet unpublished. As he points out, there was not the same interest on the part of the crown in protecting such men from criticism as there was in the case of the full-time judges; and, being untrained, the lay commissioners were more likely to go wrong. As a rule they were knights, men of the same rank and experience as the knights who were being called to account as suitors in the county courts for judgments challenged as "false"; it was natural to apply to them some of the procedures used against other knights who were called up as spokesmen for and defenders of their counties. It is a great question whether the judges of the central courts would ever have been willing to multiply their own burdens by developing an appellate review of the full-scale canonist type. At any rate, the channel

[231] S. F. C. Milsom discusses these questions in a study not yet published, "The Origins and Early History of Judicial Review in England," chap. 4, sec. C. He makes the point that the reviewing court might often have achieved sensible and fair results despite the limitations supposedly laid on their inquiries, because the procedural complexities of the times (especially in the land law with which most of the published cases were concerned) opened a wide area for judicial discretion in the reviewing court.

[232] Pollock and Maitland, HEL, II, 667. Review of proceedings by lay judges operating under royal commission is discussed also by Sayles, Introduction to *Select Cases in the Court of King's Bench* (Selden Society), II, xlvii–xlviii.

through which the new techniques were mainly developed may have preserved the tie with ancient procedure and thus helped to cripple the new infant at birth.[233]

In the second half of the thirteenth century the writ of error was given the form that was to last for centuries. Its essential faults were that no error could be shown that did not appear on the record, and that any error that did appear, however insignificant, was enough for reversal. Before these features were firmly established several changes were needed. The judges whose acts were under review ceased to appear in person and submitted instead a written report; the report instead of being specially prepared for each occasion became a mere transcript of the court's own roll; the "record" thus submitted became conclusive —that is, it was made immune not only to correction but to changes by way of addition. The bill of exceptions, introduced by statute in 1285, allowed an extension of the record on specific points as to which exceptions were saved, but this remedy may have helped to aggravate the disease by discouraging the reviewing court itself from amending the record.[234] The final stage was to develop a form of writ by which the errors to be considered would be specified. It is interesting for present purposes that this feature was probably introduced through attempts to review judgments of the London court of hustings, which resisted the intrusion of royal justices and was subdued through writs of error after vigorous contest.[235]

The narrow, rigid, and technical proceeding that was thus manufactured proved to be one of the most unhappy creations of the medieval common law. It not only survived into modern times but it became the standard mode of appellate review in all types of common law actions. It was extended to cover not only the part-time amateurs who judged as royal commissioners, but also the permanent judges sitting in the assizes or on general eyre and

[233] This contention is developed by S. F. C. Milsom in "The Origins and Early History of Judicial Review in England," 138–158, with the conclusion (p. 138) that the association of the false judgment proceeding with the correction of errors "had a lasting and damaging effect upon the development of a procedure in error."

[234] This again, is Milsom's argument in his chapter VIII, based on cases shortly before 1285 and a small residue appearing for a time thereafter, in which amendments were allowed through action by the reviewing court. The main lines of development are described by Thorne, above, note 230.

[235] Milsom, chapter X.

finally to the Common Pleas itself. For courts that were technically not courts of record—the county and hundred courts, the courts baron of the manors and the courts of the towns—there remained the writ of false judgment, subject to similar limitations.[236] By the standards of continental procedure neither one was a true appellate proceeding. Though erring judges ceased to be punished, the assumption still was that the function of review was to search out faults that were assigned against the formal record. If any faults whatever were found there must be reversal, but it was no part of the reviewing court's duty to rehear the whole case and reach its own conclusion as to what justice required.

In a field so technical as the review of judgments, it would be a mistake to attribute too much to philosophies of government. But self-denial so resolute reflects at least a narrow conception of judicial duty. Whatever may have been the motives, one can measure by the results. The first and most obvious result of the limitations imposed on the writ of error was to save time and trouble for the reviewing court. By 1300 the King's Bench had acquired a monopoly of proceedings in error. Its membership then was three justices and it continued for many centuries with a complement of four or five.[237] During this period in France the Parlement of Paris was swelling to 51 (in 1296), to 94 (in 1454) to 240 (in 1715), and by the eighteenth century the Parlement of Paris had become merely one (though the largest) of 13 similar appellate courts in France. The severe limitations imposed on the writ of error can be likened to the use of the jury for the finding of facts; the result at least, whatever the motive, was to conserve the time of trained personnel. It is true that this very use of the jury, to which royal courts were well committed a full century before, narrowed the possibilities of appellate review that

---

[236] Sayles, Introduction to *Select Cases in the Court of King's Bench* (Selden Society), II, xlix. The forms of a writ of false judgment addressed to a county court and containing many of the ancient features are given by Greenwood, *The Authority, Jurisdiction and Method of Keeping the County Court* (9th ed., 1730), 53–54. The writ of *accedas ad curiam* by which the sheriff was directed to go to a court of a franchise, hundred or court baron and "make record" in the presence of the suitors of the court plus four lawful men of the county is described and discussed by Greenwood, 56.

[237] Sayles, Introduction to *Select Cases in the Court of King's Bench* (Selden Society), I, cxxix–cxxxv, gives the list of King's Bench judges under Edward I and II.

lay open in the last thirty years of the thirteenth century. Appellate review if fully developed would have found one large avenue of inquiry blocked off, the avenue into review of facts. Yet it is easy to imagine active policies that would have brought much sooner some controls over the jury. It is still easier to imagine an appellate proceeding that would have laid open for inspection all the acts of lower courts, whether recorded in their own rolls or not. This was not the course that was chosen. In this aspect of their work, as in so many others, the royal judges of the thirteenth century, as Maitland said, had a "passive habit" that "grew on them" as time went on; the judges sat in court "not in order that they might discover the truth" but as umpires to see that the rules of the game were observed.[238]

Yet no one would wish to attribute this passivity to laziness or simple inertia. The royal judges of the central courts were busy men. Many of them had a remarkable command of a large and growing mass of technical law and were much engaged in its day-to-day administration. As the King's Bench developed its supervisory jurisdiction there came into use a variety of writs that could have been used for control, not only over courts of record, but over local courts of county, hundred, manor and town. It was surely neither energy nor means that failed. It seems rather that the judges of the central courts were content with limited objectives. They had seized control in those areas that had paramount interest for the national government—especially major crime and freehold land; they had imposed the 40 shilling limit of value, even before adequate substitutes had been developed by the common law for the local and private court remedies that were thus displaced. The vacuum thus created was filled by the gradual expansion of common law remedies and the more rapid growth of the Chancery. So far as the common law judges were concerned, they plainly were willing to leave for local administration an immense range of other matters that did not seem to be worth their time and trouble. For these other matters, important as they were to the general population, the royal judges kept merely some strategic controls that set outer limits on the power of subordinate bodies and could be used to ensure compliance with the traditional procedure that the subordinate bodies had in-

[238] Pollock and Maitland, *HEL*, II, 670–671.

herited. So long as the limits and the procedure were on the whole observed, the common law judges saw no strong reason to meddle with them.

We have no way of measuring the extent of the meddling that did occur. Such issues did not attract much attention from Yearbook reporters. The printed reports of the sixteenth and later centuries contain occasional references, but again they were only a random sampling of the work actually done by the central courts. We do have the reports of two thirteenth-century cases: one in which a county court judgment was found to be "false" because the court had been held more often than every three weeks,[239] and another in which an amercement for obstructing a highway was held to be void because imposed in a three-weekly court baron and not in the semiannual court leet.[240] Violation of ground rules like these would probably induce the umpires to intervene if anyone had funds and felt strongly enough to file a proper protest. A protest against a local court amercement could reach a common law court in several ways—if suit were brought in a common law court to collect the amercement or if the person amerced sued in replevin or trespass for a taking of his goods by way of distraint. Attempts by such means to disprove guilt or review grounds of decision in manor courts would ordinarily meet with total failure, but they might perhaps have succeeded if the object were to challenge the power of a local court to control conduct outside its own geographical area, to try a person charged with major crime or otherwise clearly to exceed its power.[241] In reported decisions of the late sixteenth and seventeenth centuries the common law courts struck down some court leet presentments on what seem to have been very technical grounds and also showed some disposition, sporadically, to impose substantive limitations on the matters that courts leet could deal with.[242] But they relied

[239] *Bracton's Notebook*, pl. 40 (1219).

[240] *Y.B. 21 & 22 Edw. I* (Rolls Series), 109, cited by Hearnshaw, *Leet Jurisdiction in England*, 344.

[241] Geographical limitations on the power of local courts were admitted in the discussion of the 1505 Yearbook case referred to above section 6g, note 179.

[242] Evington v. Brimston, *Moore* 356 (1594), amercement on the ground that "le pl' lessa ses gates open ad nocumentum inhabitantium" held to be no defense to a distraining bailiff because "n'appiert al un Leet"; Wormleighton v. Burton, *Croke Eliz.* 448 (1595), amercement for putting geese on the common held no defense to a distraining bailiff (1) because he did not show that the common was within the leet precincts and (2) because "it was not any article inquirable in a

as usual on the initiative of litigants and the few reported cases would hardly suggest that the common law judges had mounted a full-scale campaign. If a campaign was planned, the records of the local courts themselves show that it did not make much impression.

A searching test of common lawyers' attitudes was provided by the by-laws so freely made in the village communities. They were plainly legislation, often cast in general terms. They were issued by groups that acted very informally and that could hardly claim under royal charter or statute a delegated power to legislate. But on the main issue there was really no doubt—by-laws in general were assumed to be valid. The question was not often discussed, but Coke, at least, was emphatic: amercements could be imposed in manor courts for "breach of any by-law made either for the profit of the whole kingdom or for the benefit of the little commonwealth among themselves, or for default of doing suit, or for other misdemeanors, punishable by the same court, infinite in number and quality." [243]

The question left open and unresolved was a difficult one—the

---

leet nor punishable there"; King v. Dickinson, 1 *Wm. Saunders* 135 (1669), presentment in a leet for erecting a new cottage found to have technical defects and also to be beyond the court's power because the injury was only to the lord and was not a public nuisance; Hughes v. Bishop of London, 3 *Keble* 106 (1673), court leet presentment held to be bad because failure to scour ditches was alleged to be *ad nocumentum diversorum* instead of *ad commune nocumentum*.

Pigeons presented sharply the difficult issue as to the line between public and private nuisance. In Prat v. Stearn, *Croke Jac.* 382 (1616), plaintiff, a freeholder, had erected a dovecote on his land and had been ordered by a court leet to remove it. On his failure to comply he was amerced and the lord's bailiff distrained. Plaintiff then sued in replevin. During the discussion of the case a question was raised whether the erection of a dovecote was a common nuisance inquirable at a leet. Coke, C. J., was clear that it was, "but the other justices seemed to doubt thereof." The judges "all resolved" that the lord of a leet could distrain or sue in debt to collect such an amercement if the presentment was valid, but the presentment in question was held not to be valid because it had said *ad commune nocumentum* instead of *ad nocumentum legiorum domini regis*. (The same case is reported less fully in 1 *Rolle* 200). Four years later in another dovecote case a "pain" of £10 had been imposed for disobedience of a court leet's command to remove a dovecote. In an action of trespass against the distraining bailiff the whole court agreed that the dovecote was not "a common nuisance to all the people" but only to those persons whose corn the pigeons ate, so that the "pain" was invalid. Montague, C. J., added that if the multitude of pigeons inhabiting a dovecote became a grievance to the whole county the justices of assize might inquire, but the lord of the leet still could not since he could only deal with nuisances committed within the precincts of his own leet.

[243] *Complete Copyholder*, sec. 41.

effect on persons who had not been present when the by-laws were issued and who might therefore have had no notice. This question was raised, at least obliquely, in a Yearbook case of 1370. The action was replevin. The defendant, a bailiff, justified the taking as a distraint and alleged that the parishioners of a certain church, in accordance with their ancient custom, had voted to assess the members of the parish sixpence for each carucate of land and a penny for each cow that they owned, the proceeds to be used for repair of the church. In the course of the argument Serjeant Kirketon (two years later to be justice of the Common Pleas) is quoted as saying: "There is a usage throughout the land which is called by-laws, made by the consent of all the neighbors" of assessing the cost of making bridges, walls, and so forth. "And if commoners have common in a certain place they can order by assent that they shall not common in a certain parcel before a certain time and if they do they may be distrained, and this is done throughout the land. . . . And although all the neighbors do not wish to come, if proclamation was made that this would be done those who default are just as much bound as those who were present." In the end, however, the plaintiff was allowed to take issue on the somewhat different point that he had not agreed to the amount of the assessment in question or to the grant to the bailiff of a power to distrain.[244] In a Yearbook case in 1506, "all the justices of the Common Pleas" were quoted as saying that "a vill can make a by-law among themselves that he who places his beasts in the common before a certain day shall forfeit so much money; this is good and binds them but it cannot bind a stranger." [245] Yet even this last qualification was later thrown in some doubt if we can believe Croke's report of a King's Bench case in 1638. Here the by-law forbade the keeping of sheep on the common pasture land "below the meer." The plaintiff, who had pastured his sheep on this part of the common and on whom a "pain" was therefore imposed, sued in replevin and in the King's Bench asserted that "this was not a good bye-law to bind one for his inheritance. . . . But all the court held that an ordi-

---

[244] Y.B. 44 Edw. III, fol. 18–19. Kirketon's career is sketched in Foss, Lives of the Judges, IV, 63.
[245] Y.B. 21 Henry VII, 40.

nance by custom for the government of the common is good." And to the objection that the defending bailiff had not shown that the plaintiff had notice of the by-law, the court's answer as reported was: "But it being proclaimed in court, as it was alleged in the plea, he being a commoner is bound to take notice thereof, for none is bound to give him notice." [246]

The central courts thus gave some moral support for the wide-ranging activities of the local courts, but aided them most by refusing to review their activities unless the ground rules were flagrantly broken. On a few occasions they went beyond this and took affirmative action, ordering manor courts that had been in abeyance to be held at the accustomed times. For courts baron the chief motive for such orders was to enable copyholders to register transfers of copyhold land; [247] for courts leet a motive was to provide means for electing local officials and by statute in 1724 the King's Bench was specifically authorized to mandamus lords of leets for this purpose.[248] Again we have no statistics as to how often such orders were issued. If frequently used they could hardly have arrested the gradual decay of the local courts in the late seventeenth and eighteenth centuries. Even if rare, as they probably were, they at least suggest that the English central authorities had attitudes quite different from those in France,

[246] James v. Tutney, *Croke Car.* 497 (1638). In Earl of Exeter v. Smith, Carter 177 (1669), an action of debt by the lord of a leet hundred was held to be maintainable, the offense being violation of a by-law that forbade pasturing any animals on the common between Feb. 2 and Aug. 1. The by-law in question had been issued by the steward himself, but this point was not discussed. In Fox v. Amhurst, *L.R. 20 Eq.* 403 (1875), a by-law made by the homage of a court baron in 1835, regulating the rights of the tenants in common pasture lands, was not only assumed to be valid but on the basis of the by-law £2,000 were distributed to the various tenants as the proceeds of condemnation of the pasture lands for railroad purposes. Austin v. Amhurst, *L.R. 7 Ch. Div.* 689 (1877), indicates the difficulty of fitting within common law classifications the rights created by this by-law in "occupiers" who owned no adjacent land. In both cases, it should be added, the validity of the by-law did not rest on ancient practices only, since a Chancery decree of the early seventeenth century, confirmed by private act of Parliament, had empowered the homage to make by-laws regulating the common lands that would bind the users of the commons.

[247] Johnson v. Waterhouse, *Cases Decided by Lord Bacon,* 70 (1617); Moor v. Lord Huntington, *Nelson* 12 (1631).

[248] 11 George I, c. 4. Mandamus issued in King v. Willis, *Andrews* 279 (1738), and Rex v. Lord of the Hundred of Milverton, 3 *Ad. & Ellis* 284 (1835). In Rex v. Bankes, 3 *Burr.* 1452 (1764), Lord Mansfield indicated willingness to grant mandamus for this purpose but denied it in the particular case.

where the crown in the eighteenth century forbade meetings of lords and tenants without specific royal permission.[249]

If one looks beyond the central courts to other sectors of the central government one finds the same attitude of toleration, mixed with mild encouragement. As to civil litigation Parliament in 1601 sought to discourage "small and trifling suits" in the central courts "which by the due course of the laws of this realm ought to be determined in inferior courts in the country" by denying costs in amounts that exceeded the total judgment recovered; this effort to preserve the jurisdiction of local courts was largely nullified by the reluctance of common law judges to enforce this feeble sanction.[250] In dealing with minor crimes Parliament was generally careful to preserve the acquired jurisdiction of courts leet if it mentioned them at all.[251] During the sixteenth century various minor offenses, newly manufactured by statute, were expressly declared to fall within the jurisdiction of courts leet: the harboring of strangers ("inmates") who had migrated from other settlements, the use or possession of cross-bows or firearms, hunting rabbits in the snow, pasturing mangy horses on common lands, "conspiracies" of victuallers or of workmen to fix prices or wages, selling wine without license, failure to work on repair of the roads, and so on.[252] The specific new powers thus added by statute did not compare in importance with the large miscellaneous assortment inherited from the sheriff's tourn with its late medieval accretions. Nor did they compare with the deluge of new powers that were poured on the justices of the peace. But in some degree they expressed a judgment of Parliament that the courts leet in the manors and towns were useful agencies of social control. That the Privy Council took a similar view at times is suggested by instructions issued in 1630, in which the Privy Council urged courts leet to be vigorous in their traditional types of local police activity.[253]

[249] Above, note 161.

[250] 43 Eliz. c. 6, applicable to personal actions not involving land or personal assault. Similar provisions were applied to actions for slander by 21 James I, c. 16, sec. 6. Plucknett, Concise Hist., 173–174.

[251] 12 Edw. IV, c. 8 (1473); 35 George II, c. 102 (1795); 55 George III, c. 43 (1815).

[252] A list of statutes mentioning courts leet is given by Hearnshaw, Leet Jurisdiction in England, Appendix II.

[253] Quoted by Webb, ELG, II, 117.

To this broad policy of toleration there was a brief exception in the assaults on the privileges of the towns, begun under Charles II and continued under James II. Many town charters were expressly revoked or were surrendered under threat of revocation. The object was political—to secure the election to Parliament of persons who would support royal policies and to exclude from the town governments religious nonconformists. If the attacks had continued they might have destroyed self-government in the towns in the way that the French crown succeeded in doing by its capricious intervention. But the revolution of 1688 brought a return to the policy of nonintervention.[254] England went on into the nineteenth century with its town governments free of external controls, safely ruled by the very best people who firmly excluded intruders.

It has been said that the English constitution has had two fundamental characteristics—"the system of self-government and the rule of law." [255] If the law that "ruled" the local courts of manor and town is identified with the common law, it did not penetrate far. Even if one reads the "rule of law" in a larger sense as a social ordering that sets limits to power and standards for its exercise, doubts still remain as to whether the law of the judges in the central courts contributed much to the main result. Having made some broad allocations of authority and drained away all dangerous power, the common law judges in their role as umpires retreated to a distant part of the field where they seldom saw or heard the play. It was the essence of judicial controls that they be intermittent and depend on the initiative of litigants. In the absence of stronger incentives than existed in the common law judges or in litigants, the "rule" of the common law was a pale abstraction about which it is easy to romanticize. The question is whether the standards of the common law were transmitted through all levels of the population as meaningful guides and limits to action. One can raise the same question as to the justices of the peace, whose great and growing powers were subject in theory to numerous restraints enforceable by common law courts.[256] Despite these restraints the government of the counties and towns became

---

[254] Webb, II, 268–270; Holdsworth, *HEL*, VII, 210–212.
[255] Holdsworth, *HEL*, II, 405 and IV, 133–134.
[256] Holdsworth, *HEL*, X, 155–158 and 243–254.

increasingly a "rule by squires" which few cared or dared to challenge.

This merely suggests that for a very large share of the population the ordering of English society was not imposed from Westminster but developed through training and experience in self-government. The shape of local institutions was determined by decisions at the national level. As a result of these decisions ancient modes of community action were preserved, adapted and on the whole strengthened, mainly through the borrowing of the jury from royal procedure. Within the broad framework thus created, the smaller communities—especially in the manor courts—were left free to build their own systems of internal order. One can hardly call this democracy, and whatever representation there was in the main was unorganized. Yet so long as the local courts lasted—roughly into the eighteenth century—they brought genuine self-government, conducted under judicial forms by juries of the neighborhood.

CHAPTER V

SUMMARY AND CONCLUSIONS

I⊤ should not be surprising that in the past so many modes of
social action have been organized around processes of adjudication. Conflict compels thought by those who lie within its radius.
This is true whether the conflict is between particular individuals
or between a larger group (a family, the users of common pasture
land or perhaps the whole community) and an individual who is
accused of conduct harmful to the group. If the conflict is to be
ended by a lasting settlement, it will usually have to be through
application of some standard other than personal liking or dis-
taste. The standard may be available at once through memory of
a rule already formulated and well known. At times, however,
the claims asserted on either side will so challenge assumptions
and habitual practices as to require a serious reappraisal. Yet if
the use of force is to be restrained, means must be found for
achieving settlement. Institutions or procedures for dispute-settlement are primary then in a double sense—they are apt to be
earliest among the means for achieving social order and they continue to be centers for new growth as community action expands.

Even after procedures for community action have been well
organized there are various reasons that can be urged for participation by numerous persons. The most general reason would be
that the process itself is so vital a part of community organization
that the community itself has a right to share in the process. Translated into modern terms, deceptive as they may be, this is essentially a theory of political democracy applied to adjudication. In
the long record that has been reviewed only the Greeks—so far
as we know, only the Athenians—ever formulated a theory that
was so extreme. Though Greek political theories had wide circulation in Rome under the late Republic and some Romans may

have been bemused by them, the solutions adopted by the Romans fell far short of this. The persons called to judging duties came for the most part from the highest levels of Roman society. The large assembly courts used for criminal trials were created and maintained for the deliberate purpose of giving their members effective control in decisions that were important for the whole Roman people. But no such broad political motivations can be detected in the arrangements for civil litigation, of which the best known and most widely used was the single *iudex,* chosen by the praetor with consent of the litigants.

In the earlier Middle Ages the popular assemblies, organized first within kinship groups and then on a geographical basis, gave as a rule a wide cross-section. All law-worthy men, at any rate, had a right to attend and at least passively to participate. Theories of political democracy, if they existed at all, must have lain below the levels of conscious expression, however much a kind of working democracy was sometimes achieved in fact. In the course of time law-finders and other leaders emerged as custodians of community traditions, but the principle of consent by local assemblies was not obliterated. Disputes that were deemed important were still reserved for group decision. However, in societies that lacked both the theory and the practice of political democracy, the impulse to preserve a large share in dispute-settlement for the community at large was not likely to be expressed in general terms. The impulse may have been felt and in some communities it may have been strongly expressed. But the local contests for power of which we have records, such as those that occurred in the towns of the late Middle Ages, covered the whole range of community functions. So an immediate connection between political democracy and adjudication, which was so clear to the Athenian Greeks, was not preserved. As populations grew and systems of law inevitably became more complex, it became less and less convincing to assert in general terms that adjudication in all its phases should depend on popular vote.

Another possible reason for preserving lay participation is that the persons involved in disputes may accept the result more readily if they are judged by their own kind. This might be a general reason for enlisting a segment of the community, small or large,

in the processes of dispute-settlement. It would be hard to show
that it played any part in the developments that have been described. If acceptance of results is the object, this cannot mean in
most cases that the parties involved, especially the losing parties,
will express affirmative approval. On the other hand, the broad
objective of promoting acceptability in general may have been
one of the reasons for maintaining in "public" systems of adjudication an arbitral element. The Roman *iudex*, chosen by the praetor
with party consent, and the gentry employed by the English
Chancery as court-appointed arbitrators, may not have been for
the litigants men of their own kind, but at least they were in some
degree men of their own choice. Those who developed and maintained such systems may have been perfectly conscious of their
pacifying effects.

More familiar to us is a phrasing that identifies this factor as
a right of the individual—the right to be judged by one's "peers."
This interest of the individual, distinct from any interest of the
community at large, may have been a factor in developing the
praetorian procedure in republican Rome, especially if it began,
as it probably did, as part of a broader movement to set limits
on the powers of Roman magistrates. The claims of individuals
may also have worked obscurely to preserve as part of their "birth-
right" the procedures of the early Germanic assembly-courts. No
one has yet found evidence that any such claims were asserted.
The notion of "judgment by peers" moves into recorded history
in the context of feudal relationships. It was first clearly phrased
as the right of an individual vassal to be judged by his fellow
vassals, especially in contests with his own feudal lord. In France
it was well known as a special privilege of nobility and finally was
reserved for a small and very exalted group, the Peers of France.
In England the most famous provision of Magna Carta, c. 39, projected "judgment by peers" across the sky of history for all the
world to see. *Judicium parium* was expressed as a privilege of all
free men, not merely of the barons who extorted the Charter. The
generality of the phrase, plus its close connection with the com-
panion phrase, "the law of the land," enabled later generations to
make the right to "judgment by one's peers" into a symbol of human freedom, especially against oppression by government. As

originally used it was clearly not intended either as a generalized guaranty of jury trial or as a buttress for more ancient modes of community judging.[1] But it was expressed as a restraint on royal action, and despite the narrow meanings that were originally intended, clause 39 of Magna Carta deserves an honorable place in the history of constitutionalism. It was not till much later that "peers" were connected with jury trial. It was only in the United States, later still, that the right to jury trial became more than protection against government and was riveted into all litigation conducted under the forms of the common law. Our American constitutions, state and federal, now confirm the right of all our citizens to this partial form of lay participation—provided the action is at "common law." We cannot stop now to review why this happened, for the career of the common law jury would take us far on a winding path. The jury has become, especially in the United States, a special form of "judgment by peers," contained by its own elaborate rules and invested with its own ethos.

Outside the context of the common law system there is not much proof that the right to be judged by one's own kind was asserted or widely accepted. The question arises chiefly in England, for in England many courts that were not technically part of the common law system preserved, in essentials, the ancient ways. In manor courts, for example, could an individual tenant insist that his affairs, especially in contests with the lord, should be subjected to the judgment of neighbors? Magna Carta, clause 39 applied only to freemen; and even if a freeman were involved, it would have been startling to hear that the "peers" whose participation was guaranteed were the homage or jury of a manorial court. There is no reported instance in which a common law court intervened on any such ground. Yet one catches a fleeting glimpse of convictions that must have lain deep in many minds in the story of a minor peasants' revolt in the manor of Darnhall, in 1329. The manor was owned by the abbot of Vale Royal. The

---

[1] Keeney, *Judgment by Peers,* chapters III and IV, discusses the meaning of the phrase in Magna Carta and the construction it received in the thirteenth century. He gives convincing evidence that the barons never intended clause 39 to require jury trial in suits between private litigants, including themselves, but intended at most some similar safeguard in cases between king and subject. It is difficult, however, to accept his suggestion (page 68) that the "peers" referred to in the charter of 1215 were the 25 magnates appointed by clause 52 to uphold the charter.

story begins with a secret night meeting of the bondmen of the manor. They resolved that they were free men, that they would not grind their grain at the abbot's mill, that it was lawful to lease their lands without the abbot's consent, and that "it was not lawful for the abbot to punish them for any offence except by the assessment of their neighbors." This last resolution proved to be misplaced hope. At the next court of the manor, with the abbot himself present, the steward accused them of holding a secret meeting and then (as reported by the abbot's partisans) "they all, with one accord, rose against the lord in court and flew to arms." They were captured by the abbot's men, put into shackles, their goods and cattle were seised, so the men submitted. But seven years later, in 1336, twelve of the men left secretly, followed the king to the north of England and then to Westminster, where they filed a petition to Parliament asking it to review the abbot's proceedings. When the king's justiciar ruled against them, they appealed to the queen; and when the abbot was returning from a hearing before the queen "a great crowd of the country people" attacked the abbot and killed his groom. In the end the men were all subdued, after a judgment of the county court had confirmed the abbot's claim that they were all serfs.[2] There are not many such records of resistance and desperation inspired by local issues. But the story gives some clue to the meaning of judgment by "peers" in the context, not of baronage, but of the peasant settlements. The issues most vital to most of the people of England were regularly decided by the judgment of neighbors, through procedures that were well known and well understood. The right to this form of "judgment by peers" must have been deeply prized by men like the serfs of Darnhall. It must have been asserted, as it was by them, in many local contests that were far beyond the reach of Magna Carta or the common law.

Apart from the individual's right to "judgment by peers" or the claims of the whole community to vote on such matters, there may be another, quite different reason for giving laymen a share in adjudication—the total performance of the legal system may be improved if it can draw on their resources. This kind of argument might have been used in various contexts. In the interme-

[2] Ault, *Private Jurisdiction in England*, 262–264; *Ledger Book of Vale Royal Abbey* (ed. John Brownbill, Edinburgh, 1914), 31–32, 37–41.

diate stage of the English Chancery's history—the sixteenth and early seventeenth centuries—the vagueness and variability of equity doctrines opened the way to court-sponsored arbitration, which helped to make results more sensible, as well as more acceptable. Even in legal systems that have reached a higher level of refinement and precision the use of laymen in various capacities has seemed to offer advantages. It is remarkable, for example, that in Roman law of the late republic and early principate, during a period of great expansion in commerce and general prosperity, the judges were exclusively laymen; the trained jurists who were available limited their role to general guidance and advice. No reasons for preserving this system are explicitly stated by Romans in sources that have survived, but all the evidence indicates that it worked to general satisfaction. The single judge of the praetorian civil action, about whom most is known, was normally drawn from high levels of Roman society and was apt to be widely experienced in public affairs. The praetorian formula which conferred his authority was often cast in very general terms, leaving an open avenue for the convictions and ideas that circulated in the forum, the baths and other upper-class centers of concourse and conversation. It is likely that Roman law itself was enriched by this means, though few visible deposits survive.

In highly developed systems of modern law, laymen have been installed in judicial offices deliberately and for similar reasons. In Germany, in other parts of central Europe, and in Scandinavia a pattern widely adopted is the mixed tribunal, in which laymen specially chosen for short terms of office form part of the bench, sitting with one or more professional judges. These modern *Schöffen* are not merely jurors, confined to the finding of facts under instructions from the professionals. They vote on the whole case and usually can outvote the professional judge if they will. Some of the arguments for using laymen in this way in commercial cases resemble arguments often made for commercial arbitration—that technical knowledge and specialized experience can be supplied by laymen and may be needed, not only to solve the immediate problem but to provide correctives where legal rules themselves are deficient. In criminal cases, where similar lay judges are also much used, the arguments must take a different form and are likely to approach the reason we sometimes give for using our juries—the conscripting of laymen, even in a limited role, provides a means for adjusting law to the purposes and convictions of the community at large. There may lie concealed in this argument an assumption that legal rules may be not only incomplete but positively wrong, when measured against the standards evolved through broader social experience. At the least there is an assumption that law is better administered if it draws on the good sense and practical wisdom of persons in whom these qualities have not been severely warped by excessive exposure to law.

The question then arises whether any of the various reasons that might be given for installing laymen in a judging role have had a major influence on the solutions adopted. The question relates chiefly to England, for among the countries examined it was only in England that the use of laymen was preserved and expanded. In England an elaborate system of national law was developed very early by trained professional judges. Yet professionalization, occurring much earlier than in France or Germany, had the result by a strange paradox of making more room for laymen. In the English court system, viewed as a whole, their influence increased.

If the analysis I have offered is at all close to the truth, the use of laymen within the common law system was not the result of careful reflection or an appraisal of their virtues and defects; it came in the twelfth and early thirteenth centuries because of a driving need to economize on the time of professional judges. The most important and lasting of the economy measures was the common law jury. Extensive use of juries began as early as 1166, nearly twenty years before the emergence of a group of judicial specialists around the king. During the next fifty years the rapid expansion of royal remedies produced a huge volume of judicial business. When the church in 1215 threw its weight very heavily against the archaic modes of proof through ordeal and battle, neighborhood juries had become familiar and were an obvious alternative. But the use of sworn bodies of neighbors did not exclude the judges from an active role. The real question was whether the sources of the jurors' knowledge should be examined, the ignorance or partiality of their members should be exposed and other sources of knowledge explored if their knowledge seemed deficient. There were signs of hesitation, lasting for decades. It must have been plain to the royal justices in the thirteenth century that opening up such inquiries would add immensely to their own tasks, though they could not know that the decision to do so that was then being made in France would roll up such mountainous consequences. The decision to accept collective verdicts and to cut off inquiries into the jurors' sources of knowledge was not made in a moment, but we can conclude that the issue was settled by 1300. In the whole context it seems unlikely that the virtues and defects of neighborhood juries were nicely calculated. There was an immense amount of work to do and few trained men to do or direct it.

Another method of relieving the judges was the appointment of laymen to preside at trials. This method was used on a very large scale in the thirteenth century, the time when other critical decisions were being made. This kind of delegation was in effect made possible by the uses made of jury verdicts. There were no rules of evidence to administer because there were seldom any witnesses, other than the jurors themselves. Instructions to juries were minimal and most of the time cannot have been much more than a reminder to the jurors of the questions they must answer, the questions being narrowly defined by writ and pleadings. Knights of the shires could handle such tasks. It could be, of course, that their use was also partly inspired by the desire to enlist the prestige and influence they possessed in their own localities and thus to promote acceptance of the judgments rendered. Their knowledge of local affairs may also have made them useful in more obscure ways, and this is suggested by the later practice, long continued, of including at common law trials one or more "substantial" persons of the county as members of the bench. As trial procedure grew more complex, the lay commissioners were displaced more and more by judges or trained practitioners sent out from Westminster. In common law civil actions and prosecutions for major crime, the extreme forms of delegation that were first attempted had to be abandoned. But these extreme forms of delegation are a mark of the pressures at work at the critical time.

The measures adopted within the common law system to shed and to delegate judicial functions cannot be viewed in isolation. They were part of a very much broader pattern which had originated by necessity in the late twelfth century. It was then that the English crown committed itself to governing England with a thoroughness and intensity beyond anything then known in Europe. The workload problem was not confined to judges. All the king's permanent officials had the same problem. Beginning so early and attempting so much, their only recourse was to delegate. Though they had no bias toward Greek-style democracy, they were compelling the people of England to govern themselves. We should try to imagine, for example, the immense number of tasks that were needed to make the royal court system work—service of process, the tedious business of examining excuses for non-attendance (essoins), enforcement of judgments, the empanelling of jurors and making sure they were there on time. Beyond this, however, was the whole system of neighborhood security (the frankpledge system) which needed constant review and refurbishing, the hue and cry, and other procedures for capturing offenders and reporting crimes. There was royal revenue to be collected. The county and hundred courts, surviving as they had not in France, were preserved by the crown in their ancient forms but were forced to do the king's business in many ways. Even the beginnings of Parliament must be traced to this capacity of the early English kings to impose responsibility on persons who were at first, no doubt, reluctant to assume it. As Professor McIlwain has said: "Medieval parliaments everywhere were in the beginning regarded by their members as a burden, and attendance was only obtained by rulers strong enough to compel it."[3] And so we face the paradox, that the great power of the English monarchy, mobilized so early, produced in the end self-government.

The private courts in England, to which I have given much attention, have a place in this larger picture. Before they were trusted with power, the power itself had been greatly reduced. The courts of the greater lordships were hampered, restricted and supervised so that most of them were no longer worth maintaining and none could support any private ambition that was dangerous to the crown. All but a few of the franchise courts lost jurisdiction over major crime. Disputes over land title were

[3] McIlwain, "Medieval Estates," in *Cambridge Medieval History*, VII, 664, at 707.

shepherded into the royal courts and most came of the litigants' own free will. The 40 shilling limit was applied very widely. When they had thus been closely contained, the crown interposed no resistance at all to the drift of courts into private hands. The manor courts, reflecting the economic and social cohesion of the rural settlements, developed all over England. Perhaps their roots lay back in Anglo-Saxon farm communities and perhaps they were the offshoots of Norman feudalism. Their conquest of new powers, in any case, was not resisted by the crown. On the contrary, they were allowed to borrow a royal procedure, the jury both of presentment and trial. The ancient processes of community decision were channeled into the form of jury verdicts. Presentments became judgments; the juries issued legislation as well as commands to individuals and elected their own officials to enforce them both; and even the suitors assembled in the court baron (the "homage") became gradually another kind of presentment jury. The acquiescence of crown officials was for obvious reasons. They were very busy with more important matters. So long as the established limits on power were observed and the inhabitants themselves were satisfied, the crown had no reason to prevent these small communities from using mild penalties to protect and to purge themselves.

In the fourteenth century new needs emerged, needs that could best be met by judge-administrators spread around the counties whose status and powers would be intermediate—between those of the central court judges and those of the local courts. As the nature of the function became more clear there was an open contest for its control. The crown's high officials wished to name their own men as justices of the peace, and especially to include many lawyers. But the pattern of delegation to laymen was too familiar and too well established. In addition, the country gentry and the merchants in the towns were now allied in Parliament and had means for exerting steady pressure. The compromise that was adopted kept a few lawyers on the commissions, at least for a time, but made heavy drafts on the local leadership of the counties and towns. This junior aristocracy was already very heavily engaged in the management of local affairs and in status (fortunately for England) it was not sharply marked off from the higher nobility. During the next several centuries Parliament piled new duties on these men. The Tudor monarchy made them its loyal agents. After the Puritan Revolution and the restoration of 1660 the central government relaxed its vigilant supervision. The justices of the peace became in the fullest sense the "rulers of the counties." Most of their work was still done under judicial forms but almost all were laymen. Their wide powers and more flexible procedures enabled them to control the machinery of local government and gradually to displace such older institutions as the court leet, which had a wider base of popular participation. And so, until the nineteenth century, in all but strictly national matters England was ruled increasingly by "little knots of squires and parsons." They used royal powers but they were deeply rooted in their own communities, the communities that men like them had led for centuries.

The Chancery is one of the last places that one would look for similar devices for delegation. From an early stage the Chancellors used a mode of proof, examination of individual witnesses under oath, that they may have borrowed consciously from canonist models in English church courts. If they did, they borrowed very little else. They did not, like the French courts, pile up mountains of paper and police every stage of the proceedings with meticulous care. The early Chancellors probably would have said, if they had thought about such possibilities, that all this was a waste of valuable time. So the collection of evidence was farmed out to laymen. Party initiative was used in framing both pleadings and examiners' questions, with minimal controls by the court itself. Actual decision of the cases too was largely farmed out to the ubiquitous gentry, with the result that equity doctrines received a strong infusion of robust good sense and practical morality. All this worked very well, until the earlier methods of streamlining the judge's task brought basic and crippling defects in the procedure of the Chancery, the workload at the same time grew greatly, and the development of equity doctrine committed its two judges more and more to precision and refinement in its application. In the eighteenth and early nineteenth centuries the Chancery became a national scandal and deserved the bitter reproaches that were levelled against it. Through all this time the common law judges, especially in America, were receiving not reproaches but praise for their invention of the jury. The irony is that the greatest of the Chancery's calamities came from its efforts in the fifteenth century to transfer to others a considerable share of the judicial task. In this they were merely following the example of thirteenth-century common law judges when they put so much faith in common men assembled in groups of twelve.

When institutions have been organized and patterns of action have been established, their virtues can be discovered in retrospect. We in America, having inherited the jury, have developed an attachment for it and can give many reasons for retaining it. We retain it even in civil cases, though the English, who transposed it into its modern forms, have almost wholly abandoned it in civil cases. Again, the early Chancery's reforms were more widely accepted and their content was better adjusted to English needs through the active part taken by responsible laymen who had standing in their own communities. The justices of the peace were drawn from an even more circumscribed class, but they became powerful agents nevertheless in preserving and extending local self-government. Even more important for English society was the growth of self-government in the courts of the manors. Local oligarchies in a few manors may have captured control, as they soon and quite generally did in the courts of the towns. But even if they did (and this is not proved), one could never measure the gains to English society through the self-reliance and self-respect, the training for concerted action and the growing sense of responsibility that came in these close-knit farming communities, found all over England. Few of these gains could have been even dimly foreseen at the outset. With time, however, they became apparent. It was not merely because all his passion was spent that Coke in his old age expressed his hope for "a perfect union" between lords and copyholders, so that "their so little commonwealth, having all his members knit together in complete order, may flourish to the end." [4] He, and surely others before him, had seen new meanings poured into these ancient institutions, when procedures that were well established and well understood opened wide the channels for effective group action.

It would have been miraculous if these English institutions, seen in the large, had been planned by any single mind. Of course they did not provide scope for all the hopes and purposes that

[4] Quoted above, Chapter IV, sec. 6g.

modern societies have created under a wider freedom. These
institutions were built into a highly stratified society and helped
to confirm its stratifications. But as they evolved they left larger
room than was provided elsewhere in Europe for wide participation by untrained people—not only in the process of judging
disputes but in all the processes of government that clustered
around that vital center. There was wisdom, no doubt, in retaining them and in letting their meanings unfold. The contention
here is merely that the form they took was not fixed by wisdom,
foresight or master plan. The solutions adopted in England were
adopted early, because of the necessities of government in the
twelfth and thirteenth centuries.

So we return to the question why France, which started with
institutions that seemed so similar, followed in the end such a
different course. The answer that has been given centers on weakness—weakness at the critical times. The marks of weakness had
appeared very early. The community courts, analogous to the
English county and hundred courts, had been captured by local
feudal lords during the breakdown of government in the tenth
and eleventh centuries. When the rebuilding of the monarchy began, the French crown therefore lacked an important resource
that the Norman kings of England had already put to very good
use. But it was much more than this. Over large parts of France
that owed a nominal fealty to the king great territorial lords had
effective control; in them, for long, the king's writ did not run.
Even within the king's own domain there could be no massive
enlistment of free subjects whose allegiance was to the crown
as a symbol of national government transcending and displacing
the bonds of feudal tenure.

One critical decision, the adoption of the canonist inquest
as a mode of proof, might seem to be a symptom of strength,
since it called for and produced a great extension of French
officialdom. I have suggested that the French crown's decision
to use the canonist inquest was long delayed (till the year 1258)
and that in that interval of nearly 100 years the French had had
fuller experience with the canonist inquest, much fuller than
Englishmen in 1166. From this experience they had learned its
great and evident superiority over the jury as a method of fact-
finding. But the jury was also well known in France. It was a

royal procedure that could have been used; indeed it was used till late in the *ancien régime* for proof of local custom. If widely used in France it would surely have had the same advantage that it had in England—relieving royal judges of time-consuming and troublesome tasks in the determination of disputed facts. In the earlier discussion it was pointed out that the large-scale use of juries required a strong assertion of royal authority to organize means for selecting juries, to compel their attendance and to extract sworn answers on matters in which they had no personal interest. So it must have seemed far easier, as well as far more rational, to address the questions to individuals, who were usually named by the litigants. The adoption of this procedure was surely not a mark of strength. If calculations were consciously made, they would have disclosed to royal officials that the French crown lacked the means and traditions by which public duties of this kind could be imposed on reluctant subjects. It would have been very difficult, though certainly in the end not impossible, for the French crown to make the choice in favor of juries, a choice that had succeeded in England after 1166 through the overmastering power of Henry II.

The canonist inquest and the complex procedure that was being built around it moved steadily downward through the court systems of France. The new procedure for appeal, which was gradually extended over private as well as royal courts, helped to promote the full-scale adoption of the canonist system which the Parlement of Paris took the lead in organizing. I have argued that the resulting changes in court procedure bewildered the laymen in the local courts, discouraged them from attendance, and thereby shifted the power of decision to judges appointed by the crown or by feudal lords. The ancient fusion of functions did not entirely disappear; a power to legislate still adhered to the power of adjudication, but where it was used the legislation came from a single judge, often the mere servant of a court-keeping lord. This disappearance of any popular element had profound effects in destroying French local self-government and in sharpening the social cleavage that helped to produce the Revolution.

Having the great advantage of hindsight, so that the harm produced by these decisions is evident to us, we might be tempted to search for some malevolence at work. But there is no greater reason for this than for attributing benevolent foresight to the early architects of English institutions. Once patterns of administration had been established and procedures organized, reversal of trends became more difficult with each decade that passed. For the solutions adopted in France on these particular points of court procedure were also part of a wider pattern. The French monarchy in the thirteenth century, unlike the English, could not or did not mobilize large numbers of its subjects to do the multifarious work of government—as jurors, suitors, tax-collectors, part-time holders of small public offices, or as advisers meeting often in national assemblies, incipient legislatures. By comparison with the English monarchy this was again a mark of weakness. It led to reliance on permanent officials, directly responsible to and controlled by the crown. As the power of the great feudal lords was reduced or absorbed, the crown slowly emerged triumphant over its rivals, and as this occurred, the French crown found itself free of internal restraints that might come from dependence on persons whom it could not command. The lines of causation were long and complex, there were many accidents along the way. At every point there were human choices, but within a constantly narrowing range. In this sense there is profound truth in the paradox that the original weakness of the French monarchy was the ultimate cause of French absolutism, just as the original strength of the English crown forced the English people to govern themselves and produced a constitution.[5]

In Germany great changes in court organization and procedure came on the whole about 200 years later than similar changes in France. The medieval systems, based essentially on the solutions of Charlemagne, lasted in most German states into the thirteenth century. Then civil war and the breakdown of imperial authority distributed court-keeping rights in great profusion among local lords, cities and towns and the remnants of ancient communities. The internal structure of the courts took many forms and reflected shifts in the centers of power in different localities, though law-finders (Schöffen) very commonly survived as carriers of local tradition and spokesmen for their communities. The weakness

[5] This general theme is developed further in the illuminating comments of Professor McIlwain, cited note 3 above, esp. pages 709–715.

of central authority was mirrored in this confusion. In reaction to the general disorder and insecurity local leaders all over Germany developed "free" courts of *Schöffen,* who rapidly became a league of private inquisitors. Their excesses led finally to their suppression. But in the meantime the dispersal of authority meant that local custom, the basic source of German law at this stage, could not be organized and recorded as it was through the group inquests (*enquêtes par turbe*) that had been used in France. Thus there was no solid core of native tradition, processed through court decision and subjected by lawyers to systematic analysis. When the influx of Roman law reached flood proportions in the sixteenth century there were only islands of resistance, located in a few districts that had managed to record and develop their customs. The displacement of German by Roman law was preceded by a general adoption of Roman-canonist procedure. The lay judges who had survived in most places until this stage were baffled and discouraged by the new procedure, as they had been in France 200 years before. A reorganized system of appellate courts ensured the triumph of the new procedure, promoted the capture of judicial functions by "learned" professionals, and aided them in imposing on lower courts the whole massive system of post-glossators' Roman law. This complex movement, occurring much later in time, was propelled by different forces than the reception in France and occurred in an environment that the mere passage of time had greatly changed. Yet a major clue in Germany was again the weakness of central authority in the critical years —the thirteenth and fourteenth centuries. This weakness precluded the central government from preserving and remolding the ancient forms of community action and using them as a counterpoise to the growing power of a feudal aristocracy.

None of these developments was inevitable. None needed to occur, certainly, on so great a scale. Even in England, for example, where ancient institutions and practices showed such extraordinary power to maintain themselves, a shift in the main directions of national policy could have altered the prospects for local institutions. Even as late as the seventeenth century, a victory for the king's party in the English civil war could have taken England on the road toward political absolutism and reacted in turn on counties, towns and manors. One can only say that the willingness of Englishmen then to battle for their liberties and their whole commitment to representative government did not arise through a sudden inspiration. For us in America, even more than in England itself, the courts of common law have become the guardians of constitutionalism. Its source, far more than we have realized, may be found in another kind of court—the courts of neighbors, the "little commonwealths," which preserved an ancient experience that most Englishmen had shared.

INDEX

Acceptance of inquest, 50-51

Admiralty, court of, 174

Affeerment: required by Magna Carta, 192, 260; transfer of function to manorial juries, 261-263

Appeal, canonist: adoption by Louis IX, 54; adoption by Reichskammergericht, 107; as means of controlling French seignorial courts, 55-56, 60; connection in France with false judgment proceeding, 54, 62; early use in France, 53-54; early use in Germany, 107; liabilities of lower court judges in France, 61-62, 65, 77-78; use by German seignorial courts, 108-109

Arbitration: as source of Roman praetorian procedure, 23-26; in Athens, 13-14; role in introducing canonist procedure in France, 45-46; role in introducing canonist procedure in Germany, 105; use in English Chancery, 163-170

Aristotle, 10

Assemblies of inhabitants, see Local government, French

Assessors, court: advisers to late Roman judiciary, 33; in German courts, 103; use by French judges, 69

Assize of Clarendon: introduction of presentment jury, 121; source of court-leet presentments, 187-189

Assizes: survival in France, 62-63

Athenian courts, 11-14

Augustus, 19, 28, 31

Bacon, Sir Edward, steward of Redgrave manor, 224-225, 237

Bacon, Sir Nicholas: purchaser of Redgrave manor, 209; owner of Redgrave manor under James I, 222

Baillis, royal, in thirteenth-century France, 54

Beaumanoir, Philippe de: on fact-finding in thirteenth century, 52; on

false judgment proceeding, 53; on judgments by "the men," 61; on judgment by peers, 66

Botisdale manor: relation to Redgrave manor, 213; "great beast" by-laws, 221

Bracton, Henry, 123-124, 126, 186

Brunner, Heinrich, 119-120

Canonist inquest: "acceptance" of, in French criminal cases, 50-51; adoption in France, 44-53, 57-58; adoption in Germany, 104-106, 111; effect in excluding laymen in France, 64-68; elaboration in French procedure, 57-60; influence on English Chancery, 147-154, 170-172; rejection by English common law, 125-128

Canonist procedure: adoption in France, 44-66, 69-70; adoption in Germany, 103-109, 111; effect in excluding laymen in France, 64-68, 87; origin in late Roman procedure, 32-34. See also Canonist inquest

Cas royaux, 54-55

Central courts, English: early organization, 129-131; limited controls over lower courts, 278-281; personnel, 130-131; protection of copyholders, 206; review of courts leet, 257-260, 280; review of judicial commissioners, 276; scope of writ of error, 275-279

Centumviri, court of the, 20

Chancery, court of: administrative collapse, 158-159, 170-172; centralization in London, 145-146; early procedure, 148-151; methods of examining witnesses, 149-158; role of masters, 159-163; use of arbitration, 163-170; vagueness of doctrines, 163, 168-170

Charlemagne, 38-39

Church courts, English, 175-176

Coing, Helmut, 104-106

Coke, Sir Edward: as mediator in Chancery, 166-167; on affeerment, 261; on the "commonwealth" of copyholders, 264, 281, 298; on distinctions between freeholders and copyholders, 211-212; on manor court by-laws, 281; on power to hold courts baron, 210; on powers of stewards, 237, 238-239; on prevalence of copyhold, 234; on qualifications of stewards, 225

Commissions, judicial: see Judicial commissions

Copyhold: analogues in France, 242-244; early forms, 204-207; elimination of, 239-241; importance to self-government, 244; methods of transfer, 205-206, 234-235, 236-237; mortgages of, 236-237; ownership by freeholders, 211; prevalence of tenure by copyhold, 234; protection by central courts, 206; variety of local customs, 235-236

Corpus Juris, Justinian's: influence of, 33-34, 44-45

County courts, English: decline after 1500, 181; jurisdiction in thirteenth century, 179-180; organization in thirteenth century, 178-179; survival in Anglo-Saxon period, 116-117; use by crown in thirteenth century, 179

Court baron: as agency of town government, 271; distinction between copyholders and freeholders, 197-198; frequency of meetings, 200, 214; membership, 210-212; powers, 234-239; relation to court leet, 210-222

Court leet: affeerment of judgments, 192, 260-263; as agency of town government, 190, 268-271; finality of presentments, 255-260; frequency of meetings, 191, 214; jurisdiction in thirteenth century, 189-190, 202-204; membership, 191-192, 197-198, 211, 216-218; number of courts leet in sixteenth century, 213-214; number of jurors required, 191-192; origin, 187-189; powers conferred by statute, 284; private ownership, 189-191; relation to court baron, 210-222; review of presentments, 257-260; sanctions, 192, 255; subjection to 40 shilling limit, 192

Customs, French: defining jurisdiction of seignorial courts, 73-74; regulating rural assemblies, 91; requiring judges in seignorial courts, 76

Dikasts, dikasteria, 11-12

Droits honorifiques, 84

Duel, judicial, elimination of: England, 121-122, 275; France, 47-50; Germany, 97

Ecclesiastical courts, English, 175-176

Échevins, derivation from scabini, 40, 89

Enquête, see Canonist inquest

Enquête par turbe: absence in Germany, 97; use in France, 46-47

Error, writ of: as mode of reviewing courts leet, 257; origins in thirteenth century, 274-278; scope of review, 277

Examiners in English Chancery, 151-152, 154-155

Eyres: importance in thirteenth century, 132-133; abandonment, 135

Fact determination, modes of: canonist inquest in France, 44-53, 57-58; canonist inquest in Germany, 104-106, 111; in early middle ages, 43-44; in English Chancery, 149-159; in thirteenth century England, 121-128

False judgment: connection with appeal in France, 54; connection with English writ of error, 274-277; liability of suitors in French lower courts, 62, 67; restrictions on, in English seignorial courts, 186-187; use in early Germanic procedure, 53, 98, 107; use in medieval France, 53, 62

Feudal Courts: collective forms of decision in, 41-42, 60-66, 95. See also Seignorial courts, French and German

Feudalization: in English manor courts, 195-198; limited degree of, in England, 117-118, 184-186; of French community courts, 95-96, 113-114. See also Seignorial courts, French and German

Folk-moots: early Germanic forms, 35-37; effects on, of Charlemagne's reforms, 38-39; survival in England, 116-117, 178-179; survival in Germany, 94-95

Forty-shilling limit: application to county courts, 180; application to courts leet, 214; application to hundred courts, 183; application to seignorial courts, 186; effects of changing price level, 228-229; exemption from,

of copyhold title disputes, 232; instances in which limit exceeded, 248, 259; origin, 180
Frankpledge, 188-189

Gaius Gracchus, 16-19
Gislingham manor, relation to Redgrave, 213
Goebel, Julius, 39, 233
"Great beast" by-laws, 220-221
Group inquest: elimination in Normandy, 122; introduction in England, 118-122; origin, 44; use in France for proving custom, 46-47. *See also* Jury

Henry II: development of centralized justice, 129, 185; introduction of juries, 121, 187-188
Holt, Lord John: on affeerment of amercements, 262; owner of Redgrave manor, 209
Homage: fusion with leet jury at Redgrave, 216-222; role in copyhold transfers, 237-239; transformation into special jury, 218-221; unanimity as a requirement, 196, 199, 238
House of Lords, 176-177
Hundred courts, English: decline, 183; organization in thirteenth century, 182; private ownership of, 182-183; survival in Anglo-Saxon period, 116-117, 181-182; use by crown in thirteenth century, 183-184

Interrogatories, in English Chancery, 150-157. *See also* Canonist inquest
Iudex: methods of choosing, 16-19, 27-29; relation to praetor, 21-30

Judges, numbers of: in early Parlement of Paris, 56; in English Chancery, 146, 170-171; in English central courts, 71, 130-131, 278; in French royal courts, 70-71; in French seignorial courts, 79; in Germany after 1500, 111-112; justices of the peace, 142
  qualifications of: English justices of the peace, 136-137, 140-143; English town courts, 273; manorial stewards, 224-227; French royal courts, 72-73; French seignorial courts, 77-78, 86
Judgment by peers, *see* Peers, judgment by

Judicial commissions: for appointment of justices of the peace, 137-138; for arbitration in Chancery, 164-165; for members of Chancery bench, 160-161; introduction of common lawyers, 135-136; review of judgments by writ of error, 276-277; use in thirteenth-century England, 131-132
Jury: appearance of, in medieval France, 44, 46-47; crudity of early English, 123-127; early English forms of, 121-122; early use of, in Chancery, 148; early use of, in manor courts, 200-201; elimination in Normandy, 122; Frankish origins of, 44; homage as a form of, 218-220; membership of, at Redgrave manor, 216-222; origins of, in England, 118-122; requirement in England of group verdict, 122-128; restriction on use of, in English seignorial courts, 185-186; use of, in France to prove custom, 46-47; use of, in medieval Germany, 99; use of, in Redgrave manor court, 229-230. *See also* Presentment jury
Justices of the peace: control over local government, 139-140, 143-144; importance in Tudor administration, 139-140; influence on criminal law, 138; legislation by, 142-143; methods of appointment, 137-138, 141-142; numbers, 142; permanence of tenure, 142; powers, 138-140; qualifications, 136-137, 140-143; role in town government, 272

Landgerichte, transformation of, 113
Langdell, C. C., 147-154, 158
Law-finders: adaptation of, by Merovingians, 37; early Germanic forms of, 36-37; reform of, by Charlemagne, 38-39
Laxton, manor of, 252
Leet, *see* Court leet
Legislation: by courts leet in English towns, 190, 268-271; by early English manor courts, 202-204; by English county courts, 196; by English justices of the peace, 143-144; by French local assemblies, 90; by French seignorial judges, 92-93; by Redgrave manor court, 245-253; "great beast" by-laws, 220-221, 248; suitors or stewards as source, 226-227, 248-253; validity of manorial by-laws, 281-283

Local government, English: Anglo-Saxon forms, 194; attack on town privileges by later Stuarts, 285; copyhold tenure as a form of, 244; county courts, 179; courts leet in the towns, 190, 268-271; decline of courts leet, 252-254; election of officials by manor courts, 249-250, 253, 283; encouragement by medieval monarchy, 133-134, 136-137, 294-295; forms of town governments, 265-266; hundred courts, 183-184; oligarchy in the towns, 267-268; role of justices of the peace, 139-140, 143-144; role of manorial courts, 190, 245-253; role of parish, 254

Local government, French: assemblies of rural inhabitants, 88, 90; reasons for decay, 88-90, 93-94; supervision by central government, 89-92

Local government, German, 113-114

Louis IX, 47, 54

Magna Carta, provisions of: affeerment of amercements, 192, 260-261; judgment by peers, 262-263, 289-291; trial of crown pleas, 180; trial of possessory assizes, 131-132

Maitland, F. W., views of: controls over seignorial courts, 186; early English jury, 127-128; effects of juries in manor courts, 201; lay justices of the peace, 145; membership of trial commissions, 132; origins of borough courts, 267; origins of courts leet, 188-190; origins of manor courts, 195-198; passivity of English judges, 279; relations of free and villein tenants, 197-198

Manchester, manor of, 224, 271

Manor courts: administration of copyhold, 204-207, 233-236; controversies over origins, 194-198; early civil litigation, 198-201; early forms of organization, 196-198; extent of oligarchy, 219-222; frequency of meetings, 200-214; influence on American colonists, 233; late survivals, 232-233; numbers of, in sixteenth century, 213-214; powers of steward and suitors, 196-198, 225-228; relations of freeholders and villeins, 197-198; requirements for membership, 196-198; sanctions, 212, 228-229. *See also* Redgrave manor, court of

Manors, origins of, 192-198

Masters in Chancery: importance in early period, 159-160; relation to Chancellor, 160-163; service on Chancery bench, 160-163; use as arbitrators, 166

Milsom, S. F. C., 276-277

North, court in the: abolition of, in 1641, 172; jurisdiction of, in sixteenth century, 146

Numbers of judges, *see* Judges, numbers of

Oath-helpers: in ancient Germanic procedure, 43; survival in English county courts, 181; survival in English manor courts, 200; survival in medieval Germany, 97-98, 104

Open-field system: essential elements, 193-194; late survivals, 252; prevalence in thirteenth century, 193

Paris abbey courts: civil procedure in fourteenth century, 51-52; criminal procedure in thirteenth century, 49-51; frequency of sessions, 64-65; purchase by Louis XIV, 82-83; survival of augmented "assizes," 63

Parlement of Paris: influence on lower courts, 58-60; organization, 56; political activities, 83-84; procedure in fourteenth century, 56-60; size, 56-57, 70-71

Parlements, provincial, 70

Peers, judgment by: affeerment as an aspect, 262-263; in early Germanic procedure, 65; in English House of Lords, 176; in manor court procedure, 192, 260, 261-263; in medieval France, 41-42, 65-66; in Roman praetorian procedure, 27, 65; influence of Magna Carta, 260-261, 289-291

Pericles, 11

Plato, 10

Population: comparison of French and English, 71-72; distribution of English, 208

Praetor: influence of, in choice of *iudex*, 28; powers over formula, 22, 26; relations to *iudex*, 22, 26-29

Praetorian procedure: displacement of, 32; effects of, on powers of magistrates, 27-28; origins of, 23-26

Presentment jury: finality of presentments in courts leet, 255-260; homage as a form of, 218-219; number of jurors required, 191-192; offenses presented at Redgrave manor, 245-253; origin, 120-121, 187-189; review of presentments by central courts, 257-260; use by justices of the peace, 138-140; use in early courts leet, 187-190, 203-204; use in early manor courts, 190, 203-204; use in sheriff's tourn, 187-189; use in town courts, 190, 268-271; villeins as members, 197

Prévention, 54-55

Price movements: in England, 228-229; in France, 74-75

Privy Council, English, 163, 165, 168, 173-174

Provocatio, 15-17

Quorum clause: introduction, 138; degeneration, 141

Recuperatores, court of, 20-21

Redgrave manor, court of: arrangement of court rolls, 210; attendance, 215-222; civil litigation, 229-232; copyhold transfers, 235-239; frequency of meetings, 214; fusion of court baron and court leet, 214-218; history of ownership, 209; legislation by juries, 245-253; membership of juries, 216-221; procedure in civil cases, 229-232; role of homage, 218-220, 237-239; stewards, 224-226, 237; subordinate manors, 213

Reichskammergericht, 107-108, 111-112

Requests, court of: abolition, 172; centralization in London, 146; use of arbitration, 164

Roman civil courts: *centumviri*, 20; imperial courts, 32-33; Praetor and *Iudex*, 21-30; *recuperatores*, 20-21

Roman criminal courts: imperial courts, 31-32; republican assembly courts, 16-19

Roman jurists, 29

Saint Louis, 47, 54

Scabini: absorption into French feudal structure, 40-41; as antecedents of German *Schöffen*, 94-95; comparison with manorial juries, 219-220; English medieval analogues, 116, 135, 179, 267; organization by Charlemagne, 38-39; vestiges in France, 40-41, 69

Schöffen: acquisition of powers in town governments, 96; as source of Vem-gerichte, 99; derivation from Carolingian scabini, 94-95; functions in developing custom, 97, 102; Romanization, 105-106, 108-109; survival in late middle ages, 101-102, 104; use in criminal cases, 109-110

Seignorial courts, English: formation of, after Norman Conquest, 118, 184-185; late survivals, 187; restrictions by crown, 184-187

French: appeals within feudal hierarchy, 82; appellate review by royal courts, 55-56; influence on social structure, 81-82, 84-87; jurisdictional disputes, 79-80; jurisdictional limits, 73-76; legislative powers, 88, 92-93; numbers of judges, 79; Paris abbey courts, 49-52, 82-83; professionalization, 76-78; qualifications of judges, 77-78, 80-82, 86; survival of lay membership, 60

German: appellate powers, 108-109; forms surviving in eighteenth century, 109-112; influence on social structure, 112-114; numbers of judges, 111-112; Romanization of personnel, 108-109

Sheriff's tourn: origin, 182; powers, 189-190; transfer to private ownership, 182-183, 189-191

Star Chamber, court of, 172-173

Stewards, manorial: instructional handbooks for, 212, 225; powers of, in courts baron, 225-228, 237-239; powers of, in courts leet, 211; qualifications, 224-227; sources of income, 223-224

Sulla, 18-19

Terriers, renovation of, 243-244

Towns, development of, *see* Local government, English, French, German

Vemgerichte: origin, 99-100; procedure and powers, 100-101; reaction against, 101

Villeins: commutation of services, 206; protection in early manor courts, 204-208; protection by central courts, 206; relations with freeholders in manor courts, 197-198; status in France and Germany, 207

Vinogradoff, Sir Paul, 193-198, 204

Wales, Court in the marches of: jurisdiction in sixteenth century, 146;

Wales, Court in the marches of: jurisdiction in sixteenth century, 146;
abolition in 1641, 172
Warwickshire, manors of, 213
Wenger, Leopold, 24-27

Wlassak, Moriz, 23-24
Writ of error, *see* Error, writ of

York, Court at: abolition in 1641, 172;
jurisdiction in sixteenth century, 146